Tegan Zimmerman

Writing Back Through Our Mothers

D1615321

Contributions to
Transnational Feminism

edited by

Erin Kenny
(Drury University, MO)
and
Silvia Schultermandl
(University of Graz, Austria)

Volume 5

LIT

Tegan Zimmerman

Writing Back
Through Our Mothers

A Transnational Feminist Study
on the Woman's Historical Novel

LIT

Cover art: Carl Zimmermann

Printed with the support of the University of Graz.

KARL-FRANZENS-UNIVERSITÄT GRAZ
UNIVERSITY OF GRAZ

Bibliographic information published by the Deutsche Nationalbibliothek
The Deutsche Nationalbibliothek lists this publication in the Deutsche
Nationalbibliografie; detailed bibliographic data are available in the Internet at
http://dnb.d-nb.de.

ISBN 978-3-643-90560-4

A catalogue record for this book is available from the British Library

©LIT VERLAG GmbH & Co. KG Wien,
Zweigniederlassung Zürich 2014
Klosbachstr. 107
CH-8032 Zürich
Tel. +41 (0) 44-251 75 05
Fax +41 (0) 44-251 75 06
E-Mail: zuerich@lit-verlag.ch
http://www.lit-verlag.ch

LIT VERLAG Dr. W. Hopf
Berlin 2014
Fresnostr. 2
D-48159 Münster
Tel. +49 (0) 2 51-62 03 20
Fax +49 (0) 2 51-23 19 72
E-Mail: lit@lit-verlag.de
http://www.lit-verlag.de

Distribution:
In the UK: Global Book Marketing, e-mail: mo@centralbooks.com
In North America: International Specialized Book Services, e-mail: orders@isbs.com
In Germany: LIT Verlag Fresnostr. 2, D-48159 Münster
Tel. +49 (0) 2 51-620 32 22, Fax +49 (0) 2 51-922 60 99, E-mail: vertrieb@lit-verlag.de

In Austria: Medienlogistik Pichler-ÖBZ, e-mail: mlo@medien-logistik.at
e-books are available at www.litwebshop.de

TABLE OF CONTENTS

ACKNOWLEDGMENTS

This project would not be possible were it not for the lives of brave women. This book is for you. In bringing this work on transnational women's historical fiction to fruition, however, I would like to sincerely thank the editors of the series *Contributions to Transnational Feminism*, Silvia Schultermandl and Erin Kenny. Your revisions, comments, and support were invaluable throughout the various transitions and transformations the work has undergone. Your input made it a better book, and I am grateful.

Thank you to my PhD supervisory committee in the Program of Comparative Literature at the University of Alberta: Dr. Gary Kelly (supervisor), Dr. Albert Braz, and Dr. Patricia Demers you offered close readings and insightful comments, but most of all you believed in the value of this project. For my friends and colleagues at the University of Alberta, thank you for reading drafts and lending receptive ears. For Dr. Diana Wallace, your work *The Woman's Historical Novel in Britain* inspired me, and my project would not exist if it were not for your research. To my language tutors Isabel Roblez-López (Español) and Nadia Ouakil (Française) I am grateful for your expertise and dedication but most of all your patience with me.

Finally, I would like to express my gratitude to my family and friends in supporting me throughout this project. Virginia Woolf once said "we think back through our mothers if we are women" and her words were the inspiration behind this project of writing back; in thinking and writing back, we impact the future. In studying this transnational corpus (writing for women by women about women), I have, furthermore, gained a better understanding of and a special connection to my own matrilineal heritage.

INTRODUCTION

> What is her first name? she must have one –/so far she has only
> the name of a dead man,/ someone somewhere else
>   - Daphne Marlatt, *Ana Historic*

I. The Woman's Historical Novel: A Transnational Genre

The woman's historical novel, a blurring of fact with fiction or the real with the imagination, is an immensely popular literary genre. On a whole, the historical novel has not attracted much scholarship, but women's historical novels even less so. Typically, genre studies are devoted to male historical novelists and their novels (Lukács; Menton). Meanwhile feminists, who have much to say about history and fiction separately, are not as forthcoming in theorizing the historical novel or women's historical novels as one would expect. At present time a modest number of discourses centering primarily on women's historical novels are emerging (Cooper et al. 2012, Heilmann et al. 2007; Wallace 2005). These works, while offering important scholarship to the field, nevertheless, focus primarily on white British writers. Additionally, there is a growing interest in Neo-Victorian writing (Mitchell; Heilmann and Llewellyn 2010; Arias and Pulham; Kaplan 2007; King 2005), but again the focus here is Britain's Victorian era (1837-1901), and not all of the texts concentrate on women novelists. Though not concentrating on contemporary authors, other works (Stevens; Hoberman) do important work in reassessing a woman's tradition of historical writing prior to 1970. As expected, other studies, for example Von Dirke's, Light's, L. Anderson's, and Lokke's for practical reasons, are typically limited to the study of one author or one text. A truly transnational project dedicated to the genre of women's historical fiction is, therefore, missing. This book supplements current scholarship because it is a transnational feminist study on contemporary women's historical novels (post 1970). I argue that focusing on contemporary women's historical fiction constitutes a transnational feminist writing/reading project.

This project has three objectives: 1) to acknowledge and analyze a body, transnational in scope, of contemporary feminist women's historical fiction (post 1970); 2) to compare the political potential of the maternal and maternal possibilities in women's historical novels transnationally; 3) to provide a deeper understanding of the relation between transnational feminism and feminist literature.

The following chapters articulate a common goal in both transnational feminism and women's historical novels: the political act of writing back through

Is there a non-feminist whf ?

our foremothers to counter and disrupt patriarchal and hegemonic accounts of history and literature. Confronting patriarchal discourses is necessary if we are to envision and move into a new future for women, as women. Monika M. Elbert writes, "the past needs to be exorcised or healed for there to be a future or for there to be a reconciliation of the sexes" (38-39). The recuperation of maternal genealogies, voices, and figures is a sign of our indebtedness, as women, to women from the past who were brave enough to envisage reality differently. In a sense this project as a whole constitutes that which Tess Cosslett labels a "matrilineal narrative" (7). Concentrating on the maternal and the recuperation of matrilineal genealogies therefore gives this project coherence.

A matrilineal narrative either "tells the stories of several generations of women at once" (Cosslett 7) or "shows how the identity of a central character [here woman as a collective] is crucially formed by her female ancestors" (7). The phrase "writing back through our mothers" signifies this continuity with the past. The phrase is indebted to Virginia Woolf's influential statements on women's writing in *A Room of One's Own* (1929): "we think back through our mothers if we are women" (76) and "a woman writing thinks back through her mothers" (96). In women's writing "writing back" is a political action that addresses patriarchal exclusions and by doing so influences and changes women's futures. Tania Modleski refers to this matrilineage as "our cultural heritage as women" (43) and Marianne Hirsch calls it a burgeoning "maternal subjectivity" (197). These transnational writers "clearly identify themselves as a new feminist generation in relation to the maternal tradition of the past, writers for whom fathers, brothers, and husbands occupy a less prominent place, writers who are in a more distant relation to cultural and literary hegemony" (Hirsch 16). When read together, the novels create a dynamic transnational maternal discourse that challenges and contests a single and stable definition of the maternal or "mother."

I use the term "mother" more figuratively than literally. Luce Irigaray asserts "we are always mothers once we are women. ... We engender something other than children: love, desire, language, art, the social, the political, the religious, for example ... we must reappropriate this maternal dimension that belongs to us as women" (*Irigaray Reader* 43). Thus, regardless of whether women are biological or social mothers, I consider all the protagonists studied maternal figures. This transnational survey analyzes for the first time the roles of maternal figures, voices, and genealogies in the contemporary woman's historical novel.

This transnational feminist study on the contemporary woman's historical novel argues that the genre's central theme and focus is the maternal. Analyzing the maternal, disclosed through a myriad of genealogies, voices, and fig-

ures, reveals that the historical novel is a feminist means for challenging historical erasures, silences, normative sexuality, political exclusion, divisions of
labor, and so on within a historical-literary context. I discuss novels which
speak from the margins and spaces of silence within history and the genre. As
much as the works contest masculinist master narratives, they also create and
envision new genealogies. Each narrative centers on an atypical female protagonist and the role of history is not only visible but also serves as the setting for
either the heroine or the author to consciously subject patriarchal values to a
gender analysis. Furthermore, there is a maternal connection between the mi-
lieu/personal history of the writer and the subject matter/history of the novel.
Examples like those found in the epigraph to *Moi, Tituba...Black Witch of Salem* (1986) by Maryse Condé which reads "Tituba and I lived for a year on the
closest of terms. During our endless conversations she told me things she had
confided to nobody else. Maryse Condé expresses a simultaneous rewriting of
the present by recalling and reclaiming the past.

In recuperating and reclaiming the past, the woman's historical novel puts
forth a counter text or a counter version of history, but assumes, contrary to the
post-modern techniques many feminist novels employ, a historical reality and a
gendered reality that extends beyond the text and that grounds the text. Linda
Anderson claims that for feminist historians and historical novelists there is a
"powerful desire for women to exist historically in the world [and] to be more
than textually present" (131). Acknowledging and studying a transnational
corpus is, therefore, imperative for expanding and updating the genre's current
masculinist Eurocentric status and bridging new relations between transnational
feminism and literature. Collectively, the novels form a femino-centric space–
an imagined motherland or matria–wherein patriarchy, Eurocentrism, gender,
motherhood, and the nation are fiercely interrogated. The act of writing back
through our mothers is a means for making collective and personal arguments
for feminist changes; thus, this study contends that a transnational feminist
knowledge project on the contemporary woman's historical novel is necessary,
worthwhile, and timely.

Since 1970, the woman's historical novel has become a most suitable medium for writers from a plurality of transnational perspectives. This project on
contemporary works revises approximately the last 500 years of history, from
the birth of modernity in 1450 to its demise roughly in 1950 C.E. I demonstrate
the ways in which transnational topics have been used by contemporary women
writers in order to "unmask and redefine maternal roles and subjectivities"
(Podnieks and O'Reilly 5).[1] When considered as a whole, these works create a

---

[1] While maternal figures, matrifocal narratives, mother-daughter explorations, daughter-centric texts, mothering, and motherhood–all popular topics in women's literature,

politicized matrilineal genealogy that combats both master narratives and postmodern perspectives which reinforce patriarchal history, literature, and historiography. Constructing a fluid sense of the maternal and the institution of motherhood is timely within transnational feminism and allows for a more nuanced exploration of how literary studies can inform, and be informed by, transnational feminist theories and practices.

Inderpal Grewal and Caren Kaplan suggest "if the world is currently structured by transnational economic links and cultural asymmetries, locating feminist practices within these structures becomes imperative" (3). Jacqui M. Alexander and Chandra Talpade Mohanty likewise believe a transnational project will, amongst other criteria, be "a way of thinking about women in similar contexts across the world, in *different* geographical spaces, rather than as *all* women across the world (24). Transnational feminism can, thus, be understood as a heterogeneous account of women's lived experiences in specific local, national, and global contexts, which is evident in the survey of texts in this study. A "politics of location," to use Adrienne Rich's term, "identifies the grounds for historically specific differences and similarities between women in diverse and asymmetrical relations, creating alternative histories, identities, and possibilities for alliances" (Kaplan, "The Politics of Location as Transnational Feminist Practice" 139). Women's historical novels offer compelling narratives for how we can hear a plurality of women's voices without homogenizing them.

Achieved from a plurality of voices and positions, a transnational approach entails challenging national and ideological boundaries. Françoise Lionnet argues that "transnational feminism attaches much value to the questions of solidarity, for such an ethics implies that we remain respectful of differences while arguing for universal human rights in a multipolar world" (106). Lionnet's thinking provides promising directions and strategies for reading women's historical novels. Alena Heitlinger's thoughts are also worth noting:

> Transnational feminism acknowledges both the specific local and national forms of patriarchy, as well as the ways in which global economic restructuring and transnational cultural influences shape and link the material and cultural lives of women around the world ... Transnational feminism is not simply a matter of flow of ideas, but also a question of flow of money and power relations. (7)

---

predominantly novels –are now widely discussed in feminist literary scholarship (Hirsch, O'Reilly, Daly, Reddy, Brandt, Ingman, Goiogrio, Yu, Rich), a sustained discussion of the maternal in the woman's historical novel is yet to be written.

Thus, it is imperative to identify how the contemporary woman's historical novel puts forth a feminist agenda in reclaiming the maternal within a transnational context.

This study identifies the maternal as the central theme within the woman's historical novel since recent transnational times–this becomes evident when analyzing how women writers have increasingly turned to transnational topics in order to expound and explicate the maternal and matrilineal genealogies in innovative ways. The following chapters, organized roughly chronologically according to the settings of the novels, identify the most common and complex issues related to the maternal as represented by contemporary women writers: Chapter 1, Revisionist Writing: Mothers of the Americas examines several key femino-centric topics which are essential to rethinking early European women immigrating to the Americas as well as the experiences of Indigenous women encountering both European men and women in the sixteenth and seventeenth centuries. I discuss the transatlantic crossing, the notion of the woman as traitor to the nation, forced marriages for the purpose of procreation, the importance of language, and finally the ties that connect women with one another transnationally, despite patriarchal national boundaries and borders. Chapter 2, Modern Queens: Matricide, Gynocracy, and Matrophobia addresses some of the most popular figures in both history and historical fiction, e.g., Spain's Isabel la Católica, England's Elizabeth I, and Kristine of Sweden from the time period of 1450-1789. The connecting thread and transnational tie among these novels is the rule of a woman, a gynocracy, and a simultaneous matrophobia, fear of one's mother and/or mother figures. Overlapping femino-centric topics in these works include mothers who are deemed unfit, mothers who are traitors, surrogate mothers, foreign mothers, and finally the relation between motherhood and queenship as potentially irreconcilable social functions. Chapter 3, Matrilineal Narratives: Race, Memory, and Survival constitutes a counter-narrative to the Eurocentricism and elitism of chapter 2. In this chapter, women directly experiencing slavery and colonialism/imperialism from the sixteenth to the mid-twentieth century are at the forefront. In these narratives, memory plays an important part in re-visioning a maternal genealogy, particularly as it combats and disrupts hegemonic European history, racism, and the legacy of slavery.

Chapter 4, Transnational Mater-Familial Sagas: The Matriarch takes the research in a slightly different direction. I concentrate on the role of the matriarch in what I refer to as a mater-famial saga, a novel that spans across several different women's lives within a single family, the head of which is a powerful woman, a matriarch. Femino-centric topics which unite the works include forbidden romances, rebellious sisters, memory and spirituality, nostalgia, and narratives which shift between the nineteenth century past and the twentieth/twenty-first century present. Chapter 5, A New Sexual Politics of Space: Working Mothers focuses on novels from the seventeenth to early twentieth century, and, like the other chapters, examines texts from varying geo-political situations in order to stress transnational connections between representations of women's lived experiences as workers. A central idea uniting the texts is the atypical working mother and the difficulties she faces in balancing her public work with her familial duties. Topics, related to this central idea, include the dissolving of boundaries between the domestic and public realm, forbidden spaces, work as narrative, lesbian families, and women, empowered through work, coming to a new spiritual awakening. Chapter 6, Violent Women: Revamping the Gothic Novel concentrates on nineteenth century women who were either accused of or convicted of being criminals. I examine how each novel reinvents the Gothic tradition and challenges stereotypes about women, especially mothers, as the fairer sex, incapable of committing violence. Murder, unsurprisingly, plays a central role in all of the works discussed as does relationships between servants and mistresses.

Chapter 7, Feminist Mothering: The Woman's War Novel discusses a neglected area of women's writing, women's participation in war-times from the American Civil War to the Second World War. I analyze topics such as the dubious difference between homefront and battlefront, the role of nurses and doctors, mothers on enemy soil, maternal mortality, and women challenging familial traditions, expectations, and norms. The final chapter, 8, Love For/Against Art: Rebirthing our Foremothers casts its net rather wide and analyzes texts from the sixteenth century to the mid-twentieth century. This chapter brings together women artists from a variety of backgrounds and disciplines, i.e., art, music, theatre. I discuss theatre as a political medium, the role dance plays in spiritual transcendence, the importance of women educating other women, and the representation of the sacrifices many women endured and experienced in terms of their personal lives because of their love and devotion to their craft.

In addition to demarcating the chapters in the above manner, I discuss how the works in each relate to texts written prior to the transnational turn, and proceed to provide close readings of the most meaningful femino-centric aspects. In doing so, I take into account a wide range of women's social roles as mothers, daughters, sisters, wives, aunts, lovers, orphans, courtesans, storytellers, goddesses, midwives, idols, monsters, witches, traitors, healers, and mistresses. I also consider bodily experiences with childbirth, adoption, abortion, miscarriage, infertility, rape, childlessness by choice, and cross-dressing. Lastly, relationships with other women in terms of female companionship, friendship, emotional nurturing, love, sexual partners, absence, sacrifice, fear, deceit, jealousy, abhorrence, and rivalry are analyzed.

The thematic structure reflects a transnational feminist approach to the subject matter of the woman's historical novels and pays less attention to the form. I accept Joseph W. Turner's argument that "formal properties may not be the genre's distinguishing characteristic: it is the content more than the form, after all, that sets historical novels off from other fiction" (335). Grouping novels by theme is not intended to express a strict demarcation, but, in the vein of transnational feminism, fluidity. In contrast to most scholarship, this study gives shape and voice to the multi-national, multi-lingual, and multicultural nature of women's historical novels, which emerges most visibly from the 1970s.

The novels here reflect differing feminist attitudes and beliefs, thus categorizing the works according to the waves of western feminism does not make sense, especially given that many authors may openly resist the label and/or were not involved in the movement.[2] Though Irigaray's ideas on the maternal are often associated with second wave western feminism, they are the ones I draw from the most for this project. Her work on the maternal is complex enough to be updated and expanded upon when needed, for instance in terms of women's differences such as race, culture, and class. Katherine Cooper and Emma Short likewise identify "an echoing of the political ideologies behind this kind of writing, in the recent developments of female-authored historical fiction, as well as in popular women's writing more generally" (15). Similarly, Wallace shows how Irigaray's work can be used to read women's historical novels because it "symbolically map[s] women's relationship to history and their repeated exclusion from traditional forms of historiography…She [Irigaray] makes history, a female matrilineal history often most obviously expressed through myth or legend, central to that task" [of 'thinking the difference' between the sexes" and remembering/re-establishing our female ancestors (Wallace "Difficulties, Discontinuities and Differences: Reading Women's Historical Fiction," 215-16).

As this book will show, Irigaray's thinking is quite suitable for a transnational feminist knowledge project on the matenal. Nevertheless, a transnational approach to studying these novels allows for the feminism–the belief in women's equality–within the works to speak for itself; this reveals a feminism in the plural, one that can adapt and change depending on context and cirucmstance– this flexibility is to be celebrated because it expands static notions or western-centric notions of the term. The connecting thread, in all of the novels, however, is constructing and reclaiming the maternal through the act of writing back.

---

[2] See Kristeva for a useful summary of the women's movements.

My approach differs from traditional studies on the genre, which fall into the following four categories: 1) chronological and theoretical e.g., Georg Lukács' *The Historical Novel* (1932), or Richard Maxwell's *Historical Novel in Europe 1650-1950* (2009); 2) single nation, for instance Canada, see the recent *National Plots: Historical Fiction and Changing Ideas of Canada* (2010); 3) identity (gender, race, class, sexuality, for example Maurice Samuels' article "David Schornstein and the Rise of Jewish Historical Fiction in Nineteenth-Century France" (2008)); and, 4) single author studies such as Anne Green's *Flaubert and The Historical Novel: Salammbô Reassessed* (1982). The rationale for my text selection is attributed to transnational feminist thinking and themes, albeit these choices are further based on the nationality and the language of an author and/or text and the subject matter of the novel falling roughly between 1450 and 1950 CE. I balance canonical with non-canonical texts and "serious" as opposed to "popular" literature –though of course in the woman's historical novel these categories are often contended. Indebted to Stevens' approach to studying early women's historical fiction in Britain, here, I try to balance close readings of both familiar and less familiar novels with identifying "larger patterns and repeated events among a wide body" of texts (13). This egalitarian strategy detects "shared tropes, character names, stock situations, and prefatory gestures" (ibid.) among the novels, and provides a wider understanding of the genre than a close-reading of a few canonical texts does.

These chapters demonstrate differences between women, but more importantly they demonstrate feminist solidarity in making women's historical lives visible and in acknowledging them as inspirations for social transformation. While it is true the woman's historical novel does not necessarily map or fulfill all of transnational feminism's requirements, for example anti-capitalism, what justifies and validates reading as constituting a transnational feminist knowledge project is the unanimous invocation of maternal voices from the past as meaningful and meaningfully present in our present. As Rich poeticizes, the "cathexis between mother and daughter–essential, distorted, misused–is the great unwritten story" (*Of Woman Born* 225); thus, a transnational reading of the woman's historical novel writing contributes to the project of creating a maternal genealogy.

The woman's historical novel, like transnational feminism suggests patriarchy is a false hierarchy. In this hierarchy man, occupying the privileged and authoritative position over and against woman is deemed superior in all aspects of lived experience (the familial, political, social, and economic). Margaret Whitford, commenting on Irigaray's work, clarifies: "Patriarchy is … 'an exclusive respect for the genealogy of sons and fathers, and the competition between brothers'" (Section I, 24). Patriarchy, like other terms such as "Woman" has come under attack as a false universal by feminist scholars (Lorde, Mohanty, Rowbatham, J. Scott, Spivak). In contesting an essentialist conception of Woman, such critics also charge feminism with being Western, hegemonic, dominating, and colonizing/imperializing by promoting white middle-class bourgeoisie elitism which ignores the lives and activism of Black, Chicana, and lesbian feminists, amongst other minority feminists. Thus the woman's historical novel must not replace masculinist master narratives with feminist master narratives. At the same time, asking whether women's history is meaningful if we reject the category of woman or any set of shared experiences, for example patriarchy, beyond linguistic designations is meaninful.

Linda Gordon and Claudia Koontz, for instance, question if women can advocate agency in terms of social and political change without any basis or commonalities other than a linguistic designation (852-53; 19). In *Metamorphoses: Towards a Materialist Theory of Becoming* (2002), Braidotti, seeking a intermediary stance, claims, "what is most important for feminism is the 'political and conceptual task of creating, legitimating and representing a multi-centered, internally differentiated female feminist subjectivity without falling into relativism or fragmentation'" (26). She stresses the need for "embodied political practices" ("Critical Cartography" 8) because true relativism makes it difficult for feminist writers to uphold a political argument of shared embodiment or reproductive justice; after all, the laborios work of feminist historians has been, for the most part, to counter the erasure of women from and by history, claim subjectivity and agency, and to collectively undermine the hierarchical values of masculinist heterosexual societies. Feminist historiographer Judith Bennett suggests that "'women' is a slippery concept in theory, but in practice it usually acts as a stable category – for its time and place – that can critically determine a person's life chances. This practical categorization of 'women' matters today, and it has mattered in the past; it is, therefore, a proper subject for feminist thought and feminist history" (*History Matters* 9). Furthermore, she defiantly calls for a "fully historicized understanding of patriarchy as feminism's central theoretical problematic" (Morgan 6). She writes, "this division between women as victims and women as agents is a false one: women have always been both victims and agents ... Women have not been merely passive victims of patriarchy, they have also colluded in, undermined, and survived patriarchy" ("Feminism and History" 67).

Mohanty too, though attune to western feminsm's imperializing tendencies, emphasizes why feminists must build new connections. She believes "because no border or boundary is ever complete or rigidly determining, the challenge is to see how differences allow us to explain the connections and border crossings better and more accurately. My concern is for women of different communities and identities to build coalitions and solidarities across borders" (266). The transnational turn in feminism, evident in the centralizing of the maternal in contemporary women's historical novels, signals a critical engagement with precisely these questions of history as a lived event (master narrative/real) and historiography as a construct (postmodernism/construct) and how to navigate gender identity in terms of difference and solidarity across multiple locations.

In contrast to other kinds of historical novels, the woman's historical novel offers a unique gendered perspective–it is a discourse by women about women seeking feminist change. Modleski asserts that "it remains importantly the case that feminist critical writing is committed writing, a writing committed to the future of women" (47). This desire for cultural transformation aligns itself with the causes of transnational feminism and sets it apart from master narratives (one single authoritative view, traditionally masculine) and postmodern (multiple views and perspectives given simultaneously) readings of the historical novel. Despite being a vehicle for feminist arguments, transnational feminism, however, has not engaged enough with fiction (film and media excluded). Perhaps the practice of reading/writing/engaging with texts is understood as too theoretical and that the physical, political, and economic concerns of transnational feminist organizations are more urgent and pressing. Janet Lee and Susan M. Shaw's work, for instance, suggests the above, and Pascal Dufour, Dominique Masson, and Dominique Caouette, identify different types of transnational collective action, but, as is often the case, the political role of literature remains undeveloped.

Possibly the aforementioned authors believe it is too difficult to trace literature in terms of what they call "coordinated action," I argue, however, that the medium has been taken up repeatedly and simultaneously by activist women writers and readers and constitutes the practice of "mobilizing and transferring resources," "deploying discourses, and constructing collective identities" (Dufour et al. 15) the authors state as necessary. Understanding literature or literary theory as detached immateriality is misguided. There is a gendered materiality and reality outside of the text because "'gender' structures society, our thinking and our actions in fundamental ways" (Westen 7). Taking into account the gendered politics and economics of book publishing, the means to purchase books, translation, reading, etc., particularly within the last three decades of globalization, suggests a more nuanced dialogic exchange between transnational feminism and literary practices is necessary.

To summarize, this project invokes a transnational feminist commitment to reading women's historical novels from the 1970s onwards for the following reasons: we live in an age of hyper-globalization within which feminists and transnational feminists have been politically active for over thirty years (Acker

17); "the African diaspora in the 1970s, [is] the same period when the notions of "matrilineal tradition" and "female memory" newly prevailed among black feminist writers and critics" (Hochberg 3), for example, Alice Walker's influential essay "In Search of Our Mothers' Gardens" (1974); *la nueva mujer en la escritura de autoras hispánicas* [the new woman in writing by Hispanic women authors] signals a unique femino-centric voice and revises "the national imagination in Latin America" (Handley 72); feminist studies, notably psychoanalytic ones, on the mother figure and mothering become a topic of wide debate; postcolonial and marginal voices effectively question and re-write dominant western discourses while, at the same time, postmodernist perspectives that reduce history to narrative, proliferate; abortion and contraception became legal in many western countries and new technological possibilities for the maternal (surrogacy, in-vitro fertilization, sperm banks) emerged, thus contemporary writers became "able to speak about issues which were unspeakable for women of the past, notably areas surrounding sexuality and the body" (King 4); feminist rewritings in the 1970s demanded that the female subject be included in historical writing: "the recovering of women as subjects of, and agents in, the making of history and the simultaneous decentering of the male subject ... prompted widespread re-examinations of the most fundamental of historical presumptions" (Morgan 1); and, finally, the genre became a politicized medium for feminist women writers globally.

Novels from the 1970s to the present emphasize the political potential of the woman's historical novel as a transnational feminist genre; several identities such as race, class, ethnicity, sexuality, nationality, and language intersect in maternal genealogies, voices, and figures in the texts. These works unanimously suggest the maternal has been and continues to be experienced differently by women depending on context, thus challenging a normative or hegemonic sense of the maternal. All these works, however, challenge dominant patriarchal discourses and convincingly suggest that women's past lives and struggles should not be, nor are, forgotten. Therefore, women's historical experiences as manifest in a literary context should be considered sources of strength and resistance against patriarchy, provide critical literary space to women from the western and non-western world, and rethink feminist writing as a political transnational praxis.

II. Situating the Woman's Historical Novel: Master Narratives, Postmodernism, and a Transnational Context

Recently, there has been a rejuvenated debate amongst contemporary scholars on origins of the historical novel. Most critics no longer agree with Alessandro

Manzoni, Georg Lukács, Harold Orel, or Perry Anderson that Walter Scott or his novel *Waverley* (1814) is the genre's founding author/text. Maxwell, for instance, argues in its earliest forms "historical fiction is a French genre" (*Historical Novel* 65) and refers to *La Princesse de Cléves* (1678) by Marie-Madeleine Pioche de La Vergne, comtesse de La Fayette. Similarly, Wallace acknowledges La Fayette's novel as "a very early historical novel" (Wallace, *Woman's* 19). Furthermore, she looks to Lee's *The Recess, or A Tale of Other Times* (1783), a Gothic historical novel, as the progenitor of the contemporary woman's historical novel (at least in Britain). Anne H. Stevens' commendable *British Historical Fiction Before Scott* (2010) also discusses dozens of historical novels written before Walter Scott's *Waverley* (1814), many of which are written by women (Clara Reeve, Lee, Ann Fuller, Margaret Hugill, and so on). Though Maxwell expands upon Stevens' and Wallace's traditional national studies to include Europe as a whole and gives women writers like La Fayette due credit, his focus remains Eurocentric and ends in the 1950s, typically considered an unpopular time for historical fiction. Milda Danytė affirms that "it is only after the second world war and the rise of post-modernism that the historical novel again attracts the attention of major writers" (35). Convincing counter-evidence, however, suggests it is erroneous and possibly sexist to conclude genre studies in the 1950s because women writers continued to be successful. Wallace, for example, emphatically undermines claims of inertia; writers Sylvia Townsend Warner, Margaret Mitchell, Winifred Ellerman (Bryher), Virginia Woolf, Anna Banti, Jean Plaidy, Marguerite Yourcenar, Norah Lofts, Margaret Irwin, and notably Nobel Prize winning Norwegian author Sigrid Undset were all writing popular historical novels prior to and just after the middle of the twentieth century. Furthermore, women's historical novels, like many of the ones above challenge not only the traditional masculinist form but also reductivist, escapist, and complicit women's historical romances that undermine political equality. Emerging in the late nineteenth century with George Eliot's *Romola* (1862-63) and extending into the early and mid-twentieth century, works like Woolf's *Orlando* (1929), Lola Kosáryné Réz's tetralogy on a Hungarian maternal genealogy, Anna Banti's *Artemisia* (1947), and Jean Rhys' *Wide Sargasso Sea* (1966), instatiate a genre of the woman's historical novel committed to feminist political change. These early feminist novels thus serve as important precursors to the post 1970 feminist woman's historical novel.

Acknowledging prolific women writers from the early twentieth century allows one to more fully understand the post 1970 novels discussed in this study. Danytė, for example, argues that from the 1960s onwards, coinciding with postmodern essays like Hayden White's "The Historical Text as Literary Artifact" (1974), which reconceptualizes history in terms of literary devices and narrative, marginalized groups (Blacks, women, Latino/as, gbltq, feminists, the working class, and others) were beginning to recover and reclaim their histories (36). This is especially revelevant for women's novels given that "historical fiction has been one of the major forms of women's reading and writing in the second half of the twentieth century" (Light 60). Since the transnational turn, women's historical novels have been actively challenging a commitment to postmodernism and, though a postmodernist textual analysis is useful, even necessary, in exposing patriarchy as pervasive and in undermining master narratives, it cannot provide an effective feminist praxis. In this sense my project contests claims such as those found in Heilmann's and Llewellyn's Introduction to *Metafiction and Metahistory in Contemporary Women's Writing*. In this work the authors, focusing on contemporary women's novels in which "the metafictional and metahistorical combine" argue that women writers, today, are more than ever before rising to the challenge of postmodern conceptions of the past and understandings of history which support "the (in)validity of any individual account's claims to accuracy or, ultimately, objective truth" (3). I argue that this is a highly dubious claim, especially when a more diverse survey of women's historical novels, one that is transnational in scope, is considered. A social/political motivation for change drives the woman's historical novel; therefore, it cannot subscribe wholeheartedly to a master or a postmodernist position.

Wallace writes that "the historical novel has allowed [writers/readers] to invent or 're-imagine' … the unrecorded lives of marginalized and subordinated people, especially women, but also the working classes, Black people, slaves and colonized peoples, and to shape narratives, which are more appropriate to their experiences than those of conventional history" (*Woman's* 2). The woman's historical novel also "can centralize a female consciousness and explore female fears and desires" (ibid.). Wallace's survey of British women writers (1900-2000) is essential in understanding the genre, but I stress the importance of reading beyond the nation as well as distinguishing between women's and feminist writing.

I distinguish between the woman's and feminist woman's historical novel in the same manner as historiographers Judith Bennett and June Purvis differentiate between women's history and feminist history (Bennett, *History* 15). Purvis argues that women's history pertains to the subject matter of women and gender (an examination of the interdependence and relational nature of female and male identities) whereas feminist history is history informed by feminist politics and methodologies; when it is women's history in particular, Purvis refers to this as feminist women's history (7). While the links between women's and feminist history are strong, they are not interchangeable terms.

Women's history is defined by its subject matter and need not invoke a feminist perspective, whereas feminist history is defined by the very specificity of its theoretical agenda (Purvis and Weatherill 124). Many historical novels written by women–Dorothy Bonavia-Hunt's *Pemberley Shades* (1949), Colleen McCullough's trilogy on the Roman Republic/Empire (1990-2007), or *Tierra del Fuego* by Sylvia Iparraguirre (2000) – do not focus on the lives of women but on the experiences of men. On the other hand, there are many novels written by men about women; consider Richard Condon's novel *The Abandoned Woman* (1977), about Queen Caroline, the wife of George IV, or John Fowles' pastiche tale *The French Lieutenant's Woman* (1969). Novels such as these prompt questions such as whether a male author can write a feminist novel, but unfortunately are not within the scope of this study, which will focus solely on feminist women's historical novels (that for simplicity will be referred to as the woman's historical novel) since the advent of transnationalism.

Sabine Von Dirke's succinct definition of the modern historical novel is a useful point for comparison and reference with the contemporary woman's historical novel:

> Positioned between historiography and fiction, the modern historical novel productively exploits the hiatus of fact and fiction in a way most biographies and autobiographies cannot. The modern historical novel achieves transparency and self-reflexivity in its portrayal of the past as a specific gendered and political reconstruction situated between the historical record and imagination. Therefore, this genre has the potential to explode the closed text of history, i.e. the dominant historical narratives, from a variety of perspectives. Why not from a feminist one? (426)

I take up Von Dirke's challenge by suggesting the following supplement as sufficient for reading women's historical novels in a transnational context:

1) a heroine that is atypical (fictive or factual); for example, Margaret Muir's *The Condor's Feather* (2010), which narrates Thia Beresford's travel from England to Patagonia in 1885 in order to embark on an adventurous riding expedition across the Pampas.

2) the role of history is visible in the text or, as Wallace puts it, "in its use of a particular period for its fictional setting" (*Woman's* 4).

3) the heroine and/or female author consciously subjects patriarchal values to a feminist critique such as political theories of power, divisions of labor, philosophical discourse, psychological assumptions, or historical accounts.

4) the socio-historical milieu and/or protagonist of the novel relates to the transnational feminist concerns of the author.

Perry Anderson articulates that traditional definitions of the genre, such as Lukács', entail that 1) the protagonist must be a human type shaped by grand sweeping historical events, 2) historical figures appear rarely and in minor roles, 3) the protagonist is a middle of the road character, 4) the novel honors history's losers "but upholds the historical necessity of winners," and 5) human progress is completed through conflicts (24).

By contrast, my understanding allows for the use of historical figures, both famous and unknown, to be the heroine; the heroines "are the ex-centrics, the marginalized, the peripheral figures of fictional history" and factual history (Hutcheon 114) instead of middle of the road characters; historical figures do not remain at a distance (Cohn 154), and I contend that at least one "real person [be in the novel] among the fictitious ones" (Fleishman 4); finally, these novels fiercely contest the notion of historical necessity and question masculinist definitions of progress.

In their historical-literary specificity, women's historical novels suggest once again that a commitment to master narratives or postmodernism can only serve women's writing so far. The woman's historical novel as scholars (L. Anderson; Danytė; Lennox; Von Dirke) note cannot fulfill androcentric definitions of the genre, e.g., Lukács', nor fully embrace a postmodern rejection of 'History' because the woman's historical novel refuses to believe that history or gender is reducible to discourse. Chow explains,

> Even though feminists partake in the postmodernist ontological project of dismantling claims of cultural authority that are housed in specific representations, feminism's rootedness in overt political struggles against the subordination of women makes it very difficult to accept the kind of postmodern 'universal abandon' in Ross's title [*Universal Abandon*]. ("Postmodern Automatons" 103)

Von Dirke like Chow asserts that "criteria for a positive model of writing women back into cultural history, [and] thereby rewriting history from a woman's perspective, show strong affinities with the poetics of the modern historical novel" (422). The woman's historical novel ultimately aligns, more or less, with the modern historical novel but like transnational feminism seeks solidarity through women's differences.

The genre, therefore, represents a communal (feminist) political consciousness, and a means towards contesting reality as expressed by Allende's heroine in *Inés of my Soul*. Inés reflects:

> I am amazed at Alonso's verses, which invent history and defy and conquer oblivion. Words that do not rhyme, like mine, do not have the authority of poetry, but in any case I am obliged to

relate my version of events in order to leave an account of the
labours we women have contributed in Chile; they tend to be
overlooked by the chroniclers ... the hundreds of brave women
who founded the towns while their men fought the wars will be
forgotten. (66)

It is in the very possibility for reconstruction post postmodernism that a
transnational feminist critique contributes to the discussion of not only historical fiction and the historical record but also of feminist political intervention.

The aforementioned discussion, relates to identifying a visible history in a
novel. This is not straightforward. Manzoni, for example, argues that the historical novel is

[a] species of a false genre which includes all compositions that
try to mix history and invention, whatever their form. Being the
most modern of such species, the historical novel is only the
most refined and ingenious effort yet to meet the challenge, as
if the challenge could ever be met. (81)

Thus, identifying history in the novel, if one cannot separate it from fiction, as
postmodernists (White, Hutcheon, Wesseling) suggest becomes problematic.
The woman's historical novel to reiterate challenges a postmodernist rejection
of any commitment to truth in literature that is grounded in historical reality.

Dorrit Cohn, using *War and Peace* as her example, offers the most promising option for the woman's historical novel; she differentiates between the historian and the novelist in terms of representing the inner life of historical figures (154). She reads historical novels "quite literally: its noun indicates (to use
Doblin's words) that it 'is, in the first place, a novel'; its adjective points to the
fact that, although 'it isn't history,' the historical dimension is (may be considered to be) more importantly involved in certain novels than in others" (162).
Historical novels blurring the real with the fictional are often supplemented
with paratext (glossary, maps, notes) and include bibliographical or historical
records and archives (diaries, photos, newspapers, codices). Sandra Gulland's
trilogy on Marie-Josephe-Rose Tascher (Josephine Bonaparte), for example, is
an invented diary, complete with chronology, genealogy, and love letters, of
Josephine's life prior to and after becoming Napoleon Bonaparte's wife in
1796. Carol Shields' *The Stone Diaries* (1993) is also a good example because
it contains a family tree, photographs, descriptions of stones which mark
gravesites, and is written in the style of a diary by a seemingly fictional and
ordinary character, Daisy Goodwill Flett.

Wallace, in a justified response to Anderson's essay "From Progress to Catastrophe," contends that it neglects and ignores women's writing prior to
Scott, and that, in addition to the paratext, imagination is an important tool for

feminist writers because "women have been violently excluded both from 'history' (the events of the past) and from 'History' (written accounts of the past) ("Letters" 25). Women's history is also often viewed as unhistorical or ahistorical, misrepresentative, inaccurate, fantastical, anti-nationalist, and/or escapist (Wallace, *Woman's* 13, 15). Historical archives, as feminist historiographers argue, have predominantly neglected the lives of women because they have been seen as constituting the familial and personal realm. This classification suggests a hierarchy between the familial and public realms, between women's and men's lives. Women's lives, confined to the familial, are considered historically uninteresting, and unworthy of history as opposed to the public lives of men. Women's historical fictions often center on the personal and familial life of women, recognizing the personal as, not only political, but historical and, likewise, the public and political as personal. Alison Light argues that exploring "women's lives and loves, their families and their feelings" gives "the concerns of the so called private sphere the status and interest of history" (59). For example, Allende in her Bibliographical Note to *Inés of My Soul* (2006) writes: "I want to demonstrate that they [Inés's experiences] are historical fact" (n. pag.). Personalizing her historical figures, especially the Spanish conquistador Pedro de Valdivia, she writes that Inés Suárez would know him "in a way history could never know him: what he feared and how he loved" (Allende 99). The woman's historical novel, since going transnational, therefore supports Light's claims, but it also gives credence to women who like Inés were publically politically active and visible.

Crossing Borders and Connecting Women: Transnational/Translational Feminisms

Surveying women's historical novels written in a transnational context entails reading under-represented nations, languages, and writers that previously have not been studied. Though not appearing outside of Europe until the mid-nineteenth century (with the exception of possibly some written in the United States, e.g., Louisa May Alcott), this trend of historical fiction changes dramatically at the turn of the twentieth century when women began writing historical novels from almost every nation and constituting large numbers of writers and readers. A lack of criticism, therefore, is no longer acceptable. The case remains, however, that most historical novels, women's or not, are still written or translated into European languages (English, French and Spanish). While there have been recent feminist calls for crossing-borders and moving beyond Anglo-European literatures and languages, this is proving, in a time of intense globalization, a difficult undertaking.

Heitlinger, inspired by Grewal and Kaplan, argues for "the need to trace the production, circulation, reception, and mobilization of key feminist concepts and discourses within and across different political contexts" (8). Transnational feminism uniquely allows for analyzing, not only the contents of a novel but also the physical being, the book itself, and the political process of how texts are produced. Essential to any understanding of literature is the politics of writing. How women writers, especially in developing nations, get their work published and disseminated into a transnational audience is dependent on globalization (Amireh and Majaj 4). Jasber Jain cautions, however, against the marketability of certain texts geared toward specific audiences, i.e., women's historical romances and an ever increasing pressure to publish in English, for example diasporic writing.

Just as writing in English dramatically increases a work's chance of success, so too does the word "woman" carry literary currency. Disclosing covert patriarchal tactics, Jain explains how including "women" in a book's title or description plays a decisive role in the marketability of novels: "The inclusion of the word 'woman' in a title enhances its sale value but also at the same time transforms this newly gained subjecthood into a commodity, as publishers both in India and abroad are inclined to translate works which are about women or dalits [oppressed classes]" (223). Capitalism's ever extending reach over the publication of novels, particularly into English for a targeted post-feminist consumer, has enormous implications for writers and readers, both feminist and non-feminist alike. A strong indicator for this transnational turn in literary studies is Paul Jay's work Global Matters: The Transnational Turn in Literary Studies (2010). Though he traces a useful history of globalization, emphasizes fluidity across borders and discusses gender, Jay only concentrates on novels written in English.

Reading novels other than those written in English, I am concerned with, like Constance S. Richards, the opportunities and limitations globalization offers feminism and women's writing. Richards poignantly points to a challenge I face in this project, the complexity of reading texts in colonial languages. I analyze novels in three languages, either in the original or in translation: French, English, and Spanish (for example Li Chin (2010) by Shin Kyung-sook, originally written in Korean, has been translated into French). Richards acknowledges that, though the use of Fredric Jameson's term "Third World Literatures" is problematic and too simplistic, "the production of Third World literatures has punctured colonial hegemony while at the same time surrendered itself to appropriation by the global market" (8). Referencing Aijaz Ahmad, Richards writes, "canonization which inevitably favoursfavors Third World texts in colonial languages, ignor[es] the richness and nuances of Indigenous literatures in Third World mother tongues, which contain the vast multiplicity of human experiences in the former colonies" (5). For women and multi-lingual immigrant and diasporic writers in particular, the pressure to write in colonial languages is, according to Deirdre Lashgari, even more detrimental. She writes:

For a woman writing from the margins … acceptance by the literary mainstream too often means a silencing a part of what she sees and knows. To write honestly may thus mean transgressing, violating the literary boundaries of the expected and accepted. This double bind is particularly strong for women writers of color, especially so if their vision is shaped by a language other than English. What is read by the dominant group as alien, rough-edged, jolting, strident, is more likely to offend when it comes from a woman. (Lashgari 2)

On the other hand, works written in colonial languages allow for a wider and more diverse reading audience and, thus, can be a meaningful way for connecting and sharing women's lived experiences (cf. Hayot).

In light of these issues or challenges, I call, as does Richards, for a "transnational feminist reading practice" (35) as an act of "imaginative reading" (28) which seeks a middle ground between text and context, Indigenous and colonial language, all the while acknowledging the politics of one's location as either a feminist woman writer, historical figure, or reader-critic.

Women, the Nation, and the Transnational Turn

Despite women's historical novels like Allende's, which problematize national studies on historical fiction, since the mid-twentieth century studies on the genre have been focusing increasingly on national literature. Suggesting that the nation has been a fundamental glue holding historical novels together since its early manifestations in Scott's works, Lukács writes, "[t]he appeal to national independence and national character is necessarily connected with a reawakening of national history" (25). This scholarship traces chronologically historical novels and their literary changes or developments within a particular nation, for instance England or the United States. There is an emphasis on defining this literature within its own national context as autonomous from other national literatures (for instance, Dan Ungurianu's *Plotting History: The Russian Historical Novel in the Imperial Age* (2007)).

This literature stresses the importance of the nation in our era of globalization and in times of globalization in the past, which has the simultaneous if not contradictory effect of breaking down and reifying borders. Seminal works on boundaries, like Gloria Anzaldúa's *Borderlands/La Frontera: The New Mestiza* (1987), which discusses the Mexico-United States border, highlights the aforementioned paradox. Resonating with Anzaldúa's writing is the need for theorizing the woman's historical novel by examining how borders and "different nations conceive of [history and] the historical novel" from a gendered perspective (Groot 11). The focus of critical debate, including Benedict Anderson's influential concept of "imagined communities" (which has strong connections with the advent of the printing press), is that the meaning of nationhood is central to historical novels. Most often it is, however, the intersections between nationhood and gender or gender itself as an "imagined community" that takes priority in women's historical novels. Echoing Lukács' thoughts on national awakenings to history (25), there is an awakening of a gender consciousness in the woman's historical novel.

Problematizing nationalistic literary studies, Rey Chow makes a convincing case for why a comparative study, such as on the woman's historical novel, must contest notions of national languages, and national literatures ("In the Name" 109) and why when putting the nation into crisis, one cannot replace reading European texts with those from non-Western nations.Chow concludes that "[t]he issues involved in women's literature, gay and lesbian literature, ethnic literature, exceed the boundaries of the nation and national language and that they demand to be studied with newer conceptual methods" ("In the Name" 114). Supporting Chow's thinking, Margaret Higonnet argues that "to presume the primary import of national or ethnic differences both denies today's world economy in its cultural manifestations and shapes a reductive politics of identity" ("Comparative Literature" 157). Sarah Webster Goodwin further confirms that "it is by now no secret that the development of literary studies has followed closely the growth of nationalist sentiment in Western cultures. But this does not mean that the borders of modern nations coincide tidily with those of their cultures, and there are countless borderline areas" (255). Chow, Higonnet, and Goodwin's questioning of how literature and for my purposes women's historical novels can reinforce or undermine these boundaries and identity politics highlight the complex relation between national literatures and cultural boundaries.

One sees in literary scholarship a distinct split between studies which increasingly reinforce the nation as the center and those moving towards transnational texts and theorizing transnationalism. Notable examples of the latter include Jay's scholarship, Stephen Clingman's *The Grammar of Identity: Transnationalist Fiction and the Nature of the Boundary* (2009) , Nele Bemong et al.'s *Re-Thinking Europe: Literature and (Trans)National Identity* (2008) and Richards' *On the Winds and Waves of Imagination: Transnational Feminism and Literature* (2000). Jay, for one, examines "a number of contemporary literary texts produced in the context of globalization in order to develop some models for the reading and analysis of fiction that are both a product of and engaged with the forces of globalization" (6).

III. Maternal Genealogies

Establishing a maternal genealogy within the woman's historical novel is a necessary step in creating an alternative literary-history for women as has already been shown through the work of Stevens, Wallace, and Maxwell. Significantly, these three critics offer maternal genealogies that bypass Scott. Irigaray, stressing the importance of these endeavors, writes:

If we are not to be accomplices in the murder of the mother,... [we must] assert that there is a genealogy of women. There is a genealogy of women within our family: on our mother's side we have mothers, grandmothers and great-grandmothers, and daughters. Given our exile in the family of the father-husband, we tend to forget this genealogy of women, and we are often persuaded to deny it. Let us try to situate ourselves within this female genealogy so as to conquer and keep our identity. Nor let us forget that we already have a history, that certain women have, even if it was culturally difficult, left their mark on history and that all too often we do not know them. (*IrigarayReader* 44)

Femino-centric genealogies in the woman's historical novel constitute alternatives to patriarchal genealogies and encourage women to reject identification in opposition and relation to man. Braidotti asserts that when narratives develop maternal genealogies, "the specificity of the lived, female embodied experience" becomes a site for symbolic feminist change (*Nomadic Subjects* 100). Thus, a maternal genealogy is a constructive dialogue which brings together women's past lives with women's current transnational experiences and allows for a more fruitful and fuller understanding of the continuities between feminists. Studying the woman's historical novel within a transnational feminist framework provides a way to understand coalitions and continuities between the diverse social and political experiences of women.

Writing about women's historical lives decenters the established patriarchal order by undermining or exposing a false system that operates unethically on gender hierarchies and separates women from each other as rival-commodities. Irigaray poignantly asks:

What modifications would it [society] undergo if women left behind their condition as commodities-subject to being produced, consumed, valorized, circulated, and so on, by men alone –and took part in elaborating and carrying out exchanges? Not by reproducing, by copying, the 'phallocratic' models that have the force of law today, but by socializing in a differ-

ent way the relation to nature, matter, the body, language and
desire. ("Women on the Market" 188-89)

Expanding upon her earlier projects, Irigaray, working with Italian feminists, uses the term affidamento to identify not only the differences between
women but also the connections.

Creating a feeling of solidarity between women is essential in transnational
feminism and women's historical fiction. Alexander, like Irigaray, is concerned
with writing alternative genealogies that serve as bridges between time and
space. I read her theory of the palimpsest as a feminist supplement to Lukács'
dialectical model in which he argues the past is a necessary precondition for the
present (21). Alexander writes of understanding the imperfect and impossible
erasure of the past:

> As the 'new' structured through the 'old' scrambled, [a] pal-
> impsestic character of time, both jettisons the truncated dis-
> tance of linear time and dislodges the impulse for incommen-
> surability … it thus rescrambles the 'here and now' and the
> 'then and there,' to a 'here and there' and a 'then and now,'
> and makes visible what Payal Banerjee called the ideological
> traffic between. (190)

Alexander's examples can be read in congruence with women's historical novels which stress continuity between the past and present (for example Moran's
novel *Nefertiti Queen of Egypt, Daughter of Eternity* suggests Nefertiti's rule
as Pharaoh has been purposely hidden and written over but tracings of her rule
can still be perceived). Samantha Haigh believes that "the move of return and
reworking, of going back in order to go forward … [is] emblematic of the necessity for all women under patriarchy of going back specifically to explore
their relationship with their mother" (62). The woman's historical novel functions as a transnational feminist genre by writing back through our mothers.

Revisionist writing is necessary in order to reclaim a historical reality for
women while at the same time challenge reality defined within masculine parameters, or, as Serena Anderlini-D'Onofrio puts it, "conflating realism with
phallocentric representation" (167). Braidotti argues that this "amounts to a
collective repossession of the images and representations of Woman such as
they have been coded in language, culture, science, knowledge, and discourse
and consequently internalized in the heart, mind, body and lived experience of
women" (*Nomadic Subjects* 100). Also necessary is rejecting a past "colonized
by the male imaginary" (101). The importance of a femino-centric reappropria-
tion of the maternal as evidenced in the recent proliferation of women's historical novels within a transnational context is, therefore, not surprising. While
other readings or interpretations of these texts are possible, reading the femino-

centric aspects of each novel together centralizes a transnational feminist consciousness of the maternal.

Sex and Gender, Fact and Fiction

Filling in historical gaps, inventing, and imagining, all from a woman's point
of view/voice, link the novels surveyed in this book. The underlying concern is
to make visible, via a literary context, what Barbara McManus argues has been
missing from traditional studies on women's history–woman's determination of
the course of history (in daily life, both private and public). Making women's
history visible requires rereading canonical literary texts, which have subordinated, polarized, moralized, and eroticized women, in favor of "symbolic elements working to idealize the masculine" (McManus 118).

In her Author's Note to *Boudica: Dreaming the Serpent Spear*, Manda Scott
asserts that "[i]t is too late to go back and remake history. It is not too late to go
forward differently" (508). Change for women, however, is not possible without rethinking the past; seeking to establish a maternal genealogy that disrupts
patriarchal nationalism, both past and present, women's novels raise gender
consciousness cross-culturally, historically, and transnationally. Wallace writes
that such "texts all privilege the female point of view and thus expose the subjective and phallocentric nature of mainstream historiography" (Woman's 206).
Women's historical novels concentrating on gender and history supplement
archival omissions/erasures and, as such, are important feminist counter-novels
to the accepted historical record and genre of historical fiction.

The woman's historical novel not only grapples with the relation between
fact and narrative, or history and fiction, which is inherent in the genre but also
with a definition of gender. Within feminist theory and historiography, to reiterate, there is debate between strategies. Some historians of women's lives
argue for the necessity of inserting women into the past, uncovering voices and
experiences, and challenging the conceptual absence of women from our historical accounts (an example is Allende's *Inés of My Soul*). Others, historians
of gender, focus on the meaning and discourse of being a woman rather than
authentic experience and voice: "The categories woman and man are not
viewed as fixed identities or natural entities but as constructions of gender with
variable meanings across cultures and time" (Haggis 46). An understanding of
gender as constructed is supported by Wallace, who writes that:

> One of the central reasons women writers have turned to the
> historical novel ... is that a temporal viewpoint allows us to see
> that gender is historically contingent rather than essential. If
> gender roles are subject to change over time then they are

clearly socially and culturally constructed and open to the possibility of further change. (*Woman's* 8)

Wallace does not explicitly make the comparison or connection between fact as
sex and fiction as gender, but this is a worthwhile line of thinking to pursue.
Historical novels, such as Woolf's *Orlando*, often criticized for inventing history or lacking in historical truth, suggest the distinction between fiction and
history is irrelevant; it is viewed entirely as fiction. Similarly, Judith Butler
radically asserts that "[i]f the immutable character of sex is contested, perhaps
this construct called 'sex' is as culturally constructed as gender; indeed, perhaps it was always already gender, with the consequence that the distinction
between sex and gender turns out to be no distinction at all" (10-11). Facts, like
sex or history, are discursively performed according to prescriptive norms and,
therefore, have no greater a claim to 'Reality' than contingent gender roles.

For many women's historical novels, it is precisely the gap in the historical
record, between the history and fiction, and the gender and sex that is being
questioned and explored. Wallace argues that the postmodernist woman's novel
highlights not only "the constructed and multiple nature of history" but also the
historical construction and multiplicity of gender (*Woman's* 203-04). A return
to Hutcheon's definition of postmodern historical fiction and her argument that
our only access to the historical past is via narrative (114) supports Butler's
claims that our only access to 'sex' is through its texts and that sex itself becomes a text determined by interconnecting/intersubjective matrices of power.
Thus, in order to make sense of the past or materiality/corporeality, we impose
a linguistic shape or sex/gender upon that which inherently has no shape or sex
or gender (Butler 17). In Manzoni's terms, this means putting the flesh that is
fiction back on the skeleton that is fact (17), or, rather, gender putting the flesh
back on the bones of 'sex.'

Rethinking sex in relation to fact acknowledges history as a series of accepted human made-facts and a useful construction for functioning in the everyday. For example, if a bus schedule says the bus will arrive at 1pm, it is true
because time is standardized. Just as the bus in a years' time may change its
route or schedule, the meanings of sex and gender are capable of change. Historical facts, like sex and gender, are not in and of themselves necessarily true
for all time, but they are true within their own socio-historical period and can
be verified; thus, we believe in objective facts in order to function on a daily
basis: filling in one's sex on a passport is similar to catching the bus at 1 pm.
Spivak's phrase "strategic essentialism" suggests that, rather than take an ei-
ther/or position between essentialism and sex and gender as a social construct,
feminists adopt the strategy of unity for political purposes: "The strategic use
of an essence as a mobilizing slogan or masterword like woman or worker or

the name of a nation is, ideally, self-conscious for all mobilized" (*Outside in the Teaching Machine* 3).

The prevalence of cross-dressing in women's historical novels, also relates, to a consideration of sex and gender. Wallace argues that cross-dressing is a means for women writers to "cross-write as men" and to imagine "the girl masquerading as a boy" (*Woman's* 209), found, for example, in texts such as Patricia Duncker's *The Doctor* (1999), in which the renowned British military surgeon James Miranda Stuart Barry (1789 -1865) is secretly a woman. Similarly, Lau A-yin is a cross-dressing immigrant who transforms into the Chinese Mr. Lowe in Jamaica in Patricia Powell's *The Pagoda* (1998); others novels like D'Eaubonne's, Longfellow's, Piat's, and so on, all focus on cross-dressing. Cross-dressing/crossinggenders, in these novels, proves, on one hand, to be a practical necessity for survival and, on the other, a liberating experience to masquerade under a different identity.

Nevertheless, women's historical novels do not readily conform to Butler's claims on the mutability of sex. With, perhaps, the exception of Woolf's *Orlando*, an important precursor to Saracen's *Sarah, Son of God* (2011) because of its transsexual, transgenre, transhistorical, and transnational nature, sex remains a fixed category in women's historical novels. Woolf and Saracen both parody biological sex (Orlando is a man in the first half of the novel and then wakes up a woman) and history (the novel spans over the life of Orlando's 400 years); Saracen's novel narrates a lesbian love affair between a transgendered woman (Sarah, who used to be Tadzio) and Joanna, an academic who employs Sarah to help uncover the truth about both the author and the author's gender of a book published in Renaissance Venice and another woman's long-lost diary recounting Christ's final days.

Aside from these examples, however, sex is a stable category in historical novels. Butler's thinking, nonetheless, is an instructive, if not provoking, source for rethinking the historical past as a myriad of both fact and fiction, whereby one can begin to develop a feminist strategy for questioning gender and sex as mutually social construction and materiality/corporeality. Thus, the parody we see in Woolf's, Butler's, and Hutcheon's position is potentially political and strategic for women in terms of transforming rigid ideologies of femininity, sexuality, and social roles, but, nevertheless, still risks that the parody will be misread, overlooked, or go unrecognized and risks the fragmentation and loss of any identity or referent for feminism.

Women's historical novels, like those on Kristine, Queen of Sweden (portrayed as a cross-dresser upholding masculine ideals) or those on France's Marie-Antoinette (represented as extremely maternal and feminine), suggest that gender, if not sex, is unstable and demonstrate how patriarchal gender expectations seemingly lock women into subordinate positions. Subverting the inferior positions of women by laying claim to political power traditionally reserved for men, both queens, however, ultimately reinforce and buttress patriarchal ideals of gender. Neither is able to find a place for women outside of or beyond the constructed binaries of gender-sex. Audrey Macklin writes that not only are borders gendered, but that "gender is bordered" and she notes that an "enforcement of the boundaries of gender identity is sufficiently strict that crossing borders is not called migration, but transgression" (276). Kristine and Marie-Antoinette, and perhaps all women, are inscribed in discourses of gender and sex to the extent that they strive to fulfill ideals of masculinity and femininity, which in everyday lived experience as the protagonists show us can never be obtained or sustained and are indefinitely and inevitably transgressed.

Hope Jennings writes that we must:

> Think through the problems that arise when women attempt to assert a specifically feminine/sexual subject while continuing to define themselves according to male representations or symbols of femininity. She reminds us of the risks that accompany a female imaginary when it fails to remain self-conscious or critical of the position and/or premises from which it speaks; when contesting the myths of patriarchy, a feminist discourse must avoid the trap of falling for its own myths that it appropriates or sets up. (82)

If sexual difference is the question of our age (Irigaray, *Ethics of Sexual Difference* 5), the woman's historical novel proves a fruitful genre by asking what it means for men and women to be equals and how, if at all, equality can be defined?

For Irigaray, equality between the sexes does not mean women conforming to the lives and ways of men (*Irigaray Reader* 207) since "the human race is divided into two genres which ensure its production and reproduction. Trying to suppress sexual difference is to invite a genocide more radical than any destruction that has ever existed in History. What is important, on the other hand, is defining values of belonging to a sex-specific genre" (32).When women imitate men, man remains the ideal standard and norm (education, wage, public position, vote etc.) (32). Naomi Schor clarifies: "If othering involves attributing to the objectified other a difference that serves to legitimate her oppression, saming denies the objectified other the right to her difference, submitting the other to laws of phallic specularity" (48). Irigaray's work suggests that feminist literature has the potential to formulate new definitions of equality, one that understands woman in relation to man differently, and one in which woman is neither reduced (saming) nor opposed (othering) to man as the ideal.

Conclusion

This introduction situates the woman's historical novel within a contemporary transnational context. The analysis has been a way for exploring how gender is historically and literarily defined and how history and literature are shaped by gender. Traditional master and postmodern narratives do not adequately encompass the woman's historical novel, which entails an advocacy for social change across a plurality of voices, cultures, nations, and historical locations. For this reason, in a time of globalization, transnational feminism is an appropriate means for studying these diverse novels and for highlighting two issues: first, that transnational feminism operates within globalization by interlinking and forging feminist activist connections cross-nationally—here the writing and reading of texts—while at the same time challenging not only the patriarchal, capitalistic and consumptive aspects of globalization but also the centrality of the nation. Secondly, feminist novels politically undermine patriarchal authority of the past while, at the same time, they assert a truth or interpretation of the past. These novels put forth, whether consciously or not, a belief in progress (reproductive justice, religious freedom, racial, sexual, class, or political equality), for women both within literature and history. The texts argue that women have the power to change women's lives. Though historical novels deal with the past, most feminist writers are not endorsing a return to the past; history is not an escape, but an inspiration for making meaningful changes in contemporary settings. The following chapters therefore provide different perspectives on the ways in which women writers have explored the theme of the maternal through several key transnational topics and, in doing so, have innovatively used the genre of historical fiction as a feminist medium for writing back through our mothers.

CHAPTER ONE

Revisionist Writing: Mothers of the Americas

> If history is the mirror wherein generations to come shall con-
> template the image of generations that went before, the novel
> must be the photograph that records the vices and virtues of a
> people, along with a moral prescription for the former and an
> admiring homage to the latter
> – Clorinda Matto de Turner, *Birds Without a Nest: A Novel*
> (1889)

Recuperating maternal figures, our "founding" mothers, is a relatively new
theme in women's historical fiction and women's historiography. These works
constitute important feminist revisions of both known and lesser known maternal figures. In reclaiming their protagonists from derogatory historical-literary
designations such as "whore" and "traitor" or "victim," the novels complicate
the notion of who constitutes a founding mother – "who and what had made the
nation" (Jameson, "Ties Across the Border" 67) – and challenge the way dominant masculine narratives have previously appropriated maternal genealogies
for patriarchal purposes like the national imagination.

   This chapter analyzes one specific context of rewriting maternal origins in
the woman's historical novel–the colonizing of Indigenous people and their
lands/nations, the Americas, by Europeans. Though feminist historians since
the 1970s (for example, Sylvia Van Kirk's pioneering text *"Many Tender
Ties": Women in Fur-Trade Society in Western Canada, 1670-1870* (1980))
have actively rewritten traditional masculinist histories, i.e., Edgar McInnis',
Harold Innis's, or Frederick Jackson Turner's which suggest women (both European immigrants and Aboriginals) did not participate in fundamental ways to
the colonizing of the Americas (Jameson, "Ties Across the Border" 67), surprisingly, this topic is only now receiving literary attention – for example,
Crystine Brouillet's Marie LaFlamme trilogy (1990s), Suzanne Desrochers'
Bride of New France (2011) or Kathleen O'Neal Gear's *This Widowed Land*
(1993). Mothers of the Americas considers the authors' choices to focus on
femino-centric topics as deliberate and essential in understanding women's
realities – both early European women immigrating to the Americas as well as
the experiences of Indigenous women encountering both European men and

women in the sixteenth and seventeenth centuries. By discussing the Transatlantic crossing, the woman as traitor to the nation, forced marriages for the purpose of procreation, the importance of language, and finally the ties that connect women with one another transnationally, despite patriarchal national boundaries and borders, a clear feminist genealogy and revisionist history of the Americas emerges.

In this chapter, I survey Virginia Bernhard's *A Durable Fire* (1990), which describes perspectives from an Indigenous woman, Pocahontas and English immigrants to the Jamestown Colony at the turn of the seventeenth century, Colette Piat's novel on the colonizing of Québec in *Les Filles du Roi* (1998), and examples of women's historical novels written on the colonizing of Hispanic America: Laura Esquivel's *Malinche* (2006) and Isabel Allende's *Inés of my Soul* [*Inés del Alma Mía*] (2006).[3]

While criticism on women's historical novels set in early North America is still missing, María Ángeles Cantero-Rosales and Helena Araújo provide insight into the Hispanic context. Cantero-Rosales believes prejudices within Latin-American society contribute to being "*contra la literature feminine, en realidad contra cualquier aspect de la creatividad en la mujer*" 'against women's literature, in reality against any aspect of creativity in a woman' (132). Criticism on Allende like other Hispanic women writers, e.g., Angeles Mastretta, has suffered because of "*[e]l agudo sexism de la sociedad latinoamericana que, sustentada en estructuras mentales jerarquizadas, enmarca a <La Mujer> en espacios de subordinanción e inferioridad, demand de ella un rol pasivo y silencioso*" 'the acute sexism of Latin-American society, sustained in hierarchical intellectual structures which enclose "Woman" in subordinate and inferior spaces, demanding of her a role of passivity and silence' (Araújo 131). In comparing works set and written across the Americas, several important and interconnecting transnational topics emerge, all of which contribute to changing patriarchal literary-historical portrayals of women's lives during the early settling of the Americas.

Rewriting women as symbolic progenitors of contemporary and future genealogies both within and beyond the text is, thus, an important feminist political goal. Samantha Haigh writes:

---

[3] All translations from Piat's novel are my own. I use Margaret Sayers Peden's English translation for Allende's novel and Ernesto Mestre-Reed's English translation of Esquivel's *Malinche*. Chicana and Mexican feminists such as Cherríe L. Morgaga, Adelaida R. Del Castillo, Ana Nieto-Gomez, and Sandra Messinger Cypress, to name a few, have actively recuperated Malinche, but in the form of feminist plays, essays, and poetry. For some reason, the historical novel, which seems to me the most suitable medium for such a figure, has been under utilized.

> In the absence of a maternal genealogy, daughters can never
> symbolize their relation to their mother, to 'origin', a relation
> men symbolize by recreating it in relationships with other
> women. It is the resymbolization of this relationship which is
> the condition for a (re)symbolized relationship between wom-
> en. It is thus vital that a maternal genealogy be (re)discovered,
> that women be able to separate themselves from and symbolize
> their relation to be woman-mother as 'origin.' (63)

By returning to our mother as 'origin,' the authors offer inventive feminist re-
cuperations of complex figures for whom negotiating a transition from Old to
New World, in which Christianity plays a fundamental role, is necessary.

Revisionist novels, Diana Wallace argues, refashion the historical novel into
a "herstory" as opposed to history as *history*. The latter's approach is that "female historical figures were and are understood solely through male-authored
narratives [and rejects/ …] problematizes historical fiction, by and for and
about women" (Cooper and Short 3). "Herstory" narratives combat this inherent sexism by "reinsert[ing] women into history using techniques (such as first-
person narrative), which make them the speaking subjects, not the objects, of
historical narrative. Through this and their use of non-realist discourses (myth
and fantasy), they stretch the form of the historical novel well beyond the realist conventions lauded by Lukács" (*Woman's* 184). All four authors also adopt
feminist "hyperbole as a tool for creating fantasies or questioning the relationship between fiction and reality (and the impossibility, at times, of distinguishing between the two)" (Weldt-Basson 123). Targeted by Harold Bloom, however, Allende has been criticized for poorly imitating Gabriel García Marquéz's
magical realist works. As Cantero Rosales argues this ignores the fact "*la tra-
dicíon literaria moderna ha estimado la mimesis de manera despectiva, lle-
gando a acusar a quien la utiliza de falta de originalidad y carencia de preten-
siones estéticas …las formas de 'imitación' son una alternativa para socavar y
dinamitar los presupuestos ideológicos establecidos*" 'the modern literary tradition defines mimesis in a derogatory manner, accusing those who use it as
lacking originality and aesthetic merit … forms of 'imitation' are capable of
undermining and blowing apart the established ideological [patriarchal] assumptions' (134). The political potential ofAllende's mimesis is echoed by Helene
Carol Weldt-Basson, who believes what sets her "use of hyperbole apart [from
García Marquéz's] is its consistent employment with regard to feminine roles
within a context of situational irony" (123). In addition, within each novel, "the
reader is presented with two contradictory images of the protagonist … the
silent, passive, female who falls in love … or the strong, influential woman"
(Weldt-Basson 127). The protagonists fall in love at a young age and embrace

traditional femininity, but later in life practice roles traditionally associated with men such as doctoring, fighting, and speaking in public. Rewriting women protagonists (both Aboriginal and European-immigrant) from nuanced feminist perspectives undermines masculinist master discourses of Western history and national myths. As Adele Perry suggests, these novels are a testament that "we cannot separate the history of women, gender, and the family from that of lands 'explored,' proclamations made, wars fought, colonies governed, goods traded, and treaties signed or resisted (92).

Though often adhering to the traditional subject matter of historiography (e.g., wars, revolutions, conquests), these women's lives have for misogynistic reasons been ignored, falsified, or forgotten. Instead of acknowledging women's heroic contributions to the nation, studies typically focus on motherhood. Gayatri Chakravorty Spivak argues that our identity, given by the mother, our origin (both maternal and national), is coded and re-coded (*Nationalism and Imagination* 43) because of woman's assigned "plac[e] in the reproductive heteronormativity that supports nationalisms" (42). She reads nationalist narratives and discourses premised upon "women as holding the future of the nation in their wombs" (43). This propagates the belief that "motherhood is woman's highest calling" (Chrisler and Garrett 132). As is evident in the novels, the private and public spheres are problematically ruled by *patria*rchy. It is, thus, not a coincidence that motherhood plays such a formidable, albeit ambivalent, role in women's historical novels and figures prominently in this chapter on the colonizing of the Americas. Discussing the following femino-centric topics, transatlantic crossings, traitors to the nation, sexual politics, mother-tongues, racial hybridity, and new ties between women reveals the political importance of rewriting women back into a history of the Americas.

Transatlantic Crossings

In Allende's *Inés of My Soul*, Piat's *Les Filles du Roi*, and Bernhard's *A Durable Fire* the heroines, Inés, Marie, and Temperance serve as pivotal figures in an important moment not only in colonial but also women's history. Both novels narrate a European heroine's memoir of crossing. The crossing for each is physical and psychical; the Atlantic Ocean serves as a means for transmuting painful and stagnant pasts in their home countries, Spain, France and England respectively, into imaginary promised lands, complete with freedom, discovery, and love. Veronica C. Wang writes that such a comparison "provides a multivalent look into immigrant/émigré lives, which helps to sharpen for the reader the physical, cultural, and psychological displacement felt by the protagonists" (23); thus, establishing a maternal genealogy is a means for the author-reader via heroine to cope with "psychological fragmentation and cultural dislocation" caused by their transatlantic crossing (Wang 22). Allende chronicles the historical migrancy of Inés, born in Plasencia, Spain, "a border city steeped in war and religion" (6), in the year 1507, "following the famine and deadly plague that ravaged Spain upon the death of Philip the Handsome" (1). Inés' narrative is a memoir to her adopted daughter Isabel, written and dictated in the city of Santiago de la Nueva Extremadura, Kingdom of Chile, which she co-found with her lover, Pedro de Valdivia.

Piat's novel, also a memoir in the form of a letter, is dated "*Amsterdam, en l'an de grâce, le 4ᵉ septembre 1690*" 'Amsterdam, in the year of our lord, September 4ᵗʰ, 1690.' Marie Arnault's letter is to her friend, the historical figure Catherine Jérémie, a midwife from Québec who was known for her expertise in botany. Piat's fictional heroine, born in 1648 in a "*petit bourg norman non loin de Carentan*" 'a small town not far from Carentan' (13), France, is based on historical accounts of *Filles du Roi*. Also known as Daughters of the King, many women were sent from the Salpêtriere, the infamous Parisian hospital and prison, to New France in 1663 for the purpose of populating the new colony. The prison was "*une ville dans la ville; un vaisseau gigantesque de la misère humaine, où les rues, les venelles, les bâtisses s'entrecroisent, grouillant de mendiants, de folles, de filles de mauvaise vie, de voleuses, criminelles, indésirables de tous poils*" 'a city within a city, a great ship of human misery where the streets, alleys, and buildings intersect, full with the unfortunates, the insane, women of easy virtue, criminals, undesirables of all kinds' (97).

In A Durable Fire, Temperance, who sails, with her new husband, George Yardley, though they travel on separate ships, to Virginia in 1609 later describes her "choice" of journey to the Indigenous princess, Pocahontas as "we didn't come," ...we were brought" (283); her friend, Lucy, elaborates, "We came because our husbands came" (ibid.). Even the fictional character, Meg Worley comes to Virginia to discover the fate of her husband, Anthony who as part of an earlier settlement in Roanoke in 1587 disappeared and was never heard from again. Inés, likewise in Allende's text, chooses to go to the New World under the pretext of searching for her estranged husband, only known as Juan de Málaga, and Marie, a prisoner in the Salpêtriere, feels compelled, albeit not forced, to leave her family and illicit Huguenot lover, Jacob Preclair, behind.

Les Filles du Roi, Piat explains, were women who "*le Roi avait décidé d'envoyer par vaisseaux entiers des filles de familles, des ouvrières pauvres, des veuves ou des orphelines auxquelles une dot serait allouée*" 'the King had decided to send by ship–daughters from entire families, poor workers, widows or the orphans whom he would give a dowry' (*Filles du Roi* 109). One of Piat's innovative contributions is that she refutes the common belief that *Les Filles du Roi* were prostitutes. She writes:

> *Contrairement à ce que l'on a longtemps pensé, on y trouvait*
> *surtout des orphelines, peut-être quelques prostitute es, mais*
> *bien peu. Cette recherche et l'écriture de mon roman m'ont*
> *permis de rétablir la vérité historique à leur sujet, mais aussi*
> *d'écrire sur la misère épouvantable qui sévissait en France*
> *sous Louis XIV.*
>
> Contrary to what has been thought for a long time, I found
> above all that very few of the Orphans were prostitutes. This
> research and the writing of my book permitted me to reestab-
> lish the true history of this subject, but also to write on the ap-
> palling misery which raged throughout France under Louis
> XIV. (Piat, "Les Filles" n. pag.)

On account of Monsieur Brézin and her mother, Marie is chosen from the prisoners in the Salpêtriere for the first historic voyage to Québec under the guidance of Jean Talon on the *Neptune*.

Upon arriving in Québec, Marie, delaying marriage, works as a doctor for
Marie de l'Incarnation in the Ursuline's convent. She cannot, however, shirk
her duty as a *Filles du Roi* for long. She is told "*donner votre âme à Dieu*"
'give your soul to God' (152) or a take a husband. Piat suggests that, in this
patriarchal society, women's roles are defined by their relations to men; daughters, wives, mothers, nuns, and, of course, loyal subjects to the King who is like
God, *le Père*. Marie has one choice of occupation available to her: marriage–
either to an earthly husband or God.

In these novels there is migration in the physical sense but also nomadism in
Rosi Braidotti's terms, because the characters do not "hesitate to challenge their
societies. Being a nomad requires inventing oneself and not relying on the established customs" (Lagos 124). Nomadism emphasizes how "narratives [can]
show that being in between languages and cultural codes provides … a step in
the process of changing the world for women" (ibid.) and confirms the fragili-
ty-breakability of masculine boundaries. María Claudia André points out how
the heroines "deconstruct the boundaries of the space-bound stagnant female
subjects" (76); yet, we must be skeptical of this "liberatory" space-taking. In
breaking out of their confined spaces, whose spaces are these women inhabiting and taking? Whose space are the women infringing upon, and what women
are they re-enclosing into confined spaces as a result of their new found freedom? The Indigenous woman in the novel, for example, Bernhard's Pocahontas
has no recourse to her own story, and at one point in the novel she is kidnapped
and imprisoned by the English settlers; the reader, however, has more access to

Temperance's, the European heroine's, and her male compatriots', like John Smith's and John Rolfe's, accounts; thus in order for feminists to avoid imposing a new master narrative, transnational feminism alerts us to significant gaps and silences when it comes to Indigenous and other minority women's voices.

Emphasizing Braidotti's addition of embodied acts of travel and displacement to her earlier concept of nomadism, all the novels narrate a physical migration. The experience of migration for Inés first takes place in 1537, when she sails with her cousin under the captaincy of Maestro Manuel Martín. Inés, like Marie and Temperance, describes her experiences on the ship as terrible: a cramped quarter separated from the male crew only by a wooden partition, the scarcity of food, the prevalence of disease, and the threat of storms and pirate attacks. In these circumstances, all the women reveal their skills for tending the ill and wounded, but Inés, however, finds the ship's close quarters particularly difficult as she continually experiences the threat of rape from the sailor, Sebastián Romero. The prevalence of rape in this culture is seen again when the crew finally disembarks in the New World, and Inés encounters Indigenous peoples for the first time. The rape of the Indian girls signifies rape as an experience individual to its victim but a shared experience for women across race and class. The rape of the Indian girls foreshadows Inés' continual harassment from Romero, including two rape attempts, which result first in Inés putting a dagger to his neck, and then, finally, murdering him in self-defense.

Arriving in Cartagena, Inés sees "hundreds of natives, naked in chains… transporting large stones, spurred by the whips of overseers," and a cargo ship from Africa with slaves ready for market (Allende, *Inés of my Soul* 51). Allende's implicit suggestion is that the wealth generated from the slave-trade, including the slavery of women, who, likewise, make a "transatlantic crossing," allows voyages like Inés' and her compatriots' to transpire in the first place. Under the pretense of searching for her husband, Inés sails on to Panamá and continues to earn her living by healing and treating the wounded or diseased, until she discovers that Juan has been in Peru. Making her way to Peru, she arrives in Ciudad de los Reyes, where she is informed "your husband died in the battle at Las Salinas" (77).

Traitor to the Nation

If Piat's and Allende's novels are primarily about recuperating the unsung mothers of the nation, Bernhard's to some extent and Esquivel's most definitely is a rewrite of a woman known, like the biblical tale of Eve, as a traitor of the nation. Bernhard's text, at crucial times in the novel, takes up the life of a well-known Indigenous figure, Pocahontas. In the beginning of the work set in

1607, she saves John Smith's, one of the early English settler's, life. Pocahontas is introduced to the reader as an inquisitive, bold twelve year-old daughter of the chief, Powhatan, seeing a white settler, in this case Smith, for the first time: "in some curious way, she felt drawn to him" (18). Held captive by Powhatan because he is an enemy, Smith learns he is to be clubbed to death. Seconds after Powhatan's signal for the murder to commence, Bernhard describes Pocahontas intervening: "Pocahontas, panting, lay with her arms on top of John Smith's arms, and her head next to his, so close that their cheeks touched" (20). Praising Smith for his bravery in facing imminent death, Powhantan frees him and declares to Pocahontas that she will become the English man's friend and spy on his settlement. The friendship matures when Pocahontas, without the chief's permission, seduces Smith in a special love-dance. Angered by his daughter's disobedience, Powhantan refuses any contact between his daughter and Smith, and secretly plots to kill Smith and the other settlers. On false pretenses of friendship and good will, Powhantan invites the starving settlers to join in a feast and to exchange goods. Pocahontas, afraid once again for her lover's life and knowing her father's true intentions to murder the settlers, manages to warn Smith. Her punishment for betraying her father and her people is banishment for life, and as Bernhard states, "she would not see John Smith for seven long years" (30).

Bernhard shifts away from Pocahontas' story at this point, which problematically suggests her narrative is defined by English men (also evident in the material from the historical record, 1607-22, Bernhard includes at the end of the novel). Once banished, and no longer in contact with Smith, her history is silenced. Meanwhile, Bernhard centers on the young English woman, Temperance who, assuming her husband has died at sea on the transatlantic voyage, is struggling to survive in Jamestown. Ever dependent on her husband's friend, Will Sterling (one of the few fictional characters in the novel), Bernhard, nevertheless, invents a love story for Temperance which takes up a majority of the novel. Pocahontas' story comes back into the narrative only at "Potomac: 29 March 1613," (266) nearly four years since her last encounter with Smith. Unbeknownst to Pocahontas, now the wife of king of the Potomacs is that Smith is back in England, having returned after suffering from a near fatal attack on his life. Tricked into boarding an English ship manned by Captain Argall and enroute to Jameston and Henrico, so that she can be ransomed for grain and corn, Pocahontas declares: "He had played false with her, and she hated him for it. She hated all the English except John Smith" (272). It is while being kept a prisoner by Argall, Pocahontas, however, meets a widower, John Rolfe.

When Rolfe sees the poor conditions in which Pocahontas is kept, he decries, "My God, man! … You can't treat her like an animal!" (279). Effective in his plea for her care, Rolfe manages to succeed in convincing the Captain to move Pocahontas to the home of Alexandar Whitaker, a parson. During her time with Whitaker, Pocahontas is baptized as Rebecca, versed in her catechism, and dressed in English clothing. The narrative's other protagonist, Temperance, is credited with having "transformed an Indian princess into an English lady" (280). This unrealistic scene is nonetheless pivotal because it is the only one in which the two protagonists come into contact: it is telling that the transformation only works one way –Temperance doesn't show any interest in Pocahontas's language, religion, or Indigenous clothing. Also, it is only when Pocahontas takes on the ways of the English that she is deemed suitable for carrying on a relationship with Rolfe.

The reality, however, is that Pocahontas fits in with neither her Indigenous culture nor her recently appropriated English one. Declaring to Rolfe at one point in the narrative, "I cannot be English. I cannot marry with you …I will go back to my people, and they will drive your people into the sea" (309) she is firmly reminded by Rolfe, "You can't go back to Indian clothes, and you can't go back to your people" (310): this exchange prompts Pocahontas to realize "I cannot go back, but I cannot stay, either" (ibid.). Pocahontas comes to see that she is perceived as a political tool and a mere means to secure peace between the English and Indigenous tribes, especially if she marries Rolfe and bears him a child. Bernhard describes Pocahontas asking Rolfe to marry her, realizing that to give her father a grandson may appease his anger towards the English. She tells him, "I want you to marry with me so I do not have to go back to Powhatan. I want to stay with the English" (298), and she asks, "Will you take me to England?" (300). Perhaps, supposing that her dilemma is irresolvable if she remains in Jamestown, Pocahontas' seeking escape by traveling to England, nevertheless seems odd, especially because the reader is not convinced of her love for Rolfe. Pocahontas' wish, however, comes true when she sails with her husband and young son, Thomas, to England in 1616.

In England, Pocahontas is portrayed by Bernhard as Indigenous royalty, though of course she continues to dress as an English lady and speak English: "Pocahontas had never been so happy. The English treated her like a King's daughter" (366). In an intimate scene, the last one in which the reader sees Pocahontas alive, John Smith and Pocahontas re-meet in Brentford, Middlelex, in 1617. Speaking Algonquin together and remembering their past love for each other, Smith tells Pocahontas that he wishes to return to Virginia. Only a few short months later, the narrative, now back in Jamestown, sees Rolfe relaying to Temperance how his wife, Pocahontas became ill after her meeting with Smith and died on their voyage back to the Americas in Gravesend, England (374); she had wanted to be buried "on English soil" (375). Ingidenous writer

Paula Gunn Allen, in her poetry and biography refutes readings such as Bernhard's which arguably continue stereotypical portrayals of Pocahontas.

In her revisionary poem, "Pocahontas to Her English Husband, John Rolfe" Gunn Allen writes from Pocahontas' point of view:

> And you listened less,
> but played with your gaudy dreams
> and sent ponderous missives to the throne
> striving thereby to curry favor
> with your king.
> I saw you well. I
> understood your ploy and still
> protected you, going so far as to die
> in your keeping—a wasting,
> putrefying Christian death–and you,
> deceiver, whiteman, father of my son,
> survived, reaping wealth greater
> than any you had ever dreamed
> from what I taught you and
> from the wasting of my bones. (37-51)

Gunn Allen's Pocahontas clearly rejects European colonialism and refutes common assumptions about the historical figure, particularly that she is a traitor to her people. Including a quotation at the beginning of her poem from Charles Larson's *American Indian Fiction*, which probes how Pocahontas "was a kind of traitor to her people" (qtd. in Gunn Allen 670), Gunn Allen is rewriting history both fictional and factual. Bernhard's novel by contrast does not go far enough in reclaiming Pocahontas from patriarchal accounts, though she does speculate on Pocahontas' relationship with her father. She is described as having little to no affinity with her homeland after being shunned and disowned by her father, though he permits her marriage to Rolfe; the narrative does little to explain why she prefers England and the English to her own people, especially after knowing and witnessing first hand many wrongs by the English against her people in Virginia. Arguably, her father has committed wrongs against the English too, but this still does not explain her preference for the one culture over the other. Symbolically, Pocahontas' alignment with the English and her death in England foreshadows also the inevitable defeat of her people by the English; Thomas, one of the first recorded children of the Indigenous and English is also left in the care of Rolfe's family in England signifying he will be brought up English, and his Indigenous side, his maternal side, will be suppressed and ignored, if not, entirely forgotten.

When Powhatan learns of his daughter's death, he blames himself for not reaching out to her, but he also knows "if it were not for the English, my daughter would not be dead!" (380); "now that Pocahontas is gone, there is no need to play at peace with the English. I say it is time to move against them, to drive them out of the land once and for all" (380-81). Though Pocahontas is initially punished for loving John Smith and for marrying John Rolfe by her father (arguably her punishment is dying in England), she is forgiven after her death. No longer viewed as a traitor to her nation but seen as a commodity used by the English (and blind to his own use of his daughter for similar purposes), Powhantan swears his revenge against the English.

Esquivel's work similarly reimagines an Indigenous woman known for defying her people in order to protect the enemy. Esquivel revisits the historical life of Malinalli, better known as Malinche, the slave-turned interpreter, the mistress of the Spanish conquistador, Hernán Cortés and the mother of Cortés child. Jeanne L. Gillespie clarifies that in Mexican culture Malinche signals not necessarily a whore or the son of a whore, *hijo de puta* but, as Octavio Paz (74) has infamously stated, as "*hijo de la chingagada* [son of the raped or violated woman] [Sic]. … In both cases, the mother is the conduit of blame and dishonor that falls on her children" (173). The mother's only relation is to her (dis)inherited sons. Sandra Messinger Cypress writes that "Mexican women seem to be exiles in their own country if we are to accept Paz's discourse. The image of the displaced woman, exiled or disconnected from her own community and nation," is connected with Malinche's experiences (14). Malinalli, fluent in Spanish, Mayan, and Náhuatl, helps Cortés defeat Montezuma, the king of the Aztecs, and causes the fall of the Aztec Empire. Esquivel's feminist perspective, however, offers a much more complex portrayal than traditional histories (the images of *Lienzo de Tlaxcala*, Paz, Fuentes, Orozco) that blame Malinalli for the fall of her nation. In contrast to Temperance, Marie and Inés who, in Bernhard's, Piat's, and Allende's works, travel across the Atlantic for a new life, Esquivel adopts the viewpoint of an Indigenous woman witnessing the arrival of the Europeans.

Important to understanding Esquivel's work is her emphasis on gender and how gender determines one's life chances, as is exemplified in Malinalli's relationship with Cortés. Also significant is Esquivel's interpretation of the image of the serpent, which functions within both the Náhuatl (Malinalli's) and the biblical tradition (Cortés') by disrupting binaries of good and evil with Christ-Quetzalcóatl and Satan-Quetzalcóatl. The "*confrontation entre las deidades Nuevo Mundo … y el dios cristiano*" 'confrontation between the deities of the New World ... with the Christian God' (Torres Torres 378) mirrors the conflicted relationship between Malinalli and Cortés.

The centrality of the serpent is apparent from Malinalli's birth. The umbilical cord is caught in the child's mouth like a snake: "the grandmother took the sight as a message from the god Quetzalcóatl, who in the form of a serpent was coiled around the neck and mouth of her future grandchild" (Esquivel, *Malinche* 4). For her paternal grandmother, this is a positive sign because Quetzalcóatl, unlike the biblical serpent, is a beloved, though flawed deity. Within Náhuatl mythology, Quetzalcóatl is believed to have been betrayed by his brother Tezcatlipoca, a magician, who used a black mirror to show Quetzalcóatl "the mask of his false holiness, his dark side. In response to such a vision, Quetzalcóatl got so drunk that he even fornicated with his sister. Full of shame, the following day he left Tula to find himself again, to recover his light, promising to return one day" (71). The burial of Malinalli's umbilical cord in both the earth and water, for Esquivel, is a return to the cyclical nature of life as continual rebirth and a symbol of Quetzalcóatl; he, like all of the gods, is present in all aspects of life: "life was sewn anew, returning to the earth of its origin" (6).

Coinciding with Malinalli's birth is Cortés' arrival in Hispaniola (Haiti and Dominican Republic). Quickly proving himself in governing projects, Cortés has a deep desire and ambition for gold and to move onto Mexican territory. After suffering from a scorpion sting and struggling between life and death, he deliriously shouts about several events including a conjuring of the serpent image–clearly a reference to the biblical Satan, who, disguised as a serpent, seduces Eve into eating the forbidden fruit and causes hers and Adam's banishment from Paradise. Esquivel writes: "it had been a serpent, a great serpent that had bitten him, a serpent that lifted itself up in the air and flew out in front of his eyes" (12). Following this prophetic vision, Cortés is declared, "reborn" (13), which he attributes to an incarnation of the Virgin Mother, the Virgin of Guadalupe.

Jumping forward to Malinalli as a young woman and slave of the Aztecs, we find her being sold to the Spanish. Malinalli awaits the return of the god Quetzalcóatl, who will free her peoples and end the human sacrifices performed by the Mexicas. In addition, not only Malinalli but also Montezuma himself perceives the conquistadors, such as Cortés, as embodying Lord Quetzalcóatl and sent by the god to punish the Aztecs. Therefore, Cortés as a serpent lends itself to the biblical tale of Eve as represented by Malinalli, who is seduced by the deceitful snake that causes the banishment from Paradise, though she naively believes he has come to offer salvation.

Malinalli's critical decision in the novel occurs when she learns from a woman in Cholula that an insurrection against the Spaniards is being planned. Knowing that if the Spaniards are defeated, she will be condemned to death,

Malinalli chooses to inform the Spaniards about the revolt. Though Esquivel argues that Malinalli begins to doubt that the Spaniards are sent by Quetzalcóatl to save her people, she feels she has no choice but to side with them in order to survive; Cortés, for his part, strategically plays the role of a humble man transformed into a god. His decisive victory in Cholula secures his welcome by Montezuma and the gift of his throne and empire.

At the end of the novel, one senses a final transformation in Esquivel's invocation of the serpent. Cortés is still the lying seductive snake, associated with the biblical tradition, but Malinalli recognizes herself in her own culture; she must face, like Quetzalcóatl, her dark side in order to become a messiah: "To achieve this, she had to take the same journey that Quetzalcóatl had taken through the inner earth, through the underworld, before becoming the Morning Star. The cycle of Venus was the cycle of purification and rebirth" (179). In a sense Malinalli becomes her own mother through rebirthing herself – and in order to become Christ-Quetzalcóatl, Malinalli prepares to undertake a journey (more psychological and internal than physical),

> Walking into the water, Malinalli, like Quetzalcóatl before her,
> on facing her dark side, became aware of the light. Her will
> was to be one with the cosmos, and she forced the limbs of her
> body to disappear … her spirit became one with the water …
> On that thirteenth day of the month, Malinalli was born to eternity. (185)

Thus, in this critical rewrite, Esquivel offers a far more complex portrayal of Malinalli then a straightforward image of the biblical Eve seduced by a lying Quetzalcóatl-Satan-Cortés and causing the fall of her race. The novel functions as a subversive metaphor for not only European colonialism but also patriarchal Mexican historiography and history: just as Montezuma believed Quetzalcóatl had come to punish him and the Aztecs for their sins and transgressions, Esquivel's novel is a Quetzalcóatl coming to reclaim Malinalli from darkness, deception, and falsity. In this rewrite, she is a Náhuatl woman, an Eve, with a chance to speak, to be redeemed, to be forgiven, and to be reborn.

Forced Marriages, Lovers, and Sexual Politics

Women's historical novels concentrating on the conquest of the Americas narrate the inherent connection between women and the nation via marriage and reproduction. Noorfarah Merali argues that marriage is "a highly valued social institution in every part of the world" (101) and, focusing on the current rights (economic, sexual, and social/cultural) partners have within marriage across the globe, considers "the issues of consent and coercion as they relate to basic human rights of freedom of association, personal security, and the opportunities for personal development" (103). In every work discussed, the protagonist has little recourse to controlling her own body; instead, she is under the will of patriarchal authorities (God, King, Father, husband, brother). An implicit sexual politics regulates and controls women's bodies through rape, abortion, pregnancy, and virginity. This is found in the pro-natal positions and forced marriages the women in the novels endure.

Irigaray clarifies that woman is the site for man to mark himself and she bears several invisible and visible markings by her master–God, father, husband, employer, customer, and so on. Limited social roles for women include: mother, virgin, and prostitute, which Irigaray suggests fulfill the market's need/desire of the woman as commodity. Therefore:

> The characteristics of (so-called) feminine sexuality derive from them: the valorisation of reproduction and nursing: faithfulness; modesty, ignorance of and even lack of interest in sexual pleasure; a passive acceptance of men's "activity"; seductiveness, in order to arouse the consumers' desire while offering herself as its material support without getting pleasure herself. (Irigaray, "Women on the Market" 185)

In Esquivel's *Malinche*, Malinalli's life as a slave begins when her mother begins a new family. After arriving in the Spanish camps, she is first given to Hernández Portocarrero, because "the gift of an Indian woman would very much flatter him" (50). After Portocarrero, Malinalli becomes Cortés's lover. Esquivel suggests that, for both Malinalli and Cortés, their union is a life altering and perhaps pre-ordained moment: within each other, both sense "their destiny and their inevitable union" (77); her time and Cortés's time were ineluctably interconnected, laced, tied together" (117). Challenging Irigaray's thinking, Esquivel writes,

> For a few minutes – which seemed an eternity – Cortés penetrated her time and again, like a savage, as if all the power of nature were contained in his being. … She had for the time being ceased to be 'The Tongue' to become simply a woman, silent, voiceless, a mere woman who did not bear on her shoulders the enormous responsibility of building the conquest with her words. A woman who, contrary to what would be expected, felt relief in reclaiming her condition of submission, for it was a much more familiar sensation to be an object at the service of men than to be a creator of destiny. (79)

Esquivel treads a fine line between accepting the sexual passivity traditionally associated with women while not endorsing woman's role as object.

Ultimately, Esquivel emphasizes the limited choices a woman in Malinalli's situation would have had available. This is evident when Cortés arbitrarily marries Malinalli to his trusted man, Jaramillo, who will "give Marina a name, a status, and bring protection to [his] son … [who will] make history" (158). When Malinalli gives birth to Jaramillo's daughter, she realizes it is due to Cortés's will: "A child of his blood was born from my womb and a daughter from the will of his whim was also born of my womb. He chose the man who would insert his seed in my flesh, not me" (161). The sexual politics at play in Esquivel's novel are not surprisingly echoed in Bernhard's and Piat's works.

In *A Durable Fire*, Bernhard describes Termperance slowly falling in love with her husband's best friend, Will Sterling. Like Allende's heroine, Inés who has an unlawful love for Pedro de Valdivia, whom she never marries, Temperance loves Will. At various times in the novel, most often when she believes one of the men is dead, Temperance is torn between her legal husband, George and her lover, Will. Believing her husband to have died at sea, Temperance allows herself to engage in a sexual relationship with Will, who the reader quickly realizes is her true love (in many ways this also parallels Pocahontas' story because she loves John Smith but is married to John Rolfe and again stresses how gender continuities cross culturally). Temperance's illicit relationship is tolerated by the Jamestown colony until George Yardley, miraculously still alive, returns for his wife. Spying his heavily pregnant wife on the shore standing next to Will, he claims, "I ought to call you out and kill you myself, but – … that would leave your child a fatherless bastard" (196). Though Will blames himself for the situation, it is Temperance by virtue of being a woman who bears the brunt of culpability: "She was a married woman, and she committed adultery" (222). Even Temperance, herself, internalizes this guilt when she imagines what her mother in England must think of "her youngest daughter, living in sin with a man not her lawful husband, and of her newest grandchild, by English law a bastard" (258). Having no recourse to any legal rights, it is only after George tells her that he's seeking a decree of divorce that she has any means to no longer legally be his wife. As George reminds her "fornication was bad enough, but adultery was punishable by death" (450). Will's punishment or any man's for committing adultery is never mentioned – though of course the reader too knows that George has had sexual relations with Jane Wright, a serving girl also stranded on the island of Bermuda. It is only after Will's death and George saving his wife for the second time in the novel, after forgiving her, that the pair begins life together in Virginia anew.

Piat's novel likewise addresses the issue of forced marriage first with Marie's mother, and then with her step-sister Jean, who is raped by her husband. Marie, herself, is threatened with rape first by her step-father, M. Renoncour–

"*Marie, tu as le choix. Ou tu écartes les jambes, comme je te le demande, ou le couvent t'attend. Ou pire ...*" 'Marie, you have a choice, either you spread your legs like I ask, or the convent awaits you. Or worse ...' (Piat 64)–and then in Versailles by the King of France. This choice foreshadows the decision she has later in the novel between marrying or becoming a nun, neither of which reflects her true desires. Her refusal of both men sends her to the Salpêtriere and later to Québec as a *Filles du Roi*. Once in Québec, Marie is ordered to marry the fur trader, Capitaine Antoine de Boisgrévy. Angrily, Boisgrévy declares "*ma jolie, vous n'étiez pas vierge? Je ne vois pas de sang*" 'my pretty, you were not a virgin? I don't see any blood' (175). Piat underscores a patriarchal society intent on controlling women's sexuality, and the consequences women face when they do not follow social protocol.

Haigh, reading Irigaray, writes:

> Within this 'hom(m)osexual economy', the virgin and the mother are the only legitimate sites that can be occupied by women. As virgin, woman represents the possibility of exchange among men. Once exchanged (between father and husband for example), she is removed from the 'market' of between-men, appropriated by her husband and marked by the proper name, the patronym. She becomes producer of legitimate heirs and mediator of the father-son relationship, enabling the perpetuation of the paternal genealogy. Her link with her mother is broken: the maternal genealogy, the line of mothers and daughters, subsumed within that of fathers and sons. (63)

The purpose of Marie's marriage is to "*créer une patrie*," ('create a nation'; 140) and "*peupler ce pays*" ('populate this country'; 109). Piat exposes the danger or drawback against creating a maternal genealogy misinterpreted or appropriated for patriarchal economic gains.

The pro-natal stance, as feminists have identified, is very much a nationalistic position (Toinette, Marie's friend and former servant, has 11 children). The challenge in women's historical novels is, therefore, to support a maternal genealogy that symbolically and practically links women, but without simultaneously supporting patriarchal nationalism. Irigaray suggests the definition of woman as mother "is a social role imposed on women" ("Women on the Market" 185) and is a kind of matricide: "the woman in the mother is negated in favor of her maternal function" (qtd. in Rye 119). Thus, rewriting a maternal genealogy is very much an exercise in rethinking motherhood and an attempt to usurp patriarchal roles assigned to women. This is no easy task and, more often the not, the author, rather than presenting concrete alternatives, shows patriarchal genealogies as restrictive and destructive. Intimating through the actions and thinking of her heroines, cracks and slippages in the order, nonetheless, begin to appear; for example, Inés' lies about searching for her husband in order to travel to the New World are a means for revolting against the established order.

Allende's heroine, like Piat's and Esquivel's, confirms the intertwining of patriarchal religion, or more specifically a fundamentalist Catholicism, with women's sexuality. Growing up in Plasencia with her grandfather, "a cabinet maker by trade, [who] belonged to the Brotherhood of Vera-Cruz" (Allende, *Inés of my Soul* 6), famous for their inflicted flagellations, her "life was reduced to prayers, sighs, confessions, and sacrifices" (ibid.). Inés lives with her grandfather, mother, and sister because her father has deserted the family, foreshadowing Inés's husband, Juan, later abandoning her, and the overall lack of father figures in any of the novels–in all three works the paternal father is dead, leaving the child in the primary care of the mother. .

Inés meets her future husband, Juan, in 1526, during the holy week processions, in the same year as threats from Muslim attacks, "religious fervour, whipped by fear, reached the point of dementia" (7). Because her grandfather cannot afford two dowries, Inés is destined not to marry. Determined to change her fate and fund her own dowry, Inés sews and embroiders. Juan stands in juxtaposition to the holy life that denies the body and the pious life Inés has been leading; he is a womanizer, a card-player, and a drinker, with a lust for fortune that eventually fuels his desire to go to the New World. Thus, while Inés "embroidered and sewed from daybreak to midnight, saving for [their] marriage, Juan spent his days wandering through the taverns and plazas, seducing maidens and whores alike" (10). Inés confesses that it is Juan's seductive nature and her youthful love that allows her to forgive him; Allende initially portrays Inés' love as ambiguous. On the one hand, Inés embodies what Weldt-Basson refers to as "the stereotype of the female ruled by her passion for a man" (128), yet, Inés, like Pocahontas, Temperance, Malinalli and Marie, is more than the stereotypical object of love. She is also a desiring subject. Problems arise for Inés, however, when the "loss" of her virginity, though her choice and one that undermines the patriarch's law, is discovered by her grandfather. He forces Juan to marry Inés because "honour was in large measure tied to the virtue of the women in the family" (11). Irigaray suggests that "the right to virginity should be a part of girls' civil identity" and that "the right to virginity as belonging to the girl, and not to her father, brother, or future husband, should be enshrined in law" (*Key Writings* 206).

When Juan leaves for the New World, convinced he will find, El Dorado, the city of gold, Inés moves in with her mother and is forced to dress as a widow (a social symbol that she is respectable and non-marriageable). Despite severe restrictions on her cloistered life, Inés continues to engage in the few jobs respectable for women, including sewing, cooking, and visiting the hospital. In the hospital, she realizes she has, like Marie, a talent for healing by helping "the nuns with the sick and the victims of the plague" (15). With the money she makes from her labor, Inés dreams of following Juan, not out of love, but for the promise of freedom the New World offers women.

In Plasencia, Inés is tied to her husband; she cannot divorce or remarry, so she secures a permit to go to the Americas:

> The Crown protected matrimonial ties and tried to reunite husband and wife in order to populate the New World with legitimate Christian families … They issued permits to married women to join their husbands only if a family member or another respectable went with them. (17)

Swearing that she is racially pure, meaning not a Jew or a Moor, "but an old Christian," Inés secures her papers (18).

In Piat's and Allende's novels, we see two vulnerable young women who, as a result of a passionate/illicit love (Marie's love is for Jacob, a condemned Huguenot) in austere Catholic settings, face confinement and isolation in their home nations. With the prospect of a better life in the New World, the heroines challenge the stereotype of "passive and subdued traits associated with femininity" (André 77) by making their way into unknown lands. Inés, unlike Marie, Temperance, or Malinalli, further challenges a notion of motherhood. Rationalizing later in life, she says:

> I understand that the Virgin's true blessing was to deny me motherhood and thus allow me to fulfill an exceptional destiny.
> With children I would have been held down, as we women are.
> With children I would have stayed in Plasencia, abandoned by Juan de Málaga, sewing and making empanadas. With children, I would not have conquered this Kingdom of Chile. (14)

Her freedom is attributed to not having children or having to perform the duties of traditional femininity that confines women spatially. At the same time the novels do not denigrate traditional feminine roles such as healing, sewing, and cooking. The complexity of femininity negotiated by the protagonists ensures the importance of the woman's historical novel in a transnational context. Sexual freedom is also a major theme and preoccupation in women's historical novels and the women in each continually and paradoxically reinforce and grate against patriarchal notions of what does and does not constitute acceptable sexual behavior.

Proselytism and Mother-Tongues

In women's historical novels on the colonizing of the Americas, communicating with the aboriginals is imperative for survival and it is the women in the novels who understand the political importance of interpreting the other. In Allende's work, even after Inés realizes Juan is dead, she knows she cannot marry her new lover, the conquistador, Pedro de Valdivia, in the New World. Valdivia is a "famous field marshal, the hero of many wars, one of the richest and most powerful men in all of Peru" (*Inés of my Soul* 94). Valdivia senses his duty to the Emperor Charles V as colonizing/Christianizing Chile: Pedro and Francisco were grateful for their good fortune in being Catholics, which guaranteed the salvation of their souls, and Spanish, that is, superior to the rest of humankind. They were hidalgos of Spain, sovereign over all the wide and beckoning world, more powerful than the ancient Roman Empire, chosen by God to discover, conquer, Christianize, found, and populate the most remote corners of the earth. (21)

Together, Inés and Pedro share a dream for earning fame and founding a utopian kingdom in Chile, which remained un-colonized following Diego de Almagro's failed attempt and "disastrous journey" (110). The 1540 journey to Chile with Pedro entails a "handful of soldiers and the thousand auxiliary Indians" (the Yanaconas are a military force of servants) and is fraught with the perils of the desert, starvation, fatigue, internal fighting amongst the soldiers, and even a conspiracy led by Sancho de la Hoz.

The Indigenous Chileans, however, pose the greatest threat to Spanish success. As a means of necessity, Inés learns the language of the Mapuche, Mapundungu (Allende, *Inés of my Soul* 118). By comparison, in Piat's Filles du Roi, Toinette, newly arrived in Québec, notes: "*J'apprends l'algonquin, me dit-elle. Si je dois vivre ici avec Matthieu*" 'I'm learning Algonquin, she told me. I must in order to live here with Matthieu' (160). Marie de l'Incarnation who runs the Ursuline convent is also "*en train de rédiger un livre d'histoire sacrée en Algonquin ainsi qu'un dictionnaire Iroquois*" 'currently writing a book of sacred history in Algonquin and an Iroquois dictionary' (141) in order to convert the Indigenous to Christianity. Interestingly enough, though Bernhard's novel focuses on the Indigenous woman as interpreter, Esquivel's *Malinche* is the better example. Cortés asks,

> How could he be able to use his best and most effective weapon on those natives, who spoke other languages? Cortés would have given half his life if he could master the languages of that strange country … these natives were civilized, different from those in Hispaniola and Cuba. Cannons and horses were effec-

> tive when dealing with savages, but in a civilized context, the
> ideal thing was to seal alliances, negotiate, win over, and all
> this could be done only through dialogue, of which he was de-
> prived from the very start. (36-37)

Praying to the Virgin to help him triumph, Cortés sees Malinalli for the first
time "and a maternal spark connected them with the same longing. Malinalli
felt that this man could protect her; Cortés, that the woman could help him as
only a mother could: unconditionally" (49-50). Malinalli, one of twenty slaves
given to the Spanish, finds herself baptized as Marina by Friar Aguilar, who, at
her request, teaches her Spanish so they may discuss religion.

Again, in reference to the biblical Eve who desired knowledge, Malinalli's
hunger for learning brings about her downfall. Malinalli, however, interprets
the new religion, Catholicism, in terms of her own–noticing the similarities in
baptisms, symbols, and Mary, Jesus' mother, who she likens to Tonantzin "the
mother of them all" (*Malinche* 47). Cortés quickly realizes Malinalli's worth
when he learns she has a gift for languages. Known as "The Tongue," she
"translated what he said into the Náhuatl language and what Montezuma's
messengers said from Náhuatl into Spanish" (61-62). This task for Malinalli is
linked with divinity: she is literally a mouthpiece of the gods and fears "being
unfaithful to the gods" and "not being able to bear responsibility" (65). Ryan F.
Long identifies this as Esquivel's metanarrative, recognizing her "limitations as
Malinalli-Malinche's 'interpreter'" (199). Like Esquivel, Malinalli recognizes
the power of words through her role as translator and the paradoxical freedom-
servitude one experiences in this position. Esquivel writes:

> She, the slave who listened to orders in silence, who couldn't
> look directly into the eyes of men, now had a voice, and the
> men, staring into her eyes, would wait attentively to hear what
> her mouth uttered. She, who had so often been given away,
> who so many times had been gotten rid of, now was needed,
> valued, as much as if not more than cacao. (66)

Her public role is as Cortés's tongue; thus:

> La Malinche disrupted the general Amerindian curb on 'wom-
> en's tongues in public places' as well as the Christian re-
> strictions against women speakers in public. ... the use of voice
> by La Malinche, her role as a spokesperson, marks one of her
> most striking–and positive–disruptions of the patriarchy on
> both the indigenous and the European sides. (Cypress 17)

Esquivel, as writer, also becomes a kind of Malinche: "La Malinche is a 'mother' to Mexican women writers in that they are carrying out the work she began

in the public arena;" they are rebelling against patriarchal restrictions and silences (Cypress 22).

When Cortés slaughters the inhabitants of Cholula, Malinalli serves as his interpreter: "She spoke in the name of Malinche, a nickname they had given Cortés, since he always had her by his side. Malinche in some way meant the master of Malinalli" (93). This is the first time Esquivel uses the word "Malinche" and, therefore, the novel's title is subversive. Malinche, historically, is Malinalli's nickname and means traitor, but here refers to Cortés, who is defined only by his relation as the "master" of Malinalli.[4] Cortés as master symbolizes both his legal claim over the woman and the woman's words as she speaks only in patriarchal language with no recourse to her own voice– furthermore, Cortés holds sexual sway over her: she is his property.

Though Malinalli informs Cortés of an upcoming insurrection, after witnessing the destruction of Cholula, she

> [n]o longer wanted to speak, to see, to struggle for her freedom.
> Not at such a price. Not through the death of so many innocents … She rather wished that serpents would come out of her womb and wrap themselves around her body, that they would suffocate her, leave her without breath, turn her into nothing, a word in the moistness of the tongue, a symbol, a hieroglyph, a stone. (105)

Only after she is forced by Cortés on a mission to Hibueras, which means leaving her son behind, does Malinalli finally ask for her freedom (154). Cortés refuses: "accept your mission is simply to be my 'Tongue'" (ibid.). Saddened, Malinalli remembers

> [t]he moments in which Cortés's mouth and her mouth had been one mouth only, and the thought of Cortés and his tongue one single idea, one new universe. The tongue had joined them and the tongue had separated them. The tongue was the cause of everything. Malinalli had destroyed Montezuma's empire with her tongue. Thanks to her words, Cortés had made allies that ensured his conquest. She decided then to punish the instrument that had created that universe. (158)

Taking a thorn from an agave plant, Malinalli pierces her tongue in two (another symbol of the serpent) and causes Cortés's defeat in Hibueras.

Malinalli is useless to Cortés until, arriving one day at hers and Jaramillo's home, he informs her that he needs her to speak in court on his behalf. Malinal-

---

[4] Alfred Arteaga asks why Gonzalo Guerrero, Cortés's former translator is also not "Malinche" and links the answer to a "Christian, patriarchal, imperialist project" in which "a woman Malinche is more pleasing than a man" (63).

li responds, "'Cortés, I will forever be grateful for my son and the husband you gave me, the piece of land that you kindly gave Jaramillo and me so that we might spread our roots, but do not ask me to speak on your behalf, not in that tone. I am no longer your tongue, Lord Malinche'" (176). While Malinalli's refusal to do Cortés' bidding is her last dialogue in the novel with him, it has historical-cultural ramifications.

In an ironic reply to Paz's words that "she is the *Chingada*. She loses her name; she is no one; she disappears into nothingness; she *is* Nothingness" (86), Esquivel suggests that when Malinalli ceases to be "the Tongue," she ceases to exist in a patriarchal history; she transitions into the feminine world of domestic tranquility and silence, a world that eludes the archives. Unlike Gillespie and Long, Cypress argues that Malinalli "descended from 'la lengua' to become 'la matriz,' the 'womb' and in exercising that traditional female function, she was relegated to the position of a negotiable property used for political alliances and sexual exploits" (18). Gillespie and Long by contrast tentatively read the novel as "a romance novel" because "there is a 'love story,' the protagonist is fascinated by the 'wrong man,' and she is loved from a distance by the 'right man'" (178; 203). A certain amount of "domestic tranquility" is achieved, though Esquivel resists the traditional happy ending in romances– Malinalli as mother and wife leaves her family to go on a pilgrimage and sacrifices her life for the "promise of a syncretic future for her children" (Long 205). In this sense, Esquivel plays with the stereotypical dichotomous views of the mother in Mexican culture; Malinalli impossibly embodies both good and bad mothers, and in this moment she transforms from evil Eve into her opposing image, the Virgin, selfless, passive, all-loving, and all-sacrificing.

Racial Hybridity

As a result of European mobility (both male and female), sexual encounters, including rape, occur between the Indigenous and immigrants as well as amongst the immigrants (Romero's attempt to rape Inés in Allende's novel). While Bernhard's novel describes Pocahontas' marriage to John Rolfe as a potential means to secure peace between the English and Indigenous in Virginia, Piat's *Filles du Roi* describes how this mixing between colonizer (French) and aboriginal is met with ambivalence in Québec. Marie de l'Incarnation believes that:

> *Un Français devient plus facilement sauvage qu'un sauvage Français. Monsieur Talon exulte mais ne peut ignorer le nombre de jeunes gens qui abandonnent leur famille pour vivre à l'indienne, faisant le véritable métier de bandits. Et pire en-*

*core ... Les garcons courent les Indiennes et les <bois brû-
lés>se multiplient.*

A Frenchman becomes more easily Indian, than an Indian becomes French. Mr. Talon rejoices, but he cannot ignore the
number of young men who abandon their family for living with
the Indians, like true criminals. And worse still … the boys are
copulating with the Indians; the mixed-bloods are multiplying.
(144-45)

Fernando Ortiz's term "transculturation" aptly describes this kind of cultur-
al/racial "mixing" as a process or phase that not only involves the loss or up-
rooting of a previous culture" (qtd. in Rama 19) but also the "creation of a new
cultural phenomenon" (ibid.). The woman's historical novel, thus, challenges
terms like "acculturation" or "colonization" by addressing racial hybridity as a
process of transculturation in national genealogies.

Piat's text inverts the stereotype of sexual relations between Indigenous
women and French male settlers. She narrates the experiences of a French immigrant woman's sexual encounters with an Algonquin thereby complicating
the origins of the Québécois. In the New World, Marie is attacked and kidnapped by the Iroquois when she accompanies her clandestine lover, Jacob
(who has come from France to find her) and the historical figure, Robert
Cavelier de la Salle on an expedition to found new territory along the Missis-
sippi. The Iroquois, upon discovering Marie's female identity (because she is
disguised as the doctor M. Robert who *"saura se vêtir en coureur de bois"* [will
be dressed as a woodsman] (227), decide not to kill her, but adopt and marry
her into their community. Desired by an Algonquin, living with the Iroquois,
named Silence, Marie finds herself, in order to stay alive, consenting to the
marriage. After ten moons, Marie claims, *"J'apprenais peu à peu l'iroquois et
quelques mots d'algonquin, devenant peu à peu Tiskawamis, la femme de Silence que je commençais d'aimer"* 'I learned little by little the Iroquois language and some words in Algonquin, becoming little by little Tiskawamis, Silence's woman; I began to love him' (234). Marie's relationship with Silence,
like Malinalli's with Cortés and Pocahontas' with Smith, follows closely what
Mary Louise Pratt cautions is a sentimentalized "transracial love plot" wherein,
when the lovers are separated, the European returns to his/her culture more or
less intact and "the non-European dies an early death" (95). Silence's fate remains unknown while Marie, once able to escape, reunites with Jacob and discovers she is pregnant.

Having given birth to a boy named Samuel, an homage to the explorer Samuel Champlain, one of Marie's neighbors observes *"pour mignon, il est mignon.
Mais à mon avis, il n'est pas de chez nous … Il n'a pas le tête de chez nous…*

Je le vois bien" 'Cute, he is cute. But in my opinion he doesn't look like us ...
He doesn't have our face, I see that clearly' (241). Piat complicates, like Homi
K. Bhabha's theory of cultural hybridity that rejects the notion of pure racial or
national origins, the myth of Québec's founding mother. Marie's familial lineage, like many other descendants of the *Filles du Roi*, has Indigenous blood,
which is often not (but must be/should be) acknowledged by the historical archives.[5]

In Esquivel's work, racial hybridity is of central importance. As Cortés'
slave and lover, Malinalli has little access to her own desire and, following
Cortés's triumph over Montezuma's empire, gives birth to a son (145), who is
symbolically, though not historically, the first mestizo in Mexico. Esquivel
writes: "She knew that in her womb there was beating the heart of a being that
would unite two worlds. The blood of Moors and Christians with that of the
Indians, that pure, unmixed race" (146). Unlike Malinalli, who perceives her
own race as pure in contrast to the Europeans, when the child is born, Cortés,
though relishing an heir, considers his son a bastard and a "mestizo" (147).
Thus, part of Esquivel's objective in *Malinche* is engaging the Indigenous past,
the maternal past, seen as inferior to their European father that Paz believes
perpetuates the statehood of Mexicans as orphans "wandering in the labyrinth
of solitude" (Cypress 19).

Related to the Mexican condition of orphan-hood described by Paz as lacking a positive identification with the mother, Allende provides a perspective on
Chileans. Allende suggests that a lieutenant in the New World "kept thirty Indian concubines ... the norm in the New World, where Spaniards take Indian and
black women at their will" (78). Characterized by Pratt's term "contact zones,"
"social spaces where disparate cultures meet, clash, and grapple with each other" (*Inés of my Soul* 7), for Allende , European, Black, and Indigenous women
in the New World "meet" and "clash" under the rule of men. These zones in the
woman's historical novel stress that, ultimately, men are the dominating power,
not nationhood, over women's lives.

Inés, like Marie and Temperance, is one of the first European women to undertake a voyage to the New World; Inés is one of a few European women living in Peru: "at that time, the number of Spanish women in Peru could be still
be counted on one's fingers ... they were wives or daughters of soldiers, and
had come at the insistence of the Crown, which was attempting to reunite families and create a legitimate and decent society in the colonies" (79). On route to
her final destination, Chile, Inés admires Pedro because he "never doubted his

---

[5] The focus of her sequel, *Dans les plaines d'Abraham*, chronicles the life of two of
Marie's descendants, Louis de Préclair–a surgeon in Québec –and his correspondence
with Marie–a lecturer at the court of Versailles.

mission: to populate Chile with Spaniards and to evangelize the Indians" (127). The Spanish feel "the best way to serve [their] majesty in the Americas was to people it was mestizos ... the solution to the problem was to kill all males older than twelve, sequester the children, and patiently and methodically rape the women" (135). This view explains the celebrations when Cecelia, an Inca princess and part of the Chilean entourage, gives birth to Pedrito Gómez, the first Chilean mestizo. Thus, the intersection between religious conversion, territorial expansion, and the lives of Aboriginals during the time of the founding of the Americas plays a pivotal role in understanding the woman's historical novel.

Part of this understanding comes with narrating the women's actions. Bernhard's female European characters commit few violent acts (though they are victims of Indigenous attacks), but Esquivel relates Malinalli's role in the massacre of Cholula, and both Marie and Inés play a violent part in establishing the nation. When Toinette "*hurlant: - Les Iroquois nous attaquent!*" 'screams: -the Iroquois are attacking us!' (214), Marie exclaims, "*ce fut la première fois que je devais tuer des hommes; je le fis sans scruples. Entre eux et nous, il n'y avait point de choix*" 'it was the first time that I had to kill men; I did it without thinking. It was either them or us, I had no choice' (ibid.). Tensions between the new European settlers and Indigenous peoples over territory and dominion is a primary theme in these works and is mirrored in Allende's novel when Valdivia is away from the settlement of Santiago and Inés is forced to act militarily.

Facing imminent defeat against a Mapuche assault, Inés descends into the prison where "seven captive caciques [were] spurring on their warriors at the top of their lungs" (*Inés of my Soul* 199). Inés, thus, orders the prisoners to be killed. When the soldiers seem reluctant to execute "the governor's hostages" (200), Inés, taking matters into her own hands, beheads the caciques with her sword and throws the heads into the midst of her enemy, prompting a speedy retreat. Surrounded by the ruins of Santiago, Inés is haunted by her deed and begs for forgiveness for her violence, though she is heralded as a hero and savoir of the city.

Both Allende and Piat refuse to romanticize their heroine's murdering ways, and Inés laments that the Spanish, including Spanish women, will "eventually exterminate the natives of this land, because they would rather die free than live as slaves" (Allende, *Inés of my Soul* 119). Inés' sentiment is echoed in Piat's novel when Marie, working in the convent and then as a rural doctor (under the guise of being a man), witnesses the natives devastated by European religions, wars, and diseases, including sexual ones (Piat, *Filles du Roi* 143, 210). Malinalli's true desire in Esquivel's work is to be free from servitude, though she regrets her means to achieve it: she despises herself for having "'looked at myself in your [Cortés'] mirrors, in your black mirrors'" (Esquivel, *Malinche* 178).

After the uprising in Allende's novel, Pedro, upon his return, tells Inés he wants to persevere and found Chile with her, naming her "Inés of my soul" (*Inés of my Soul* 208). Valdivia's utterance is important. Not only does Allende's title stem from these words, but they are also the final words of the novel. Upon Valdivia's death, Inés, suffering from a fever, hears him in a dream whisper "Farewell, Inés of my soul ..." (313). One must ask of Allende, like of Esquivel, whose story is really being written? Cortés is, after all, Malinche. In Allende's work, the voice is Inés', the memories are of her life and the founding of Chile, but Allende's choice of Valdivia's words for her title implies either that this is actually *his-story*, that Inés forms her identity based on her relation to Pedro, or Allende has appropriated for herself the same endearment–Inés is a maternal figure, a Chilean ancestress of her twenty-first century soul.

Forging New Ties: Woman to Woman

A prominent feature of these novels is their creation of woman to woman kinship. Cantero Rosales writes: "*Si en la novella tradicional el amour heterosexual era la preocupación fundamental de la heroína, ahora esta narrativa propone un Nuevo circuito de comunicacion en el que la Amistad entre mujeres es la clave en torno a la giran las vidas de las protagonistas*" 'If in the traditional novella heterosexual love was the fundamental concern of the heroine, Allende now proposes a new narrative communication circuit in which the friendship between women is the key to turning around the lives of the protagonists'. Cantero Rosales' thinking suggests that these women's historical novels secure the bond between women both in friendship and in motherhood.

In Bernhard's novel Temperance's friendship with fellow settler, Meg Worley is unmatched by any man, especially given that the men spend long bouts of time absent from the settlement, leaving the women to fend for themselves. Temperance's affinity with Pocahontas is also highlighted after the latter, a prisoner, is moved to the parsonage. As already mentioned this scene marks the first time the two heroines of the novel come into contact and despite being difficult to image, Bernhard emphasizes that the women are, however, prohibited from taking care of Pocahontas because of a shared sense of gender. The Captain explains to John Rolfe, "You know how women are. I don't much trust them. They'd just as soon help her escape" (278). Though Pocahontas and Temperance come from different worlds, they share similar gendered experiences within patriarchal societies. The implicit suggestion is that Temperance, as a woman who has also suffered because of patriarchal notions of marriage and sin, sympathizes with the unjust treatment Pocahontas is subjected to; therefore, she would set her free.

In Esquivel's *Malinche*, Malinalli's grandmother plays the prominent maternal role and tells her granddaughter that "[t]he earth is our mother, who feeds us, who reminds us where we came from whenever we rest upon her. In our dreams she tells us that our bodies are earth, that our eyes our earth, and that our thoughts will be earth in the wind" (23). It is for this reason that Malinalli later tells Cortés, when he declares that his God does not have a wife, that this is impossible: "Without a womb, without darkness, light cannot emerge, life cannot emerge. It is from her greatest depths that Mother Earth creates precious stones, and in the darkness of the womb that gods and humans take their forms. Without a womb there is no god" (62). The image of the Virgin Mary also awakens Malinalli to a

> [n]ostalgia for the maternal arms, a longing to feel enveloped, embraced, sustained, and protected by her mother, as at one time she must have been; by her grandmother, as she definitely had been; by Tonantzin, as she hoped she would be; and by a universal mother, like that white lady who held the child in her arms. (47)

At the end of Esquivel's novel, Malinalli, on her pilgrimage, not only enacts the rebirth of Quetzalcóatl but also realizes a femino-centric desire to create a new maternal genealogy, "a link in the feminine chain created by countless generations of women" (6).

Malinalli upon her grandmother's death buries precious objects, including some kernels of corn, while praying to Tonantzin, "the Aztec goddess of fertility" (Paz 84), to "nourish those grains" (182). Symbolically, Malinalli is on the hill where, in the future, Juan Diego will witness the Mexican Virgin of Guadalupe. Paz suggests that a "return to the ancient feminine deities … is a return to the maternal womb" (84-85). Unlike Paz, however, who juxtaposes the Virgin Mother against "the *Chingada*," Esquivel transforms Malinalli[6]; she "becomes the mortal equivalent to the spiritual convergence of culture and spirituality represented by the Mexican Virgin of Guadalupe" (Long 204). In Esquivel's novel, the old female goddesses never die; they simply transform, which stress-

---

[6] Paz adds the goddess Cihaucóatl, *La Llorona* "the long-suffering Mexican mother" to this Mexican mother triad (75). Esquivel writes that this goddess "at nights wandered through the canals of the great Tenochtitlán weeping for her children. They said that those who heard her could not go back to sleep, so terrifying were her mournful, anxious wails for the future of her children. She shouted out all the dangers and devastations that lay in wait for them. Malinalli, like Cihaucóatl, wept at not being able to protect her harvest" (18).

es the importance of breaking patriarchal cycles. Esquivel's and Bernhard's emphasis in their texts on women forging bonds with women is also highlighted in Allende's and Piat's works.

When Inés' husband is confirmed dead, she decrees, "Juan Malaga was dead and I was free" (Allende, *Inés of my Soul* 85). Like Marie's husband, who is fur-trapping and fighting the Iroquois, Toinette knocks on Marie's door one day declaring, "*Ils l'ont trouvé gelé près de la rivière Richelieu*" 'They found him [Antoine] frozen near Richelieu River' (Piat, *Filles du Roi* 189). Antoine's quest for wealth in the New World results in his death and marks for Piat's heroine another chance for rebirth in New France. In this new life, Marie meets Catherine Jérémie, renown for her science of plants, who, like Inés' new Quecha Indian servant, Catalina, knows "many remedies and enchantments" (86). Together, the women do medicinal work. As in Piat's novel, Allende gives Catalina's knowledge of herbal plants and women's bodily experiences (abortion, pregnancy, birth) an equal, if not privileged, knowledge position. Vrinda Dalmiya and Linda Alcoff in "Are Old Wives' Tales" Justified?" challenge masculine-dominant notions of epistemology by referencing traditional women's knowledge as a "gender-specific experiential knowing as a species of the more general 'experiential' knowledge" (228). This gender knowledge, Dalmiya and Alcoff claim, stems from a basis for experience among women, such as childbirth and pregnancy. It is called *determinable* because "there are some gender-specific 'subjective facts' that are not accessible to subjects who are not of that gender" (Dalmiya and Alcoff 229) and they suggest that midwives, like Jérémie in Piat's novel and Catalina in Allende's, possess this type of "G-experiential knowledge" (231). Piat writes that "she was magic" in opposition to the formal training and propositional knowledge of male doctors. Though we see a positive evaluation of traditional women's knowledge in the novels, traditional hierarchies such as race and class, particularly in the form of servitude, between women remain intact. For example, though Inés' relationship with her friend and servant Catalina has a magical and spiritual quality, she is still a servant – this theme is also echoed in Bernhard's novel when Temperance has a special relationship with her black slave, Ata, but she remains a slave.

Catherine in Piat's work, because she is of the same race and class, figures as more or less Marie's equal. Piat's novel concludes with Marie, after re-meeting and marrying Jacob in Québec, recounting her return to France with Jacob and her son Samuel in order to avoid religious persecution, only to discover France is expelling, murdering, and converting non-Catholics. Piat references the Edict of Nantes, which was supposed to put an end to the war of religions in France and grant the Huguenots rights and religious freedom, but on "*le 19 octobre 1685, le Roi signa un «édit de Fontainebleau» dont la teneur fut répandue dans toutes les provinces: l'édit de Nantes était révoqué*" 'October 19th, 1685, the King [Louis XIV] signed the edict of Fontainebleau, the contents of which spread across all regions; the Edict of Nantes was revoked' (*Filles du Roi* 248). This revocation explains Jacob's and his father's death at the hands of Louis XIV's army for refusing to convert to Catholicism. Marie, forced to escape, is exiled in Amsterdam, where she finishes her letter by signaling she may indeed return again to New France, because, as an exile and twice widowed woman, Marie and her children are nationless/homeless: "*mais, ma chère Catherine, hélas, vous étiez loin de moi. Et mon pays. Quel pays?*" 'but, my dear Catherine, alas, you are far from me. And my country. Which country?' (254). There is a sense that Catherine Jérémie, the famed mid-wife and "*la magicienne de ma vie au Québec*" ("the magician of my life in Québec"; 163), and the sorority Marie shares with her are the center of Marie's life; Marie's return to Québec is, essentially, a return, not to a nation, but to a woman. The woman to woman relationships evident in Bernhard's, Piat's, Allende's and Esquivel's novels are effective because, as in many women's historical novels, "a female duo replaces the phallic hero at the center of the frame of representation" (Anderlini-D'Onofrio 162). Fusing the past with the present, the woman's historical novel written and set in the Americas constructs a revisionist matrilineal narrative, which establishes a new symbolic order for women.

Conclusion

The woman's historical novel on the colonizing of the Americas marks a transitional period in history and the new imagining of national boundaries and borders, often "separating people of shared ethnicity and kinship into residents" of different political territories (Jameson, "Connecting" 7). Women's roles in shaping nations and territories, however, have been marginalized and underwritten. Writing "herstories" not only "historicize women's experiences and identities," but force us to revise and rethink who has made the nation (Perry 83). The transnational maternal genealogies in Bernhard's, Esquivel's, Allende's, and Piat's works challenge both national origins and a definition of motherhood/maternal origins. Each novel "radically open[s] up the idea of the 'mother' to indicate that this is above all a positioning rather than an identity, and one any woman might adopt or reject according to her voluntary desires" (Jennings 82). Breaking with traditional historical novels by adopting a feminocentric focus, the writers show the difficulties women in the Americas faced in transitioning from an Old World into a New World (for Inés, Marie, and Temperance this is symbolized by the transatlantic crossing, while Pocahontas and Malinalli confront colonialism by the Christian Spaniards and Christian English in their own lands – only Pocahontas in Bernahard's novel makes the reverse crossing – though of course she dies in the country of her people's enemy and is buried on English land (perhaps, suggesting colonization only works in one direction and an Indigenous woman cannot survive in England). Nevertheless, taken together as a whole, the novels disrupt masculinist master narratives and emphasize a feminist reimagining of the history of the Americas: this reimagining centralizes women's experiences and shows how gender connects women's lives cross culturally, nationally, linguistically, and racially.

CHAPTER TWO

Modern Queens: Matricide, Gynocracy, and Matrophobia

> A dominant male culture has intervened between mother and
> daughter and broken off a loving and symbolic exchange
> – Luce Irigaray, *I love to you*

A stark comparison with the protagonists in the previous chapter (who come
from modest or humble origins – with the exception of Pocahontas who is a
chief's daughter), the noble and royal women discussed in this chapter are familiar figures in mainstream historiography and novel writing. Representing
one of the most popular categories of contemporary women's writing is novels,
taking place roughly between 1500 and 1789, on monarchs. A transnational
focus can be attributed to the fact that this period heralds a historical renaissance of women ruling the nation, here referred to as gynocracies. Gynocracies
during modernity seriously question the relation between divine and natural
law, both of which traditionally "forbade government by a woman" (Jordan
128). Megan Cassidy-Welch and Peter Sherlock, however, believe that, though
a gender hierarchy existed, "early-modern patriarchy was flexible and could
exalt individual women above men where necessary to underpin further the
whole social organization of power" (325). Though the novels I discuss do not
always strictly pertain to a woman as sole ruler of her nation, her political influence as queen is indisputable. Thus, I offer a mix of women who were indeed the monarch and those who were strictly speaking, queen consorts. The
benefit of offering both perspectives, monarch and consort, is identifying how
women across different nations/empires negotiated similar gender expectations
such as fertility, beauty, and weakness (body and mind) which they were as
women, typically, meant to embody.

   The connecting thread between female monarchs and consorts, which the
contemporary woman's historical novel highlights, is an inconsistent stance
when it comes to gynocracies during the modern period. A gynocracy places a
woman as the head of a national lineage or genealogy but each female ruler
discussed in this chapter is separated from her mother – essentially the potential
of a familial gynocracy is preempted, and furthermore, matrilineal primogeni-
ture is considered unacceptable: the mother-ruler's daughter never replaces her
mother. There is a deep distrust and fear of the mother, which Adrienne Rich

refers to as a "fear not of one's mother or of motherhood but of *becoming one's mother*" (*Of Woman Born* 235-36). By contrast, Deborah D. Rogers believes that a matrophobia is indeed a "fear of becoming a mother," and "fear of identification with and separation from the maternal body" (Rogers 1) – Rogers traces this fear/disdain to patriarchal culture's attitudes towards women, femininity, and sexuality. In the novels, matrophobia precedes and sustains the gynocracy (again, marked by a mother's physical and emotional absence in her daughter's life). In short, these works identify a characteristic of the maternal that cuts across national boundaries; it is a period characterized by a deep longing for and hyper-anxiety towards the maternal and is symbolized best by the French queen, Marie-Antoinette's, the most maternal of all the figures discussed in his chapter, execution.

The post 1970s woman's historical novel centers primarily on these atypical women rulers and their relationships with their mothers. In so doing this corpus responds to the works of notable forerunners such as Finnish writer Kaari Utrio's romantic historical novel *Kartanonherra ja kaunis Kirstin* (1968) on Kristina of Sweden, Norah Lofts' *The Lost Ones* (1969) that chronicles the fragile psyche of Queen Caroline Matilda in eighteenth century Denmark, Jean Plaidy's trilogies on France's formidable Catherine De Medici and Spain's Isabella of Castile, Evelyn Anthony's 1950s Romanov trilogy on Catherine the Great's rise to power as Empress of Russia, and Margaret Irwin's successful trilogy on the woman most often represented in women's historical fiction, Elizabeth I. A plethora of works devoted to two queens and mothers executed for treason and adultery: Elizabeth I's rival – the "foreign regnant queen," (Allinson 104) – Mary, Queen of Scots and Elizabeth's mother, Anne Boleyn also exist. [7] The emphasis in these earlier works is on women exercising power and desire (including a preoccupation with adultery, desire for the mother, and sexual desire, which Diana Wallace argues epitomizes the 1940s British woman's novel) (*Woman's* 85) and yet, we see this concern carrying over into contemporary writers again but this time cross nationally.

In addition to rewriting the above popular figures (Alison Weir, for example, offers a less emotional and romantic version of Elizabeth I than Irwin), the lives of queens outside the European-Christian tradition–e.g., Jyoti Jafa's *Nurjaha* (1979), on Nur Jahan, the chief consort of Emperor Jahangir and Empress of the Mughal Empire, or Chitra Banerjee Divakaruni's *The Palace of Illusions* (2008) which rewrites the Hindu epic, *Mahabharata* from a woman's perspective–expand and amend the genealogy. Indu Sundaresan explains her motivation for her Taj Mahal trilogy: "there are few mentions of the women these

[7] See, for example, Elizabeth Byrd's *Immortal Queen: Mary Queen of Scots* (1956) and E. Barrington's *Anne Boleyn* (1932).

kings [six main Mughal Emperors] married or of the power they exercised. *The Twentieth Wife* seeks to fill that gap" (383). Sundaresan's novel also unwittingly or not, amends racial blind spots in current contemporary writing on monarchs. Her work is a welcomed shift away from the Eurocentrism which dominates the genre.

Recuperating a concern with sexual desire found in Britain's 1940s further connects with the "captive wife," a theme Wallace also explores in relation to women's fears in the 1960s of "being recaptured and imprisoned within home and family – in short being forced to repeat her mother's life" (*Woman's* 140). Wallace writes that "these texts engage with the ideology which condemns female adultery, but they also express the understanding that marriage and traditional gender roles may entrap and stifle women's sense of their own identity" (86). There is a constant negotiation between sexual repression and liberation at play in these texts, suggesting that women's fear of sexual repression and also their fear of too much desire is once again a prevalent concern for contemporary women.

The novels I survey, Françoise D'Eaubonne's *Moi, Kristine Reine de Suède* (1979), Helene Lehr's *Star of the North* (1990), Elena Maria Vidal's *Trianon* (1997), Sundaresan's *The Twentieth Wife* (2002), Christina Hernando's *Isabel la Católica* (2007) and lastly Weir's *The Lady Elizabeth* (2008), highlight this dilemma nicely. Each work narrates the personal lives of rebellious, independent, learned, and unconventional daughters determined to break the cycle of becoming their mothers – thus the heroines commit matricide, symbolically. Though the daughter often identifies with the father while, paradoxically, sympathizing with her mother and blaming her father for her mother's misfortune (Wallace, *Woman's* 135).

In contemporary works "the erasure of her [daughter's] matrilineage" (Wallace, *Woman's* 98) is accelerated by a mother portrayed as a traitor, mad, weak, powerless, and/or neglectful and absent in her daughter's life; the mother figure is vilified-victimized. Forced to reject her mother, the heroine daughter either becomes extremely maternal (loving, nurturing, self-sacrificing) (Isabel, Mehrunnisa, Marie-Antoinette) or outright rejects this role (Elizabeth, Kristine, Catherine). Susan C. Staub notes that, in this early modern period, "sexuality is not separate from motherhood but is actually the locus of maternal anxiety" (18); thus, women were viewed as possessing:

> '[A] powerful, potentially disruptive sexuality requiring control
> through rigid social institutions and carefully nurtured inhibi-
> tions within the woman herself.' One way to control that sexu-
> ality was to valorize motherhood, encouraging women to marry
> and have children; another was to demonize it, transforming

mothers into 'anti-mothers,' whether as witches or seductress-
es. (Staub18)

Staub identifies the anxieties about mothering as correlating to anxieties about
female power (19). Marianne Hirsch, however, reminds us that the daughter's
narrative subjectivity often comes at the price of her mother's: "To speak for
the mother, as many of the daughters ... do, is at once to give voice to her discourse *and* to silence and marginalize her" (16). For Hirsch, the daughter's
narrative perpetuates the objectification of the mother and continues the tradition of mothers and daughters "becoming objects of the desire of/for the father," meaning an authentic desire of/for the mother is never realized (*Irigaray
Reader* 52).

Focusing on familiar political figures in mainstream historiography (primary
sources such as letters or visual representations of the protagonist exist), the
novels in this chapter relate the unknown aspects of their personal lives; the
"subject's inner life [depicted] through realistic fictional strategies" (Rozett
123) emerges and indicates a complex relationship with the character and her
mother and/or her experiences as a mother.

While recuperating Britain's preoccupation with maternal sexuality in the
1940s and a 1960s' fears of women being imprisoned in the family, the novels
approach the question of what/who constitutes an acceptable mother slightly
differently. They suggest a contemporary fear and preoccupation with the dis-
solution of the nuclear family and the mother's traditional maternal role. Prevalent transnational themes include the mother as immigrant, mothers living separate from their families, mothers marrying foreigners, mothers abandoning their
children, and women losing their status as mothers. Rhacel Salazar Parreñas
refers to these issues as the new reality of many families who are transnational
(80) and for whom "mothering from a distance" is now common (116). Thus,
there is a contemporary resurrection of a relevant transnational maternal past.
The femino-centric topics I explicate to shed further light on the interconnected
themes of matricide, gynocracy, and matrophobia include hysteria, separation,
betrayal, surrogacy, foreigners, and the relation between motherhood and
queenship. This last topic is an important aspect because the relation between
woman as mother and the nation as mothered is analyzed.

A contributing factor to this last component, as the well as the others, is the
definition of modernism. Within modernism, an evolving and more secular
consciousness of nations and nationalism emerges, social mobility becomes
possible, and even gender roles–particularly rethinking the definition of motherhood–becomes negotiable. John Frame, referencing Richard L. Pratt, defines
modernity as:

1) Truth is discerned primarily through rational and scientific investigation under the guidance of rationalistic philosophers and scientists, 2) Ultimate reality is the physical world. If a spiritual world exists at all, it is ephemeral and uninvolved in the events of the physical world. This is also a period for intense religious reformation, 3) Individuality of the independent objective scholar (transcendent subject) is prized over conformity to received traditions, 4) Heavy reliance on written communication, especially paper, due to rising literacy and publishing technologies (printing press), 5) Widespread rational and scientific meta-narrative depict history as progressing toward utopia. (28-29)

The novels, moreover, suggest that not only queens but also women in their everyday lives (consumerism, trade, mercantilism, guilds, church, writing, family and so on) contribute to our understanding of this period.

On the one hand, modernity is depicted in these times and places as golden ages of empire i.e., the Mughal Empire in *The Twentieth Wife*. There is cultural flourishing with the invention of the Gutenberg Press during the Elizabethan Age and when Kristine crowns Sweden the "Versailles of the North;" Kristine's tolerance for diverse religions during a time of religious reformation is similarly atypical: her conversion to Catholicism and abdication caused a scandal. Scientific discovery and territorial-transnational trade and expansion are also seen in Christopher Columbus' voyages, patronized by Isabel of Spain, to the new world.

One the other hand, this time in history has intense slavery such as in the New World and increased serfdom during Catherine the Great's reign. Religious persecution-conversion and territorial wars are equally evident in Isabel's conquest of Grenada by defeating and expelling the Muslim ruler Boabdil. Emphasizing a racial hierarchy, Isabel orders the Muslims and Jews to either convert to Catholicism or suffer the consequences, thus, leading to the infamous Spanish Inquisition that Inés recounts in Allende's novel *Inés of my Soul*. Vidal's novel on Marie-Antoinette marks the end of this chapter's modern period by narrating the French Revolution (1789) and Marie-Antoinette's murder by guillotine in 1793.

According to Anthony Smith, one cannot underestimate the role of the French Revolution "as a *nationalist* (and not simply a bourgeois) revolution (*Nationalism and Modernism* 126). For Lukács, too, the French Revolution is a pivotal event in both history and the origins of the historical novel genre. During the French Revolution, the masses experienced a historical awakening and, Lukács insists, in such key moments, the people realize "that there is such a thing as history, that it is an uninterrupted process of changes and finally that it has a direct effect upon the life of every individual" (23). Philosophers like Georg Wilhelm Friedrich Hegel sought to prove the "historical necessity" of this event and suggested that "history is [and must be] the bearer and realizer of human progress" (Lukács 27). Lukács' Marxist approach, which emphasizes the role of the individual through class struggles and in being shaped/shaping the course of history, is comparable and compatible with a twentieth and twenty-first century feminist perspective that centers on the awakening of a gender consciousness, but cautions against an uncritical mass consciousness as evidenced in Vidal's sympathetic portrayal of Marie-Antoinette as a mother devoted to her family.

Unfit Mothers, Hysteria, and Separation

The transnational novels in this chapter show how patriarchal society could effectively deem a woman a hysteric and an unsuitable mother and, consequently, separate her from her children. Irigaray suggests that "if a woman cannot express her relation to her mother and to other women, she may become 'hysterical'" (Whitford, "Section II" 77). Contrary to accepted belief, "there is a revolutionary potential in hysteria" because the hysteric, always a woman, exhibits "a movement of revolt and refusal, a desire for/of the living mother who would be more than a reproductive body in the pay of the polis, a living, loving woman" (*Irigaray Reader* 47). The hysteric is a woman imprisoned in a patriarchal society, and, thus, a "re-evaluation of hysteria as the unheard voice of the woman who can only speak through somatic symptoms" is necessary (Whitford, "Section I" 26). Hernando's novel achieves this rereading of hysteria; it opens in Spain, 1451 with Isabel de Portugal giving birth to her daughter Isabel. Isabel de Portugal is Juan II's second wife (14), as, Hernando argues, the king's most trusted advisor don Álvaro de Luna poisoned his first wife, María de Aragón (17, 51). Paranoid of suffering the same fate, Isabel demands that her husband imprison his loyal friend. The imprisonment and execution of de Luna, however, causes the king's health to decline and he dies a few months later (Hernando 52). Isabel of Portugal, thus, "ella se creía la única responsable de la muerte de don Álvaro y más tarde, de su esposo Juan II de Castilla" 'believed herself responsible for the death of don Álvaro and later, her husband Juan II of Castile' (52). Isabel de Portugal's vulnerability after the death of her husband becomes clear.

Following Juan II's death, his son Prince Enrique by the late María de Aragón becomes King Enrique IV of Castilla and León (Hernando 23). Hernando writes, "Su primera orden fue muy clara: Isabel de Portugal, junto a sus

dos hijos, debía abandonar su residencia de Madrigal de las Altas Torres y diri-
girse a Arévalo" 'His first order was very clear: Isabel of Portugal and her two
children must leave their home in Madrigal de las Altas Torres and relocate in
Arévalo' (23). Irigaray describes this process of banishment as "women 'in
exile', 'like ghosts' in the masculine phallic imaginary" (Irigaray Reader 72).
Ghost-like imagery haunts Hernando's novel as well as the young Isabel. Her
childhood is austere and tinged with the sadness of her mother, who after losing
her status and being forced into exile, frequently walks aimlessly in the night
and interrupts the children's games by shouting " Don Álvaro, don Álvaro"
(28, 47). Thus Isabel de Portugal is reduced to being merely a shadow of her
former self.

Her daughter realizes, "mi madre está cada vez más cerca de perder la
razón, pero nadie parece querer hablar del tema" 'my mother is increasingly
nearer to losing her mind, but no one seems to want to speak about it' (Hernando 32). Insisting that her governess doña Beatriz de Bobadilla disclose Isabel's
family's history, she is told who don Álvaro was, how he died, and why her
mother cannot live with her guilt. Isabel de Portugal's situation worsens where
her step-son, Enrique IV divorces Blanca de Navarra and marries Juana de
Portugal. Upon his new marriage he summons Isabel and her younger brother
Alfonso back to court. Isabel de Portugal is helpless: "Yo, que hace siete años
era la reina de Castilla y podia ordenar cuanto se me antojarse... ahora no pue-
do impeder que os arranquen de mi lado... ni aun suplicando de rodillas.¡Ay,
mis niños!" 'I was for seven years the queen of Castilla and could order when it
suited me ...now I cannot even order to keep my children by my side .... Not
even begging on my knees. Oh, my children!' (ibid.). Ultimately, Enrique IV's
motives for having Isabel and Alfonso near him are to protect the interests of
Juana, his daughter's claims to the throne, and to suppress any uprisings in
favor of his step-brother and/or step-sister. On travelling back to the court, the
infanta Isabel questions how the new queen Juana de Portugal, expecting her
own baby, "era capaz de separar a unos hijos de su madre, ni entendía cómo las
mujeres regias jugaban un papel tan pobre" 'was capable of separating children
from their mother, nor could she understand how royal women could set so
poor an example' (ibid.). The displacement of her mother, according to Hernando, deeply affects Isabel and, after this initial separation, she only sees her
mother once more, six years later, just prior to Alfonso's suspicious death. Isabel like the other women in this chapter lacks a maternal figure and suffers
from a forced separation from her mother.

D'Eaubonne's novel exemplifies both of the above themes: Moi, Kristine
Reine de Suède, (the only work in this chapter written in the style of a memoir), like Sigrid Grabner's Christina von Schweden: Die rebellische Konigin

(1992), begins with a dying Kristine, who through a series of flashbacks, is recounting her life as the former Queen of Sweden. Kristine, akin to Marie-Antoinette, is unique because, unlike the other monarchs who have ambitions to be queen, she abdicates her throne. Her decision to denounce her throne is not only tied to her wish to convert to Catholicism but also to her maternal heritage and, essentially, is an act of abdicating from motherhood.

Kristine is described as having a great love for her father Gustave-Adolphe. D'Eaubonne, portraying him in relation to Kristine's mother, writes, "L'ombre insignifiante de ma mère disparaissait auprès d'un tel soleil" 'the insignificant shadow of my mother disappeared under such a sun' (19). When Kristine is six years old, her father, famous for his success on the battlefield, is called by the Protestants to come to their aid in the Thirty Years War (ibid.). Upon his departure, he makes arrangements so that if he dies Kristine will be left in the care of his chancellor Oxienstern and his sister Katrine, not her mother, Marie-Éléonore. Kristine, also, is to be educated and raised as a boy, suggesting rigid gender boundaries can be manipulated by those in power. The novel, then, shifts to Gustave-Adolphe's death and Kristine remembering seeing her mother again. Much like Isabel, she fears her mother is losing her mind, because following her husband's death, Marie-Éléonore uncharacteristically channels her energies and interests to Kristine: "ce débordement de passion maternelle, au lieu de m'attendrir, me glaçait" 'this overflowing maternal passion, instead of softening me, froze me' (23). Denying her husband's death, Marie-Éléonore has Gustave-Adolphe embalmed and "avait placé son coeur dans une urne d'argent" 'his heart placed in a silver urn' (24). She, also, brings Kristine to live with her in Nykoping.

Kristine witnesses her mother praying, crying, and wandering from room to room like a ghost. Like Isabel's mother, Marie-Éléonore becomes a spectral figure –viewed by the daughter as both neither inside nor outside the sentient world. Patriarchal society murders the mother to the extent that becomes a shadow.

Once older, however, Kristine reflects that as a woman she can now relate to the pain of her mother:

Á l'heure de mon agonie, j'évoque sans doute mon passé de la même façon que jadis Marie-Éléonore dans les nuits blanches de Nykoping. Je sais, grâce aux récits de mon cousin Charles-Gustave (qui les tenait de son père) quelle fut la trame pathétique et agaçante de la jeunesse, du roman d'amour et du mariage de ma pauvre Allemande de mère"

In the hour of my agony, I evoke without doubt my past much in the same way that Marie-Éléonore did in the white nights of Nykoping. I know, thanks to the stories from my cousin Charles-Gustave (who had them from his father) which was the pathetic template and annoyance of youth, the romance and the marriage of my poor German mother. (27)

Irigaray believes that when daughters realize they "must liberate themselves with their mothers" (Whitford, "Section I" 26), it marks a crucial point in a woman's life; Kristine realizes this claim when she relates the early life of her own mother and the heated arguments surrounding her marriage as a Prussian Calvinist to the Swedish King, a Lutheran whose territorial wars over Poland were criticized.

Despite her mother's, Anne de Brandenburg's, wishes, Marie-Éléonore marries Gustave-Adolphe. The difference in ideologies, however, affects Kristine's own interpretation of her country. When Oxenstiern, Kristine's governor, comes to Nykoping, he learns of the cloistered existence Kristine has been living, much like Isabel. The mother's care is deemed unsuitable and Kristine is removed and taken, as promised, to her aunt Katrine in Upsal (ibid.). D'Eaubonne writes, "En vain ma mère se frappe la gorge en poussant des cris de sarcelle atteinte d'une flèche; en vain elle s'indigna de connaître que l'éducation de sa fille serait remise, entre autres mains" 'In vain my mother hit her throat, squawking like a duck stricken by an arrow; in vain she was outraged to know that the education of her daughter would be in the hands of others' (43). In exchange for Kristine's transference, Marie-Éléonore is compensated, like many other royal mothers in this time period, monetarily and she is allowed to see her daughter only a few times a year (ibid.). Marie-Éléonore's influence on her daughter, like the other mothers in this chapter, is considered threatening: matrilineal affinities can disrupt patriarchal power. The mother's influence in the text is strikingly highlighted once more in spectral terms by primarily her absence in her daughter's life.

While Kristine's father's legacy may be secure, it is her mother's sentiments which also exert a powerful force on the child's thinking, especially her anti-Swedish complaints (61). Acknowledging her mother, Kritstine declares, "il faut pourtant me souvenir à l'heure de la vérité que j'ai aussi ce sang-là [de ma mère] dans les veines" 'I must remember at this time of truth that I also have that blood [my mother's] in my veins' (ibid.). Thus, Kristine writes:

J'essayais de tout coeur de m'attacher à ce people que le hasard de ma naissance m'avait appellée à gouvener. Je déplorais la médiocrité du commerce, l'absence de toute société cultivée et policée, le faible développement des manufactures d'armes dans un pays célèbre sur tous les champs de bataille d'Europe.

I tried with all my heart to attach myself to my people, who by chance of my birth, called upon me to rule. I deplored the mediocrity of trade, the absence of all cultivated and ordered society, the poor development of the manufacturing of weapons in a country celebrated throughout all the battlefields of Europe. (63)

Kristine's feelings for Sweden are, thus, conflicted due to her maternal heritage.

When her mother unexpectedly visits her in Stockholm, seemingly having cast off her dedication to mourning Gustave-Adolphe, she shows her daughter "beaucoup d'affection" 'a lot of affection' and a new robust appearance. Oxenstiern informs Kristine that her mother has been corresponding with Sweden's enemy, Kristian IV, King of Denmark. Marie-Éléonore's affair with the Danish king ends with her being humiliated and handed back to her family in Brandenburg 66, 67). Feeling betrayed as a daughter and as Sweden's future ruler by her mother's affair, Kristine recalls her mother from her relatives, gives her money, and sends her back to Nykoping with the right to die slowly: in a sense Kristine punishes her mother in a patriarchal manner. As if speaking to her mother, Kristine writes that she confines her mother to "cette terre suédoise que tu détestait mais qui avait au moins l'avantage de t'éloigner des tiens" 'that Swedish land that you hated but which had the advantage of keeping you away from your kin' (68). Banished, this time by her matrophobic daughter, Marie-Éléonore figures little in the novel until Kristine's abdication because René Descartes, Kristine's tutor, dies in her court during this time, as do her mother and Oxenstiern.

Betrayal, Mothers as Traitors

Similar to Kristine's mother, who has a forbidden affair with the King of Denmark, Elizabeth I's mother Ann Boleyn is accused of marital infidelity and treason. As daughters of so-called adulteress mothers, Kristine and Elizabeth are forced to distance themselves from their matrilineage. Irigaray writes :

desire for her, her desire, that is what is forbidden by the law of the father, of all fathers Fathers of families, fathers of nations, religious fathers, professorfathers doctor –fathers, lover-fathers, etc. Moral or immoral, they always intervene to censor, to repress the desire of/for the mother. For them that constitutes as good sense and good health. (Irigaray Reader 36)

Weir's novel begins with Elizabeth's half-sister Mary (the daughter of Catherine of Aragon and the granddaughter of Isabel la Católica) arriving at Hatfield under their father King Henry VIII of England's orders to deliver the news of Boleyn's death.

Mary asks the governess Lady Bryan what she believes the three year old's reaction will be and if the child knew her mother well. Lady Bryan replies, "I'm afraid she did. Her Grace–I mean the lady her mother–kept the child with her, more than was seemly for a queen. If you remember, she even refused to have a wet nurse" (Weir 5). Boleyn is portrayed as monstrous because of her maternal desire and the pleasure she gains from a corporeal connection with Elizabeth. Mary's feelings toward Elizabeth, however, are complex: "because of Elizabeth's mother, that great whore, Anne Boleyn … Mary had lost all that she held dear in life: her own mother, the late sainted Queen Katherine, her rank, her prospects of a throne and marriage, and the love of her father the King" (ibid.). Weir's work ultimately recounts the loss of both daughters' respective mothers. It is a novel of matricides and, with the recent death of her mother, Elizabeth's fortunes and Mary's futures are now the same; both are considered illegitimate, despite the fact that Henry "had been king of England for twenty-seven years, … [he] still had no son to succeed him" (14). She is no longer Lady Princess, but simply Lady Elizabeth (6, 7).

In Elizabeth's earliest memories, she sees a special occasion celebrated by both her parents because "some old harridan was dead" (11). The "harridan" is, of course, Mary's mother (14). All three are dressed in yellow and Elizabeth remembers her mother's beauty. Weir writes that "[t]o Elizabeth, her mother was the ideal queen, beautiful, poised, and kind, and her love was tinged with reverence and awe" (ibid.). Her next memory is a fight between her parents. Held in her mother's arms, she hears her father "calling her mother a witch, among other unkind names" (12). The result of the argument is that Boleyn lifts Elizabeth up, forcing the King to acknowledge that she is his daughter and heir , and Elizabeth is returned to Hatfield with "a new doll in her arm–a parting gift from her mother" (13). Weir, then, picks up the narrative with Mary's memories of Boleyn and the accusations of her affairs, one of which was with a lute player named Mark Smeaton , whom some at court believe to be Elizabeth's father.

Signaling Elizabeth's illegitimacy, Mary identifies the unmistakable physical likeness of Elizabeth to her mother. She tells Elizabeth that "[her] mother committed treason against the King [their] father, and she has suffered the punishment. She has been put to death" (16). Recovering from this painful news, Elizabeth is informed that she is to have a new stepmother, Jane Seymour . This new marriage entails that, at court, Mary must face the humiliation of denouncing her mother Catherine of Aragon as rightful queen, a position Katherine, in life, refused. She must:

Accede that her mother's marriage had been incestuous and unlawful, and that she herself was therefore a bastard, but she also acknowledged her father the King to be the Supreme Head of the Church of England under Christ … she had abandoned all the principles she and her mother had held most dear. (18-19)

Thus, Mary is forced to erase her matrilineage and Elizabeth must, like Isabel at a young age, rely on clandestine information to piece together her mother's past.

Elizabeth asks Mary to divulge her mother's crimes and how she died. Matter-of-factly, she tells Elizabeth that her mother was unfaithful to the King, plotted to murder him, and, in return, was put to death by the sword . Throughout the novel, Boleyn's absence marks her as an important protagonist, one who influences much of not only Elizabeth's but also Mary's decisions. Striving to replace her mother, Elizabeth latches onto her sister Mary, her governess, and her new step-mother Jane Seymour.

Henry VIII's marriage to Seymour, nonetheless, is short-lived because she dies in childbirth (Weir 33). Lady Bryan is ordered to take care of the new prince Edward and Elizabeth likens the resultant absence to the loss of her mother: "In all but blood, she had been a mother to her, the person who had cared for her, nurtured her, comforted her, and disciplined her" (44). Elizabeth, however, realizes that the decision to move Lady Bryan is not only her father's, but also Lady Bryan's: "once again, the universe had shifted, as it had done violently when she had learned of the awful fate of her mother, and less so when Queen Jane had died" (ibid.). Elizabeth, "made motherless several times over," begins to piece together a constructed definition of motherhood, one that is unstable, contingent, and full of pain and loss (Wallace, Woman's 98).

The new governess, Mistress Champernowne, called Kat, however, proves an admirable replacement as a maternal figure in Elizabeth's life. A distant cousin of Elizabeth's "through [her] lady mother's family" (Weir 46), Kat believes in Boleyn's innocence and takes Elizabeth to Hertford to view a portrait. Elizabeth muses, "So this was her mother. She had never seen a picture of her, had only the dimmest memory, and had often wondered what she looked like" (72). Seeing that she resembles her mother–"only her red hair marked her as a Tudor" (ibid.), Elizabeth secretly takes the painting as she has no other keepsake. In her Author's Note, Weir comments that "Elizabeth's admiration for her father and reverence for his memory are also well attested. However, we have virtually no evidence for her feelings about her mother, and no means of knowing if she believed Anne Boleyn to be innocent or guilty" (477). The lack of historical record allows Weir to invent this missing mother-daughter relationship and weave together, like in Robin Maxwell's The Secret Diary of Anne Boleyn (1998), Elizabeth's feelings toward her mother. For Martha Tuck Rozett, this constitutes "a revisionist account written to contest the politically motivated Tudor history that represents Anne as a wanton woman and adulteress" (127). Elizabeth, drawing upon memory and silences, for "it is only in/through her silences that she circulates" (Irigaray Reader 60), renegotiates a maternal relationship through historical places/objects associated with Boleyn.

After Henry VIII's annulment from his fourth wife Anne of Cleves, the former Queen invites Elizabeth to her new home in Hever Castle. When Elizabeth sees another portrait of her mother in the long gallery, she is informed that this was her mother's childhood home. Weir writes, "Wherever Elizabeth went at Hever, there were reminders of her mother. Her memory was there in every room, every garden walk, every shady arbor" (78). Piecing together a counter history of her mother, through memory and her mother's objects, with that of the 'official' history of her father and court, Elizabeth declares, "When I grow up, I am going to be like her!" (ibid.). As if responding to her daughter, at the end of her Hever visit, Elizabeth sees a vision of Boleyn's ghost (79): "'Mother?' she whispered, trying out the sweet, unfamiliar word on her tongue. The irresistible conclusion, the only one she wanted to believe, was that Anne Boleyn's shade had come to her" (80). Weir stresses the importance of Boleyn in her daughter's life, even if comes from a spectral presence – her father may have murdered her mother but her objects, historical artefacts, including her ghost, a former vision of her past life, continue to haunt and shape Elizabeth's present.

Like Isabel who must defeat the supporters of her niece Juana for the throne of Castile following the death of her brother-king Enrique, tensions between Elizabeth and her sister Mary intensify after Henry VIII's death as Edward, the heir, has also died. Mary, a staunch Catholic, rises to the throne, but Protestant supporters, who first put Jane Grey, Elizabeth's cousin and a popular personae in women's historical fiction, on the throne (after which she is quickly imprisoned and executed), soon after favor Elizabeth. This results in charges against Elizabeth for conspiring with the enemy and committing treason against not only a sister, her family, but also her queen and her nation (366). Mary sentences Elizabeth to the Tower, "[j]ust as her mother had [been], all those years ago. And Anne Boleyn had not left it alive, had instead suffered the agonies of confinement and faced a terrible death" (367). Accordingly, Elizabeth is imprisoned in the same rooms where her mother was kept prior to her death. Weir writes, "It was like having a ghost standing just behind her. It has been surprisingly easy seeking out memories of her mother in the lush, leafy paradise at Hever, Anne's former home; but here, where she had met her fate, the very stones spoke of tragedy and doom" (377). During Elizabeth's first restless night in the chamber, her mother's ghost appears once again. Elizabeth believes that "her mother Anne [has] come to give her comfort and strength in her ordeal" (ibid.).

In a sense, Elizabeth asks, "so what is a mother? Someone who makes the stereotypical gestures she is told to make, who has no personal language and who has no identity. But, how as daughters, can we have a personal relationship with or construct a personal identity in relation to someone who is no more than a function?" (Irigaray Reader 50). Boleyn's presence as a maternal link in her daughter's life enables Elizabeth to become a great queen. Unlike her mother, Elizabeth is pardoned by Mary and, as the only surviving Tudor, is named Queen upon Mary's death (473). Queen Elizabeth restores the country to the Protestantism inaugurated by her father, not necessarily out of love for him, but because it allowed her mother to marry legally; thus legitimating her own claims to the throne. Elizabeth suggests that a subversive "daughter/mother relationship [which] constitutes a highly explosive nucleus" has the power to emancipate women "from the authority of fathers" (Irigaray Reader 50).

A perceived betrayal of patriarchal nationhood and motherhood is also prominent in Lehr's novel Star of the North by Catherine the Great's mother. The Russian Empress Elizabeth Petrovna, daughter of the Great Tsar Peter, is examining a portrait of the Prussian and Lutheran princess Sophie Augusta Fredericka of Anhalt-Zerbst as a potential match for her nephew Peter Fedorovich, the Grand Duke of Holstein and heir to the throne. Much to the dismay of Count Bestuzhev, who would prefer "his sovereign to choose the Princess of Saxony, to choose anyone, for that matter, except a Prussian" (10), the Empress summons the German princess for the sole purpose of producing an heir: "She was young and, from all accounts, healthy; no doubt she would easily produce children. And that, after all, was the only reason for this union" (11). Part One of the novel, titled "The Girl, 1744," marks the arrival of the fourteen year old destined to be the grand duchess, summoned by her marriage to her cousin the grand duke (the only living male Romanov). Yet, unlike Peter who stands firm in his preference for Prussia, Catherine quickly adopts Russia as her mother-country.

Her devotion is quickly tested, however, when it is discovered that her mother has been sending secret letters to the enemy, King Frederick of Prussia. The Empress asks Sophie if she wishes to return home with her mother, reiterating to the newly titled grand duchess Catherine Alexeivna that her duty is to marry and have sons. Believing Catherine innocent in her mother's betrayal, considered here as a maternal betrayal, the Empress demands that Catherine's mother return home immediately after the wedding. With the symbolic loss of Catherine's blood mother, she gains the Empress, Russia's 'Little Mother,' as her new mother. Adopted by the Empress as her daughter and heir, she is essentially considered Russian, thus, reifying a patriarchal preoccupation in these works with the interconnection between nationhood and motherhood.

Surrogate Mothers: The Contest of Custody

In novels from this period the custody of children is highly contested. In Lehr's novel when Count Bestuzhev insinuates that Catherine is still a virgin, the Empress, desperate for an heir (for by now six years of marriage have passed), arranges for Catherine to be seduced by Serge Saltikov, a handsome, married aristocrat. The Empress states that "there must be a child ... by any means available" (83), suggesting that an illegitimate heir is better than none at all. Catherine's failure to reproduce sons is unacceptable and could result in her dismissal from Russia. After having an affair with Saltikov, fulfilling her marital/national duties, Catherine at last gives birth; the Empress exclaims, "A son! ... Peter, you have a son!" (123). The maternal is denied in order to fulfill patriarchal ideology/property and Catherine, no better than an exploited surrogate, is left abandoned in her room while the child is whisked off in the arms of the Empress. Upon asking when she will be able to see her son, Catherine learns that a wet nurse has been found for the baby (thus, her own body is unnecessary) and that "the crown prince is in the apartments of the Empress" (126), for "the child is to remain with the Empress ... He ... is to live there" (127). Learning of this maternal betrayal, like so many of the other mothers in this chapter, the grand duchess falls ill. The people, however, come out in droves to "pray for her recovery their Russian hearts saddened, for they all adored her" (129). The Empress, for her part, delivers a gift of money and precious jewels–a theme consistent in this chapter–as monetary compensation means mothers are to cease interfering in their children's lives.

Staring at the coins she has received in exchange for her body, her love (Serge has been relocated to Sweden), her child, and her innocence (virginity), Catherine vows she will never love another man again. She resolves that "one day that crown would rest upon her own head, and never again would anyone manipulate her life" (Lehr 133). Lehr ends the first half of her novel with a rite of passage signaling the transition from girl to woman through the bodily act of childbirth. Childbirth plays a central role in the text. For example, later in the novel, after the Empress' death, Catherine is urged to act against Peter but she refuses because she is pregnant with her illegitimate third child, Alexis Gregorovich Bobrinsky. The child is taken to a couple in the country, in response to which Catherine bitterly observes, "Three times I have borne a child. ... But yet I am childless!" (214).

In her brief epilogue, Lehr writes:

The animosity, pronounced even early on, between Catherine and her son, Paul Petrovich, grew more so with each passing year. Deprived of her children during their formative years, Catherine gave vent to her maternal feeling by lavishing all her love and attention on her grandchildren. Ironically, she removed her first two grandsons from the care of their parents in much the same manner as Empress Elizabeth had spirited away her own two children. (264)

Catherine's rupture with her son Paul leads to her naming her eldest grandson Alexander I her successor. A similar anti-maternal stance occurs in Yolanda Scheuber's Juana la Reina, loca de amor (2010), when Isabel la Católica's daughter Juana, an extremely educated and intelligent woman, marries the Habsburg prince, Philip of Flanders. As Isabel's heir, Juana is separated from her maternal family and is continuously declared mad and incompetent to rule by her father and husband. Scheuber, however, defends Juana against madness and attributes her unhappiness to patriarchal confinement and control over her life. In the end, her son Carlos V, the future holy Roman Emperor, rules.

In Lehr's novel, despite Catherine's wishes, four years after her death, her son Paul becomes ruler and loses no time in reversing his mother's policies and undermining/erasing all that she stood for–after all, he believes she murdered his father Peter in order to take the crown. Lehr ends the work by informing the reader that on March 11, 1801, Alexander I overthrew his father and, in the process, Paul was assassinated. The novel suggests that the temptation of surrogate mothers to repeat the process by procuring for themselves the child of another woman can be attributed to the prohibition/matricide of a loving maternal relationship in patriarchal societies.

This theme is continued in Sundaresan's novel The Twentieth Wife. The protagonist Mehrunnisa, by virtue of the position of her father Ghias Beg (who fled from Persia to India after the assassination of Shah Ismail II in 1578) in Emperor Akbar's court, is permitted to serve the Empress Ruqayya. Summoned, Mehrunnisa meets the Empress' son, Khurram (the future Emperor Shah Jahan). The child, flinging himself on the Empress' lap, demands, "'Ma sweets'" (Sundaresan 65). Mehrunnisa is surprised because the Empress has no children; in a way that resonates with many women's historical novels' declarations of plural mothering, Mehrunnisa modifies her position:

to be sure, there were hundreds of 'mothers' for every baby born in the zenana, but she had never before seen any child wrap the autocratic Padshah Begam around his little finger as this one had. ... "'Yes, he is mine. All mine. ... I may not have given birth to him, but he [is] nonetheless my son." (ibid.)

Khurram, Mehrunnisa learns from her mother Asmat, is the prince Salim's (Akbar's son and heir) third son by his second wife Jagat Gosini, but the Empress has custody of him. A sign of her friendship and trust, Ruqayya invites

Mehrunnisa to the harem every day to help mind Khurram. Sundaresan states, "The usually levelheaded Ruqayya was obsessed with the child, to such a point that his mother, Princess Jagat Gosini, was permitted only brief weekly visits" (67). Thus, the consistent theme of mothers being separated from their children is related to other women acting as, for all intents and purposes, the maternal figure for personal and political gain. Mehrunnisa, also, faces this temptation when, after miscarrying twice, she discovers her husband Ali Quli has impregnated one of the servants.

Ordered by her father and the Emperor to marry Ali Quli, a soldier, Mehrunnisa watches "her dreams slipping away" (83). Though married, she has no children. Mehrunnisa thinks, "It could not be so. It was unimaginable –this life without a child, this life Ali Quli had sketched out for her as the barren wife of a common soldier" (122-23). Her servant's pregnancy, meanwhile, progresses and Mehrunnisa can only "watch her husband's child in another woman's body" (147). When Yasmin goes into labor, however, a mid-wife cannot be found because she "is not married" (ibid.). Taking command of the situation, though inexperienced, Mehrunnisa feels pity for the orphan slave-girl laying on a bed of straw in the hen-house.

She realizes that "she had no choice. They were all –this slave girl, the servants, Mehrunnisa herself –the property of her husband. How could this girl have denied him anything?" (149). After the difficult birth, Mehrunnisa, holding the baby in her arms, wonders, "[i]f Ruqayya could command a child away from a royal princess, why shouldn't she from a penniless orphan maidservant? She could always pension Yasmin off and send her to some remote village. She would never talk. Mehrunnisa had brought the child into this world. He must belong to her" (151). Musing over the decision, Mehrunnisa declares that she "yearned desperately for a child –but her own child, not the fruit of some other woman's womb. So she gave the baby back to Yasmin and sent her away" (168). Unlike Mehrunnisa, who refuses the son of her servant and eventually gives birth to a daughter, Lehr suggests Catherine mimics the actions of the Empress by later appropriating her own son Paul's child, Alexander I. Women's historical novels such as Sundaresan's and Lehr's re-emphasize the need for understanding the complexity of motherhood in relation to patriarchal restrictions on desire and parenting. Catherine is unable to see that the patriarchal ideology she subscribes to and perpetuates once she takes the crown entails her forfeiture of personal-maternal desires and that control over women's bodies resides outside of themselves.

Foreign Mothers: Sexual-Political Alliances

The woman's historical novel on modern queens emphasizes the importance of transnational marriages for political security (Wilkinson 21). Marriages to foreigners were a strategic political decision and meant an implicit truce and loyalty between respective nations. This is seen in both Lehr's Star of the North and Vidal's Trianon, in which the queen's sexuality, unlike her more androgynous predecessors, such as Kristine, "was now described as totally maternal, a symbol of motherhood rather than monarchy" (Wiesner-Hanks 20). As queen consort "'in motherhood and in her household … as well as through her family' she remained firmly engaged 'in the political community'. The fragility of her sexual reputation as a woman ensured that she remained a potential scapegoat for the failings of her husband and her kin" (Oakley-Brown and Wilkinson 16). In Star of the North, Lehr suggests the fragility of Catherine's position as queen consort, but she innovatively reverses stereotypical pairings of the "the patriot versus the enemy; the loyal citizen versus the disloyal immigrant" (Alexander 5) by contrasting Peter with the Prussian-born Catherine. Catherine lives in Russia, her birth nation's enemy, and Prussia and Russia are soon to be at war. She is an immigrant and, like most immigrants, she must negotiate the complexity "of a pure 'home'" with "a 'contaminated' diasporic location" (Grewal and Kaplan 16). Catherine's position is frequently described as being unstable and the threat of being sent back 'home' by her adopted mother/family/nation always looms. In Eva Stanchiak's The Winter Palace (2011), for instance, Catherine is essentially spied upon from the moment she arrives by her servant Barbara, who works for the Empress and Count Bestuzhev, stressing that being obedient and becoming Russian for Catherine is necessary for survival. Lehr describes that four years into the marriage, practically under house-arrest, and still without child, Catherine is approached by Count Bestuzhev:

His gaze traveled about and rested at last upon Catherine's writing table. With some surprise, he noted the works of Voltaire and Montesquieu; heavy fare, indeed, he thought to himself. He picked up another book, one dealing with the history of Russia, and now he regarded her with open curiosity. (73)

Surprised by her learnedness in contrast to the duke who plays with toy soldiers and spends hours training his dogs, Bestuzhev feels admiration for the duchess.

Sensing approval, Catherine remarks, "I am deeply interested in the history of my country" and the Count asks, "And just which country is your country, madame?,") to which Catherine answers, "Russia is my country, Chancellor" (73). Pressing the issue one step further, Bestuzhev inquires, "And should the day come when we are at war with Prussia ... where will your sympathies lie?"

(ibid.). After a short silence, Catherine reassures the Count that her allegiance to Russia need never be questioned and if war were to arise against Frederick, she, unlike her husband and mother, would be prepared to strike him down. Catherine's political devotion to Russia and her ability to speak "faultless Russian" is juxtaposed with her husband who openly supports Frederick, speaks German fluently, and Russian poorly.

When Bestuzhev explains that he's had a troubling report from General Apraxin, whose troops are failing against the Prussians, he asks Catherine to communicate with the general. This correspondence, as Catherine knows, will undermine the Empress' orders. Bestuzhev claims, "Some time ago ... you told me that Russia was your country. If that's true, then she needs your help now as never before" (148). Bestuzhev's inscription of Russia as a woman suggests how women and nations both fall under patriarchal governance and anchor the national imagination. According to Geraldine Heng, this posits and naturalizes "a strategic set of relationships linking land, language, history, and people to produce a crucial nexus of pivotal terms 'motherland,' 'mother tongue,' ... that will hold together the affective conditions, the emotive core, of nationalist ideology and pull a collection of disparate peoples into a self identified nation" (31). Bestuzhev also explains there are plans to draft a Manifesto altering the succession from Peter to his son Paul, with Catherine reigning as regent until Paul comes of age. Shocked by Bestuzhev's act of treason, Catherine reminds him "I ... am Prussian" and Bestuzhev asks, "Are you?" to which Catherine replies, "only by birth" (151) and so agrees to write the letter.

The forbidden letters (reminiscent of her mother's betrayal), Jacqui Alexander suggests, signify that guilt lies not in any act but in suspicion, which explains "the demarcation between citizen and immigrant" (237). As an immigrant, Catherine is always a suspect when contrasted with the loyal citizen. Taking her fate into her own hands, Catherine sends a plea to the Empress to send her home, back to Prussia (Lehr 167). Dressing modestly beneath her station, emphasizing the power of bodily appearance, the Empress is reminded of Catherine's girlhood and her innocence. Though disappointed that Catherine has been writing letters without permission (to congratulate a general on the birth of his son), the Empress also observes that she cannot believe Catherine would betray her: "I do believe you actually regard Russia as your country. ... For this we forgive you much Catherine Alexeivna" (175). This intimate scene between two women (daughter-mother) continues as the Empress reflects that she does not have much longer to live. Fearing Catherine's life will be in danger when Peter seizes the throne, she declares, "Your husband will kill you if he can" (177). Catherine tenderly calls the Empress "Little Mother" (ibid.), inscribing her in patriarchal discourse as her personal mother but also as the collective mother of the nation.

When the Empress dies, Peter ends the war with Prussia and plans a celebratory banquet. Meanwhile, the people are still mourning for "their revered Little Mother" (Lehr 199). Count Panin, who has been plotting with Bestuzhev to alter the succession in favor of Catherine's son Paul, exclaims, "the tsar has not only sent word to Frederick that all his lost lands will be returned to him, he has apologized for taking them in the first place!" (203). Even Panin pleads with Catherine to act against the grand duke, but she refuses. Catherine realizes that, in order to achieve her goal, she will need to win the people over. Morning after morning, Catherine sinks to her knees and bows her head in prayer for the loss of the Empress. This act of loyalty not only moves the people but also the members of the Imperial Guard (205). By comparison, when the casket is sealed in order to be taken to Kazan Cathedral, Peter is described "cavorting through the street, his booted feet tapping out a gleeful dance to a rhythm accompanied by music only he could hear" (207). Peter's actions appall the people, who whisper and murmur in the streets, "He plans to turn us all into Prussians... Long live our new Little Mother...God grant us her Imperial grace" (ibid.). Lehr suggests that Peter cannot rule Russia because he is considered unpatriotic and disloyal and he is unable to merge his sexuality in a way that motherhood (devoted to her children and her nation) allows a woman.

Orlov, a lieutenant in the army and Catherine's greatest devotee, declares that, if given the word, the regiments will fight to place her on the throne. Catherine asks, "And what makes you think that the soldiers will follow me? ... I'm no more a Russian than is Peter" (Lehr 209). Orlov, however, shakes his head and claims, "You are a Russian, Catherine!" (ibid.) and reminds her that her son is, also, Russian by birth. The question of what it means to be Russian or mother becomes less about biological birth than about adopting wholeheartedly the ideological customs and beliefs, language and religion, and historical imagination of that nation.

Peter, ordering Catherine's exile to Peterhof, declares she will soon be banished to a nunnery. Women's historical novels, like Lehr's, confirm patriarchal restrictions on a woman's body; her sexual life is always regulated by others, whether by the Empress in producing children or the denial of a sexual life altogether by Peter. Met by Orlov on the outskirts of Peterhof in Mount Plaisir, Catherine finally decides to act militarily. Reaching Ismailhov and met by thousands of military supporters, Lehr describes in sexual terms how "the men, without exception, gazed at their beautiful tsarina with adoring eyes, each of them prepared to lay his life at her feet" (237). Catherine "felt the love of the people embrace her like the passionate arms of an ardent lover and gave herself up entirely to the feeling it generated within her" (238). Entering Kazan Cathedral, Catherine is met with a teary eyed Archbishop. Kneeling, Catherine accepts the crown from the archbishop. As Panin notes, "it wasn't the rightful successor that the people wanted to take the place of their hated tsar; it was the foreign woman who had so blinded them with her charisma that they were all willing to overlook her origins!" (239). Reborn as the newly crowned Empress and Autocrat of Russia, Catherine appears "wearing the uniform of the Preobrazhensky Guard" (240). Lehr explains that "[s]o proud was her bearing that another great cheer erupted from the onlookers when they caught sight of her. 'A long life to [their] Little Mother!'" (240). Quickly mounting her horse and leading it in a great circle around her regiments, Panin, watching, declares, "He had always suspected that Catherine's interest in history was exaggerated. But he now saw that she had done her homework well. The act she was performing was as old as the Cossacks and hussars. The meaning was clear, to him and everyone witnessing it: She was publicly displaying her intent to take command" (241). Lehr ultimately suggests that Catherine's knowledge of history and the military as well as her ability to use her body as a mother and cultural translator secures her rule of Russia, despite her Prussian birth.

By comparison, Marie-Antoinette is described in Vidal's novel Trianon as detested by the people of France. Marie-Antoinette, born in Austria and the fifteenth and penultimate child of Holy Roman Empress Maria Theresa and Holy Roman Emperor Francis I, is arranged to marry the Dauphin of France at a young age, before they have even met. Though she is revered for her famous beauty and grace, she is referred to by the French as the embodiment of her nation: "l'Autrichienne" ['the Austrian'] (with a playful linguistic link in French to the "Austrian Dog/Bitch" (49, 73). Unlike Catherine, who wins over the Russian people, Vidal's narrative centers on the increasing alienation and isolation Marie-Antoinette experiences in being away from her own mother and in relation to the French people whom she cannot win-over because of her dislike for Versailles, French etiquette, and French politics. Marie-Antoinette, however, experiences a domestic happiness and a seemingly genuine love for her husband which neither Catherine nor any of the other monarchs do.

Focusing on a time in the Queen's life that is rarely given attention, her final years between 1787 and 1793, Vidal offers several perspectives on the Queen's past life and those relevant to her domestic life in Trianon. A gift from her husband (83), Trianon is a romantic pastoral escape for the Queen, though "jealous courtiers called it 'Little Vienna'" (52). Through women close to the queen, including two chapters by Marie-Antoinette herself, Vidal paints a sympathetic portrait leading up to and following the execution. For example, the Prologue: Portrait of a Queen begins with the voice of the court painter Madame Elisabeth Vigée-Lebrun, famous for her domestic scenes of the Queen with her children (106).

The artist, pregnant at the time, reflects:

In many ways, Marie-Antoinette was still the child-bride, separated so prematurely from her mother and homeland. Her innocence and sincerity made her open prey for devious minds. She had blossomed, with a rich and ripening beauty that came not from midnight dancing at the opera ball, or having Monsieur Léonard dress her hair, but from domestic tranquility and maternal fulfillment. (Vidal 17)

Vidal suggests that motherhood changes Marie-Antoinette, but her former "misdemeanors"–"card parties, "appearances at horse races," "acting in her private theatre at Trianon," "huge sums spent on diamonds" (ibid.)–make her an ideal scapegoat. She is considered a personal failure as a mother and a political failure as France's mother (84, 95).

The King's sister and Carmelite nun Madame Louise of France, however, supports Vigée-Lebrun's narrative. She suggests that despite the "gazettes full of complaints against her," such as false accusations of the Queen throwing lavish parties at Trianon "for a select group of friends" (28), and her sexual promiscuity with Axel von Fresen, she believes "motherhood has enriched her character, and sorrow, too. She lost the great Empress, her mother, in 1781, and just last summer, she lost a child" (29). The death of her young child Sophie is described by Marie-Antoinette's eldest daughter, who says, "Maman had wept as never before. She had not shed so many tears even during the terrible disturbance of the diamond necklace" (35). Vidal's novel suggests a maternal role is at the heart of the queen's life.

Vidal's Marie-Antoinette tells her sister-in-law, "Mercifully, only a man can inherit the throne! Women are happier when busy with domestic matters. Leave the politics for men!" (60). Unlike the other women discussed in this chapter, Marie-Antoinette wishes to remain outside of politics, though it becomes increasingly clear this is impossible: "a bundle of pamphlets was found, containing vicious cartoons of the Queen … there were underground presses in the palace that were printing some of the same filth (91). Vidal's narrative juxtaposes public politics with the Queen's domestic life.

Vidal describes the Third Estate in 1789, which "wanted to abolish all class distinctions and privileges of rank … [they] demanded the restructuring of society" (100), in the context of the death of Marie-Antoinette's son Louis Joseph (101). This suggests only fiction can bring history into focus, into "the heart of things" (Butterfield 18). History's inadequacy, Vidal intimates, in the vein of Herbert Butterfield, is that it cannot accurately document the "human touches" of the past that fiction can make us feel (Butterfield 21). Amidst grief for her dead child, Marie-Antoinette declares, "in the minds of many, the King was no longer the representative of God, but the Nation had become a god, and Antoinette knew that a false god was demon" (Vidal 108). Rejecting pleas from her husband to flee when "Paris is marching on Versailles" (110), Marie-Antoinette declares she will face the dangers head-on (109, 122).

Following the decision of the Assembly, the Queen, her husband, and their children are imprisoned in the Temple (Vidal 124). On "January 8th 1793, the King was sentenced" (125) and executed thirteen days later (138). The Queen's trial takes place in October and she is questioned about her past deeds and the few objects that remain on her person, including lockets of hair from "[her] dead and living children, and from [her] husband" (150). Accused of politically influencing her weak husband, spending large sums at Trianon, conceiving "the project of uniting Lorraine with Austria" (153), having a Sacred Heart badge in her possession, and refuting the testimony of her son against her, the Queen is pronounced guilty (154). Vidal uses the eyes of the Queen's servant Rosalie to describe how Marie-Antoinette is taken in a cart for cabbages to the guillotine (164). The novel ends with Marie-Antoinette's only surviving child, Thérèse, being informed, much like the young Elizabeth in Weir's novel, that one year ago her mother "was guillotined, her corpse was thrown onto the grass of the cemetery of La Madeleine, the head between the legs, without funeral services or proper Christian burial" (170). As the only one spared, Thérèse, in order not to garner royalist sympathy, is taken to Austria in exchange for some French prisoners (172). Consoled by her religion, Thérèse ends the novel with the memory of her childhood:

In her heart, she had found her way home to Trianon, home to the garden of childhood peace and innocence … She had found an interior garden where she could live, regardless of the vicissitudes of life, and turmoil of events that swirled around her. With her there danced again the serenity and joy she once possessed when as a little girl she had played so happily at Trianon. (187)
Vidal, thus, ends her revisionist novel on Marie-Antoinette by showcasing the Queen's maternal bond, her religious devotion, and by reclaiming Trianon, not as a house of ill-repute but as one of domestic happiness for her protagonists

Motherhood and Queenship

The woman's historical novels suggests that "by and large queenship operated within a primarily 'familial context' … and royal daughters, sisters, and more distant female kin might be highly prized as brides on the international marriage market" (Oakley-Brown and Wilkinson 14). Within this "familial context," we can also read the frequent and willful erasure of a woman's, a future queen's, matrilineage as male anxiety about the threatening power of the maternal towards masculinity and patriarchal rule. Irigaray writes:

If we are not to be accomplices in the murder of the mother, [it is necessary] for us to assert that there is a genealogy of women. There is a genealogy of women within our family: on our mother's side we have mothers, grandmothers, and great-grandmothers and daughters. Given our exile in the family of the father-husband, we tend to forget this genealogy of women, and we are often persuaded to deny it. Let us try to situate ourselves within this female genealogy so far as to conquer and keep our identity. Nor let us forget that we already have a history, that certain women have, even if it was culturally difficult, left their mark on history and that all too often we do not know them. (Irigaray Reader 44)

Weir's The Lady Elizabeth and Sundaresan's The Twentieth Wife assert the importance of maternal figures in the young lives of future queens. In the case of Mehrunnisa, Sundaresan narrates her unlikely birth in a desert tent, her parent's failed attempt to abandon her, and, finally, her family's good fortune in being welcomed into Emperor Akbar's court after fleeing Persia.

In Akbar's court, Mehrunnisa meets Prince Salim, the heir to the throne. Much to both the Prince's and her own despair, Mehrunnisa is arranged to marry the soldier Ali Quli, a marriage that is ultimately a failure. Arriving in Bardwan (Ali Quli's punishment is exile for supporting the Emperor's son Khusrau instead of Salim), Mehrunnisa gives birth for the first time. Sundaresan writes, "'Maji ...' Mehrunnisa whispered over and over again, wanting the cool comfort of her mother's hand on her brow, wanting to tell her of the fears that ambushed her" (216). The midwife is kind, but Mehrunnisa laments that "she was not Maji" (Sundaresan 216). Like many protagonists in the woman's historical novel, Mehrunnisa loves her mother, but she is, by virtue of marital duties, absent in much of her daughter's life. Giving birth to a girl, much to Ali Quli's dismay, Mehrunnisa names the child, "Ladli. One who was loved" (217). It is only after Ali Quli's death (likely ordered by the Emperor (296)) that Mehrunnisa's desire to marry Prince Salim, now Emperor Jahangir, is realized.

Refusing to be a concubine in the harem, Mehrunnisa defies precedent because she is a thirty-four year old single mother born in an Afghanistan desert, and now is being granted the role of Jahangir's final and twentieth wife and the title Nur Jahan "Light of the World" (Sundaresan 379). Mehrunnisa muses over her ambition to rule the empire and cites Elizabeth, though not by name, as a source of inspiration: "European queens shone in court beside their husbands. Why, there had been one English queen who ruled alone, who had come to the throne in her own right as the daughter of a king" (380). Realizing her ambition, she determines "to be the force to reckon with behind the throne. She wanted to be the power behind the veil" (ibid.). The novel ends with Nur Jahan's wedding and the beginning of what the Afterword declares will be the unprecedented power of a woman within the Mughal Empire. Weir, like Sundaresan, exploits the many historical gaps in her protagonist's early life prior to becoming a powerful monarch.

Weir relates the young princess Elizabeth's life, beginning with the death of her mother and later her father. Unlike other historical novels, such as Susan Kay's Legacy (1985), which denies the sexual relationship between Elizabeth and Thomas Seymour, the brother of Jane Seymour, the third wife of Henry VIII, (and later husband of Henry VIII's final wife, Queen Katherine), Weir plays upon speculation that, in Elizabeth's early life, she became pregnant by the Admiral. Elizabeth also refuses the Admiral's marriage offer because, as Weir reiterates throughout the novel, "I have resolved never to marry" (168). Following Elizabeth's rejection, the Admiral pursues his former love (173) and, in less than four months after the king's death, he and Katherine Parr are wed (177). As guests at Chelsea Palace, Katherine and the Admiral adopt Elizabeth and become her guardians.

Weir describes the Admiral's inappropriate behavior as including entering Elizabeth's bedchamber early in the mornings (185-190). On a Sunday morning, Weir imagines, the Admiral and Elizabeth decidedly staying home from church. The Queen, however, catches them in bed together (228). Disgraced, exposed to gossip, and pleading Katherine's forgiveness, Elizabeth is sent to Cheshunt where her governess' sister resides (230). Attempting to hide her pregnancy (240), Elizabeth confines herself to her rooms until she notices one day that she is bleeding (248). Contrary to Ella March Chase's novel The Virgin Queen's Daughter (2008), which imagines Elizabeth secretly giving birth to a daughter, Elinor de Lacy, Weir's Elizabeth suffers a miscarriage (249): "Never again, she vowed, would she risk her reputation, let alone allow any man to come near enough to get her with child" (250). Acknowledging her escape from scandal, Elizabeth reaffirms, "I will never marry" … I will never again allow love to blind me to all good sense and reason" … I will be circumspect in the future" (251); "I will continue to wear sober clothes and be a virtuous Protestant maiden" (ibid.). When Kat declares that she can, technically, never be a maiden again, Elizabeth replies, "Nay, but the world must think it … I will never give anyone cause to doubt it. I will flaunt my virginity as others flaunt their charms, and lead a godly life from now on" (ibid.). This incident, according to Weir (and other novelists like Edith Sitwell), solidifies Elizabeth's decision to never marry and is symbolized by the tapestries of St. Ursula that hung in the Virgin Chambers in Greenwich where she was born (49).

Ursula, a saint beheaded, reminds Elizabeth of the unjust treatment of her mother, the deaths of her father's wives, and the risk of childbirth. The novel ends with the young Elizabeth being crowned the Queen of England upon her childless sister's death; she will never marry or have children, but she will construct her own maternal identity and be personified by others, such as in Walter Scott's *Kenilworth* (1821), as the queen without sexual desire. She is pious, chaste, intellectual, and authoritative–the opposite of her licentious mother, a "Virgin Queen." Staub writes that:

Though she rejected literal motherhood, Elizabeth manipulated it metaphorically to serve her political agenda. Seemingly affirming traditional gender expectations, maternity provided a stratagem to turn the biological reality of her womanhood to her advantage by transforming her anomalous political authority into a socially sanctioned nurturing maternal authority. (17)

Suggesting motherhood can be constructed, Elizabeth embodies the Virgin Mother, whose English subjects will be her holy children. Her virginity is linked with divinity; the purity of the virgin, who is untainted, she is juxtaposed with her mother's sexuality which is deemed monstrous, a destructive womb.

The decision not to marry is also found in D'Eaubonne's focus on Kristine as a virgin queen–"an authority figure, untainted by the sin of Eve" (Oakley-Brown and Wilkinson 16)–and holy mother to her Swedish people. Kristine references Elizabeth as a source for not marrying: "je préfère me passer d'époux, comme le fit Élizabeth d'Angleterre" 'I prefer to pass on having a husband, like Elizabeth of England did' (D'Eaubonne 121). Like Weir, D'Eaubonne ties this decision to an event during Kristine's adolescence. Secretly engaged to her cousin Charles, Kristine is shocked when she sees that"[i]l était couché sur la Tzigane" 'he was on top of a gypsy' (86). Though she never tells Charles what she witnesses, she ends the engagement, deciding to never let her personal feelings as a woman overrule her duty as queen or lower herself to marry a subject (99). She declares that she will rule alone and identifies herself with Diane, the Roman goddess "de chasteté et de chasse" ('of chastity and the hunt'; 100).

Kristine's astrologer believing she is under a sign of change and mobility (by rule of the moon, a symbol for both women and Diane) contributes to her religious conversion to Catholicism (D'Eaubonne 165). Kristine, however, not only masquerades as Diane and worships her as a source for not marrying, but she also embraces cross-dressing (93) and sporting an androgynous look. Drawing on Constance Jordan's work Renaissance Feminism: Literary Texts and Political Models (1990), Merry Wiesner-Hanks writes that "defenders of female rule clearly separated sex from gender, and even approached an idea of androgyny as a desirable state for the public persona of female monarchs" (18).

Androgyny in Kristine's life is present when she has a love affair with Ebba Sparre (D'Eaubonne 91), when Charles Gustave refers to her as "Kristian," (72, 73), and when she declares that, instead of being a queen, "je serai roi!" ('I will be king!'; 50).

Wiesner-Hanks argues that all concepts of masculinity, such as "physical bravery, stamina, wisdom, duty" (20), are "important determinants of access to political power" (18). Unlike Elizabeth, who embodied these attributes and also never married or had children, the weight of being a Swedish mother proves too much for Kristine to bear. Converting to Catholicism, Kristine abdicates her throne and names Charles her successor. Her break with the Swedish people is evident when they accuse her of hating her country (D'Eaubonne 263) and she fails to win their approval for reclaiming the throne when Charles dies . D'Eaubonne's novel, like Hernando's and Lehr's, narrates not only the early life of her protagonist but also her rise to power and her life in older age.

All of these monarchs disrupt patriarchal rule. Following the defeat of her husband Peter and his subsequent death, Catherine, in Lehr's novel, declares she will not to re-marry, but "rule alone" (261). She is revered and loved by the Russian people for her devotion to her country in a similar way to Elizabeth, Kristine in her early years, and Isabel when she takes the crown of Castile. Isabel's success in becoming queen is attributed by Hernando to her questioning of patriarchy:

'Mi madre', reflexionaba, 'fue desplazada del trono¡tan solo por enviudar! Y yo me vi desplazada en la línea sucesoria a la corona de Castilla tan solo por tener un hermano menor. ¿Por qué? ¿Por qué somos de menos valor que un varón? Grandioso future es el que depara el destino a la sangre real si tiene nombre de mujer', ironizó. 'Mi suerte sera ser reina… pero no más que reina consorte. El rey de Castilla, aunque sea mi hermano Alfonso, me prometerá con algún rey extranjero para sellar quién sabe qué alianza políca; viviré en tierras extrañas hasta mi muerte, convertida en reina consortee o…', su rostro adquirió gravedad '…despojada de todo mi poder y relagada al olvido si tengo la desdicha de enviudar, como mi madre.¡Pero mi destino no será distinto si algún diá o heredo la corona de Castilla! Deberé desposarme consangre real extranjera para dar descendencia que perpetúe la dinastía. Mi marido gobernará estas tierras, que no son las suyas, mientras que yo permaneceré a su sombra… a pesar de ser la propietaria de cuna de este pueblo. ¡No debería ser así! ¡Es injusto y menosprecia el valor de las mujeres!'

'My mother,' she reflected, 'was displaced from the throne for being a widow! And I see myself displaced in the line of succession to the crown of Castile by having a younger brother. Why? Because we are of less value than a man? A great future is what destiny holds for the royal blood if she has the name woman', she said with irony. 'My fate will be to be queen ... but no more than queen consort. The king of Castile will be my brother Alfonso, I will be promised to some foreign king to seal a political alliance; Living in foreign lands until my death, converted into a queen consort or ..., ' her face became serious '... stripped of all my power and regalia, forgotten, if I have the misfortune of becoming a widow, as my mother. But my fate will be no different if someday I do inherit the crown of Castile! I must wed foreign royal blood to give offspring to perpetuate the dynasty. My husband will rule this land, which are not his own, while I will remain in his shadow ... despite being born in this homeland. This shouldn't be! It's an injustice and discourages valor in women! (55-56)

The treatment of her mother, including losing her lands (Hernando 144-45), instills in Isabel the conviction to disavow being reduced to reproductive purposes and as subordinate to her husband.

Isabel proves her determination by untraditionally marrying Fernando d'Aragón in 1469 without her brother, the king's, consent. When Enrique IV dies, Isabel seizes the crown of Castile and is named "como reina de Castilla" 'as queen/ruler of Castile' (191); her husband is merely "el rey consorte de estas tierras" 'the king consort of these lands' (192). Fernando, recognizing the unprecedented power of his wife holding "la espada ... el símbolo del poder 'the sword, the symbol of power' (196), rather than forsake her, commends her: "¡Asombrosa mujer! ("Amazing woman!"; 194). Isabel's love for Fernando, much like Mehrunnisa's in Sundaresan's novel, appears genuine and she has Fernando crowned king of Castile in a small ceremony (195) so that they can rule together as equals. Conversely, the hatred of a people for their queen reaches its greatest heights in Marie-Antoinette's life, though, in Vidal's novel, the queen's devotion to her religion and family is steadfast. Thus redefining the sexual/political definitions of motherhood, the family, and rule ordained for them, Isabel and Nur Jahan marry for love, Kristine and Elizabeth never marry, and Catherine becomes the 'foreign' Russian mother-Empress, while Marie-Antoinette, embracing her domestic role as private mother, refuses to play publically the role of Queen as mother to her foreign people.

Conclusion

Women's historical novels on modern monarchs suggest that a transnational definition of motherhood is flexible, contingent, and linked with the politics of sexuality, nationhood, and religion. Contesting the gender conventions of their times and places, the heroines' ability to play a plurality of gender roles is a testament to the constructed nature of both nationhood and motherhood. Yet, in many ways, the woman's novel also suggests that, if a woman fulfils her political duties, she neglects her family and vice versa; she cannot be present in both, which is evident when analyzing their personal lives. Similarly, when the mothers lose their political status, they simultaneously lose their children: they are no longer mothers of the nation nor mothers of the family. There is a powerful fear and preoccupation with losing the mother, of the mother being erased, of the daughter becoming mother and suffering the same fate as her mother in each text. In order to break this patriarchal chain, Whitford, emphasizing Irigaray's position, suggests there must be "the possibility for love of self on the side of women, and the recognition of the debt of the mother, thus freeing the mother to be a sexual and desiring woman, and freeing the daughter from the icy grip of the merged and undifferentiated relationship" (Whitford, "Section II" 77). The femino-centric topics of hysteria, separation, betrayal, surrogacy, foreigners, and the relation between motherhood and queenship all reveal the dissatisfaction with modern conceptions of mothers. While the form and function of queenship and the maternal undergo changes, the denigration of the maternal, of the queen's mother and queen as mother, remain held in low estimation. She is relegated to an abject space. Thus, there is a need for a new woman's desire, a new gynocracy, not recognized "only when enveloped in the needs/desires/fantasies of others, namely, men" (Irigaray Reader 136). To break this code is to break women's silences and to establish a matrilineage that celebrates desire for women as mothers and daughters.

CHAPTER THREE

Matrilineal Narratives: Race, Memory, and Survival

> So many of the stories that I write, that we all write, are my
> mother's stories
> – Alice Walker, *In Search of Our Mothers' Gardens*

This chapter concentrates on contemporary women writers who establish transnational matrilineal genealogies by putting forth revisionist, anticolonial novels
on African, Caribbean, and Aboriginal women from the seventeenth to the
twentieth century. Serving, like chapter one, as an alternative genealogy to the
privileged, mainstream figures in chapter 2, this writing centralizes the lives of
women experiencing racial prejudices, slavery, and other colonial practices.
Memory, personal and collective, recent and historical, plays an important role
in this corpus and stresses the necessity of telling narratives of women's survival – for survival. Coinciding with "an emergent national awareness" and the
postcolonial independence of several nations during the twentieth century
(Zwicker 9), essential to these contemporary works is returning to the past in
order determine the role of women in the new, current nation. There is a belief
that confronting and recognizing women's history is necessary if women's
lives in the present are to improve. I analyze Judith Gleason's work *Agotime:
Her Legend* (1970), Nancy Cato and Vivienne Ellis' novel *Queen Trucanini*
(1976), *I, Tituba, Black Witch of Salem* (1986) by Maryse Condé[8], and *Nervous
Conditions* (1988) by Tsitsi Dangarembga. Jerome de Groot believes that Walter Scott's influence has "obscured other historical fictive writing, particularly
that of non-Western cultures" (13). Groot, referencing Kimberly Chabot Davis,
writes that "novelists interested in the 'particular concerns of marginalized
communities haunted by a history of oppression' use historical fiction to 'insist
on the political urgency of rewriting history from the perspective of the disem-
powered'" (148-49). As Kathleen Gyssels claims with regard to the historical
Tituba, "Condé rewrites her voice to enable her to claim power and become
master of her own narrative. Tituba, accused, misnamed, and distorted by history, has overturned the Puritans' power and knowledge by speaking for herself"
(65). Authors like Condé and Dangarembga who politically engage in voicing

---

[8] I am using the English translation of *Moi, Tituba, Sorcière ... Noire de Salem* by
Richard Philcox.

historical silences through fragmented "first-person retrospective narratives" subvert traditional master narratives of Western progress and domination and establish a "literature of revolt" (Androne 271).

Embracing a *"testimonio"* style, the works when read together form a unique women's "resistance literature" that stresses the need for contemporary social change from the perspective of Indigenous, African, and Caribbean women (ibid.). However, as Rey Chow reminds writers of (fictional) history, when we resurrect the past, we cannot simply translate the native's experience and struggles: "That silence is at once *evidence* of imperialist oppression and what in the absence of the original witness to that oppression, must act in its place by *performing* or *feigning* as the preimperialist gaze" ("Where Have" 38). Continuing a pre-1970 genealogy of anti-colonial, anti-patriarchal historical novels (such as Catherine Edith Macauley Martin's *The Incredible Journey* (1923), in which two aboriginal women cross the Australian desert to retrieve a child kidnapped by a white man), these works employ historical imagination by writing the Indigenous and Black woman back into recorded history; they call into question how the historical record has been and always is already con-structed while "lay[ing] claim to their own stories" (Newman 24) by creating a new maternal genealogy. Edward Said argues that postcolonial texts "are in effect a re-appropriation of the historical experience of colonialism, revitalized and transformed into a new aesthetic of sharing and often transcendent re-formulation" (*Orientalism* 351). These authors suggest that, despite coloni-al/hegemonic history's attempt to enslave, murder, and erase, the maternal not only has endured but is essential to survival.

Memory is also necessary for survival and a prevalent theme in the wom-an's historical novel. In Gleason's *Agotime*, for example, which narrates Ago-time's crossing as a 19th century slave from Dahomey to Brazil, Edna G. Bay argues that how Africans who remained in Africa during the slave-trade were affected is also a meaningful pursuit. Bay draws upon memories from both sides and discusses recent government sponsored projects in Benin: "these projects were specifically linked to the collective memory of the descendants of those who remained in Africa and of those who were taken" (43). Gleason also suggests both memory and destiny are collective: "memory animates, finds words to summon sleeping forces" (9) and refers to "our collective destiny" (97). This destiny is to "find a way, in the new world" (Gleason 99). Bay ar-gues that "in Africa, collective memory preserves a record of the trauma of the trade to African societies and speaks directly to the question of the meaning of the trade to Africans" (45). Highlighting what many writers, including Gleason, perceive as an inherent tension between accounts from collective memory and those of the official record, Bay attempts to bridge the two approaches:

Good history is built by historians who document, cross-check, and search out corroborating pieces of evidence. History is nevertheless always an interpretation of the past tied to historians' understandings in and of the present. Collective memory works from signs of the past in the present: our empathy for what we know of the past, our sense of who we are and where we come from, and our study of rituals, symbols, and actions that could plausibly be linked to a former social or political condition. Collective memory assumes that conscious memory will gradually fade, but its signs endure. Those understandings are worthy of consideration and evaluation by a historian. (49)

Bay shows two possible understandings of the slave trade in Dahomey: one of collective memory during a time of intense insecurity and uncertainty and the other focusing on the individual experience, for example the politically-minded Agotime whose banishment is documented in historical sources (58).

Gil Zehava Hochberg sees the relation between history and personal memory along gender lines:

By assigning mother [...] the role of a 'medium' through which an alternative narrative emerges as a direct confrontation with history, 'woman' (as mother) is aligned with memory as an alternative to history. This promising role of the mother is promoted through a gendered mobilization of the radical division between 'history' and 'memory.' (2)

Hochberg recognizes the powerful role mothers play in women writers who are African and of the African diaspora. She writes that "the centrality of the maternal figure as the originator of women's alternative voice and as a transmitter of memory is an outcome of the particular history of black enslaved mothers" (ibid.), which is evident in woman's historical novels like *Agotime* and *I, Tituba, Black Witch of Salem*. Considering the convergence of memory, race, and maternal survival in each text within this chapter as a basis, I develop these postcolonial themes more fully through the lens of the following subtopics: hegemonic history and women's imperialism, the arrival of the Europeans, exile, bad women, patriarchy within and without, and maternal survival.

Hegemonic History: Rewriting Women's Imperialism

Criticizing hegemonic Western history, postcolonial or anti-colonial writers (Franz Fanon, Said, Homi Bhabha, Spivak) have influenced and been influenced by postcolonial/anticolonial woman centered novels by Flora Nwapa, Jean Rhys, Zaynab Alkali, Ifeoma Okoye, Buchi Emecheta, and Nadine Gordimer. Analyzing the socio-political impact of a discourse of Empire on colonizer and colonized, these writers, in varying ways, seek alternative identities and new ways of imagining relations between races and nations. A new relation to history becomes of great value, as does the power for speaking in one's own voice. Gayatri Chakravorty Spivak, critiques not only Western history as hegemonic, but many of the above postcolonial theorists for their inherent sexism.

In her influential book *A Critique of Postcolonial Reason* (1999) and her essay "Subaltern Studies Deconstructing Historiography," Spivak writes of the challenges in re-writing India's colonial history from the point of view of the peasant insurgency, which she calls the "subaltern." Like much of women's history, also included in the subaltern, Spivak is all too aware of a lack of records. Spivak, working with the group *Subaltern Studies*, a collective of historians, claims that the only existing records (diaries, memoirs, newspapers, etc.) belong to the colonial subject ("Subaltern Studies" 212). Spivak argues that "a hegemonic nineteenth-century European historiography had designated the archives as a repository of 'facts' and [she] propose[s] that they should be 'read'" (*Critique of Postcolonial Reason* 203). As an example of the incomplete archive or the production of evidence, Spivak invokes the life of the Rani of Sirmur and the records of the East India Company, "the first great transnational company" (220).

The Rani, the wife of a deposed and banished king-husband and mother to a prince is an example of "agent-as-instrument" in patriarchal industrial capitalism and in, what will later become, transnational capitalism. The Rani is mentioned, albeit briefly, Spivak argues, because of her interest both territorially and commercially to the East India Company. One worker/writer for the company in particular, Captain Geoffrey Birch, signals that "the truth value of the stranger [Birch, a man,] ... is being established as the reference point for the true (insertion into) history of these wild regions" (*Critique of Postcolonial Reason* 213) and that "here what is one narrativization of history is seen not only 'as it really was,' but implicitly 'as it ought to be'" (222). Spivak's analysis of women who have been seen not as they really were but how they ought to be is seen again when Birch asks in a letter to interfere with the Rani's private wish to be a *Sati*.

For Spivak, the Rani signifies a commodity, exchanged by men for men, that marks the movement from a "feudal" society to a "modern/imperialist" one (*Critique* 235). As Spivak notes, the Rani may be within the margins of Western history, but even the Rani herself is a woman of relative privilege and not among marginal women. Dangarembga's novel *Nervous Conditions*, which narrates the life of Tambu, a young Rhodesian woman transitioning between tradition and modernity, supports Spivak's thinking. Spivak argues that the marginal woman, "'the third-world woman," is caught, frozen, between two polarities–patriarchal tradition and patriarchal development, subject and object–the result of which is "the figure of woman disappears" (304). While the colonial authorities, Spivak suggests, may be responsible for the near historical erasure of women like the Rani, it is the "emancipated" women and men of contemporary India who are complicit in silencing women today; therefore, contemporary women's historical novels are invaluable in re-writing and re-reading the accepted views of history and literature.

Jean Rhys' historical novel *Wide Sargasso Sea* (1966) supports many of Spivak's claims and is an important forerunner of the novels I discuss in this chapter. Rhys suggests that a critical feminist perspective evolves not only out of a rejection or retelling of the masculinist dominant discourse such as Walter Scott's but also evolves from the popular woman's novel–regardless of whether it is a "classic." Charlotte Brontë's *Jane Eyre* (1847) is reinterpreted in anti-imperial feminist terms in *Wide Sargasso Sea* in such a way that it is almost impossible not to re-read the original. Jane's agency in the novel, which is heralded by later Western feminism, comes at the lack of agency granted to Antoinette (Bertha) Mason, Rochester's first wife. Rhys gives Bertha Mason a story, an identity, and a humanity that draws the reader's attention to the sexism, racism, exoticism and Orientalism within Brontë's original tale, which Caroline Rody calls a "mother-text" (145). The idea of a mother-text further plays on the fact that Rhys' novel chronologically is the prequel, not the sequel, to *Jane Eyre*, though it was written much later. Rhys, thus, puts forth her own original work while simultaneously transforming/subverting Brontë's mother-text.

Similarly, Jane Haggis in "White Women and Colonialism: Towards a Non-Recuperative History" examines the role women have played in colonialism/imperialism. Haggis' strategy places, in light of anti-colonialism criticism such as in women's historical novels, three narratives side by side: 1) the subject (the British missionaries), 2) the missionaries' Indian subjects, and 3) her own purpose, a feminist post-colonial history (175). Refusing to romanticize the white-woman's point of view "allow[s] the historical figures to live within their context rather than to rewrite history to conform more exactly with current received notions" (163). By doing so, Haggis acknowledges the danger of universalizing women's experiences or fragmenting and losing any sense of reference at all. Her project incorporates individual voices, but in concert: "Thus history becomes by analogy, expressive of difference and interrelatedness 'everybody talking at once, multiple rhythms being played simultaneously, but held together in a particular narrative, by the explicit awareness of inter-relatedness" (165). Haggis writes that "by showing how the image of the Indian woman victim acted as a literary device and artifice of missionary women's representation to their home audience in England, [she is] able to suggest the fictional quality of the missionary portrayal of women" (181). This kind of thinking, which Spivak refers to as 'reading' and Haggis as 'translating,' is meaningful for a feminist study of historical novels such as Barbara Kingsolver's *The Poisonwood Bible* (1998). The novel is told from the point of view of an American Baptist missionary's wife and her four daughters (and their increasing criticism of colonialism) after arriving in the Belgian Congo in 1959. One cannot ignore the participation of women in colonialism; Bertha Mason's dramatic death in Rhys' novel is a case in point, thus, analyzing the ways in which women's lives and narratives meet and converge within the novels is imperative.

The Arrival of the Europeans: Dead Mothers and Wayward Daughters

An important aspect in retelling colonial narratives pertains to the encounters between Indigenous women and European men. In Cato and Ellis' and Condé's novels, a pivotal moment in the protagonists' lives occurs when their mothers are murdered upon the early arrival of Europeans to their island homes, Tasmania and Barbados respectively. Cato and Ellis' novel opens with the happy birth of Trucanini to her mother Waubelannina and her father Mangana, Chief of the Bruny Island Tribe. Coinciding with the birth are sightings of "*ria* or *rae*," "the white man, who had come to hunt the whales and seals of the Southern Ocean, and cut down the forests of Van Diemen's Land for timber" (Cato and Ellis 7). When Trucanini is still a young child, the tribe is ambushed by the whalers. Waubelannina is raped and stabbed to death when she fights back (9). Her mother's death and the kidnapping of her sisters, who had "been sold to a sealer on distant Kangaroo Island in South Australia, to live as his slaves and concubines" (13), however, do not deter Trucanini. As if learning from her mother's death that those who fight back are punished and die, Trucanini engages in relationships with the whalers, who are multiplying in numbers and setting up permanent residences.

Cato and Ellis suggest that, while some of the women were sold as slaves, others, like Trucanini and her friend Pagerly, "went to the whalers' camps by choice" (14). Tensions between the new settlers and natives arise, however, after the natives are forced out of the towns. The natives' position became "an uncompromising hatred of the white invaders [... and] replaced the courteous welcome given by the natives to the first explorers. Every white man, every single one, must be killed or driven back into the sea he came from!" (17). Likewise:

> The settlers, the newspapers, the officers of the Van Diemen's
> Land Company in the far northwest, all clamoured for action.

> The treacherous, savage black men were stopping them from
> getting on with their lawful business of clearing the bush, rais-
> ing sheep and exterminating the unique fauna such as the Tas-
> manian tiger and the native cat. Reasoning with the natives had
> proved useless. Every one, every single one, must be killed or
> driven into the sea! (18)

Governor Arthur, wanting to avoid the extermination of the aborigines, decides
to woo them with food stocks and for a permanent storekeeper to live on Bruny
Island.

George Augustus Robinson, seeking social mobility, is awarded the job.
Robinson believes it his job to civilize "the black on Bruny" (21) by introduc-
ing "them to the Christian religion" and "the women, who … less fierce and
more tender-hearted than the men, may later act as missionaries and ambassadors to members of their race in other parts of the main island" (21). For this
reason, Trucaniniis sent to accompany Robinson back to Bruny so he can instruct her in his language and religion: "George Robinson had outlined his
great plan for 'ameliorating' the natives to Lieutenant Gunn. The plan was to
take a party of civilized blacks with him as interpreters on a friendly mission
the wild tribes of the unexplored bush. He would take no arms; and he believed
he could persuade the natives to come in peaceably and give themselves up"
(29). Thus, Trucanini willingly becomes Robinson's chief translator and guides
his expedition.

Condé's novel, *I, Tituba, Black Witch of Salem*, by contrast, reimagines a
popular subject in contemporary women's historical fiction, seventeenth century witch trials. Condé's work reimagines all these axes converging in the life of
the historical figure Tituba, a West Indian female slave from Barbados. Though
Tituba is a plantation slave, her life is known in historical records for surviving
charges of witchcraft in Salem, Massachusetts in 1692.The novel begins with
the lines "Abena, my mother, was raped by an English sailor on the deck of
Christ the King one day in the year 16** while the ship was sailing for Barbados. I was born from this act of aggression. From this act of hatred and con-
tempt" (Condé 3). Tituba tells the reader that her mother, upon arriving in
Bridgetown, is bought by Darnell Davis so that she can entertain and look after
his wife who pines for England. Edouard J. Glissant describes the experiences
of "transplanted" (112) slaves like Abena as constituting "shock," "painful
negation," and "brutal dislocation" (62). Glissant also refers to a "nonhistory"
(61-62) that exists outside master narratives of History that prevents "'the collective consciousness' of the colonized from absorbing the totality of this tor-
tuous genealogy" (Thomas 87). Writing nonhistory is a means towards realizing a collective memory and consciousness. As Jennifer R. Thomas clarifies,

"nonhistory can emerge as history for peoples of the Caribbean with the help of the writer who cultivates a historical consciousness unlimited by the traditional chronological and hierarchal understandings of experience" (88). Thus, Condé's writing of Abena engages with nonhistory by delving into a relatively unknown African-Caribbean past.

When Davis learns that Abena is pregnant, however, he banishes her from the house and gives her to one of his slaves, Yao, who is also an Ashanti. Condé writes: "While Abena stood there in front of him her head hung low, Yao's heart filled with immense compassion. It seemed to him that this child's humiliation symbolized the condition of his entire people: defeated, dispersed, and auctioned off" (5). Together Yao and Abena find reciprocal peace and support. Though Yao fervently loves Tituba when she is born, Tituba suspects her mother feels differently. She surmises, "when did I discover that my mother did not love me? Perhaps when I was five or six years old. Although the color of my skin was far from being light and my hair was crinkly all over, I never stopped reminding my mother of the white sailor who had raped her" (6). As a slave, Abena is also cautious of loving a daughter too much.

A slave's life is unpredictable and subject to the whim of a white master, which is evident when Tituba recounts a day her mother takes her to the yam patch and, unexpectedly, they meet their master Davis. When Davis tries to rape Abena, Tituba hands her mother a cutlass that she uses to strike the man (8): "They hanged my mother. I watched her body swing from the lower branches of a silk cotton tree. She had committed a crime for which there is no pardon. She had not killed him, however. In her clumsy rage she had only managed to gash his shoulder. They hanged my mother" (ibid.). Following Abena's death, Yao commits suicide and Tituba finds herself taken in by an old slave woman named Mama Yaya (9).

Mama Yaya is a powerful woman with a gift for prophecy, healing, and making potions; she has an innate connection with nature. She also has the ability to see and communicate with the dead, which she teaches to Tituba. Following her death, Mama Yaya appears to Tituba and teaches her the skill for seeing herself (Mama Yaya) and her mother (10). Living as a recluse on the edge of a pond, Tituba practicing Mama Yaya's magic inspires fear in the other slaves, including John Indian, who thinks she is a witch. After John Indian's invitation to a local dance in Carlisle Bay, Tituba returns home to summon Mama Yaya. Though Tituba desires John Indian's love, Mama Yaya warns against it. Mama Yaya "shook her head. 'Men do not love. They possess. They subjugate'" (14). Abena seconds this opinion in an exchange with her daughter: "'Why can't women do without men?' she groaned. 'Now you're going to be dragged off to the other side of the water'" (15). Despite "Mama Yaya's reluc-

tance, and [her] mother's lamentations," Tituba meets John Indian at the dance
(16). John Indian declares his desire for her to live with him in Bridgetown.
Similar to Trucanini's sexual feelings towards Mr. Robinson, Tituba desires
John Indian's love, though she acknowledges that "therein lay [her] misfortune" (18). Tituba muses:

> My mother had been raped by a white man. She has been
> hanged because of a white man. I had seen his tongue quiver
> out of his mouth, his penis turgid and violet. My adoptive fa-
> ther had committed suicide because of a white man. Despite all
> that, I was considering living among white men again, in their
> midst, under their domination. And all because of an uncontrol-
> lable desire for a mortal man? Wasn't it madness? Madness
> and betrayal? (19)

Fully knowing the dangers that lay ahead, Tituba takes her meager belongings
and sets off for John Indian in Carlisle Bay.

After arriving at Susanna Endicott's, John Indian's mistress, Tituba's bap-
tism is arranged; she is given commands for the cleaning of the house and she
takes bible instruction as the new young wife of John Indian;

> The slaves who flocked off the ships in droves and whose gait,
> features, and carriage the good people of Bridgetown mocked
> were far freer than I was. For the slaves has not chosen their
> chains. They had not walked of their own accord toward a rag-
> ing, awe-inspiring sea to given themselves up to the slave deal-
> ers and bend their backs to the branding iron. That is exactly
> what I had done. (25)

Tituba becomes increasingly conscious of the mistake she has made and the
pain she will suffer. Her epiphany comes when her mistress accuses her of
being a witch. Susanna Endicott's accusations serve as a precursor to future
claims against Tituba that she is a witch. As punishment, Tituba and John Indian are sold to a minister leaving for Boston the following day (35). Unable to
abandon John Indian, Tituba knows she is being essentially banished to America as an act of revenge, but that she will, in turn, enact her own revenge–she
will tell her story. Both Condé's and Cato and Ellis' novels provide a glimpse
into the life of a young woman whose complicity with patriarchy determines
their suffering. Despite the deaths of their mothers at the hands of white male
colonizers, Trucanini and Tituba persist to engage in this dangerous world for
the love of a man. The outcome of this love is that both women are indoctrinat-
ed into a Christian religion and education and taught the English language,
whilst being exiled from their native lands and enslaved in the service of the
colonists.

Exile and Rewriting the Myth of Aeneas

The theme of exile is not only central in women's historical novels but also Virgil's classic Roman epic *The Aeneid*. Virgil writes: "I impose no limits of time or place. I have given them an empire that will know no end" (Book I-278-9). Building on Homer's *Iliad* in which Aeneas is also a demi-god, the *Aeneid* is the tale of his exile and survival after the burning and capture of Troy by the Greeks. Both Cato and Ellis and Gleason draw from this founding myth when writing the lives of two relatively unknown historical nineteenth century queens: the sole remainder of the Indigenous Tasmanians, proclaimed Queen of the Tasmanians, Trucanini (c.1812–8 May 1876) and the West African Queen of Dahomey (now the Republic of Benin), Agotime (reign 1789-97). The jacket sleeve to *Agotime* likens Agotime to a "womanly Aeneas" carrying her gods and vodu to a new land.

Amidst Troy burning, Virgil depicts Aeneas carrying his father Anchises on his shoulders, leading his son by the hand, and saving the Trojan gods. Like Aeneas, Agotime's odyssey as a slave from Dahomey to Brazil is one of wandering. Surviving slavery, Agotime escapes and lives in Casa Xelegbata, São Luis for a time. Virgil's immortalization of Aeneas in the founding history of the Roman Empire is analogous to Agotime, who founds her eventual Rome in Brazil–according to Gleason she does not, contrary to some historians/tales, return to Dahomey once her son Gãkpe takes power.

Bay argues that Agotime's fate is uncertain and it is unclear that she ever returned to Dahomey to become the recorded *kpojito*, Queen Mother, "though survival and return, then, seem to have had a particular importance in Dahomean thinking –almost as if exile as a captive in a foreign land was perceived as a period of trial or testing" (56). According to Gleason's account, Agotime remains steadfast in Brazil. The last line of the novel reads "No, when she left Casa Xelegbata, she was headed towards the interior –" (Gleason 293). Agotime's destiny, like Aeneas', is imposed by the gods. Her decision to put down new roots, the author through a contemporary narrator suggests, makes finding traces of her life and spiritual power possible.

Gleason is not the only one, however, who rewrites the tale of Aeneas from a postcolonial feminist perspective. Cato and Ellis re-interpret the most famous scenes between Aeneas and his lover Dido in the personages of Mr. Robinson and Trucanini. In Book I, Aeneas is ship-wrecked onto the shores of Carthage, a city ruled by Queen Dido. Up until now, Virgil has portrayed Aeneas as the quintessential Roman hero: steadfast in his respect/duty towards the gods, homeland, and family. In Carthage, Aeneas sees the city newly being built with citadels and temples dedicated to Juno. The high walls also depict the fall of

Troy. Aeneas sees his King Priam and the events of the war before him, including himself in combat. Dido, nonetheless, welcomes the Trojan Prince and tells him, "I, too, have known ill fortune like yours and been tossed from one wretchedness to another" (Book I-628-29). In Virgil's text, Aeneas and Dido's fates are intertwined and Aeneas will eventually cause the ruin of Dido and her city. Dido's love for Aeneas is solidified when Venus sends her son Cupid to inflame Dido with a fiery poison/potion, ultimately a destructive love. Thus, a mad passion, Virgil argues, will cause Dido's downfall, much like it does for Trucanini when she meets Mr. Robinson.

Cato and Ellis' Trucanini, enlisted by Robinson, helps round-up the remaining natives on the island. The government's plan is to domesticate and civilize those natives who are willing and to kill those who are not. During their trek through the bush, Robinson's life becomes endangered by hostile natives seeking him out, which causes him to jump into a river. Essentially, Trucanini saves Robinson's life and the pair takes refuge in a cave before making love (82). This mirrors Virgil's text when, while out hunting, Dido and Aeneas are driven by a storm into a cave for shelter and where ultimately the lovers "cave" into their desires. The cave offers temporary protection for its lovers. It symbolizes secrecy because in a sense what occurs inside the cave between the lovers cannot exist outside the cave's walls –it is an interior space outside of politics and law. The etymology of the word "cave" is akin to Greek *koilos* for hollow and also *kyein* to be pregnant – the womb, a place of primordial darkness, is a fearful yet protective place where sexual desires remain uninhibited: the moment these desires, these lovers, leave the cave, social norms and rules on class, race, and nation and of course gender forbid and arguably incriminate. The storm is caused by Juno (the goddess of marriage), who is trying to make an alliance with Venus for Dido and Aeneas to marry and co-rule. Virgil writes: "that day was the first cause of death, and first of sorrow. She [Dido] gave no thought to appearance or her good name and no longer kept her love as a secret in her own heart, but called it marriage, using the word to cover her guilt" (Book IV-171-74). Cato and Ellis do not suggest Trucanini believes she is marrying, but a similar cultural mistranslation occurs. The love of a 'foreign queen' is null and void; Trucanini is neither white nor British, just as Dido herself is Carthaginian, the sworn enemy of Rome during the time in which Virgil is writing.

Both women are 'engaged' and in love with what patriarchal rules of nationhood/society have deemed enemies of their peoples. Is Trucanini, like Dido, a traitor to her nation? According to Ellis, "[t]he Aborigines thought little of Trucanini. They were inclined to regard her more as a traitor than a savior for her exploits with the Friendly Mission" (145). This view is supported in the novel by the few times Trucanini helps her people against the whites . The narrative, thus, offers a complicated protagonist whose allegiance appears to be torn. She is never portrayed as despising her own people, but she is also not a glorified heroine. She is naïve, trusting, and has sexual feelings for Mr. Robinson that convince her that change and a better future for her and her people are possible–she does not have the clairvoyance to know what colonization and submission to the whites in the future will actually entail.

The sobriquet "Queen" also highlights the tension between Trucanini and her people; to the whites, in old age, she becomes a local celebrity as "people believed that she really was a queen, and considered her a heroine, the saviour of her race" (145). Ellis suggests that the facts about Trucanini have been obscured and that she was only granted the ironic title after the death of her people (though of course this refers to recorded history only and also does not take into account the children of Indigenous and Europeans). She is a queen without a kingdom, rights, or citizens. The empty appellation problematically also signifies her allegiance to the whites. The sexual affection between Trucanini and Mr. Robinson, like Aeneas and Dido, is short-lived; Aeneas forgets his fate and his oath to the gods, in this case to track and capture the natives for the government. Coincidentally, Robinson's first wife Maria dies, like Aeneas' first wife Creusa, and he remarries after his affair with Trucanini and lives with his new wife Rose in Rome (238)–just as Aeneas, after his time with Dido, marries his destined Latin bride, Lydia.

Analogously, Milton in *Paradise Lost*, describes Satan as an empire-builder; he is ambitious, a colonizer, and an adventurer, which, according to Heather James, are positions Aeneas holds in Virgil's epic (2552), and I argue Mr. Robinson possesses in Cato and Ellis' novel–according to an older and wiser Trucanini, he is "a Rageorapper, a devil!" (235). Does this characterization also fit Agotime? Does Agotime re-enact the colonizing-imperializing process, though she is a Dahomean slave, when she spreads her vodu throughout Brazil? Like Aeneas, she is not seeking a return to her original home, nor does she ever return to Dahomey, but she, also, is not a war-monger in the way Aeneas is portrayed. Agotime does, however, install the gods from Dahomey in Brazil and continues her Dahomean familial lineage in a way similar to that which Aeneas does with Ascanius, his Trojan son. Though her only biological child remains in Dahomey, in Brazil, Agotime adopts a son named Luiz Braga, a romantic poet who is half black (262) and speaks Portuguese. Much like Piat who complicates Québec's history in *Les Filles du Roi*, Gleason challenges Brazil's history and suggests it cannot ignore and erase its African past. Gleason's narrative suggests that Agotime's legend and her gods are still alive and visible today and that she warrants a feminist novel worthy of preserving her heroic life in the epic manner of Virgil's *Aeneid*.

The imperializing aspect of Agotime in Gleason's novel is ambiguous because her cult is subjugated and limited by the dominant discourses; she must
find imaginative/alternative ways to express her beliefs. By comparison, Mr.
Robinson's imperializing role in Cato and Ellis' novel is clear. Derogatorily
nicknamed by the other colonists as "Black Robinson" for his affection for
Trucanini, he must, like Aeneas who puts his personal feelings aside when he
flees Carthage and sails for Italy, dis-engage himself from Trucanini and return
to his wife and children in Hobart Town. When Dido reminds Aeneas of his
marriage pledge to her, Aeneas claims that he has not held the torches of a
bridegroom, "nor [has he] offered [her] marriage or entered into that contract
with [her]" (339-40; Book IV), though "[i]t is not by [his] own will that [he]
still search[es] for Italy (361-2; Book IV). Unlike Dido who, when Aeneas
leaves in the night, ritualistically burns all of Aeneas' clothing and belongings
before laying herself atop the pyre, Trucanini does no such immediate act. In
fact, hers is a slow-death. Maintaining a quasi-friendship with Mr. Robinson
over a period of years until his eventual return to England, she suffers poverty,
exile to Flinders Island, racism, and, finally, as the only member of her race
still alive, the annihilation of her people. Towards the end of the novel, Mr.
Robinson pays a visit to his old friend Trucanini , who barely acknowledges his
existence, bringing to mind when, in Book VI, Aeneas pleads with honeyed
words to Dido in the Underworld, but she only stares back, emotionally un-
moved, and flees, his enemy, "hating him" (474-75).

Patriarchy Within and Without

Among the challenges the women in Gleason's *Agotime* and Dangarembga's
Nervous Conditions face is patriarchy within their own cultures as well as patriarchal prejudices from imperializing European forces. In *Nervous Conditions*, the protagonist Tambu and the women in her Zimbabwean family (formerly Rhodesia) are subject to the rules of her father and uncle. In the case of
Agotime, she faces patriarchal discrimination from her own Dahomean culture.
Gleason's novel introduces Agotime just prior to her exile:

> She was at a crossroads now. Frightening though her prospects,
> she willingly committed herself to change, for nothing could be
> worse than the dismal path the last five years had taken. When
> her husband King Agõglo died, she, unlike those childless
> wives required to immolate themselves upon the bier, had
> passed with come fourscore others into the keeping of
> Adãdozã, his son and successor. However, unknown to the

commonality, this customary transfer had in her case implied
immediate imprisonment. (8)

Confined to the panther-wives' compound, Agotime awaits her banishment,
while her son Gãkpe is in exile on the banks of the Weme.

Prior to her departure, Agotime secretly consults the oracle of the Bokonõ.
The Bokonõ tells Agotime, "adapt to circumstance; be discreet, adept at disguise, change of place and you will survive to accomplish that which Fa has
decreed" (Gleason 33). When Agotime is brought before her stepson, evidence
of a transatlantic exchange between European, Brazilian, and Dahomean cultures is clear. Adãdozã sits on a throne, "a gift from his 'brother' George III"
(43), and there are Dutch canons that had been given in exchange for "one
hundred slaves apiece" (48) surrounding the procession. Agotime, also, muses
on the name that each canon bears, as if its maker were a king: "No Dahomean
smith would dream of affixing his name to one of the artifacts ... [but] she
would have liked, before she died, to leave upon something somewhere a little
brass plate that said *Agotime made me*" (ibid.). On the other side of the Great
Gate are the *caboceers* and slave traders. Gleason writes: "Victims of a lan-
guished trade, some of these ex-sailors and adventurers, accidently captured in
the course of Dahomean raids along the littoral, had remained unransomed
prisoners as long as twenty-five years in Abomey" (49). At her late husband's
bidding, Agotime learns Portuguese from Innocencio, a caboceer whose name
ironically translates as "innocent," and undertakes a religious education from
the priests (ibid.).

Standing before Adãdozã, Agotime is accused of telling stories, naming the
king a tyrant, and, like Tituba in Condé's novel, being a witch. Possibly too
powerful to execute because of her access to the supernatural (Bay 53), the
outcome is that Agotime is sentenced to Whydah Beach as an anonymous slave
destined for Brazil (Gleason 59). Bay, in her study on the effect of the slave
trade on African societies such as Dahomey, argues that "the ruling elites
themselves lived with the possibility of becoming victims of the trade. Being
traded overseas was one of the several documented punishments for losers in
political struggles at court" (52). Thus, Agotime is sold, like many Dahomean
slaves, by her own stepson into the hands of European and Brazilian traders.

In *Nervous Conditions*, Dangarembga stresses the patriarchal limits her protagonist faces when pursuing her dream to be educated. The novel begins in an
existentialist fashion with the female protagonist Tambu telling the reader, "I
was not sorry when my brother died" (1). In a sense Tambu benefits from
Nhamo's death in 1968. As the second eldest child in the family, Tambu is only
permitted to attend the missionary school in Umtali where her uncle is head-
master after Nhamo dies. Tambu argues, "Though the event of my brother's

passing and the events of my story cannot be separated, my story is not after all about death, but about my escape and Lucia's; about my mother's and Maiguru's entrapment and about Nyasha's rebellion" (ibid.).

Tambu recounts how, at an early age, her family only had enough money to send Nhamo to school: "my father thought I should not mind. 'Is that anything to worry about? Ha-a-a, it's nothing,' he reassured me, with his usual ability to jump whichever way was easiest. 'Can you cook books and feed them to your husband? Stay at home with your mother. Learn to cook and clean. Grow vegetables'" (15). These rigid gender roles based on sexual difference continually attempt to limit Tambu's life choices, but she knows education can help her situation:

> My mother said being black was a burden because it made you
> poor, but Babamukuru was not poor. My mother said being a
> woman was a burden because you had to bear children and
> look after them and the husband. But I did not think this was
> true. … I decided it was better to be like Maiguru, who was not
> poor and had not been crushed by the weight of womanhood.
> (16)

Planting and growing her own maize in the year 1962, Tambu affirms to her family that she will raise her own school fees (17), despite her father's disapproval and her mother's conviction that she will fail.

The success of her maize is accredited not only to her hard work and determination but also to her late grandmother who "gave [her] history lessons as well. History that could not be found in the textbooks" (ibid.). History plays an important role in the novel and Tambu finds herself torn between dominant master narratives and the point of view of the colonized; she also begins to questions why women's knowledge and history in both is missing and unrecorded. This struggle plays itself out, literally, when Tambu discovers that Nhamo has been stealing her mealies. After attacking Nhamo on the playground, Mr. Matimba offers to help Tambu sell her mealies to the Whites in the town. Earning enough money to pay for all her school fees, much to Nhamo's jealousy, Tambu comes top of her class in Sub A and, the following year, in Sub B. It is, also, at this time that Tambu's uncle Babamukuru and his wife Maiguru, after five years of living and studying for Master's degrees in England, return home with their children Chido and Nyasha.

Babamukuru decides that Nhamo will live with him and attend the missionary school. When Nhamo unexpectedly dies from what is believed to be mumps while in his uncle and aunt's care, the family is distraught and full of guilt. Though Tambu's father sees little point in educating her, Babamukuru says, "I will not feel I have done my duty if I neglect the family … Tambudzai

– must be given the opportunity to do what she can for the family before she goes to her husband's home" (56). In favor of Tambu's education, Babamukuru still clings to an idealized conception of woman, whose roles include, first and foremost, marrying and having children. Thus, Tambu not only has to overcome the future her mother and father have already mapped out for her, but she must also negotiate the expectations of her aunt and uncle who, in some respects, adhere to traditional gender divisions of labor and, in other respects, embrace Western materialism and ideals such as career, education, home, automobile, religion, clothing, etc.

Learning to navigate her new lifestyle at her uncle's, conforming to a school with white children, and adapting to the ways of the missionaries proves alienating for Tambu (105). Tambu reflects, at the end of the novel, on being accepted to a prestigious Young Ladies College of the Sacred Heart (195) where she learns European languages, plays sports, and avidly reads literature (199). According to Tambu's mother, it is this:

> 'Englishness,' in which one must tread carefully: Be careful, she had said, and I thought about Nyasha and Chido and Nhamo, who had all succumbed, and of my own creeping feelings of doom. … I was beginning to have a suspicion, no more than the seed of suspicion, that had I been too eager to leave the homestead and embrace the 'Englishness' of the mission; and after that the more concentrated 'Englishness' of Sacred Heart' (207).

The novel concludes with Tambu asserting her increasing criticisms of colonialism and patriarchy within both her own family and foreign influence. The woman's historical novel becomes the medium for her catharsis, once again suggesting its suitability for women writers (208).

Bad Women

In all of the novels discussed in this chapter, women's transgressions of a hegemonic and idealized image of the good woman as wife and mother are described–Trucanini lives with the whalers and Mr. Robinson, Agotime dares to undermine her son-in-law's authority, and Tituba is incarcerated as a witch in Salem. Several of the female characters in Dangarembga's *Nervous Conditions*, in particular, however, are referred to as "bad women." In this section, I focus on the characters Nyasha and Lucia. Nyasha, Tambu's cousin, is a self-proclaimed "hybrid" (Dangarembga 79) negotiating, with difficulty, her Shona culture and an English one. She is not fully accepted in either culture. When Nyasha returns from England she is unrecognizable to Tambu. Unlike Tituba, for whom returning to the Barbados is a kind of justice, for Nyasha, returning to Zimbabwe proves difficult. For one, Nyasha barely understands Shona, thus, making conversation nearly impossible. Tambu, like her other family members, disapproves of Nyasha and judges her ungrateful, critical, and spoiled.

The relationship, however, begins to improve after Tambu moves to live with her aunt and uncle and the cousins share a room. Tambu, though, cannot understand why her cousin talks disrespectfully to Maiguru, to which Maiguru apologetically says, "They are too Anglicized … they picked up all these disrespectful ways in England" (74). As Tambu notes, however, she is unsure if her aunt is "censoring Nyasha for her Anglicized habits or [Tambu] for [her] lack of them" (ibid.). Tensions between cultural and gender expectations continue as Nyasha rebels against her parents. She smokes cigarettes, starves herself, is outspoken, and reads English novels voraciously (84-85). Tambu knows that "beside Nyasha [she] was a paragon of feminine decorum, principally because [she] hardly ever talked unless spoken to, and then only to answer with the utmost respect whatever question had been asked;" thus, "Babamukuru thought [Tambu] was the sort of young woman a daughter ought to be and lost no opportunity to impress this point of view upon Nyasha" (157). This is not entirely accurate, however, as Tambu criticizes her own mother in the text more than once, such as over the dirty latrine (125). Tambu's relationship with her mother, a personal and political figure, influences her relation to the mother-country and mother-tongue.

As Katrina Daly Thompson notes, "[t]he mother tongue in *Nervous Conditions*, then is no mere metaphor for first language but also a linking of Shona to the character of Tambudzai's mother" (52). Learning English as a language and lifestyle means a distancing and separation from her mother. Nyasha also feels alienated from her mother, who she views as a wasted talent. Tensions between Nyasha and her parents reach a climax at the same time that she reaches sexual maturity. After attending a school dance, Nyasha stays outside with a boy named Andy (Dangarembga 113). Tired of waiting, Tambu and her cousin, Chido go into the house. When Babamukuru discovers Nyasha is still outside, he fetches her and cries, "No decent girl would stay out alone, with a boy, at that time of night" (115). Babamukuru continues to argue, "Why can't you behave like a young woman from a decent home? What will people say when they see Sigauke's daughter carrying on like that?" to which he repeats, "[I] cannot have a daughter who behaves like a whore" (116) and he strikes her for talking back to him. In retaliation, Nyasha hits her father and they struggle until Chido is able to hold Babamukuru and Nyasha escapes to the servants' quarters (117). Tambu remembers:

> Thinking how dreadfully familiar that scene had been, with
> Babamukuru condemning Nyasha to whoredom, making her a
> victim of her femaleness, just as I had felt victimized at home
> in the days when Nhamo went to school and I grew my maize.
> The victimization, I saw, was universal. It didn't depend on
> poverty, on lack of education or on tradition ... What I didn't
> like was the way all the conflicts came back to this question of
> femaleness. Femaleness as opposed and inferior to maleness.
> (118)

Tambu's realization jump-starts her feminist consciousness and continues afterward when she, Nyasha, Maiguru, and her uncle travel/drive to visit her family for Christmas.

It is at this point that Lucia is introduced into the narrative. Lucia is Tambu's mother's sister and is described as "a wild woman" (127); Dangarembga writes: "Look at Lucia! Ha! There is nothing of a woman there. She sleeps with anybody and everybody, but she hasn't borne a single child, yet. She's been bewitched. More likely she's a witch herself" (128). Tambu sees the contradiction of these claims.

Lucia is criticized for not being a good woman, thus, losing the social status of the categorization; her being childless also seems to exclude her from being a woman. Her sexuality is deemed a threatening supernatural power for which she is called a witch. Adding to Lucia, her "shame" is that she becomes pregnant with Takesure's child (meaning it is a distant cousin of Babamukuru's) and is sleeping with Tambu's father (129). When Jeremiah says that he'd like to take Lucia as a second wife, Babamukuru refuses the marriage based on the fact that bigamy is sinful and "would bring the wrath of God down on the entire family" (129). The "problem" of Lucia prompts a serious family meeting that the women, including the accused, are not permitted to attend.

With the women fighting amongst themselves, Lucia finally strides into the room of men to defend herself and set the record straight (146-47). The patriarchy decides that a cleansing ceremony is necessary for the family, for which two ideas are put forth: a traditional witchdoctor or a Christian wedding between Tambu's parents. In a way reminiscent of the minister Samuel Parris in Condé's novel wherein he insists upon marrying Tituba and John Indian on the ship bound for Boston, Babamukuru insists upon a Christian marriage. Tambu, in response to the wedding, tells Nyasha:

> The more I saw of worlds beyond the homestead the more I
> was convinced that the further we left the old ways behind the
> closer we came to progress. ... When I confronted Nyasha with
> this evidence of the nature of progress, she became quite an-

noyed and delivered a lecture on the dangers of assuming Christian ways were progressive ways. 'It's bad enough,' she said severely, 'when a country gets colonised, but when the people do as well!' (150)

In the end, Tambu refuses to attend the wedding (170).

Tambu's refusal causes Babamukuru to equate her with Nyasha. He tells Tambu she is ungrateful, disrespectful, and evil: she is "a bad girl" (169). Her punishment is two weeks of the servants' chores. Lucia, on the other hand, is able to somewhat redeem herself when she suggests to Babamukuru that she would like a job. Unable to secure one for herself, Babamukuru finds Lucia a position working at a hostel, for which Lucia is forever indebted. Though she defiantly defends Tambu in her decision not to attend the wedding, Lucia is able to make her living as a single mother and prove to Babamukuru that she can be "good." Nyasha, on the other hand, is described at the end of the novel as having a breakdown.

On holiday from school, Tambu sees the decline in Nyasha's health. Tambu hears Nyasha internalizing and crying in the words of her uncle: "I'm not a good girl. I'm evil. I'm not a good girl" (203). She rips her history book into shreds declaring, "Their history. Fucking liars. Their bloody lies" (205). This behavior sends Nyasha to Maiguru's brother in Salisbury and, later, a clinic (206). Nyasha suffers, literally and metaphorically, from starvation. She is hungry for change. Dangarembga suggests that this hunger is a symptom of a nervous condition, which is not only the title of the novel but also is included in an epigraph from Fanon's *The Wretched of the Earth* that reads: "the condition of native is a nervous condition." Thompson explains that "Nyasha cannot articulate her illness because it occurs in a language which is not part of the culture surrounding her, the 'bewitching master narrative', English" (57). Nyasha's problems, once again, are attributed by Tambu's mother to her "Englishness."

Tambu senses the contradiction to this claim; it is as if as her body deteriorates, her thoughts become more lucid. Nyasha's "English" education alerts her to the sexist and racist historical record and culture she lives within, one which distorts and ignores history from the point of view of the Black Zimbabwean, particularly Black Zimbabwean women, and is myopic when it comes to the future. Nyasha envisions gender equality and, therefore, she is also, like Tambu, "critical of her mother's sacrifice of self for her father's ambition" and his colonializing and Puritanical way towards women's sexuality (Shaw 9-10). Derek Wright argues that "puritanism is the principle ingredient of the colonial education that Babamukuru enforces upon his children" (122). This highlights the complicated relation the girls have with sexuality, colonialism, and family customs. Returning to school (206-07) at the end of the novel, Tambu, a young woman, reflects on the process of self-realization and being caught between traditional and modern colonial patriarchies in Zimbabwe.

Maternal/Historical Survivals and Metanarrative

Women's historical novels insist upon women's survival, individually and collectively. As Adrienne Rich notes "re-vision – the act of looking back, of seeing with fresh eyes, of entering an old text from a new critical direction – is for women more than a chapter in cultural history: it is an act of survival ... We need to know the writing of the past, and know it differently than we have ever known it; not to pass on a tradition but to break its hold over us" (*On Lies, Secrets, and Silence: Selected Prose 1966-1978* 35). Rich's words encapsulate the politicized feminist strategies adopted in the novels in this chapter. It is one thing to tell a previously unknown history for the first time but another thing to retell and revision canonic texts.[9] In Dangarembga's *Nervous Conditions*, the novel ends with Tambu seeing her education as a ticket to freedom, albeit not without problems. She witnesses the death of her brother Nhamo, the decline of her cousin Nyasha, and the wayward ways of her other cousin Chido, who dates a white girl. These family members serve, for Tambu, as painful reminders of the dangers in becoming Anglicized and, at the same time, raise questions of what it means to have an authentic existence. Tambu, thus, is very much torn between her African heritage and assimilating to the ways of the whites. Her story is a quest for a sense of self and a means for making sense of the racial and patriarchal limitations imposed upon her. The initial joy she feels for taking charge of her own life by escaping the homestead and the mission and, later, exiling herself to the college is juxtaposed with the preordained exile in Gleason's novel *Agotime*.

Agotime, a former Dahomean queen and later exiled slave, is celebrated as a woman of tremendous power and courage. In the Foreword, Gleason writes: "the gods she brought to a new world have known a modest survival. This is her story, an exploration of her unsung destiny" (v). According to Gleason, Agotime's legacy, however concealed, persists in São Luis, Brazil in the Casa das Minas "by which they mean the Dahomean cult house" (4). Though Agotime's name is inconsistent in the formal records, Gleason suggests that evidence of her life has been preserved, such as a pair of sandals, a spear, her courtyard, the drums, and the room where she was interviewed by ambassadors who tried to persuade her to return to Dahomey. For Gleason, these potential

---

[9] See Peter Widdowson's "'Writing Back': Contemporary Re-visionary Fiction" for an account of this kind of writing in contemporary British historical novels.

objects/texts signal the preservation of Agotime and a female genealogy in the community's memory. Defiantly, Gleason appropriates Agotime's life as both mythical and historical: "it was not a dream" (3).The importance of preserving her story is emphasized when she claims:

> The brand on the boat: that was unreal. There it was, still on her breast, but she had never accepted it. No, she was growing old, and she might be recaptured and sold many times, but she had never and would never be a slave, not in that sense any-way. To have been clawed by the unseen, however, and to have survived to tell the tale, even if it could never be told, this made an honest woman of her! (251)

Gleason highlights that physical restrictions will not imprison her mind; in her mind, Agotime is and always will be free. She rejects the name "slave" that has been imposed upon her by authorities whom she refuses to recognize.

Jacqui Alexander articulates this history of "the Crossing" seen in Gleason's and Condé's novels on the life of Kitsimba, a slave who "numbered among those who through the door of no return were shuttled from the Old Kongo kingdom to the Caribbean circa 1870" (6). The forced journey in Gleason's novel suggests that the promise of a future articulated by the European hero-ines' "crossing" in chapter one must be read in the context of slavery. Alexan-der reads Kitsimba's story as a way for reconciling the embodied with the dis-embodied sacred or spiritual and, therefore, disrupting accepted boundaries of episteme, geography and nation. She promotes multiple pedagogies as they relate to re-understanding history as a dialectics, a palimpsest, and the Crossing is "meant to evoke/invoke the crossroads, the space of convergence and endless possibility … it is the imaginary from which we dream the craft of a new com-pass" (Alexander 8). Thus, Agotime's legacy persists in Brazil while, in Con-dé's novel, Tituba eventually returns to the Barbados, her motherland.

Tituba originally arrives in Salem, Massachusetts because she and her hus-band John Indian are owned by Samuel Parris, a Puritan. Tituba notes: during this time "thousands of our people were being snatched from Africa. I learned we were not the only ones the whites were reducing to slavery; they were also enslaving the Indians, the original inhabitants of both America and our beloved Barbados" (Condé 47). Mixed-race, Tituba has an African mother and a Euro-pean father, who, literally and figuratively, dominates the former through rape. Tituba, however, only embraces her maternal African side and, born in Barba-dos, she feels a strong love for the country. This is amplified when she arrives, first, in Boston and, later, in the village of Salem. In Salem, Tituba is criticized for her vast knowledge of plants and herbal remedies as well as for the color of her skin, all of which help verify she is a witch and a "visible messenger of Satan" (65).

Condé does not deny that Tituba is a witch, but rather problematizes how a word can have a single denotation–Tituba's magic heal and cures as well as causes injury and harm. In addition, the spirits of Tituba's mother and Mama Yaya offer comforting words: "Out of them all, you'll be the only one to survive" (86). Ann Armstrong Scarboro suggests that the use of the "I" in the novel's title as well as the "first-person narrative point of view empowers the heroine, making her a survivor rather than a victim" (214). Though presented as a slave narrative, Gyssels reminds us, "there are virtually no autobiographies of African slaves" (71). Tituba will survive, but she will also be forgotten: "I felt that I would only be mentioned in passing in these Salem witchcraft trials about which so much would be written later, trials that would arouse the curiosity and pity of generations to come as the greatest testimony of a barbaric age. There would be mention here and there of a 'slave originating from the West Indies and probably practicing 'hoodoo'" (110). Condé's narrative allows Tituba to speak through the author as a conduit into the present while, at the same time, reminding the reader not to be seduced by so called facts or the narrative authority of the "I." Putting into question linguistic designations, in this case "Afro-Caribbean," "woman," "slave," and "witch," and how the individual I's story relates to and can speak for the collective is one of the novel's strategies. An example of what Linda Hutcheon calls "historiographic metafiction," Tituba's narrative is open equally to interpretation and falsification as are other accounts in the record –but the novel cannot be a parody of the suffering the historical Tituba endured; this is the dilemma women's historical fiction faces.

Highlighting omissions in the historical record, Condé puts a postmodern twist on her narrative by imagining Tituba meeting Hester Prynne, the infamous and fictional protagonist of Nathaniel Hawthorne's novel *The Scarlet Letter* (1850), in prison. Hester, a self-proclaimed "feminist" (101), a sign of Condé's deliberate insertion of the American present into the past, tells Tituba about being accused of adultery and that, though she is pregnant with her lover's child, she plans to commit suicide (98). Jane Moss argues that Condé "is killing off Hawthorne's heroine at a point before his classic novel begins. Here is another act of revenge against the American intellectual establishment" (10). In a way that invokes Rhys' rewriting of *Jane Eyre*, Condé, through the character of Hester, is able to challenge Western discourses, including feminism.

Playing with relations of power, the author imagines Tituba and Hester as both having been accused of transgressing Puritan values; thus, Condé often gives the reader a novel of "self-conscious clichés" and stereotypes expected in female slave narratives (Moss 9) to criticize these imbalances. The insertion of

the fictional Prynne is juxtaposed with the scant historical record, allowing
Condé to question how reality and whose reality is constructed. Despite the
complexity and contradictory claims Condé puts forth,[10] the novel still holds
onto certain truths and a belief in social transformation based on revisiting the
past. Zubeda Jalazai rightfully argues that "Condé's engagement of Tituba and
her shifting allegiance to historical accuracy also illustrate that appeals to history still carry authority, even for those creating self-referential fiction, or harbor-
ing a postmodern 'incredulity toward metanarratives'" (423). Tituba's court
testimony also includes extracts from the actual trial.

In a footnote, Condé writes that "[t]he original documents of the trial are
kept in the Essex County Archives" (104). The trial coincides with Hester's
determination to hang herself and the end of Tituba's marriage to John Indian,
whom she never sees again. Imprisoned in Salem Town, Tituba reflects not
only on the loss of Hester's child but also her own unborn child, which she
aborted because she could not bear the pain of bringing an innocent child into a
life of slavery and abjection. Released seventeen months after her incarceration, Tituba learns she must pay her debts for being in prison, which necessi-
tates being bought as a slave by a Jewish widower named Benhamin Cohen
d'Azevedo. Under his roof, Tituba cares for his nine children and helps him
communicate with his dead wife. Tituba and d'Azevedo become lovers and,
together, they find consolation in their respective persecutions (Jewish and
black). Crises arise, nevertheless, when, harassed by anti-Semitic townspeople,
d'Azevedo's house is set on fire and his children die. He decides to leave for
Rhode Island and grants Tituba her freedom and the right to return to Barbados.

Tituba's narrative stresses the importance of survival, particularly when she
is recognized by a Nago sailor named Deodatus on the ship. Deodatus asks
Tituba if she is the daughter of Abena who killed the white man and Tituba
remarks, "I had forgotten the ability our people have of remembering. Nothing
escapes them! Everything is engraved in their memory!" (136). The power of
collective memory is echoed again when Condé writes, "Our memory will be
covered in blood. Our memories will float to the surface like water lilies"
(168). The defiance of Tituba's mother serves as a powerful impetus for her
own revolt against slavery when she finds herself living with maroons near
Bellaphine (143). Without a family or home, Tituba's odyssey back to the Barbados makes her a "sort of female hero, an epic heroine, like the legendary
'Nanny of the maroons'" ("Interview" 201). Condé continues, "I hesitated between irony and a desire to be serious. The result is that she is a sort of mock-
epic character" ("Interview" 201). While ambiguity manifests itself throughout

---

[10] See Condé's claim that "Tituba is not a historical novel. Tituba is just the opposite of
a historical novel" (Condé, "Interview" 200-01).

the novel, there is rebirth for Tituba when she returns to the Barbados and reconnects, once again, with her maternal ancestors.

The beginning of Tituba's political career is signaled when she publically begins practicing her magic powers and organizing slave revolts. After spending time with the maroons, Tituba, pregnant, returns to Mama Yaya's cabin. She reasons, "If the world were going to receive my child, then it would have to change!" (159). Her rebellion continues when a slave-boy named Iphigene (a name similar to Agamemnon's daughter whom he sacrificed to the gods) is brought to her for healing. Iphigene tells the story of his mother's death at the hands of their master, which resonates with Tituba's own life-story. Together, the pair prepare for a revolt.

Betrayed, Tituba and Iphigene are captured by the planters and taken to the gallows. Tituba is accused of her crimes and is the last to die; at the moment of her death, she sees Mama Yaya, Abena, and Yao waiting for her. The Epilogue follows, in which Tituba claims, "And that is the story of my life. Such a bitter, bitter story. My real story starts where this one leaves off and it has no end" (175). Surviving in the hearts of her fellow Barbadians, Tituba urges them to keep fighting and to refuse submission and subordination. Like Gleason's Ago-time, Condé writes: "I do not belong to the civilization of the Bible and Bigotry. My people will keep my memory in their hearts and have no need for the written word. It's in their heads. In their hearts and in their heads" (176). Denied motherhood, Tituba explains how she chooses a girl named Samantha to be her descendant, learn her art of communicating with the dead, and possess the special power of plants and animals: "a child I didn't give birth to but whom I chose! What motherhood could be nobler!" (177). Believing she is one with her island , Tituba shows herself for those who can perceive her presence in the last lines of the novel: "the twitching of an animal's coat, the crackling of a fire between four stones, the rainbow-hued babbling of the river, and the sound of the wind as it whistles through the great trees on the hills" (179).

By contrast, Cato and Ellis reveal the impossibility of the Tasmanian's survival when Trucanini dies in *Queen Trucanini*. After spending several years in exile on Flinders Island, Trucanini and the remainder of her peoples ("fourteen men, twenty-two women, and ten children, mostly part-white" (230)) are brought to Oyster Cove: "their new home was an old probation station for convicts" (231). Oyster Cove proves the final breaking point for the settlers; the dream of returning to their old homes and ways of life clearly becomes impossible. Disheartened, subject to living in abject poverty and prone to alcoholism, the settlers know they have been "left to die" (236). Cato and Ellis suggest that by 1866, with the certain extinction of the race, Trucanini and the four others are treated as objects and likened to animals: "the world was at last beginning to take an interest in the unique race of the Tasmanians, now that it was almost too late. Like the *Thylacine*, the marsupial wolf or 'Tasmanian Tiger', which had been hunted almost to extinction, they were suddenly valuable – even dead ones" (239). A photograph taken of the last known five peoples marks this historical event, supported by an article in the Hobart *Mercury* that "noted that only four people remained of the 4, 000 to 7, 000 original inhabitants. 'The Tasmanian natives as a race are now virtually extinct ... As savages they were found, as savages they lived, and as savages they perished'" (242). The last recorded member of her race, Trucanini is given the ironic title of Queen and, with the last man, her husband, is photographed for postcards. When Trucanini's husband dies, however, his body is stolen and exhumed for medical purposes . Thus, "added to the burden of being the last of her race was the nightmarish fear of being mutilated after death" (247). Alone, Trucanini reflects on her love for her island, in a similar way to Tituba in Condé's novel, and equates her separation from her island as a separation between mother and child:

> This was her country. She alone had come back to it. She had no mother, no father, no brother, no uncles, no aunties, no sisters, no children; and now she had no husband. She was solitary as she had been in her mother's womb, before her aunties called her into the light. Yet she was surrounded by her own country, and it sustained her as a mother's blood sustains the unborn child. (248)

The novel ends solemnly with Trucanini's death in 1876 and the Royal Society losing "no time in making its move to get custody of the body" (251).

Conclusion

Postcolonial women's historical novels describe protagonists experiencing exile from their homes akin to a maternal exile. While Agotime continues her legacy in Brazil in Gleason's novel, Tituba lives in the memory of Barbadian slaves and their descendants, though Condé refuses to mythologize her as a founding mother. Tituba dies by hanging like her mother before her because she rebels against slavery. Trucanini, likewise, witnesses the death of her mother by the colonists and, as the sole survivor of her race, becomes a historical artifact of Tasmania's imperialist past (a stamp was dedicated to her as a part of the Famous Women series appearing in 1975 (Ellis 159)). Tambu, living in 1960's Rhodesia, inherits this maternal past. Initially, as an adolescent, she rebels against her own mother and mother-tongue, but, by the end of the novel, she questions her uncritical and hasty rejection and her unknowing participation in acts of racism, sexism, and imperialism from a new perspective. By writing and re-writing the Indigenous, Black, and Caribbean woman back into recorded and (fictional) history, these post 1970's women's historical novels call into question the historical record as construction but also the reality of trauma and suffering within history. Poignantly, Julie Neman argues that "[f]or some stories there can be no revisions" (40). This becomes clearer when analyzing the role of hegemonic history and women's imperialism, the arrival of the whites, exile, bad women, patriarchy within and without, and maternal survival in each of the novels.

CHAPTER FOUR

Transnational Mater-Familial Sagas: The Matriarch

> Let it be myth then...Whether the Golden Age of Matriarchy ever existed in history is not important: what is important is that the myth exists *now*; that there is a story being passed from woman to woman, from mother to daughter, of a time in which we were strong and free and could see ourselves in the Divine, when we lived in dignity and peace
> — Ann Carson, *Feminist Spirituality and the Feminine Divine: An Annotated Bibliography* (1988)

A revival and updating of primarily British family sagas from the 1930s, such as Vera Brittain's *Honourable Estate: A Novel of Transition* (Wallace, *Woman's* 55), the contemporary woman's historical novel now concentrates on the establishment of a transnational maternal genealogy in what I call the "mater-familial saga." Today, mater-familial sagas[11] revolve not just around the family, as in typical familial sagas, but distinctly around the transnational lives of women and, in particular, a powerful mother or grandmother figure. The role of the mother figure in literature is a familiar topic (Hirsch, Adalgisa Giorgio, Irigaray, Lori Saint-Martin, just to name a few), but scholarship, specifically on the matriarch in women's historical novels is rare. In women's historical novels, matriarchs figure prominently in two literary-historical time-frames: premodern utopian societies, for example Joan Wolf's series on a prehistoric matriarchal society in southern France (1991-93) or Mary Mackey's Earthsong trilogy (1993-98), and the long twentieth century. In this chapter, I focus on the latter time-frame because it is the same time frame invoked by the 1930s family sagas identified by Diana Wallace, the works do not portray matriarchies in a utopian light as many premodern novels do, and a distinct transnational maternal genealogy emerges. I discuss Laura Esquivel's *Like Water for Chocolate* (1989), Adhaf Soueif's *The Map of Love* (1999), Uyen Nicole Duong's *Daugh-*

---

[11] Consider Colleen McCullough's *The Thorn Birds* (1977), V.C. Andrews' prolific series *Dollanganger* (1979-86), Barbara Taylor Bradford's *Emma Harte Saga* (1979-2009), Philippa Gregory's Wideacre trilogy (1987-1990), Joan Chase's *During the Reign of the Queen of Persia* (1983) or Marianne Fredriksson's *Hanna's Daughters* (1994).

ters of the River Huong (2005) and Padma Viswanathan *The Toss of a Lemon* (2008).[12] The matriarch in these novels is an ambivalent and unconventional figure; similarly, the family is once again experiencing a time of radical transition. This transition is reflected in the life of the matriarch, who, as a complex mother figure, is revered and resented, respected yet feared, challenged, sometimes loved, and often pitied by her family.

Mater-familial sagas today are multi-vocal, multi-perspectival, crossnational, and collapse/combine different historical eras into a unified narrative. Mary Green argues that there is "an opportunity to turn back to her place of origin, to her mother, and to her mother's mother, allowing her to insert herself within a female genealogy" (98). Gill Rye describes this process as chronicling "women's relations *with* their mothers through to women's experiences *as* mothers" (118). These novels assert the political potential of the woman's historical novel through the process by which a woman inserts herself into a female genealogy and her rememoriation of the past. These memories express an insider's perspective to colonization/globalization, as opposed to the national enthusiasm the protagonists in chapter one share in their respective New Worlds. For example, in *Daughters of the River Huong*, the narrator highlights the devastating effects of war on women's lives when she makes her escape from war-torn Vietnam by marrying an American journalist.

Male absences, often attributed to death, are the norm in these novels. In Viswanathan's novel *The Toss of a Lemon*, Sivakami's husband dies while she is still a teenager and Goli, the husband of her daughter Thangham, is a wandering father who sees his children once every few years. Soueif's protagonists Omar and Sharif in *The Map of Love* die; Andre Foucault's death in Duong's novel can be read as not only a personal freeing from a man but also as the symbolic death of French colonialism in Vietnam; and in Esquivel's work, the heroine, Tita, dies while making love to Pedro (she is only heroine whose death is dramatically marked in these novels).

The matriarch's freedom or power–political, religious, social, economic, familial–arises from male absence. Hirsch argues that in contrast "to the female family romance prevalent in nineteenth-century novels" that revolved "around the attachment to a male figure" and the female family romance of the 1920s that subscribed to "compulsory heterosexuality … the feminist family romance of the 1970s de-emphasizes the role of men … the concentration on motherdaughter bonding and struggle, and the celebration of female relationships of mutual nurturance leave only a secondary role to men" (133). Gil Zehava Hochberg, drawing on the work of Hortense J. Spillers and the African-

---

[12] I'm using the English translation of Esquivel's *Como Agua Para Chocolate* by Carol Christensen and Tom Christensen.

American woman's narrative, writes on women writers of the African diaspora, such as Simone Schwarz-Bart's historical novel *Pluie et vent sur Télumée Miracle*; Hochberg claims that:

> With the absence of the symbolic patriarchal figure ... 'the monstrosity' of a strong maternal figure ('with the capacity to name') offers a radical identity position for (African American) women and an alternative narrative of female empowerment, based on the specific (destruction of) the African American family during slavery. (2)

In the textual analysis to follow, in addition to the notable absence of men, I examine forbidden romances, rebellious sisters, rememoriation, exile, mirrors, and sacred objects, all of which figure prominently and elucidate an understanding of the matriarch's role in transnational maternal genealogies.

Forbidden Romances and Matriarchs

Warning against matriarchal societies that merely reverse patriarchy, Luce Irigaray writes that in these cases "[t]he mother commands, the daughter is to listen and obey. The elder seems to repeat to her daughter what has been forced upon her as a woman" (*I Love to You* 130). Similarly, Hope Jennings suggeststhat "matriarchal myths are more often than not equally as oppressive as their patriarchal counterparts, since those feminisms that express a desire for the maternal as a source of inherent female power do not so much grant women freedom from phallocentric parameters but, in fact, help keep them in place" (66). Elleke Boehmer warns African women writers who inscribe the continent as "Mother Africa" (4-7) of the risk in imagining an idealized, mythologized, "homeland in the Motherland" (James Alexander 10). In addition, noting the dangers in essentializing reproductive roles for women, Jennings claims that what can be a source of power for women can also enslave women (66). Her insights are particularly true of Esquivel's novel *Like Water for Chocolate*, which centers on the matriarchal figure of Mama Elena and her daughters Rosaura, Gertrudis, and Tita.

In Esquivel's novel, the dominating force of the United States is clear. The De la Garza family lives on a ranch on the US-Mexico border during the time of the Mexican Revolution (1910). Mexico's national struggles within the novel serve as an important backdrop in this mater-familial saga and parallel the battles between Mama Elena and her daughters. Eric Skipper suggests that the Revolution itself plays such an essential role in shaping events that it ultimately functions as a protagonist and should be treated as such (186). Skipper identifies Mama Elena and Tita as representing the two opposing sides of the Revolution: Mama Elena as matriarch runs her household according to patriarchal authority, traditions and customs; she stands for the Federal troops and the dictatorship of Porfirio Díaz while Tita symbolizes the revolutionaries (ibid.). The relationship "can be classified as a colonized relationship between the colonizer and colonized in which the (powerful) mother fits the profile of a colonizer and the (powerless) daughter is the colonized" (James Alexander 19). Mama Elena is a dictator in her family, and forbids Tita from marrying her lover Pedro, because the youngest daughter, according to Mama Elena's Mexican tradition, is to be a caretaker.

Mama Elena is also portrayed with physical strength, skill, and calculating coldness, for example, her ability to kill chickens or crack sacks of walnuts without tiring (Esquivel, *Like Water for Chocolate* 230). Tita, on the other hand gains confidence as the novel progresses. Her rebellious nature supports the revolutionaries, who desire socialist change, and a dismantling of the old systems (Skipper 187). Tita resents her mother's ways until the end of the novel when she discovers Mama Elena once had a secret lover, José Treviño, who was murdered. This revelation invokes compassion, if not pity, within Tita for her already deceased mother. It is significant that first Mama Elena, (including her ghost) and then Tita, after her mother's death and after making love to Pedro, dies. The De la Garza ranch burns as a result of Tita's and Pedro's lovemaking, which was so impassioned that it literally burns the household and the lovers themselves to the ground.

Mónica Zapata confirms that the army is, indeed, the background, but that, for her, the domestic scene is the central focus of the text (71). This is not necessarily a reversal of traditional historical novels, for example Scott's *Waverley* or Tolstoy's *War and Peace* that clearly gives textual space to the domestic, but, here, the familial takes center stage and, in doing so, reflects the state of the nation during the Revolution. Zapata writes that "*[c]omo agua para chocolate est l'un des premiers romans écrits par des femmes qui déplace complètement le lieu d'où émane le discours en même temps qu'il instaure une temporalité parallèle et plus féconde que celle du calendrier 'officiel'*" 'Like Water for Chocolate is one of the first novels written by women, which completely displaces the place from where the discourse originates, and at the same time it establishes a parallel temporality more fruitful than the one of the 'official' calendar'' (72). There is a sense of irony in Zapata's words because Esquivel sets her novel in conjunction with her recipes, according to the months of the calendar. Highlighting the cyclical aspects of her narrative, (also present in *Malinche*) Esquivel ruptures history as chronological and linear: "time as project, teleology, linear and prospective unfolding; time as departure, progression, and arrival-in other words, the time of history" (Kristeva 17) is suspended when recuperating maternal origins and maternal time.

Painting a complicated picture of the past, on the one hand, Esquivel's novel implies through the ranch burning that the past cannot repeat itself–is not wanted to repeat itself. On the other hand, because of the fire, a chance for rebirth and renewal for the De la Garza family emerges. Tita's great niece, the anonymous narrator of the novel, claims that "all they found under the remains of what had been the ranch was this cookbook ... they say that under those ashes every kind of life flourished, making this land the most fertile in the region" (246). The narrator describes her own relation to the land, after her mother has an apartment rebuilt on the site, by recounting her mother's cooking of the Christmas Rolls. The narrator clearly is tied to her mother, but in a healthy or more nourishing way than the previous generations; she connects her intimate relationship with her mother as linked with her great-aunt Tita, "who will go on living as long as there is someone who cooks her recipes" (ibid.). In a sense, Esquivel writes a matricide so that, like a phoenix from the flames, a more promising, loving, and productive maternal genealogy–ending with Mama Elena and commencing with Tita–can begin.

That cooking is meaningful in creating this genealogy, Anna Marie Sandoval argues, is clear: "it is a literal border narrative. It also crosses borders through its form, one that has traditionally been associated with women – the recipe book" (58). Encapsulated in the novel's subtitle, *A novel in monthly instalments with Recipes, Romances, and Home Remedies*, Esquivel transforms a woman's space and her traditional labor with food from an imposed patriarchal space/labor into a mode of resistance and creativity. Tita uses cooking as an emotional outlet, seen for example when her lover Pedro marries her sister Rosaura. She cries so many bitter tears into the wedding cake batter that the guests get food poisoning and vomit.

Traditionally a woman's space, the kitchen is a way for Tita to bond with another woman, Nacha, the family's Indigenous servant (mirroring Catalina in Allende's novel). Nacha breastfeeds Tita as a baby because Mama Elena is still in shock from the death of her husband (he dies shortly after discovering her secret affair) and cannot produce milk: a symbol of her spiritual and physical maternal lack. This scene mirrors when, later in the novel, Tita magically produces milk for Roberto, Rosaura's and Pedro's son, because Rosaura cannot. Incidentally, Mama Elena forbids Tita from feeding Roberto any longer, which constitutes nothing less than infanticide in Tita's eyes because Roberto dies of starvation shortly after Pedro and Rosaura, under Mama Elena's orders, move to Texas.

Roberto's death causes Tita a nervous breakdown and her relocation to the house of the local doctor, Dr. Brown, who nurses her back to health. It is only, however, at the end of the novel, after Mama Elena's death, that Tita comes to terms with her mother. Tita opens a hidden box:

> It contained a diary and a packet of letters written to Mama Elena from someone named José Treviño. Tita put them in order by date and learned the true story of her mother's love. José was the love of her life. She hadn't been allowed to marry him because he had Negro blood in his veins. A colony of Negroes, fleeing from the Civil War in the United States, from the risk they ran of being lynched, had come to settle near the village. Young José Treviño was the product of an illicit love affair between the elder José Treviño and a beautiful Negress. When Mama Elena's parents discovered the love that existed between their daughter and this mulatto, they were horrified and forced her into an immediate marriage with Juan De la Garza, Tita's father. (137)

The narrator explains that "[t]he action didn't succeed in stopping her from keeping up a secret correspondence with José even after she was married, and it seemed that they hadn't limited themselves to that form of communication either, since according to the letters Gertrudis was José's child and not her father's" (ibid.). Like Marie's son, Samuel, in Piat's novel and Malinalli's in *Malinche*, Esquivel, once again, complicates the issue of racial origins in Mexico. Esquivel describes Mama Elena as a matriarch who inflicts the pain of her own life upon the lives of her daughters. Forbidden her true love and desires, as an act of vengeance, she forbids her daughters this experience. Esquivel underscores there is an inherent violence in the matriarchy, both physically and emotionally, when it operates essentially as a patriarchy.

Rebellious Sisters

Desperate for an escape from matriarchal rule, Esquivel's and Duong's novels include the rebellious sisters of the protagonists, who serve as foil characters. In Esquivel's novel, Gertrudis, unlike Tita, courageously stands up to Mama Elena. In one of the most memorable scenes of the novel, Getrudis takes a cold shower in order to suppress her sexual desires heightened after eating Tita's Quail in Rose Petal Sauce. Inflamed, she spontaneously runs naked through a field and is swooped up in dramatic-romantic fashion by one a rebel leader. Drawn to Gertrudis and the scent of rose petals, he believes "a higher power was controlling his actions" (Equivel, *Like Water for Chocolate* 55). Esquivel's parody of the popular romance novel's rescue paradigm is evident, particularly when Getrudis later works "in a brothel on the border" (58), a "transgressive" location and occupation for a woman. Gertrudis is in the process of forging "an underlying theme of rebellion, change, and momentum in the gender politics of the novel and confronts Mexican popular myths of femininity within the bloody conflict" (Dobrian 57). Susan Lucas Dobrian, writing on Getrudis, reaffirms Skipper's and Zapata's arguments that the backdrop of the Mexican Revolution serves as a sign of imminent political change. She writes:

> By placing the armed revolt within the context of female domesticity and frustration, Esquivel defines as a political act Gertrudis's revolt against her mother and the repressive demands of a rigid society. Gertrudis is successful not only in escaping the preordained female domesticity demanded by society, but she also achieves success in the male world, where might makes right, as she rapidly distinguishes herself as a *generala* of the Revolution and commands a regiment of men. (63)

Gertrudis' rebellion against traditional femininity (weakness, peace-loving, maternal) is clear, but this theme also finds resonance in Duong's novel *Daughters of the River Huong* with the defiant Aunt Ginseng.

Aunt Ginseng is Simone's great aunt who she never meets. She is described by Simone's mother, Dew, as a "black-clad tigress whose fate belonged to the Vietnamese goddess" (Duong 103) and, is compared to the infamous historical gold-armored Lady Trieu "fighting a war for the good of all of us" (101). Ginseng is portrayed as a "patriotic feminist," to use Djurdja Knezevic's term (67), because the first time she meets Dew she is dressed as a revolutionary soldier wearing black pajamas, sandals, and a straw hat (Duong 102). During this brief respite from the grim Indochina War between France and the Viet Minh, Ginseng declares her mother, the Mystique Concubine, a traitor to the nation. She tells her sister, Simone's grandmother, Cinnamon: "She betrayed all of us … Face up to reality, your revered mother slept with the enemy for wealth and security…People are dying every day and you are well fed!" (100). Like Malinalli, the protagonist of Esquivel's *Malinche*, the mother in this novel is portrayed as a traitor to the nation. In this case, however, we see the mother defined through her daughter's eyes.

As if in retribution for her mother's sins, Ginseng pays a price for national independence, seen on her return from Hoa Lo prison and the war in 1949. She is severely disfigured: "part of her upper lip was missing," "one little finger was missing," "a stooping, limping old woman with dead eyes and a scarred face," "scar tissues on her breasts. The nipples were missing" (Duong 104-05).

Duong's use of anaphora emphasizes Ginseng's loss of femininity and her physical identity as a woman, which stands as a contrast to her sister's and her mother's physical beauty. Psychologically traumatized, Ginseng repeatedly asks, "Do you have a womb and a pair of breasts?" (105);" her bodily mutilation and loss of identity result in her suicide and, though she sacrifices herself and her body for her people, in the end she is betrayed. Novels like Duong's, which contrast Ginseng's painful experiences with the very different lived experiences of the other women in her family, incite a re-read of Getrudis in Esquivel's novel. Dobrian maintains that:

> The diversity of female participants in the Mexican Revolution has been eclipsed and reduced to two common stereotypes: the submissive servant and the erotic enticer. Within this context, Esquivel's presentation of Gertrudis's escape from domesticity into war, where she successfully rises through the ranks, restores the image of the warrior woman that has been eliminated from history and myth. (64)

Dobrian's support for Esquivel's protagonist is questionable considering Gertudis' transformation at the end of the novel when she returns to the ranch for Esperanza's wedding: "in a model T Ford coupe … Stepping out of the car, she nearly dropped the huge wide-brimmed hat trimmed with ostrich feathers she was carrying. Her dress with its shoulder pads was the most daring, absolutely latest thing" (Esquivel 234). Esquivel's once rebellious warrior is now a beautiful sophisticated lady and mother who stands as a romanticized portrait, the same one Simone's mother once held for her own aunt until the grim reality of the war transformed her into the real Aunt Ginseng, a disfigured revolutionary.

Untouchable: Romance, Race, and Religion

In Viswanathan's novel *Toss of a Lemon*, the matriarch differs from both the Mystique Concubine and Mama Elena. Sivakami, unlike the Mystique Concubine, never has another sexual relationship after the death of her husband and she is in many ways less cruel and calculating than Mama Elena. Her strict adherence to her religious caste system, however, creates problems not only for herself but also for those in her family. Sivakami is thrust into her role as matriarch when her father marries her to Hanumarathnam, a man whose astrological signs signal a short-life. When the prophesized death becomes reality, Sivakami, after eight years of marriage, is left to run her household and raise her two children, Thangham and Vairum. Viswanathan exemplifies the rigidity of Sivakami's belief system when, upon his death bed, Hanumarathnam sits up straight and beckons Sivakami towards him, to which she responds that "no middle-class Brahmin wife with any kind of breeding walks through the main hall and talks to her husband in front of guests" (61). The Brahmin code, also, does not permit Muchami, the local boy Hanumarathnam has hired to help Sivakami run his fields and land after his death, to walk on the Brahmin street without being accompanied by a Brahmin . Sivakami, who refuses to let anyone see her cry after Hanumarathnam's death, embraces her instructions on operating the fields though she is not permitted to physically traverse them. While she has known other women who do the family accounting, she admits "she is the first she has known whose husband has trained her at these tasks, shown faith and approval in her abilities" (50). On her husband's death, Sivakami, still a very young woman, accepts her social destiny as a Brahmin-widow.

In a traditional ceremony, she is escorted through the street by her father, eldest brother, and son. On the riverbank, her brother tears her blouse and she exchanges her bright clothing and pendants of wifehood for "two white cotton saris that will be her only garments and her badge" (64). The most important aspect to this ritual from *sumangali* to *aamangali*, however, is the shaving of her hair. The loss of Sivakami's hair symbolizes her Brahmin-status of widow-hood as well as poses a threat to it as the barber is an untouchable: "From now on, she will be *madi*, maintain a state of preternatural purity from dark to dark, so that no one may touch her after her pre-sunrise bath until the sun sets. And she will be as invisible as any untouchable in the Brahmin quarter (65). The novel, in many ways, narrates Sivakami's struggle with consistently adhering to her new lifestyle and the spaces to which she is confined. This includes not being able to touch her own children before and after certain times and when her daughter Thangham marries she is not permitted to participate in, or even witness, the wedding (99).

The primary conflicts in the novel, however, are Sivakami's constant confrontations with Vairum, who has over the years renounced traditional Brahmanism. As a Brahmin, he is "to be married to Brahmin girls, live in Brahmin quarters, [and] eat only with Brahmins" (102). When her brother insists that Vairum attend a paadasaalai, a school for Brahmin priests instead of the secular one, Sivakami daringly decides to leave her father's household and her brothers to return to Cholapatti and run her former house with the aid of Muchami. Sivakami's defiance against her family stresses once again the protagonist's constant negotiation between a role that has been imposed on her and one that she in turn imposes upon herself, a strict traditionalism in combat with modern allowances for change.

Rememoriation: Feminist Mirrors, Hybrid Narratives, Spaces, and Histories

Feminist change in the women's historical novels in this chapter is recognizable by the "politically activated countermemories" (Braidotti, *Nomadic Subjects* 105). Hochberg adds that:

> With all the official evidence and records erased, it is the telling and re-telling of these memories alone that testifies to this painful past and keeps its memory alive … The act of passing down the memories is therefore a unidirectional process of creating knowledge, for it makes the past 'known' to both the teller and the receiver. (4)

In Viswanathan's novel, Sivakami's, the matriarch's, story is told in chronological order. Beginning with Sivakami as a ten-year-old Brahmin bride in the village of Cholapatti, India, the work ends with Sivakami's anonymous great-granddaughter retelling her own life in Canada and Sivakami's death in Pandiyoor, India (post British colonialism), 1966. The maternal genealogical link is made clear when the narrator reflects that "the tale has transmuted, passed from my great-grandmother into my mother into me, from old world into new" (616). While Viswanathan's novel is multi-vocal, it is told from a third-person perspective until the Epilogue when the narrator speaks in the first person. She writes, "my story, too, may no longer exist for those who lived it, because it is in English and they knew only Tamil, maybe some Sanskrit … So it is that I sit here with you, the book of our lives between us, telling my story, and my people's, in lands and languages I know but that are not my own" (ibid.). In *Toss of a Lemon*, geographical/linguistic/religious distances separate the women and the narrator is a Canadian immigrant.

Duong's heroine, Simone, is a refugee having fled the political and economic circumstances of her Vietnamese homeland in the 1970s to the Americas. As Renny Christopher notes, refugees:

> Came to it [the new country] not necessarily because of its own allure, but to escape often life-threatening circumstances, usually political or military, in the home country. Unlike immigrants, refugees perceive themselves as temporary residents in the new country waiting for the opportunity to return home. (70)

Simone's experiences as a refugee entail a looking back to her homeland and Vietnamese past while simultaneously living her present in the United States; in this way, the novel's crossing of time and geography creates a dynamic dialogue and transcultural bridge. Simone's memory plays an integral part in her life and narrative, as it does in all of the novels.

Christopher identifies that the trope of haunting is an important aspect of memory in Vietnamese and Vietnamese American literature. Referencing Kathleen Brogan, Christopher writes that "ghosts serve a different function than those in traditional Gothic narratives: working toward the 'recuperation of a people's history,' they register 'a widespread concern with questions of ethnic identity and cultural transmission'" (77). Clearly, the past and the wars of the past haunt Simone, but she attempts to reconstruct her identity by confronting her shared past by physically returning to Vietnam, her motherland, at the end of the novel and enacting a rememoriation of her female ancestors.

Simone's desire to create a maternal genealogy adheres to what Hochberg describes as a form of resymbolization. The tracing back in Duong's work is achieved by analyzing, first, the 'uncomfortable' marriage of Simone's great-grandmother to the King of Annam and her affair with the French Resident Superior, Sylvan Foucault. The novel, then, traces Simone's relationship with Foucault's grandson Andre and her marriage to Christopher, an American journalist.

A recurring dream prompts Simone to realize that "it must be my cultural subconscious mind that created those dreams and all my nostalgia … I bear in me the collective subconsciousness of an extinct culture, with all its tragedy" (Duong17). Christopher reminds Simone that it is not just this interpretation that explains her unhappiness as a war refugee-American immigrant but also the always present prehistory of a Vietnamese duchess who was "sold off in exchange for the Cham's lands" (ibid.). The importance of memory (in this case, a memory of historical-mythical women), in the feminist novel is manifest; just as Sivakami and the women in her family are imagined in her great-granddaughter's story, Simone establishes a generational and historical connection between herself and the Vietnamese women in her family, beginning with her great-grandmother the Mystique Concubine.

Returning to mythology, the purpose of Duong's work, like Irigaray's, is "not in order to recover a lost, authentic, feminocentric 'origin' which lies behind and before patriarchal appropriations of myths but in order to reread, to (re)invent and reappropriate" (Haigh 63). The Mystique Concubine, Simone's great grandmother, is formerly known as Huyen Phi, an orphan making her living by paddling passengers across the River Huong. Huyen Phi relates how "we, the Chams, are the disappearing Hindu minorities of central Vietnam (Duong 41). Her family, originally traders in cinnamon and ginseng (later the names for her children), was forced to relinquish their living with the advent of French colonialism. Beginning a new way of life as a river paddler, Huyen Phi rationalizes her art as being tied to the loss of her Champa Kingdom and learning the folk songs of her people. The Champa Queen, in particular, holds significance for Huyen Phi:

> The Viets captured the queen of Champa and transported her by boat back to the north. The exodus began in the rivers of our kingdom. Under a full moon, the captured queen, crying for the defeated, jumped into the river and drowned herself. The surviving Chams called out to after her, Mee-Ey, Mee-Ey, meaning 'that noble woman.' The sound Mee-Ey entered history and was mistaken as the name of the Champa Queen ... The Chams believed Mee-Ey's soul never left the water. (42)

The River Huong is connected to the maternal lineage and matriarchal figure evident in the novel's title *Daughters of the River Huong* and subtitle: *A Vietnamese royal concubine and her descendants*.

The River Huong, located in Hue, Vietnam, is described by Duong in maternal terms. It is personified as a woman, a Spirit (33) whose perfume or scent–the literal translation of the word "Huong" (25) – lingers. The river, also, serves as a motherland in the text. Huyen Phi, the Cham descendent who earns a living like her ancestors paddling passengers across the river (41), meets her future husband in this manner. She ferries him from shore to shore whilst singing the songs of her people and past. Enamored by her charm, the King of Annam quickly marries her and settles her in the Royal Palace. The Mystique Concubine (1895-1930) and the River Huong meld together, expressing a fluidity of identity, and create a matriarchal figure and setting for the novel. Huyen Phi's eunuch servant, Son La, tells his new mistress that "Cham societies are matriarchal, my Lady. The Cham woman takes control of her household" (73). His claim reverberates in the novel cross-generationally.

Simone's memories of her great-grandmother carry over to her "real" memories of her grandmother Que (Cinnamon) who, during the period of civil war, runs the family's silk business. The business, the reader learns, was started by Huyen Phi and her royal chambermaid Mai, after the King of Annam abdicated and was exiled. Cast out by the French and forced to make a living, the women's struggles mirror Simone's for financial/emotional independence following the war with America. Simone begins and ends the novel with her memoirs as a lawyer living in New York 1985 and New Jersey 1994 respectively. Unlike canonical historical novels, many women's historical novels containing maternal genealogies are not chronological and they begin in the living time of the author. Duong's is one example, and Soueif's novel is another.

Amal, the co-protagonist in *The Map of Love*, a position she shares with Anna Winterbourne, lives in Cairo while her brother Omar, a famous playboy conductor, diaspora intellectual, and Palestinian supporter (Omar is commonly believed to be a portrait of postcolonial theorist Edward Said), lives in the United States with his on-again-off-again girl-friend Isabel. Similar to Duong's and Viswanathan's novels, the narrative switches between past and present in retelling two simultaneous cyclical tales: Amal's own contemporary life in the twentieth century and the story of her British-Egyptian great-aunt Anna Winterbourne in the nineteenth century. Fulfilling what Suzanne Keen identifies as a "romance of the archive," the novel's plot unfolds when Isabel brings Amal her great-grandmother's trunk. It is Amal's job as quasi-detective to unravel the family's secrets by piecing together her relative's life from the contents of the trunk as/since many pieces are written in Arabic; as translator, Amal's "'research features as a kernel plot action, resulting in a strong closure, with climatic discoveries and rewards" (Keen, *Romances* 35). Amal's actions, likewise, evoke history by "looking back from a post-imperial context" and put into question methodologies for accessing the past (35), which suggests history does not create the archive–the archive creates history. As a novel reconstructing the archive and official history through a gendered lens, it is also very much an explication of a transnational past and family.

Waïl S. Hassan, in his discussion of translation theory, notes the similarities between the converging plots:

> The British military occupation of Egypt (1882–1956) and, later, United States foreign policy and its self-serving advocacy of free-market globalization. Each story involves an Egyptian political activist and a woman—English and American, respectively—who travels to Egypt. The 1990s lovers, Omar al-Ghamrawi and Isabel Parkman, discover their kinship to the 1900s couple, Sharif al-Baroudi and Anna Winterbourne. Thus, the principal characters represent branches of a multinational family that extends from Egypt to England, France, and the United States, undercutting the myth of autonomous national or cultural identities. (757)

Hassan, however, fails to point out the 'incest' of this kinship in the novel, which winds around the family.

Omar, after having a sexual relationship with Isabel in New York, reveals he also had a sexual relationship with Isabel's mother, Jasmine, many years ago. The novel is unclear as to the possibility that Omar may, in fact, be Isabel's father. The possibility of incest complicates the dynamics of the family, particularly when Isabel gives birth to Omar's son, Sharif (Soueif 468). Perhaps the implication in the novel is that politics and family are intertwined and anchored in history more than we typically imagine; therefore, the mater-familial saga suggests before a nation's politics can change, a re-examination of the family is necessary.

Important within Soueif's transnational family is multi-lingualism. Both Anna and Isabel begin to learn Arabic, Amal and Omar speak Arabic, Anna and Sharif each speak French (this is initially how they communicate), and Isabel, Omar, and Amal converse in English. The learning of an other's language is a path towards understanding in the text and extends to the reader. Soueif provides a ten-page glossary (a common form of paratext in women's historical novels) at the back of the novel highlighting for the reader textual references to Arabic idioms and vocabulary. It is a means for culturally linking the novel to the reader and the life of the protagonist Anna Winterbourne in Egypt. Anna makes the shift in the novel from the position of, what seems at first, the straightforward travel narrative of a colonizer and English widow (her husband Edward, horrified by his fighting in Sudan, dies), to the anti-colonial wife of an Arabic man and active participant in Egypt's political scene, including the fight for independence.

Hassan also connects with the act of translation Anna's cross-dressing (Soueif 761). Anna, in order to escape the enclave and insularity of the British in Cairo, dresses as a man so that she may explore the city. This unique vantage point allows her access into a world in which she would normally be forbidden. The dangers of this masquerading, however, culminate when she is mistakenly taken prisoner as a British officer by Egyptian nationalists. The kidnapping does, however, warrant her first occasion for meeting a native Egyptian woman, Layla al-Barudi (Amal's maternal grandmother), and Layla's brother, Sharif. Meeting the brother and sister allows Anna entrance into an unfamiliar world, including the harem, and a personally guided trip to Mt. Sinai, where she falls in love with Sharif. Yet, as Hassan argues, "they pay a price for carving out this transgressive, translational space in the ideologically stratified world of empire: her compatriots shun her, and his suspect him of collaborating with the occupation; this suspicion leads to his assassination" (762). The other aspect of Sharif's campaign that causes much controversy and hatred is his advocating for female education, perhaps showing that cultural influence is a two-way street in that Anna is a highly educated woman.

Anna's journal, also a sign of her education, serves as a way for Soueif to dispel Orientalist myths and imagery associated with EgyptThe stereotype of the repressed/oppressed harem woman, an image that initially seduces Anna into travelling to Egypt in the first place is characterized by Catherine Wynne. Wynne writes:

> Soueif's text reappraises the Victorian female traveller in the
> context of empire and as such mirrors current feminist ap-

proaches to women's travel writing. Sara Mills argues that the
writings of female travellers do not fit neatly into an Orientalist
framework and often seem to 'constitute an undermining voice'
within the colonial discourse. (61)

By realizing the complexity of historical realities during British occupation and
national instability, at the end, Anna fulfills Sharif's deathbed request that she
return to England with their daughter Nur (Soueif 513).

In all of these novels, there is a firm resistance to perpetuating the painful
past. Hochberg notes that "as long as the centrality of mother (as a source of
one's name, past, identity, genealogy) is based on the commitment to a past of
suffering, loss, and exclusion, it keeps women attached to the place of the
wound" (6). There is the need for return, knowing that one cannot ever truly
return, in order for there to be departure; as the narrative must move beyond its
confines, so, too, must the status of women in the mater-familial saga. Anna's
departure for England, thus, need not be interpreted as a failure or a regressive
return to colonial times. She finally returns 'home' changed, and with her entire
knowledge system altered and shaken. The novel is a way for Soueif to suggest
that history is repetitive if we want it to be, but it can also be altered. By layer-
ing Amal's story with Anna's, there are clearly textual overlaps, but also there
are divergences. If Soueif's novel is to be trusted, she suggests that current day
tensions between the Arabic and Western worlds can be disrupted and inter-
vened upon most effectively by women. Women are the key in remapping
these new relations and serve important roles as cultural mediators, translators,
and interlocutors.

The past serves a reflective basis for the reader, writer, and protagonist to
shape her identity, suggesting identity (and a sense of self) is fluid and always
in transition. The authors in this chapter suggest the use of mirrors is foundational in women's historical novels. Mirrors effectively blend or blur fiction
and fact as well as the past and present. Like Malinalli, who in Esquivel's *Malinche*, regrets defining herself through Cortés's image of her, transnational
family sagas emphasize a maternal lineage both within and outside of the text
by explicitly linking the past to the present, often to the effect of obscuration.
Though there are concurrent narratives in the same novel, the overall whole is
one of layered unity.

In Duong's novel, Simone's affairs with the Frenchman Andre and the
American journalist Christopher mirror the Mystique Concubine's illicit affair
with Sylvan Foucault, the Frenchman proclaimed Vietnam's enemy. When
looking at exotic-erotic postcards of her great-grandmother, Simone notes, "I
recognized myself in those photographs. It was also the face. The woman had
the same face as mine, as though I were in the portrait" (218). When she sees

her grandmother Que and great-aunt Ginseng sitting on Foucault's lap, she remarks, "I saw again, my own face on the two little girls" (219). Simone's reflections occur just prior to her return to Vietnam, whereby she hopes to re-establish the family and give legal aid to poor Vietnamese. Duong's technique of blurring one life with another resonates with Irigaray's thinking in *This Sex Which is Not One*, wherein she articulates that a recognition and separation between women is necessary:

> Contiguity was the figure for mother and daughter: the two lips represented (among other things) the two women continually in touch with each other. But even then, Irigaray was warning that contiguity in patriarchy could mean fusion and confusion of identity between women, and thus the impossibility of relation-ships between them (since they were not separate enough for the 'between' to exist), and the impossibility of a maternal ge-nealogy. (Whitford, "Section III" 161)

The strategy of mirroring found in Simone's reading of her great-grandmother's journal, as recorded by Son-La, also occurs in Soueif's novel when Amal reads Anna's journal.

Mirroring is evident as Amal traces her life back to her British ancestor An-na and the spaces the novel occupies. Just as Tita and Sivakami negotiate des-ignated woman's spaces, "through the representation of the harem as desirable domestic space Soueif's revisionist project advances a positive vision of nine-teenth-century Arab-Muslim domesticity and culture" (Wynne 56-57). Anna's experiences with Layla, who authors some of the letters Amal reads, convey a sense of mirrors and space. When Sharif invites a number of prominent politi-cal leaders in support of ending the Occupation to his home, they quickly turn to discussing what Anna spells as "*Al-Mar'ah al-Jadidah*, 'The New Woman'" (Soueif 374). Layla, ecstatic about how quickly Anna is learning Arabic, asks her to translate by changing two diacritics. The word is "Mir-aah," which Anna recognizes after a gesture to a large mirror. She asks, "why are the words so close? ... 'Woman' and 'mirror'" (375). The answer is accounted for in the novel, as "drawing attention to the maternalist, quasi-feminist roots of political and religious terms" (Heilmann and Llewellyn, *Neo-Victorianism* 96) but also suggests Soueif's linking of woman with visibility and woman as a reflection of society.

One of Sharif's compatriots has recently argued for women to be educated in the same way as men and to have a choice whether or not to wear the veil. In order to listen to the conversation more closely, Anna and Layla enter in a small box behind heavily drawn curtains, "in front of them the mashrabiyya that looks down to the salamlek" (Soueif 377). Soueif relates this secret space back to her description of the question of the New Woman and the veil. Layla and Anna, much like when they wear the veil, have the power to see men without being seen. Mariadele Boccardi writes that Anna takes "on the very characteristics with which 'the classic scene of [western] travel literature' invested the Orient in an 'unexpected reversal of the gaze'" (109). A view from within, rather than outside the harem, which is the common western viewpoint, is "made possible by the fact that Soueif's protagonist is a woman" (Boccardi 110). Boccardi adds that "the harem occupied a privileged place in the Western imaginary as the epitome of all that is most desirable because forbidden, exotic because socially most different … about the Orient" (ibid.). The veil women wear is, by extension, like the harem, a sign of the exotic and the forbidden for westerners.

Anna, a British woman married to an Egyptian and living in Egypt, views her compatriots from within the harem and normalizes this space. Imparting her own gaze, she also blurs the boundaries between "Orientalism" and "Occidentalism" and gender objectification. This unfamiliar act/space further reminds her of being in an Italian church confessional, again emphasizing the clandestine, sacred, and forbidden. With Anna, there is an ongoing exchange of her Victorian social code transferred-translated into an Egyptian one with different constraints, such as the haremlek. Though Amal's contemporary tale no longer invokes the harem Anna experiences, Wynne suggests that Soueif does create "a female-centred, hybrid family in which the child promises regeneration at least within a familial context" (64) and concludes that "*The Map of Love*'s return to domesticity and family provides only transient respite from the relentless political exclusivity of East and West" (65). Soueif's linguistic connection between "woman" and "mirror" in the novel, once again, implies that women are the mirrors of social ills and national tensions, and that the domestic, whether formally/officially divided or not, is never separate from the political.

Politics of Exile; Nostalgia

The nostalgic longing for home the heroines experience is manifested symbolically, psychically, and physically in these transnational mater-familial sagas. For example, Sivakami, the matriarch in *Toss of a Lemon*, in the most important episode in Viswanathan's novel, is banished by her son Vairum from his house because she cannot accept his modern ways, for instance eating dinner with non-Brahmins (544). Sivakami initially travelled to Vairum's grand city-house in Madras because Vani, his wife, by means of a miracle in the eyes of the family, is pregnant. Sivakami, like many of the women discussed in this work, is known as a skilled mid-wife and for her luck with births; thus, Vani, who views Sivakamias a mother, summons her (534).

After a lengthy period of time during which Vani has still not given birth, Sivakami, finally, confronts Vairum. Unwilling to discuss the matter, he commands her to "go" (546). Viswanathan writes: "this is the first time in sixty years that she has gone anywhere alone. She feels naked, invisible, petrified" (547). Though nighttime, Sivakami makes her way to the train station and onto a train. The space typically granted to a Brahmin-widow is a fantasy and she is forced to stand pressed against the bodies of others. Her inexperience with travelling also shows. In the early morning she makes her stop at Kottai to change trains, but is robbed while washing her face: "Her bundle is gone – her money, her ticket, her Kamba-Ramayanam" (551). Viswanathan suggests that traditional Brahmins must confront a changing India–it is a time when a Brahmin widow will be robbed, have their sacred texts stolen, and Brahmin sons will kick their own mothers out of their homes.

Sivakami's journey is a forced journey and she must find her own way home to Cholapatti without any money, provisions, or urban awareness. Attempting to grasp her bearings, she decides to find her grand-daughter's Saradha's house in Thiruchi, reasoning that her best bet is to follow the train along the railway tracks, symbolizing modernity and the break-down of the rigid caste system in India as well as the woman who has lived within this socio-framework. Sivakami is an aging woman; like the inevitably aging body and the crumbling shrine to Ganesha Sivakami prays to on her journey, Viswanathan suggests change in a new India cannot be stopped. This is evident in several places in the novel, but notably in the celebrity success of Bharati, Goli's illegitimate daughter, who becomes a movie star. Despite Bharati's stardom, Sivakami refuses to acknowledge her. Even after she is invited by Vairum, to the horrors of all the others, to eat in Sivakami's home, at the end of the novel, in Sivakami's eyes, this means; "the house is defiled" (609).

Changes continue to rapidly occur, among which are increasing violence against Brahmins (582-83) and Janaki, the most traditional of the grandchildren, moves into her own household instead of living with the family under one roof. Viswanathan writes: "It is mid-August when finally the two couples move into their own homes, the week India gains independence and Pakistan splits off: a country born, a country split, parturition and partition. Northern corridors run with blood – families abandon homes, families abandon families" (570). As in so many women's historical novels, the disintegration of the family mirrors the fragmentation of traditional national values and social codes, in this case India's. The trek, like most (including Sivakami's final choice not to hurl herself under an oncoming train), prompts her existentially questioning her own purpose and lifestyle: "she has always thought of her life as a series of submissions to God. What if she has been making her own decisions all along" (556)? She finally arrives, confused, at Saradha's house, who, stupefied by her appearance, takes her in, allows her to recover, and has her escorted back "home" again–like Anna's return to England, and Tita's from Dr. Brown's house, and Simone's decision to relocate back to Vietnam, a forever changed woman.

The transnational mater-familial saga suggests the refugee-immigrant's deep desire to always return to the birth nation (evident, even if romantically, by the future generation no longer living in its maternal ancestor's homeland, i.e., the Canadian narrator in Viswanathan's novel) and the difficulty or impossibility in truly ever being able to fully culturally assimilate to the culture or nation of an other. Samantha Haigh writes:

> The quest for Motherland embarked upon by the narrator ... becomes a continuation of that attempt to articulate an undefinable 'homesickness' ... This homesickness, emblematic of women's social and symbolic dereliction, can be articulated only through a (re)invention of the maternal genealogy, that broken line of mothers and daughters which the narrator is here attempting to restore. (69)

Once returned to her home, Sivakami's final transformation occurs. Bharati and Goli, the father no one has seen in years, are invited to eat by Vairum. Vairum beckons Sivakami to cross the main hall in the same manner as Hanumarathnam had previously, only this time she concedes:

> No Brahmin widow walks through her main hall in front of guests. How the neighbours would talk! But Sivakami is not the woman she used to be. Her house is not defiled– this is not her house [technically Vairum's]. And she left her fear walking a train track near Thurichi. She can't lose her son the way she lost her husband: without a word. She goes to Vairum. (611)

The result of Vairum forcing his mother to face Goli and his illegitimate child is Muchami and Sivakami simultaneously suffering strokes. They are, literally, paralyzed and the maternal bond between Sivakami and Vairum is forever severed.

"Magical Feminist" Objects and Spiritual History[13]

Integral to exploring the potential of women's domestic spaces and forming a maternal genealogy in the woman's historical novel is identifying the im-

---

[13] "Magical feminist" is the title of an Interview between Allende, Jennifer Benjamin and Sally Engelfried (1994).

portance of magical heirlooms or objects connected with the mother or the motherland. Hochberg stresses the liberating potential of the maternal ability:

> Not only to remember but also to invent stories about the past, both the immediate and the mythical, as a way to transcend the horrors of women's daily existence. Imagination, storytelling, and magic, rather than 'real memory,' seem to be the means through which women ... [can] strive to displace, or at least to survive, history. (8)

Though typically associated with Latin American historical novelists, magical realism or magical feminism occurs in many women's historical novels. Antonio Planells argues "magical realism" is *una categoría de la literatura fantastic a que reacciona contra el realism literario*" 'a category of fantastic literature that reacts against realist literature' (9). Fusing fantasy or magic with accepted reality, feminist novels like Esquivel's or Allende's have prominently shaped historical fiction, though they are often overshadowed by male authors like Gabriel García Márquez.

Caroline Bennett expresses the limitation of this view point: "Latin American fiction in the magical realist style, despite its authors' expressed desire to find a voice for oppressed people, frequently adopts a patriarchal tone, ignoring the role of women in society" (171). Thus, feminist writers attempt "to redress the balance by exploring women's colonization and repression by patriarchy, and the means by which they endeavor to resist the oppressive, dominant ideologies in which they are inscribed" (ibid.). Patricia Hart defines magic feminism as a "femino-centric magic realism" (105):

> Magic feminism occurs in works in which real and impossible (or wildly improbable) events are juxtaposed, when this juxtaposition is narrated matter-of-factly, and when the telling of the apparently impossible events leads to the understanding of deeper truths that hold outside of the text. In addition, conventional notions of time, place, matter, identity, or logical cause and effect are often challenged. The result of reading this may very well be to change the reader's perceptions of what reality is or should be. When these processes occur in a feminocentric work, a work centered on women, their status, and their condition, we may speak of magic feminism. (105-06)

In Duong's *Daughters of the River Huong*, it is her great-grandmother's objects, the "four symbols of her heritage–the jade phoenix, the two ivory plaques, and the lacquer divan" that fulfill this magical role (167).

Nguyễn Thị Hiền discusses the importance of spirituality and its relation to memory in Vietnam. She writes that "[f]olk beliefs were regarded as backward practices and were officially banned" (Hiền 544) from the time of 1946 to 1986 which explains Simone and Grandma Que's clandestine activity in visiting Mai, her former servant. Mai has an altar dedicated "to the female deities and goddesses of Vietnam" as she has "developed the psychic ability to communicate with the dead, review the past and foretell the future" (24). Engaging in a séance with Mai leaves Simone feeling embodied by the history of her ancestors: "that was how the Spirit of the River Huong first spoke to me in 1965, through Mey Mai's wrinkled mouth and eyes, in the clear voice of a young woman. The spirit told me that she resided in the river and would wait for me there. She went on to tell me her life story as the Mystique Concubine of the Violet City" (33). The importance of visionaries in Vietnam's history, Thị Hiền suggests, is the reason for the state, in 2004, finally recognizing that "'the activities of folk beliefs are activities representing the veneration of ancestors, commemoration and honoring of those who had great merit towards the country and people; the veneration of spirits, traditional symbols and other activities of folk beliefs which are typical for good values in history, culture and social ethics'" (547). Reappraising spirit mediums and their undeniable influence on the Vietnamese psyche is, thus, one of the tasks the novel sets out to accomplish.

Spirituality also informs Viswanathan's *Toss of a Lemon* and the life of Sivakami. It is the ancient palm leaves of Hanumarathnam, the only man in any of the novels to truly work as a natural healer, that have "recorded mysteries of the universe" and her children's astral portraits" (71). The importance of astrology is reflected in the novel's title as the toss of a lemon marks, for Hanumarathnam, the exact time a child is born; the midwife is to throw the lemon out of the window as a sign so that he may record the child's future–which, of course, directly influences his own future (and forebears his eventual death).

One of the most symbolic items, carrying this cultural weight, in Soueif's *The Map of Love* is the tripartite panel Anna weaves – her weaving, her "subversive stitchings," like so many women's historical novels, is "a metaphor for the feminist project of revision" (Heilmann and Llewellyn, *Neo-Victorianism* 91). The tapestry of the ancient Egyptian Goddess Isis, her brother Osiris and "between them the infant Horus" is a symbol of Anna's "contribution to the Egyptian renaissance" (Soueif 403). In the novel's present, Omar sends Amal his part of the panel, Isis, while Amal has Osiris. The third piece, however, is missing until Isabel declares she has magically found it in her bag (495). Isabel reasons that the missing panel was slipped into her bag when she paid a visit to the Baroudi's family residence in Tawasi (292). Making her way into a courtyard, Isabel, greeted by a woman, is led to a tomb guarded by a man wearing "the white turban of a sheikh" (294). The couple shares a drink with Isabel and converses in Arabic before she leaves. When Amal and Isabel return to the house the next day, the shrine is locked: "[l]ocked and padlocked and covered in cobwebs as it had been before" (307). They are, likewise, informed that there is no sheikh in charge and there hasn't been one for over a year. Isabel, upon finding the missing panel in her bag months later, claims, "the woman in the mosque. Umm Aya. She put it there" (500). Amal denies this possibility and Soueif never provides a concrete answer for Amal's uncertainty, only that she, over a hundred years later, finally, has the whole panel, and the continuity between past and present lives (Ancient Egyptian, Christian, Muslim) is complete.

Sharif's death signals the initial separation of the panel, and is reversed by the end of the novel with Omar's probable death. Osiris, in the Egyptian myth, is torn into pieces, has his body scattered by his brother Seth, and is gathered later by his faithful Isis, who searches for and collects his dismembered pieces. Susan Gubar and Sandra Gilbert suggest that "the traditional figure of Isis in search of Osiris is really a figure of Isis in search of herself" (99); in Soueif's novel, this symbolizes a new beginning, a new myth for Isabel (Isis) and her son fathered by Omar, Sharif (Horus). This resonates with the words of Mabrouka, the Baroudi's Ethiopian maid: "from the dead come the living, the branch is cut but the tree remains" (516). The family (possibly incestuous given Osiris and Isis were brother and sister and Omar could be Isabel's father) is, finally, reunited on the eve of the twenty-first century, suggesting, much like Esquivel's novel, a chance for rebirth.

In Esquivel's *Como Agua Para Chocolate*, special objects share specific meaning for women. Stephen Butler Murray notes that the Catholic faith and God play a minor role in Esquivel's novel due to the narrative importance of female ancestors such as Nacha, Mama Elena, and Luz del amanecer (John Brown's Kikapú grandmother) in the form of spirits. These spirits meaningfully shape the physical world, which leads Murray to conclude that "the ending affirms that the spiritual legacy endures, informing the cultural inheritance and the artefact of the cookbook that bears them witness" (103). Thus, the cookbook is an artefact bestowed with spiritual meaning and serves as a sign of woman's cultural heritage.

Elisa Christie suggests that the "cookbook-journal is a physical archive for the gendered knowledge and culture of the kitchenspace" (113). An alternative archive to traditional history is offered; a maternal archive that caters to women's knowledge and experiences is passed down across generations, including after Tita's death. The only item to survive the fire, her cookbook becomes an invaluable source of inspiration and identification for her Chicana niece Esperanza and Esperanza's daughter, much like how Mexican/Chicana readers might identify with Esquivel's characters today.

Tita's nurturing relationship with food and cooking begins with Nacha. María Teresa Martínez-Ortiz writes that it is the "power of the 'curandera' (the female healer of the Mexican Indigenous mythology), … who becomes her nurturer and spiritual guide from birth" (175). From Nacha, Tita learns that plants and vegetation have a dual purpose–consumption and healing–and, in life, women are responsible for knowledge of both. Tita preserves this episteme in her memory and in her associations of specific foods, including their smells, tastes, and touch, with specific memories. Efraín Garza believes that "*el personaje que más muestra esa capacidad de relacionar el presente con el pasado por medio de una perceptión olfativa es Tita* 'the character that best shows this capacity for relating the present with the past through her olfactory perceptions is Tita' (9). Unable to translate the sensuality and sensory pleasure food awards her, Tita writes her recipes down. Is this why Gertrudis, whom Tita tells to follow the recipe exactly, cannot effectively make the cakes? Getrudis does not possess the kind of knowledge that only comes through culinary experience. Dobrian argues that "culinary activity involves not just the combination of prescribed ingredients, but something personal and creative emanating from the cook, a magical quality which transforms the food and grants it powerful properties that go beyond physical satisfaction to provide spiritual nourishment as well" (60). Sensuality is, also, an important aspect to cooking, and, as Rosaura's marriage to Pedro shows, requires more than mechanics.

For Tita, cooking and the spaces of *la cocina* offer an escape from her matriarchal mother. Christie suggests that "the gendered nature of the 'kitchenspace' and the gendered knowledge transmitted to younger generations within its realm are essential elements in the fictional and real world of Mexican society" (106). She further argues that "kitchenspace" becomes an important site for women "in establishing alliances and maintaining reciprocity networks" (Christie 108). The dynamics of the kitchenspace, embodied by women and constituted as feminine, are played out in Esquivel's novel; we see a variety of experiences and social hierarchies (a familial microcosm in the political macrocosm) within this domain ranging from Rosaura's and Getrudis' relative lack of skill and uncomfortability to Tita's and Nacha's expertise and sense of respite or refuge.

The objects in these novels not only connect back to a maternal source but also carry spiritual significance. The means to heal through food is central to Esquivel's novel, evident when the ghost of Luz del amanecer heals Tita after her nervous breakdown caused by the death of Roberto. John Brown, also, serves as a rare example of a male healer interested in traditional-Indigenous methods inherited from his grandmother combined with his formal medical training. While healing, Tita confronts her mother in life, and she faces her mother's ghost. Tita tells Mama Elena she hates her, a sentiment that has the effect of both dismissing the ghost for good and causing Tita's menstruation to begin (after she was certain she was pregnant with Pedro's child). Mama Elena's final retaliation is to knock candles over, which burn Pedro severely, though Tita nurses him back to health with the aid of Nacha's herbal remedies.

Supernatural objects and occurrences in conjunction with the experiential gendered knowledge the novels employ suggest what Pamela Butler and Jigna Desai refer to as the only possibility for the protagonists to create a sense of belonging or identity in a globalized world (22-23). The authors maintain that through the use of magical realism "the possibility of counter-hegemonic visions of social realities" can be imagined, thus, "the use of the supernatural here subverts dominant notions of reality in an unjust world, allowing minority visions and perspectives to be realized" (Butler and Desai 23) in addition to alternative epistemes. As is the case for many protagonists in the mater-familial saga, Tita's relationship with her niece Esperanza supports Haigh's claims that "in order to find herself, she must first find her mother" (65). The transnational mater-familial saga suggests that women must invent a future for themselves by revisiting and sharing the maternal past. In order to make this *affidamento* more than an imaginary space, Irigaray suggests that "women must love one another as mothers, with a maternal love, and as daughters, with a filial love" (*Ethics of Sexual Difference* 89). The woman's historical novel allows for a unique vantage point in critiquing matriarchal societies that are run and operated by women along patriarchal parameters and celebrating those which break with patriarchy in favor of symbolic relationships and exchanges by women between women.

Conclusion

This chapter explored, through the sub-themes of forbidden romances, rebellious sisters, rememoriation, exile, mirrors, and sacred objects, the role of women in the nineteenth and twentieth centuries as complex matriarchs and the difficulty for women-as daughters in both distancing and recognizing themselves in their mothers. Esquivel, more so than other authors, shows the suffocating aspect of this family organization in *Como Agua Para Chocolate*. In Viswanathan's *Toss of a Lemon*, Sivakami copes as best she can with the matriarchal role in which she is thrust, though her son ultimately cuts the umbilical cord: "the first bond with the mother," "before any cutting, any cutting up of their lives into fragments" (*Irigaray Reader* 39). Though her daughter Thangham and her grandchildren respect and revere her, they, too, regard her Brahmin traditionalism as old-fashioned and not a way in which they want to live. Both Duong's *Daughters of the River Huong* and Soueif's *The Map of Love*, by contrast, emphasize the positive attributes of a matriarchal figure and pay particular homage to the maternal for their protagonists' own sense of identity, memories, and belonging. The novels share a questioning and searching for maternal origins within a transnational-transgenerational context, a search that bears directly on the present narrator-author as émigré-exile-refugee. There is the implicit argument that woman cannot move forward without negotiating and confronting her past, both in a shared and personal sense; thus, history plays an indispensable role as a critical mirror in these texts. Rethinking the mater-familial-saga as a means for creating communal ties with women, these novels take up the challenge of working towards feminist social change and are a promise for rebirth and reconnection with our maternal ancestors through writing our own lives alongside their lives.

CHAPTER FIVE

A New Sexual Politics of Space: Working Mothers

> The overthrow of mother right was the world historical defeat
> of the female sex
> – Friedrich Engels, *Origins of the Family, Private Property,
> and the State*

A timely and popular theme in women's historical novels is revisiting the working mother. Post 1970s novels narrate, from a variety of transnational positions and perspectives, the similar economic circumstances of working women and the potential to make the transition from poverty to wealth, not by marriage, but by employment. The time-setting circa the Industrial Revolution in Britain remains the most popular background for women's historical novels centered on working mothers. For example, Catherine Cookson's *The Rag Nymph* (1991) narrates the life of an English rag and bones woman in the 1850s who takes in a young girl whose mother is incarcerated for prostitution, in Posie Graeme-Evans' *The Dressmaker* (2010), Ellen Gowan goes from poverty to wealth by owning her own dress-making business in 1850s London, and, finally, Elizabeth Hickey's *The Wayward Muse* (2008) narrates the life of Jane Burden's social rise as a model and muse for artist Dante Gabriel Rossetti. I take a broader approach starting with the end of the seventeenth century in Iran to the mid-twentieth century in the United States, to show how diverse writing on gendered divisions of labor is. Shifting away from industrial Europe allows for a transnational focus on the working woman to be centralized; it also allows one to see how women writers are representing both differences and similarities across cultures and time periods between women, which is evidence of a deep contemporary concern for the very real problem of the feminization of poverty on a global scale.

In centering on the life of a working mother, considered a social taboo in all of these works that range from seventeenth century Iran to the American South in the 1960s, the novels depict the complexity of designating spaces as gendered and social uncomfortability both then and now with women, particularly mothers, who work outside of the home. As Anita Ilta Garey notes, since the Industrial Revolution, there has been a social trend rationalizing the claim that "employed women with children are seen as less than fully committed moth-

ers" (7). Relatedly, Ann Taylor Allen suggests that, in the 1970s, a new feminist epistemology (Simone de Beauvoir, Germaine Greer, Juliet Mitchell,
Adrienne Rich) took hold in Western Europe and challenged the nuclear family. Many women rejected motherhood as irreconcilable with being employed
and began "repudiating the cult of patriotic motherhood [and] they defined
childrearing as an individual choice" (Allen 233). Given this view, at the same
time, "the work of married women outside the home had begun to be accepted
by public opinion" (225). Reconciling or balancing one's traditional maternal
duties (childrearing, household chores, cooking etc.) with a career continues,
however, to be a difficult challenge and both motherhood and women's work
require continual redefinition.

The texts analyzed here foreground and draw from this feminist movement
by highlighting subversive sexualities and mobilities between domains by the
heroines, which, the authors suggest, could not be possible if the women did
not have the love and support of other women and the opportunity to earn an
income. Within each work, like in chapter four, the father figure–the patriarch
as breadwinner, head of the family, legal citizen and owner of his wife and
children–is dramatically displaced and questioned. I examine critical approaches to divisions of labor between men and women within the home and the public sphere, and how women are described as either "work oriented or family
oriented" (Garey 6) in relation to Alice Walker's *The Color Purple* (1982),
Belinda Starling' *The Journal of Dora Damage* (2006), Bett Norris' *Miss
McGhee* (2007), Anita Amirrezvani's *The Blood of Flowers* (2007), and Joyce
Lebra's *The Scent of Sake* (2009). Adrienne Rich notes that in the nineteenth
century, as is evident in Starling's and Lebra's novels, "women's work was
clearly subversive to the 'home' and to patriarchal marriage; not only might a
man find himself economically dependent on his wife's earnings but it would
conceivably even be possible for women to dispense with marriage from an
economic point of view" (*Of Woman Born* 49). I read the concerns identified
by Rich as reappearing in today's novels as contemporary fears and anxieties.

In addition, each work resonates with a transnational feminist concern for
legally redefining marriage and the family. This includes refuting the suprema-
cy or supposed normalcy of heterosexuality. Jacqui Alexander compares the
"fear of a queer nation" (213) with the "heterosexualization of family and of
morality" (3). Her point is illustrated in the United States' recent defense of the
sanctity or purity of heterosexual marriage (for example, the 1993 Defense of
Marriage Act): a union between a man and a woman for the purpose of producing heterosexual children. Alexander writes that "at a time of empire [such as
the US'], heterosexuality emerges as the nexus of Judeo-Christian fundamentalism and militarization to uphold ostensibly natural teleologies of propagation

and of market capitalism simultaneously, both of which require privatized heterosexuality and, increasingly, privatized homosexuality as well" (221). In Bett
Norris' novel, the sexual privatization that Alexander describes as well as violent responses to Mary McGhee's homosexuality are seemingly justified by the
US constitution upholding morality, law, tradition, natural sex, and nation-
al/personal integrity (Alexander 220). This chapter articulates exactly how
women taking up untraditional roles and jobs typically reserved for men undermine patriarchal authority. In order to show this better, I focus on the femino-centric topics that unite these works: gender boundaries, forbidden spaces,
weaving as storytelling, illicit sexuality, and woman's spirituality. In each novel, the breakdown of the traditional patriarchal family, inaugurated by women
working in the public sphere of men and breaking sexual taboos, is significant.

Boundaries Dissolving

As mentioned above, many women's novels focus on the nineteenth century
industrialization of England and Starling's work *The Journal of Dora Damage*,
which narrates the protagonist Dora taking over Peter's, her husband's, bookbinding business after he succumbs to rheumatism, is an excellent example.
The novel, presented as Dora's diary that has later been edited by her daughter
Lucinda in 1902, describes both the recent rise of industrialization and Peter's
subsequent accrual of debts and loss of respectability. The Damages are in dire
financial trouble and, with Peter not well enough to continue working, Dora,
desperate, begins to slowly learn and take over his trade. Initially, a curtain
separates Peter's workshop from the rest of the house and family (Dora and
their only child Lucinda). In the house, Dora is responsible for all domestic
duties (childrearing, washing, cooking, cleaning, and so on). Not oblivious to
his debilitating illness, Peter tells Dora, "It perturbs me to mention the affairs
of men's business within these four walls, and with my wife … but we are in
trouble" (20). Starling also undermines traditional associations of femininity
with weakness and masculinity with power when she juxtaposes Peter's illness
and physical frailty with Dora's strength. Peter, unable to pull himself to a
standing position, is dragged by Dora to his feet. Starling writes:

> Perhaps he had never noticed how much I had to carry our
> long-limbed daughter around, or even that she was no longer a
> baby. It was as if he did not know that muscles could be made
> strong through the labours of housework or factory work, mus-
> cles that could rise up and crush the languid, unmuscled rulers
> of their sex. Did they not have to work an eighteen-hour day

and more, and tumble into bed at the end of it, too tired even to
dream?" (22-23).

Over a period of months, Dora pawns her valuable belongings in order to pay
the rent and keep food on the table. Unable to find solutions to their economic
situation, Dora braves the streets and risks her reputation by visiting Charles
Diprose, who might be willing to give her husband some work binding medical
anatomy books.

Lying, Dora tells Diprose that her husband has sent her in his stead (59) and,
when she returns home with the commission, Peter rages and demands to know
where she has been; he asks "how a mother can leave her house, her husband,
her child? With no *prior* explanation?" (63). Disheartened by Peter's claims,
Dora makes her way into the kitchen and puts Lucinda's bed in front of the
stove, full-knowing that the family is "going to have to start living out of one
room for warmth, like the poor unfortunates who had no choice but so to do"
(64). Margaret Higonnet clarifies that, during the mid to late nineteenth century
in England:

> While the poorest women lived in quarters so cramped that
> segregation by sex was scarcely possible and privacy a dream,
> the architecture of wealthy women's 'private' domains subdi-
> vided into private and public arenas, such as dressing rooms
> and salons. The home had a very different configuration of pri-
> vate and public for a mistress or a maid, for an aristocrat or a
> peasant, 'upstairs' and 'downstairs,' in a city or on the land.
> ("New Cartographies" 4)

Higonnet's research, supported by Starling's novel, suggests men and women's
domains within the spheres are relational and permeable.

Speaking on the Industrial Revolution and the breakdown of the "bourgeois
family" within Britain, the arguments put forward by Friedrich Engels and
amended by Ann Taylor Allen in *Feminism and Motherhood in Western Europe 1890-1970: The Maternal Dilemma* are relevant for this work. Allen suggests that, during the "latter decades of the nineteenth century" in Western Europe, patriarchy as an absolute was challenged; it was no longer believed to be
"a universal aspect of human civilization" (20). She also claims that a new
consciousness for women arose:

> Mothers had not always lived a life of abject dependence –they
> had once been independent, self-supporting, and even powerful
> … if the father-headed family was not a God-given and univer-
> sal order, but merely a political arrangement that had risen in
> response to historical circumstances, then it might also come to
> an end. (20)

This kind of thinking is further supported in Engels' *The Origin of the Family, Private Property and the State* (1884). Engels rejects the belief that divisions of labor founded on hierarchical sexual difference are ahistorical. He concludes that, if the rise of the wife in modern day capitalist societies "over the husband, as inevitably brought about by the factory system, is inhuman, [then] the pristine rule of the husband over the wife must have been inhuman too" (*Communist Manifesto*, note 36). Society must destroy "the twin foundations of hitherto existing marriage – the dependence through private property of the wife upon the husband and of the children upon the parents" (Engels, qtd. in Jones, "Introduction" 67). For Engels, woman's equation with the womb and synonymy with the home is challenged within modern capitalism by the rise of the working woman outside of the home.

Though Engels, as well as Karl Marx, recognized the quasi-liberating potential of capitalism for working women, both writers were aware of what Zahra Karimi suggests is still occurring in today's now globalized world–the exploitation of women workers. Cheap female labor entails "lower wages and inferior working conditions" as well as long hours, insecure employment, flexibility, and sexual harassment (Karimi 169). Though attune to the public sphere, a serious consideration of the domestic sphere as an economic realm is missing in Marx and Engels' work. The domestic is considered non-economic and outside of the domain of production: it remains under the rubric of reproduction, as noted in Starling's novel. Contemporary women's historical novels supplement Marx and Engels' conception of production by revealing that women's domestic roles contribute considerably to a household's wealth and, therefore, the wider economy's (i.e., city, state, nation, empire).

Despite Peter's objections, Dora informs him that, whether he likes it or not, she will re-open the business and do the bookbinding herself, though she will disguise the work as his (65). Dora disrupts the neat division between workspace and domestic domain and the realm of husband and wife–symbolized when she has the curtain separating the workspace from the home removed.

The removal of the curtain invites reflection on the nature of gendered boundaries and gendered divisions of labor. Leonore Davidoff and Catherine Hall's *Family Fortunes: Men and Women of the English Middle Class, 1750-1850* (1987), theorizes middle-class men and women as inhabiting separate spheres. Scholars, such as Janet Wolff, however, believe this study needs revising. Wolff argues that "the simple equation of men/public and women/private, of course, is quite wrong … men also inhabited the private realm of the home. Working-class women always, and necessarily traversed the public sphere of work and the street" (118-19). Amanda Vickery, likewise, describes a fluid and relational understanding of the separate spheres. She believes that an uncritical commitment to the separate domains "fails to capture the texture of female subordination and the complex interplay of emotion and power in family life" (401). A theory of separate gendered spheres within the familial realm and the workspace is, this chapter argues, and Starling's novel highlights, at best, complex and specific to certain cultures, times, and places.

Discontent with women taking up new positions is clear, however, not only in Peter's reactions, but in Diprose's when he pays an unexpected visit to the Damages. Dora knows "[they] would have got away with it had Jack [the apprentice] been here, had [she] not sent him out to deliver [their] trade card to a stationer's in Holborn. But to someone who knew, like Mr Diprose, it would have been apparent, from the hammer in [her] hand and the jar of freshly made paste on the bench, that [Dora] was doing men's work" (Starling 92). Dora's entrance into the working world, however, is not unique. Peter, himself, is initially against women working in professions assigned to men, such as bookbinding. He exclaims, "They laid off twelve men – *twelve men* – today at Remy's, including Frank and Bates. They've taken on twenty women – or girls, I should say – since Christmas, and they're all staying. It's an outrage, an utter disgrace" (17-18). Women are only suited for "lower-quality work" (18) and "steal from honest workers and their poor families, threaten[ing] the very structure of the family life upon which England became great" (64). Peter adds, "Their standards are lower. They will sell shoddie work, for less. And their expectations are lower" (19). Continuing with his tirade, Peter concludes, "Too many machines … Machination equals *fem-in-i-cation*" (19).

Marx and Engels, similarly, characterize the period of the Industrial Revolution with these consequences: "the less the skill and exertion of strength implied in manual labor, in other words, the more modern industry becomes developed, the more is the labor of men superseded by that of women. Differences in age and sex have no longer any distinctive social validity for the working class" (*Communist Manifesto* 28). Marx and Engels, like Peter, describe the modern capitalist worker stripped of his trade and vocation in production and reduced to non-skilled factory work with machines—but this machine work also incentivizes women to leave the confines of the home. Engels argues that women are emancipated by entering into public industry and believes that the "quality possessed by the individual family of being the economic unit of society be abolished" (*Origin of the Family* 83). Women are, therefore, permitted to work in these roles because they are considered cheaper labor than men and increase business profits.

Marx aptly summarizes the paradoxical situation for women in this time:

> However terrible and disgusting the dissolution of the old fami-
> ly ties within the capitalist system may appear, large-scale in-

dustry, by assigning an important part in socially organized processes of production, outside the sphere of the domestic economy, to women, young persons and children of both sexes, does nevertheless create a new economic foundation for a higher form of the family and of relations between the sexes. (*Capital* 620-21)

This change occurs within the Damage household. Refusing to succumb to the workhouse or whorehouse, Dora begins to put the bookbinding business back on track and earns enough for the family to survive. Playing with gendered spaces, Starling makes Dora the sole breadwinner, spending long hours in the workroom and Peter increasingly withdraws from his former space until he is eventually confined completely to the domestic realm.

Exemplifying several dilemmas of the working mother, such as what Allen calls "the double burden" (1) and of which Marx and Engels were unable to anticipate nor fully theorize, Dora struggles with balancing her public binding work with her domestic duties, especially nursing Peter and childrearing her epileptic daughter (epilepsy being much understood during this time/place). As Ann Heilmann and Mark Llewellyn suggest Dora, invoking a feminine aesthetics "must make do with the materials she has on hand; that she does so successfully bears witness to her talent. Her failure as a housewife stands in marked contrast to the skill with which she masters the craft of bookbinding. Unsurprisingly perhaps, Dora's expertise in feminizing this traditionally masculine trade prompts marital discord and the threat of union action for breach of the prohibition to employ women as binders" (*Neo-Victorianism* 134). She remarks, "I knew Lucinda was suffering from my absence … a child needs her mother in ways far greater than a workshop needs its binder, a house its cleaner, or even a husband his wife. Not to mention that the river ran in both directions: I was suffering from Lucinda's absence no less" (Starling 98). Finding the transition from a working mother within the home to one outside proves difficult.

Allen claims that Dora's challenge continues today: "women still assume the chief responsibility for the family, and do most of the work of reproduction and childrearing" and that " this maternal dilemma "restricts their participation in economic, social, and cultural life and is now the major source of gender inequality in Western societies" (1). Dora, however, cannot afford not to work as a binder, nor can she pay someone to help her in the home; it is necessary for the family's survival that Dora do it all. She must learn and master the craft while tending to her domestic duties and, in the process, must abandon any sense of what she believes is womanly propriety or moral purity.

Initially taking on commissions for bibles and books deemed appropriate for her sex, Dora soon discovers that binding anatomical books, illegal pornographic catalogues, and those with an imperialist/colonial subject matter such as tribal customs in Africa or interracial sex such as in *The Lustful Turk* pay much better. Producing pornographic and racist works for Sir Jocelyn Knightley and his gentlemen friends (modelled on historical figure Richard Burton (Muller 123), Dora embodies the contradictions capitalism entails. Dora rejects traditional women's work by running the business herself (particularly necessary after Peter dies) and she challenges Victorian ideals of women's moral superiority or innocence as well as a lack of sexual desire. Her desire as Nadine Muller attests, is awoken primarily through her viewing of illicit material – though the material has little in common with "real" sex, which Dora realizes when she has a romance with a fugitive slave named Din (123); Starling, furthermore, suggests that "any sexual power or liberty women imagine they possess through the enactment of heterosexual sadomasochistic practices is, ... merely subject to and created for the satisfaction of male desires, and is therefore artificial and degrading, rather than an emancipatory or liberating, nature" (Muller 127). The novel, therefore, tackles a contemporary feminist concern for women's sexual identities and how pornography, now widely available, is being increasingly misconceived as empowering for women; Starling, through representing Dora's life and revisiting her past, elucidates how the issues of sexual and racial, exploitation converge in pornographic texts. This furthermore highlights how pornography perpetuates "women's physical and psychological subjugation in society" (Muller 128) and the complex relation between sexual/textual politics.

Forbidden Spaces

Just as sexual expression perplexes the characters, dilemmas about gendered divisions of labor affect every single protagonist in women's historical novels. The protagonist of Lebra's *The Scent of Sake*, Rei, is a quintessential example. The novel is set throughout several decades of mid-nineteenth century Japan. Beginning in 1825, Rei is described scrubbing wooden sake barrels outside her family's brewery. In her Note to Readers, Lebra writes, "the real economic strength of Japan is in the hands of the prosperous merchant class, the chonin, and among them sake brewers are the most powerful." The novel is very much about the rise of the merchant class in Japan's increasingly capitalistic economy, which brings new, though limited opportunities for women (Ueda 14). Women workers are subservient to men and, in 1908, still limited to fifteen suitable occupations: "flower girl, telephone operator, drugstore attendant, babysitter, professional storyteller, wet nurse, woman gangster, concubine, prostitute, dancer, seamstress, masseuse, laundress, office secretary, and circus girl" (Ueda 14-15). Rei defies these restrictions by working for her family's brewing house, but traditional boundaries remain intact, such as the division between business and family.

Like the Damage's household, there is an outer office, an inner office, and, then, the rooms for the family. Rei is permitted to work outside of the brewery, but not inside: "[w]omen were never to enter the forbidden door that gaped darkly before her. 'Let a woman enter the brewery and the sake will sour,' the old ones always said" (Lebra 1). When Rei's father discovers she is working too close to the door, he bellows, "Get back to the kitchen!" which Rei interprets as "the place of women. How unreasonable of her father to expect her to be only a confined 'girl in a box'" (3). Divisions of labor according to gender are clearly marked out, though, as the only heir to the Omura House, Rei envisions a more active role for herself in the business; she desires to make Omura House the number one brewery in Kobe, Japan.

Following Rei's banishment to the house, she is informed that she is now engaged to an apprentice name Jihei, though she is secretly in love with Saburo Kato, the third son of another brewing house. Lebra writes that "for a merchant class family, marriage was a matter of momentous import … Choice of spouse depended on many factors, least among them the emotional preferences of the two individuals" (183). Similar to Dora who initially strives to fulfill a Victorian ideology of maternal and domestic perfection, "the angel of the house" (Starling 305), Rei's mother gives her this advice: "You must try to be a good wife, Rei. Be compliant. Your feelings must not intrude … Women often find it necessary to 'kill the self.' Otherwise life becomes too difficult" (Lebra 7). Rei as wife-mother is "enslaved in self-sacrificial roles that suppress the expression of desire" (Rogers 4). Though Rei chooses to obey the wishes of her family, she also commits to pave a new destiny for herself.

Lebra writes:

> She thought suddenly of the way her father banished her to the kitchen, wanted to keep her away from the business side of the brewery, especially transactions involving cash, something to which women of Kansai merchant houses had no access. How was she to fulfill her responsibility to the house if she wasn't allowed to be involved in the business of brewing? (9)

Married to a man she does not love, Rei is, nonetheless, responsible for producing an heir. She consents to this obligation, but she also negotiates for the inner office within the brewery to become "her own sphere" (18) so that she can concentrate on the business. Rei's entrance into the forbidden world of her husband and father is a slow process, but she begins by learning from the clerk Kin-San, to whom she quietly puts forth suggestions such as increasing their market to Edo. Rei's dreams are put on hold, however, when she miscarries and discovers her husband, who has little business sense, has produced another heir with a geisha named O-Toki. Failing to give birth to her own child is attributed to Rei's "constant involvement in the affairs of the house" (44); thus, by working, which is considered unnatural for a woman, she sacrifices her perceived biological duty to be a mother and upsets the traditional division between work and home.

The decision to adopt O'Toki's child is made by Rei's father, much to Rei's despair. The child's arrival, however, coincides with the death of Rei's mother, suggesting that the cycle of birth and death, the family, and the business are interlinked. Much later, when Rei does have her own children, including a granddaughter, she declares, "The family and the brewery are equally important to me ... They are really one and the same" (239). Adopting O'Toki's child, Yoshitaro, under the pretense that she is his biological mother, Rei understands that this will benefit the business. Yoshitaro, eventually learning the truth of his adoption, thinks to himself, "*I really have two mothers, my natural mother here in the Sawaraya and Rei, the virtual head of one of the most powerful houses in all Kobe*" (201). Rei's desire for the house to succeed necessarily involves her taking on the role of mother to both her family and the business.

As the business expands, so too does Rei's family: unprecedentedly, she adopts two more of Jihei's illegitimate children, Kazu and Teru , has a secret affair with Saburo Kato, gives birth to his daughter Fumi , and, later, has a son by Jihei named Seisaburo. When Rei's father dies, as per his instructions, she is given the family seal, ostensibly giving her power over the running of the business. Despite her powerful position, as a woman she still cannot attend the Brewers Association meetings or ever enter the kura. Lebra never has Rei, much to the reader's disappointment, undermine this rule. Thus, while some gender boundaries are outright rejected, other traditional ones remain intact. Lebra further suggests, like many women's historical novels such as Starling's, that Rei's unusual power is solidified because her husband is weak. When Jihei dies after a night of drunkenness, it is because, as Yoshitaro notes, "he'd always moved in Mother's shadow" (202). The transition of power from a man to woman is also linked with political and economic changes occurring in Japan.

Domestic borders, divisions of labor, and relations with foreign nations were becoming more flexible within Japanese society. Pressured militarily by Western forces with their "black ships and guns" to resume trade, Japan, on guard against foreign imperialism, is, nonetheless, in the process of moving away from an isolated feudal society (The Tokugawa period (1603–1868) to the Meiji or Enlightened era). In terms of the business, Rei decides that White Tiger should buy its own ships and run its own shipping company, though no brewer has ever done so. Able to adapt to changes, Rei's survival and success amounts to White Tiger taking the number one position by the time she is eighty-eight years old. Though Rei is, for all intents and purposes, responsible for the economic success of her family and the business, history will not be kind.

Rei knows that in "the name tablets of the generations of Omuras" she, nor any woman, including her very capable daughter-in-law, will be included (363). A similar omission is conceded by the protagonist of Amirrezvani's heroine, a beloved carpet maker who says ""I will never inscribe my name in a carpet like the masters in the royal rug workshop who are honored for their greats skill … [when they sit on my carpet] my heart will touch theirs and we will be as one, even after I am dust, even though they will never know my name" (360). Thus, women's historicals identify gaps and silences but also presences in alternative creative outlets.

Weaving the Work of Women Storytellers

Women's historical novels like Lebra's *The Scent of Sake* and Starling's *The Journal of Dora Damage* describe the ways in which patriarchy exercises power within and outside of the home. Though women's experiences within the domestic sphere can be dramatically different, for instance isolating, imprisoning, or confining, feminist historiographers such as Carroll Smith-Rosenburg and Nancy Cott believe women's domestic spheres can, also, be sites of affirmative "women's culture." Thus, gendered divisions of labor have the potential for creating "an autonomous, homosocial female world bound together through kinship networks and women's shared life experiences of marriage, family and religion" (Morgan 7). As Sue Morgan clarifies, critics of this approach, such as Ellen DuBois, regard "the sometime romanticized portrayal of female domesticity as an ineffective way to challenge patriarchal structures, reminding readers that any form of women's culture still existed in a world whose contours were largely determined by men" (8). This kind of empowered women's culture within the parameters of a patriarchal society is found in Starling's *The Diary of Dora Damage* when "the afterlife of the characters offers a personal-cum-political solution to the sexual colonization of women. By starting to give bookbinding lessons for women and founding a female bookbinding union Dora helps to establish a viable career pathway that will enable women to move beyond the bleak choice of whorehouse, workhouse, madhouse" (Heilmann and Llewellyn, *Neo-Victorianism* 139). Amirrezvani's novel *The Blood of Flowers* and Walker's *The Color Purple*, however, exemplify needlework as not only a positive experience for women but as a means for storytelling and recording one's life in history.

Set in seventeenth century Iran, Amirrezvani's novel describes a renaissance in carpet weaving (Karimi 175). The text begins with the anonymous narrator and her mother living in poverty without a protector. The young narrator asks her mother if, this time, she can recount the story of her and her mother's past. Moving into the past, Amirrezvani portrays the narrator as a young girl living in a village making a carpet to sell for her dowry. Marriage plans continue until her father suddenly dies. Without a patriarch, the narrator and her mother Maheen are subject to abject poverty and they must sell the family's valuables, including the carpet, in order to survive. The narrator and her mother decide to leave their village for the first time and move to Isfahan, Iran's capital.

Their only relative, her father's half-brother Gostaham, lives in Isfahan as a master carpet maker. Amirrezvani writes: "My father could no longer protect us, and no one else was duty-bound to do so. My mother was too old for anyone to want her, and now that we had no money for a dowry, no one would want me" (31). When the daughter and mother arrive at Gostaham's house, impressed by its grandeur, they are ushered to meet his wife, Gordiyeh. Unlike the rest of the family, the narrator and her motherare taken to a "tiny room squeezed between the kitchen storerooms and the latrine. There was nothing in it but two bedrolls, blankets, and cushions" (38). The "I" of the story realizes that she and her mother, without having a male protector, are essentially servants.

A brief respite from servitude arises when the protagonist is allowed to work at the Great Bazaar, which is closed to men twice a year "so that the ladies of the royal harem could shop in freedom" (54): "[a]ll men had been ordered away under penalty of death, lest they should catch a glimpse of the unveiled women" (55). Starling's, Lebra's, and Amirrezvani's novels suggest that experiences differ depending on whether or not a woman is in the city or the village, the urban or the rural, but, in both instances, there are some semi-respectable spaces for middle-class women. For example, in the cities in Victorian England the theatre, park, or department store were respectable and, in Rei's case, she visits Japan's flower exhibits, while the narrator of Amirrezvani's novel visits her friend Naheed, the hammam, and the bazaar, provided she is properly dressed.

Slippages in rigid gendered spaces and divisions of labor in the woman's historical novel, however, are linked to capitalist economics. This is shown as the protagonist's beliefs transform from one supporting the separation of spheres until, for economic reasons combined with personal desire, she transgresses gendered divisions of labor and space. The narrator and her mother prove admirable negotiators for Gostaham and secure several important and profitable commissions when they work his bazaar shop. Gostaham rewards the narrator by taking her to visit the normally forbidden royal rug workshop. The narrator's ambition and love for carpets is clear, but, as her uncle knows, love is not enough: "What a pity you're not a boy! You're the right age to apprentice in the workshop" (63). Attempting to find a way around this gender exclusion, she asks to assist her uncle with his projects at home. Her uncle grants his consent provided she does not shirk her household chores. Unlike a boy, who would only devote himself to the craft, she is forced to balance her domestic duties with her work, for which she is forced to steal time on the side to complete; considered a semi-respectable woman, she can only practice this craft within the home. In this way, the narrator as a carpet weaver contributes to an increasing cottage industry in Iran made up of mostly women, which will, in later centuries, become increasingly threatened and industrialized (Karimi 170).

Tired of being berated by Gordiyeh for their backward and clumsy village ways and for draining the household's resources, the mother-daughter team decide to save for another dowry by selling medicinal herbs and beginning a new carpet. The narrator's fate changes, however, when, one day, returning from the hammam, she enters her uncle's home and carelessly removes her picheh and head scarf. Unbeknownst to her, a stranger wanting to commission a carpet for his daughter is watching; horrified she shouts, "well, don't just stand there looking!" and retreats to the *andarooni*, "the part of the house where women were safe from male eyes" (71). The protagonist later learns that the stranger is a wealthy horse trader named Ferydoon. Though her mother knows "marrying [her] is the only way [they] can hope to live on [their] own" (81), once again emphasizing women's socio-economic dependence on men during this time and place, this opportunity is cut short when Gostaham receives a letter from Ferydoon offering to make his niece his wife. But it is "not for a lifetime marriage contract. It's for a *sigheh* of three months" (117). Maheen knows a *sigheh* is a fancy word for a prostitute and that "once [her] daughter's virginity is gone, who will want her then?" (ibid.). Ferydoon has the option of renewing the sigheh indefinitely and must pay an agreed amount of money to the family each time,. Gordiyeh reminds them, "How can two penniless women expect more?" (123). With this new arrangement, the mother-daughter continue to live under Gostaham's roof, while the narrator increasingly learns more from her uncle about making carpets.

Waiting for Ferydoon's summoning, the narrator works on a carpet for a commission her uncle has with a foreigner, a Dutch man of the Dutch East India Company. The trade with the Dutchman signals, as in Lebra's novel, initial interactions and trade with the imperializing and soon to be industrial West and, for the protagonist, an opportunity for economic independence. With her mother helping, she has a "bold idea: What if I could find a few women knotters and hire them to make my designs? That's exactly what they did in the royal rug workshop and in the rug factories that dotted the city" (179). An all-woman workshop, though keeping in line with gendered divisions of labor, is innovative and allows for a new solidarity between working women. For example, one of the women named Malekeh is commissioned because her husband is ill and unable to work. Though the protagonist enjoys some sexual pleasure with Ferydoon and he renews his sigheh for a second time, things change when the girl learns her best friend Naheed is arranged to marry him. Feeling guilty about her sigheh with Ferydoon, the narrator is, nonetheless, required to keep it concealed. In exchange for her secrecy, she blackmails her aunt. The aunt promises the narrator that she will be allowed to make a rug so she can sell it and keep the profits. When Naheed eventually discovers that her husband has a sigheh with her best friend, the friendship dissolves; Naheed informs her that "[a] respectable married woman like me does not associate with someone who sells sex for silver" (247). Realizing her role as an economic pawn–by virtue of the fact that she is female, unmarried, fatherless, and poor–within her family, the narrator intercepts Ferydoon's offer to renew the sigheh and decides, on behalf of her uncle, to, unprecedentedly, reject it. Discovering that the girl has renounced the sigheh in his name, Gostaham banishes the mother and daughter to the streets.

Cast onto the streets, the narrator finds Malekeh, who agrees to take them temporarily into her home, which consists of a small room for the entire family. The economic situation of working women, the woman's historical novel suggests, is not always one of social mobility. Sally Zigmond's work *Hope Against Hope* (2009) details the lives of two sisters who must sell their pub to make way for a railroad. One ends up working in a brothel, while the other is sexually harassed in the boarding house where she works. Erica Eisdorfer's *The Wet Nurse's Tale* (2009) traces the life of Susan Rose, forced to become a wetnurse when she loses her job though she struggles to feed her own baby. Her son is, later, sold to another family by her father. In Amirrezvani's text, the plight of the mother-daughter worsens and, without a meager income, they are slowly starving. When Maheen falls ill, the daughter is forced to go into the streets to beg. Propositioned by a butcher for a sigheh for an hour or two in exchange for meat to make her mother a healing soup, she has no choice but to consent, though she postpones the meeting. Rather than sell her body in exchange for food, the daughter is forced to grovel in front of her aunt and uncle, upon which she is given enough money to repay the butcher and buy some medicines to sell. Thus, it is her wealthy uncle again who guarantees her survival.

Her uncle, also, commissions some carpets from her and allows her to show them at the bi-annual harem's bazaar. Within the harem, the girl finally wins the favor of the Shah's favorite Maryam and declares, "I had finally achieved what I wanted: sold a carpet on my own, of my own design, on my own terms" (351). The narrator's success continues because, as a woman, she is permitted to visit the harem, which brings her business opportunities her uncle or any man cannot imagine. Upon leaving the harem one day for her own modest home, the narrator reflects:

> As each of the thick wooden gates slammed behind me, I thought about how richly dressed Maryam was, how soft her hands, how glittering her rubies, how perfect her face, how lovely her red hair and tiny red lips. And yet, I did not envy her. Each time a gate closed with a thud, I was reminded that while I was free to come and go, she could not leave without an approved reason and a large entourage. She could not walk across Thirty-three Arches Bridge and admire the view, or get soaked to the skin on a rainy night. She could not make the mistakes I had, and try again. She was doomed to luxuriate in the most immaculate of prisons. (358)

Amirrezvani envisions a gendered freedom and creative outlet for her narrator that is only possible, first, by her uncle's economic situation and, then, her own economic independence, her autonomy within a non-patriarchal family, and the support of a social network of women: her employees, employers, friends, and, most important of all, a master of story-telling, her mother.

Sewing also contributes to the success of Walker's protagonist Celie in *The Color Purple.* The climax of the novel is when Celie discovers from her lover Shug that her husband Mr._____ has been keeping her long-lost sister's, Nettie's, letters from her. In an attempt to refocus Celie's anger, Shug suggests: "us ought to do something different … let's make you some pants" (Walker 146). Shug notes that Celie's the one out in the field every day, doing a man's job in a dress, and she deserves practical clothing. As Lin Yu notes, the other protagonists discussed here fulfill the tasks many African women already perform: "the dual function of being both a provider and a nurturer to their children" or family (137). The pants also signify a new sense of empowerment for Celie and a forthcoming power shift in her relationship with Mr._____, who remains referred to primarily throughout the text as Mr. followed by a blank line, a sign of historical racism but also a play on gender because typically women are the ones without names and/or are simply known by their husband's namesBy contrast, Celie is known only by her first name. Sewing, for Celie, is a means for identity, independence, and healing. Together, she and Shug sew the pants while reading all of Nettie's letters. When they finish, Shug tells Mr. _____ that she's bringing Celie to live with her in Memphis.

In Memphis, Celie's pants sell well. Like Amirrezvani's narrator, Celie becomes successfully self-employed and hires some local women, creating a feminine workspace. Understanding the importance of being an artist, Shug tells Celie, "Let's us just go ahead and give you this diningroom for your factory and git you some more women in here to cut and sew; while you sit back and design. You making your living, Celie, she say. Girl, you on your way" (214). Celie's liberation through finding a woman to love combined with her capitalist endeavors, however, brings to the forefront what many feminists identify as the paradox of capitalism: it permits individual economic independence necessarily at the price of an other's economic servitude and exploitation. It is unclear from the text how Celie will resist, if she can, the kind of gendered commodification capitalism requires. Celie's success continues when her stepfather dies and she returns to Georgia to reclaim the house and dry good store that her biological father used to own before he and his brothers were lynched for taking business away from white merchants. Will Celie suffer from the same kind of racism when she, taking Shug's advice, uses her parents' store to sell her pants? Walker implies that Celie, an independent black woman, will triumph despite living in a racist, sexist, classist, homophobic society.

Illicit Sexuality: Lesbian Mothers in the South

The novels in this chapter describe a working protagonist's forbidden sexuality and transgressions of the traditional patriarchal family. In Starling's novel, Dora falls in love, first, with a recently freed American slave named Din who works in her bookbinding workshop and she lives with her former employer's wife Sylvia (443), with whom she raises her daughter Lucinda. In Lebra's *Scent of Sake*, Rei secretly meets Saburo Kato for one night of passion and Amirrezvani's protagonist, like Starling's, takes her sexual life into her own hands. After being briefly "married" to Ferydoon, the narrator proclaims, in similar terms to Malinalli in Laura Esquivel's *Malinche*, that she will never desire a man who sees "in [her] only a mirror for his own pleasure" (364). Bett Norris' novel *Miss McGhee* and Alice Walker's *The Color Purple*, however, both reject patriarchal relationships by focusing on the forbidden romances of two working lesbian women. These novels make up a sub-genre of lesbian historical fiction and historical fiction in which heterosexuality is rejected as normative. Other noteworthy novelists in this genre include Shan Sa, Sarah Waters, Michèle Roberts, Justine Saracen, and Penny Hayes, to name a few.

The novels bring visibility to the lesbian subject, which many historians and theorists of lesbianism (Faderman, Rich, Rupp, Vicinus, Wittig, Zimmerman, and others) argue has been erased and excluded from dominant discourses, including feminism. While Norris' text narrates the experiences of a white lesbian woman living in Myrtlewood, Alabama, Walker's novel narrates the experiences of a black lesbian living in Georgia. I categorize the novels as lesbian according to Lillian Faderman's broad definition in *Surpassing the Love of Man: Romantic Friendship and Love Between Women, From the Renaissance to the Present* (1981):

> 'Lesbian' describes a relationship in which two women's strongest emotions and affections are directed toward each other. Sexual contact may be part of the relationship to a lesser or greater degree, or it may be entirely absent. By preference the two women spend most of their time together and share most aspects of their lives with each other. (17-18)

Though Faderman's definition ignores lesbian relationships outside of monogamy or those of a purely sexual nature, her description aptly characterizes Norris' and Walker's novels.

The time-frame of *Miss McGhee* moves from post WWII in 1948 to the 1960s Civil Rights Movement and tells the story of Mary McGhee, a promising employee from a Texas Oil Company who has just been hired to get a local lumber mill, in operation since the Civil War, back on its financial feet. Resonating with Norris' epigraph, which "is dedicated to all those strong ladies who never married and who somehow made their own way in the world in a time when it was not easy to do so," Adrienne Rich points out:

> The fact is that women in every culture and throughout history have undertaken the task of independent, nonheterosexual, woman-connected existence, to the extent made possible by their context, often in the belief that they were the 'only ones' ever to have done so. They have undertaken it even though few women have been in an economic position to resist marriage altogether. ("Compulsive Heterosexuality" 635)

An atypical woman, Mary finds success working for an oil company prior to being transferred to her new employer Tommie Dubose, who, she quickly realizes, is unfit to run the business.

Like Rei in Lebra's text who bypasses her husband Jihei, Mary keeps Tommie busy while, essentially, running the business on her own (Norris 13). Mary is informed by a local girl, "My mama says you got a big mess to straighten out, but she don't see what one woman alone can do. She says there ain't a chance in a hunnerd a woman can set that lumber yard back to rights. It's a man's job. They ought to have hired a man, my mama says" (16). In light of Tommie's inabilities, Mary suggests, much to the chagrin of Gerald Buchanan, the Dubose's banker and bank president, that Tommie's wife Lila become active in the business. Lila will also have access to the checking account for the first time. At this point, the reader is still unaware as to why Mary has come to Myrtlewood. It is only after she retreats to a small fisherman's cabin in Mobile Bay and reflects on how and why she has come to Alabama to work for the Duboses that her past is revealed.

Mary recounts a past of fear and violence experienced because of her homosexual relationships, which have been more debilitating than her being a woman working in a man's world. She remembers being caught by her father in the hayloft with another girl and being beaten: "the sound of the fist meeting flesh, the crunch of the bone in her nose, the animal whimpers she emitted" (50). Forced by her father to leave in the middle of the night, without being able to say goodbye to her mother, Mary's memories next turn to Samantha, the daughter of her Texan employer, Big Sam: "She could recall with minute detail the look on Big Sam's face when he burst through the door and stood, his hand still on the knob, staring at them in bed, sitting up in surprise at his entrance, Sammie naked and defiant, smiling at him, almost triumphant, but unable to hide the fear her pride tried to mask" (51-52). Unlike her father, Big Sam gives Mary a train ticket, a large amount of cash, and "a job in a backwater, forgotten town, working for an imbecile" (52), which is likened to exile, not only in the geographical sense but in a psychological one.

As a lesbian, Mary is in exile and pretends to follow heterosexual norms and expectations. When Sammie visits Mary, she wonders if their lives "would have been easier if we could ignore this and live like normal women?" (88). Mary's use of the word "normal" is problematic because she suggests her homosexuality is unnatural; lesbians are not normal women as women are heterosexual. Though Mary internalizes the patriarchal language of heterosexuality as normality, she reveals to Sammie, again in terms of exile, that now with Lila she is "caught once again by emotions and desires it would be foolish to indulge" (89). She continues, "I feel trapped, Sammie, because I crave what is not acceptable. Exiled to the back of beyond, isolated, and yet it happens again" (ibid.). Meanwhile, Lila, working with Mary in the office several mornings a week, begins to question her heteronormative role as Tommie's caretaker and wife.

> I never sat around dreaming about getting married, like I suppose most girls do. When I thought about it, I always imagined

> I would be married, but I dreaded it. I felt like, that's what I'm
> supposed to do, so I'll just do it, but I never was eager about it
> … Isn't there some other choice, some other way to live? Look
> at Miss McGhee. Is there some kind of law that says this is
> what women have to do, and that's it? (58)

It is not until after her weekend with Sammie that Mary finally decides to disclose her past to Lila and reveal that she is in love with her, though the relationship will have to be concealed and conducted in secret, mostly at Mary's cabin in Mobile Bay.

As the relationship blossoms, so does the business, though Buchanan continues to insist they need a male manager to run the mill. Norris writes: "It don't look right, a woman hiring and firing men. We need a man in here, somebody that knows timber and land and how to run a sawmill and boss the men. Somebody Mrs. Dubose can depend on" (155). Buchanan's idealizations of the patriarchal workplace and family are further frustrated when, after Lila's husband Tommie dies (Norris 203), Mary moves in with her. Tired of sneaking around, Lila claims that, for a town in denial of homosexuality, together they will be rationalized as "a widow sharing a house with a spinster" (222). A homophobic Buchanan tells them, "People wonder, and they'll start to talk about what two women do, shut up in that house together every day. Every night" (225). The emphasis on night is clear; night is the time of sexual acts, thus, no two women should spend a night together.

Norris further describes the sexual relationship in the rhetoric of economics so that the sexual or personal household converges with the public business relationship. While Mary tells Lila, "I want to be a real partner in the business, not a secretary. I don't want to feel like an employee anymore" (227), Lila responds with her own interpretation of partner, rejecting the way Mary always rescues and protects her, thinking her naïve, childish and feminine . Lila insists upon democracy between them and a shared equality: "I want to feel like a partner too, and not just in the business" (228). She continues in feminist terms:

> Mary, it's time we changed the way we do business. You're
> not my teacher any more. I'm not your student. I am your lov-
> er, and we are equal partners in this relationship. We live to-
> gether, honey. You're not here to look after me, to oversee my
> every move and approve my decision. You're here because I
> love you and I want to live with you (254).

It is Lila's optimism and her feminist belief in an individual's ability to make real social change that finally convinces Mary to publicize the private and no longer suppress her lesbian relationship with Lila, though both know the path towards recognition and rights will not be easy.

In *The Color Purple*, Walker also describes the importance of female companionship, both physically and emotionally, in the lives of her protagonists, particularly Celie and Shug. An epistolary novel that "interweaves the African American oral tradition with that of the white-identified epistolary novel" (Lauret 109), *The Color Purple* begins when Celie, only fourteen years old, is raped by her father Alphonso, though later in the novel she learns he is her stepfather. Celie, like Dora, uses the format of diary entries to explain that, because of rape, she has given birth to two babies, though they have been forcibly taken away from her (the reader learns later that her children have been adopted by a Reverend and his wife who, having also taken in Celie's sister Nettie, travel together to Africa as missionaries and return at the end of the novel to reunite with Celie). Early in the text, however, Walker makes Celie's sexual preference for women known. Celie claims: "He [father] beat me today cause he say I winked at a boy in church. I may have got something in my eye but I didn't wink. I don't even like mens. That's the truth. I look at women, tho, cause I'm not scared of them" (5). Maria Lauret believes that Walker "rewrites the early epistolary novel's script of rigidly fixed gender roles and compulsory heterosexuality" (102). When a man only known as Mr._____ in the text, asks for Nettie's hand in marriage, Celie takes her place and learns about Shug Avery.

Celie stares at a picture of her future husband's former flame and mother to three of his children; she was "the most beautiful woman I ever saw" (6). Knowing Nettie shows promise at school and wanting to protect her from a violent life, Celie marries Mr._____ in her stead. Her father sweetens the marriage deal by throwing in a cow and telling Mr._____ that "she can work like a man" (8), again suggesting a fluid sense of gendered divisions of labor. Being unfeminine, normally considered a drawback for a woman, in this case is considered valuable– Celie's ability to work contrasts stereotypical feminine weakness, which is considered useless and unprofitable.

Things change for Celie when Shug, very much a professional entertainer, comes into town to sing at a local club. When she falls ill, however, Celie notes that "nobody in this town want to take the Queen Honeybee in. Her mammy say She told her so. Her pappy say, Tramp. A woman say she dying– maybe two berkulosis or some kind of nasty woman disease" (43). Finally, Mr._____ decides to take Shug in and Celie is tasked with looking after her. Celie reflects, "the first time I got the full sight of Shug Avery long black body with it black plum nipples, look like her mouth, I thought I had turned into a man" (49). While Celie nurses Shug, she also works on a quilt with a pattern called Sister's Choice. The pattern is poignant given that, by this point in the narrative, Celie's sister Nettie has run away in pursuit of her freedom and a better life, though Celie has no idea as to her whereabouts and is emotionally suffering in her marriage. The title of the quilt also suggests Celie's choice to marry in her sister's place. Shug is the one gleam of happiness Celie possesses.

When one of Mr.'s_____ children, Harpo, builds a jukejoint, Shug is urged to start singing again and she dedicates a song to Celie in gratitude for her kindness. Though Shug sleeps with Albert, Celie's husband, Celie doesn't care because she doesn't love Mr._____; her sexual feelings are only for Shug. Seeing Shug perform just prior to her leaving for a road tour, Celie says "I feel my nipples harden under my dress. My little button sort of perk up to. Shug, I say to her in my mind, Girl, you looks like a real good time, the Good Lord knows you do" (81). Upon returning from the road, lying in bed together, Celie tells Shug that she was raped by her father, her mother died, her two babies were taken away, and then she was bartered to Mr._____ , who doesn't love her and assaults her. Shug informs Celie that she loves her and kisses her before they make love. Unlike Mary, who experiences violent repercussions because of her lesbianism, Celie doesn't seem to suffer from any homophobia. bell hooks questions how the text can justify not showing lesbianism as socially problematic for the other characters in the novel, given the historical setting and time-frame.

Celie's happiness with Shug is disrupted, however, when Shug falls in love with a young musician. Unable to understand her attraction to a man, Celie describes Harpo's and his wife Sofia's attempt to set her "up with some man" (260) as misguided. Celie says, "They know I love Shug but they think womens love just by accident, anybody handy likely to do" (ibid.). For Monique Wittig, Celie's lesbianism as a Black woman provides her with a double kind of freedom; it is a freedom from what Rich calls "compulsory heterosexuality" and slavery. Wittig writes:

> Lesbian is the only concept I know of which is beyond the cat-
> egories of sex (woman and man), either economically, or polit-
> ically, or ideologically. For what makes a woman is a specific
> social relation to a man, a relation that we have previously
> called servitude, a relation which implies personal and physical
> obligation as well as economic obligation ('forced residence,
> domestic corvée, conjugal duties, unlimited production of chil-
> dren, etc.), a relation which lesbians escape by refusing to be-
> come or to stay heterosexual. We are escapees from our class
> in the same way as the American runaway slaves were when
> escaping slavery and becoming free. (20)

At the end of the novel, Walker shows a counter-discourse to the heterosexual family. Shug tells Celie that she is coming home for good: "I missed you more than I missed my own mama" (283). Shug's statement reflects a change in understanding the family, including one's mother, as the one you choose out of love, not necessarily the one from whom you are born. The family is not a fixed entity; it is fluid. An argument for redefining the family as an economic unit that began with Marx and Engels in the mid-nineteenth century, is renewed through contemporary works like Norris' and Walker's, but, with a shift in understanding the family in terms of mutual love and respect, both heterosexual and homosexual, and as flexible in its gender roles.

Woman's Spirituality

In the woman's historical novel, often there is dissatisfaction with religion and the church defined and organized according to patriarchal parameters. There is a search for God and spiritual meaning through an alternative maternal geneal-ogy of divine history; for example, a female prophet is imagined in Stevie Da-vies' *Impassioned Clay* (1999) and Donna Woolfolk Cross's controversially claims in *Pope Joan* (1996) that a medieval woman disguising herself as the monk John Anglicus reigned as Pope John VIII until her pregnancy when she was discovered and murdered. Irigaray suggests that women must reject patri-archal religions that determine "the gender of God, the guardian of every sub-ject and discourse, [as] always *paternal and masculine*, in the west" (*Irigaray Reader*, 186). Such discourses deny the existence of a "Mother God" (186) and reduce women to silence (166). Women must reinvent the divine through "body and soul, sexuality and spirituality" (Irigaray, *Irigaray Reader* 173), and at the same time insist that "the maternal should have a spiritual and divine dimension, and not be relegated to the merely carnal, leaving the divine to the genealogy of the father" (Whitford, "Section III" 159). Therefore "the divine and the maternal genealogy" together have the radical potential of "ending women's status as sacrificial objects" (159). As discussed in the Introduction, feminist rewrites of Biblical women are now emerging, for example, Ki Long-fellow's novel on Mary Magdalene but many figures from other religions like Muhammad's wife A'isha are also being imagined for the first time

Religious fundamentalism, racism, classism, and sexism intersect in many women's historical novels, but Norris' and Walker's novels reflect this conver-gence particularly well by focusing on rethinking the family, woman's eco-nomic independence, and woman's spirituality. Each novel opens with refer-ences to God; Walker's novel begins with her step-father's words: "*You better not tell nobody but God. It'd kill your mammy*," and then Celie's undated letter begins with "Dear God," (1). Norris begins each chapter with a message in italics from the Ku Klux Klan in the form of a "*Report to the Grand Dragon*" (3). Following this brief report, the novel states the words "FEAR GOD"

(Walker 3). Mary McGhee reads these words on a sign along the highway as she arrives in Myrtlewood, Alabama in 1948. The presence of God haunts and permeates each novel set in the early and mid-twentieth century America.

Walker explains in a later 2003 edition's Preface that the novel "remains for [her] the theological work examining the journey from the religious back to the spiritual." She believes readers have not recognized this important aspect of the novel because of the "pagan transformation of God from patriarchal male supremacist into trees, stars, wind, and everything else" it may have "camouflaged for many reader's the book's intent." Walker's claim is supported by her protagonist Celie who, as I already stated, begins the book with a letter addressed to "Dear God," "written in the African American vernacular of black Southern speech" (Lauret 90), and continues in a confessional style. This changes, however, when Celie discovers that her sister Nettie and her children are still alive. The letters then switch almost exclusively to an exchange between Nettie and Celie, who, each not knowing if the other is reading her respective words, are writing to one another in faith; God receives few letters. When Celie learns from Nettie the truth about her family, she writes to God for the penultimate time: "my daddy lynch. My mama crazy. All my little-half brothers and sisters no kin to me. My children not my sister and brother. Pa not Pa" (177). Some pages later, Celie declares to Nettie, "I don't write to God no more. I write to you" (192). Confronted by Shug, Celie retorts: "What God do for me?" and continues to explain:

> He give me a lynched daddy, a crazy mama, a lowdown dog of
> a step pa and a sister I probably wont ever see again. Anyway,
> I say the God I been praying and writing to is a man. And act
> just like all the other mens I know. Trifling, forgetful and low-
> down … If he ever listened to poor colored women the world
> would be a different place, I can tell you. (ibid.)

Celie realizes that she has never searched for God on her own terms.

Celie has only passively received what others have dictated, which is also true of her understanding of women. She has, for the most part, accepted and internalized patriarchal roles for women; thus, the novel is very much a coming to terms not only with one's self as a woman but also the self's relation to a higher power. Writing is essential to Celie's journey or pilgrimage to finding herself and her God, though Lauret argues that, for Celie, writing is a last resort for when speech fails.

According to Lauret, this encapsulates an important difference between "the dominant (white) culture's valorisation of writing as against speech" (107). Such writing includes "white women's literature, which tends to take *writing* as the mark of liberation from patriarchal oppression" (107-08). Therefore,

"Walker undermines the ground of *written* discourse upon which her own work rests" (107), while at the same time stressing the importance of the African-American woman's domestic narrative, like Celie's, which has been excluded from hegemonic literature and history. Though Lauret privileges Celie's increasing ability to speak as a black woman, Carmen Gillespie believes that, through her letters, Celie finds:

> A validating outlet through which to express her anguish and also to assert her morality, innocence, and outrage at injustice. This ability resonates with the traditions of African-American slave narratives and echoes the long and pervasive history of the African-American literary tradition of correlating the acquisition of literacy and voice with the attainment of freedom. (59)

Rather than privileging one form of text over the other or pitting them against each other, a stable hierarchy between speech and the written text is continually put into question and played with by Walker, evident in her discussions of God.

Shug explains that, for her, "she doesn't worry about pleasing God by going to church, she just does the best she can and to feel loved by God" (Walker 193). When Shug asks Celie to describe her God, Celie replies, "He big and old and tall and graybearded and white. He wear white robes and go barefooted" (194). Explaining that she, too, used to see the God that Celie describes, Shug knows the image is only the "one that's in the white folks' white bible" (194). A white God she clarifies, like white people, is not interested in the prayers of colored people; this is why, she says, "God is inside you and inside everybody else. You come into the world with God. But only them that search for it inside find it. … She say, my first step from the old white man was trees. Then air. Then birds. Then other people" (195). The transition from thinking about God as a man carries over for both Celie and Shug into everyday life.

Walker suggests that patriarchy dictates most of life's experiences because "Man corrupt everything … He on your box of grits, in your head, and all over the radio. He try to make you think he everywhere. Soon as you think he everywhere, you think he God. But he ain't" (197). This androcentric thinking suggests the importance in establishing a maternal relationship with the divine. A feminist reappraisal of the divine is evident when Shug tells Celie that, in order to critically reject her former white God, she must think about nature instead. Simultaneously, in Africa, however, Nettie is working as a missionary to spread Christianity and the word of God to the Olinka peoples .

Valerie Babb argues that Nettie's writing to Celie "alters literacy and takes it out of its imperialistic function of dominating oral cultures and allows it to record an oral history that would otherwise be lost" (79). Both Celie and Nettie (and I would add Walker) transform writing from a "device traditionally used by a white male culture to ensure its authority" (Babb 75) into a means for surviving. However, the Olinka are unable to tell their own tale; it is only through Nettie, an African-American, that the reader learns that the African Olinkas are being displaced and their traditional ways of living threatened by English builders using the village as a rubber plantation headquarters. Nettie also realizes that her preconceived notions of kinship between Africa and America are fragile at best. This is evident in her thoughts on God that change after her experiences as a missionary.

Nettie describes Africa's history of selling Africans as slaves and a history of western colonialism/capitalism in conjunction with the Olinka's patriarchal practices such as scarification and female circumcision. For Walker, "'Africa,' despite its almost mythical presence in the novel, is not celebrated as some idealized space outside the history of women's oppression, but then neither is America held up as a locus of liberation" (Lauret 108-09). Walker suggests that patriarchal oppression is trans-cultural and trans-national. Constance Richards concurs that "Walker's critique of patriarchal practices against the bodies of women transcends the politics of white versus black, colonizer versus colonized, and addresses forms of cultural nationalism that appropriate traditional African patriarchal practices as anticolonial strategies" (104). For this reason, Nettie reflects on her own complicity in the colonial project and comes to believe that God is, now, for her, "more spirit than ever before, and more internal. Most people think he has to look like something or someone –a roofleaf or Christ- but we [I] don't. And not being tied to what God looks like, frees us [me]" (Walker 257). The last letter of the novel comes full circle back to the opening letter, only this time Celie is empowered.

This final letter coincides with Nettie returning with Celie's children back to Georgia. Gillespie writes that "Celie is able to reclaim–through narrative and, ultimately in reality–her stolen, lost, sold children. Through Celie's knowledge about her children and ability to read their lives, Walker addresses and tries to rewrite, even redress, the historical loss of black women's children" (64). At the end of the novel, Celie is able to forgive Mr._____ for keeping Nettie's letters in a way that makes her a Christ-like figure. The final letter is marked "Dear God. Dear stars, dear trees, dear sky, dear peoples. Dear Everything. Dear God" (285). Celie's return to God, albeit from a new critical perspective, shows both spiritual transformation, forgiveness, and a sense of the self-reimagining Walker's Preface envisions.

The spiritual shift that occurs for Celie and Nettie can be described to a certain extent as returning to the legacy of slavery and "African-based cosmological systems" (Alexander 290). Jacqui Alexander argues that "housed in the memory of those enslaved, yet not circumscribed by it, these Sacred energies made the Crossing" of the Atlantic during the slave-trade (292). Celie may possibly be reviving traces of the practices of Winti, "in which one becomes oneself in the process of becoming one with the Sacred; and they manifest their sacredness in nature as well as in their relationship with human beings, both of which take shape in a process of mutual embodiment" (Alexander 301). With Celie and especially Nettie, who returns to Africa and then makes the Crossing back to the United States again, an alternative maternal spirituality survives.

Alexander, like Walker, suggests that "the idea, then, of knowing self through Spirit, to become open to the movement of the Spirit in order to wrestle with the movement of history … are instances of bringing the self into intimate proximity with the domain of Spirit" (295). Thus, the feminist statement that "the personal is not only political but spiritual" (Alexander 7, 295) is particularly relevant when reading *The Color Purple*. The renewed spirituality seen in *The Color Purple* continues Alexander's argument that feminism's, particularly a postmodern one's, preoccupation with the secular has meant a costly neglect of the sacred and, thus, a reappraisal of the sacred–"spiritual labour and spiritual knowing" (15)–is essential to transnational feminism because it plays such an important role in shaping/healing women's lives.

Norris' novel, similarly, touches on the issue of religious fundamentalism when she discusses segregation between the whites and blacks living in her town and the events leading up to the Civil Rights Movement. Mary's own involvement is clear when the local doctor tells her that the town is completely divided between rich white people and poor blacks who live "down there, red mud and dust and outhouses and shacks. Poverty, disease, misery" (Norris 81). Norris writes that "Mary was appalled. The Depression was over. How could people live like they did here, completely ignoring an entire segment of the population, effectively confining them in a camp as though they were prisoners of war?" (81). Though Mary can recognize oppression based on race, she is unable to face her own oppression based on lesbianism and she does little to further the visibility or the rights of homosexuals. Repressing her sexual desires, she begins going on regular walks through the town so that she can meet more of the "Negroes" (144) and understand their situation better.

Giving money to the black school for textbooks and blackboards (Norris 144), Mary is also accosted by one of Lila's brothers for "hirin' niggers to do white men's work" at the lumber mill (150). Buchanan echoes the man's sentiments when he explains that they need to hire a male mill manager, "somebody who knows how to hire the right kind of people" because "some of the men don't like working side by side with niggers. That's just a fact. And there's good people who need work and they see these Nigras taking jobs away from them, and they got families to feed" (155). Mary, knowing what it feels like to be discriminated against for taking a man's job, defends her decision: "'The men I've hired need the work and have families to feed too.' And some of them had lost their land and farms to the bank, Mary didn't bother adding" (155).

Norris's novel is similar to racial/class tensions epitomized by slave revolt novels like Allende's *Island Beneath the Sea* (2009) or *Property* (2003) by Valerie Martin, set on a sugar plantation near New Orleans during the 1830s.. The argument in Norris' novel involves Lila, who doesn't question racial segregation and is upset when it's disclosed that Mary is giving the black men skilled work and paying them a wage equal to the white men's (157). Lila's opinion about the situation changes, however, when her beloved maid Annie, a black woman, is accosted for riding in Lila's car. The garage owner asks her, "why don't you git out and walk like all your friends in Montgomery?" (Norris 181). The speaker is referring to the recent protests against racial segregation on the buses and a refusal to take public transportation until things change.

Together Mary and Lila start working for the cause of equality. By 1965, Mary's and Lila's involvement causes them to be the target of several raids, particularly by the local townspeople and members of the Ku Klux Klan. Things come to a climax in the novel when Annie's house is burnt to the ground and Mary and Lila are violently involved in the struggle. As Mary begins to lose faith in the fight, Lila stands defiantly by her, encouraging them to continue working. Mary's determination to combat injustice is restored when "down the street, two cars full of black people from Annie's church pulled up at Miss Louise's house and began picking through the rubble that sill smouldered. Watching friends she hadn't realized she had, Mary said, 'Maybe we should call Annie and Ben, see if they want to ride with Selma with us'" (285). Ultimately Norris, like Walker, suggests spirituality need not be confined to discriminatory patriarchal parameters and definitions. Lila and Mary fight for racial equality, basic human rights, and the equality of others while remaining tied to their Christian faith. Norris, thus, ends her novel with hope. An individual feminist woman and feminists in solidarity can transform a community and combat oppression in all its manifestations, such as race, sexuality, class, religion, and gender.

Conclusion

Analyzing women's historical novels across different times and places on working women shows a disruption and transformation of gendered spaces and spheres, including the patriarchal family, patriarchal public roles and jobs, and heterosexuality. The novels discussed stress the importance of a woman being able to earn and keep her own income, as financial independence is a means to guaranteeing other forms of social independence, including not marrying. Essential to this freedom is, also, the love and support of other women: for example Dora with Sylvia and her daughter Lucinda in Starling's novel, Lebra's narration of Rei with her daughter Fumi and daughter-in-law Tama, Amirrezvani's narrator with her mother Maheen, and friend/co-worker Malekeh, Celie and Shug in Walker's work, and Lila and Mary as life and business partners in Norris' novel. At the same time, we can read these works as expressing historical and contemporary fears about the breakdown of traditional patriarchal society, which is threatened by women, lesbians, and mothers who work outside of the home. As Rich suggests, such beliefs are reactionary and strive to decree that "the home, its cares and employments, is the woman's true sphere" (*Of Woman Born* 49). The struggles of working women are clear when reading the femino-centric topics of boundaries, spaces, weaving, romance, and spirituality in the woman's historical novel from a transnational feminist perspective.

CHAPTER SIX

Violent Women: Revamping the Gothic Novel

> No man who oppresses a woman can be free
> – Karl Marx as quoted by Luce Irigaray, *Democracy Begins Between Two*

Having roots in Sophia Lee's *The Recess* (1783), Charlotte Smith's *Emmeline* (1788), and Ann Radcliffe's Gothic novels, including *The Mysteries of Udolpho* (1794), the historical novels discussed in this chapter resurrect the early woman's Gothic historical novel as a contemporary "vehicle for expressing terror and fear" (Groot 16). More specifically, this chapter analyzes how contemporary writers such as Margaret Atwood are rewriting the Gothic genre through historical female characters. Wallace argues that "women writers have used the Gothic as 'a mode of history' precisely because it expresses their complex and ambivalent relationship to history as both events and narrative" (*Woman's* 20). Lee, in particular, in her novel on the fictional daughters of Mary Queen of Scots, "uses the Gothic mode to stage a coded but sustained (and angry) political protest against the ways in which women have been excluded from history" (*Woman's* 20). Maria Vara argues Lee's work exemplifies the "persecuted heroine – the maiden in flight" so characteristic of classical Gothic in the eighteenth century; she believes that the genre transforms itself, however, in the nineteenth century when works like Charlotte Brontë's *Jane Eyre* (1847) provide insight into a new trope: the "mad woman in the attic" (172). Inspired by both types of literary foremothers, persecuted heroine/woman confined, the contemporary writers in this chapter, "examine gender difference and the problems and anxieties involved in being female" (Rogers 37) from a transnational feminist perspective. The past for these writers, is not only dark, incriminating, sexualized, mysterious, and charged with fairytale and supernatural elements but also reveals woman enclosed in suffocating stereotypes – not surprisingly, the women rebel, act out violently, try to flee, but suffer imprisonment, both psychically and physically.

Gothic works expose "the dark side of conformity, alternatives to the status quo[;] it is contradictory, providing social critique and highlighting what lies beneath everyday behaviors, what hidden contradictions, dreams, fantasies, and fears undermine the ostensibly familiar and ordinary" (Wisker 95). Other characteristics include an isolated and isolating domestic setting, a rural land-scape/wilderness, the presence of ghosts or spirits, a deliberate play with ideal-izations of romance, a focus on maternal figures, and a detailed analysis of class conflicts, particularly between the mistress and maid, and wife and prosti-tute. The partners in each pair, however, deny a binary set-up and display a propensity for violence and murder. Perhaps, most importantly is how the nov-els play with and undermine notions of women's "innocence, virtue and exces-sive passivity" especially when it comes to sexuality (Vara 176); though Vara argues that some contemporary women's novels like Alice Thompson's *Justine* (1996) challenge the "feminist imperative of the 1970s to feature strong and active women characters" (ibid.) in the novels discussed in this chapter, this reading is not entirely accurate; though initially obscured by a façade of femi-nine innocence, obedience, and decorum, the heroine's active agency, high-lighted by the violent acts she commits, is evident. Each character embodies a combination of agency and passivity, implying a complete break with this bina-ry altogether is favored by contemporary writers.

Nevertheless, this liminal position confirms Vara's belief that the Gothic can divest "the persistent myth of the 'Perfect Woman' of its allure" (179). For Katherine Cooper "the re-telling of maternal narratives is a popular device of the gothic" (163) primarily because it allows for gender identification: "the discoveries they [female protagonists] make about their maternal histories help them to understand their own lives and their own experiences as women" (164). Maternal narratives allow for continuity between protagonists as women or mother-daughters but between writers and readers as well. These sentiments support feminist criticism which argues for a plurality of women's experiences and voices speaking from a shared sense of gender. Poignantly Donna Heiland recognizes the popularity and suitability of the gothic as a genre for women writers, transnationally. She writes, "Gothic fiction at its core is about the transgressions of all sorts: across national boundaries, social boundaries, sexual boundaries, the boundaries of one's own identity" (3). Therefore, the genre "'is the mode par excellence that female writers have employed to give voice to deep-rooted fears about their own powerlessness and imprisonment within pa-triarchy'" (Brabon and Genz , qtd.in Cooper, 153). Thus contemporary women historical novelists are challenging both inaccurate and fantastical representa-tions of Woman in both literature and history (179) and offering a more diver-sified understanding of women's oppression in each.

Kate Mitchell reminds us, despite the fact that many early historical novels suppressed the fantastic, for example, Walter Scott's *Waverley*, "its appearance in contemporary historical novels suggests its productive possibilities for his-torical recollection" and offers writers the ability "to give voice to vanished or silenced elements of the past" (123), which includes the female heroine's voice. Though Mitchell is correct in her thinking about contemporary writers, one could argue that the reason the Gothic is believed to be downplayed or missing in traditional historical novels, is because the critic is not seriously taking into consideration early women's historical novels such as Lee's: this is a point Wallace emphasizes when starting with Lee's gothic novel in tracing a genealogy of the woman's historical novel in Britain. In one sense, the Gothic woman's historical novel succeeds because it recasts mainstream narratives; it turns them inside out and shows us alternatives. The suppression of the fantastical, often used to characterize women's history, can also be read as a political strategy privileging the masculinist tendency to prefer realism and "scientific truth-telling" (King 175). As author Shelley Jackson tells us "what literature has edited out: the feminine"–the contemporary gothic historical novel is about retrieving and rewriting the feminine and feminine history in a way that is no longer feared, denigrated, or defined by patriarchy, e.g., as maternal, weakness, and/or fantasy, i.e., non-history.

Notable contemporary authors drawing on the gothic and thereby creating a new literary space in the genre include Ann Rinaldi's *The Color of Fire* (2005), which describes the life of a white servant who witnesses a fellow black servant being accused of treason and subsequently put to death. In Carol Birch's novel *Scapegallows* (2007), the historical English protagonist, Margaret Catchpole, is a former servant and "a smuggler's trollop" (174) sentenced to hang two separate times before being pardoned and exiled to Australia "for life" (418). Angela Badger's *Charlotte Badger: Buccaneer* (2002) and Zana Bell's *Forbidden Frontier* (2008) chronicle the life of English convict turned pirate Charlotte Badger, who, after being transported to Australia, became one of the first known white women to live in New Zealand. *Newes from the Dead* (2008) by Mary Hooper narrates the historical life of Anne Green, a London maidservant, hanged in 1650, but miraculously is revived when doctors at the Oxford Medical School prepare to dissect her body. In all of these Gothic historical novels, women are indirectly and directly involved in criminal activity, and when read together the works challenge norms of sexuality and gender.

Rather than condemning their respective protagonists for breaking the law, the authors contextualize and predominantly defend their heroine's choices. Laura Sjoberg and Caron E. Gentry suggest that such "stories contradict the dominant narrative about what a woman is generally and about women's capacity for violence specifically" (51). The authors argue that "mother, monster, and whore narratives exclude the possibility that women can choose to be violent because violent women interrupt gender stereotypes. 'Real' women are peaceful, conservative, virtuous and restrained; violent women ignore these boundaries of womanhood" (Sjoberg and Gentry 50-51). Such restrictive roles confine women's acts to being rationalized as "vengeance, insanity, and sexuality" (216). The act of confining ignores the political impact/justifications of women's violent actions. Nevertheless, Sjoberg's and Gentry's triad conforms with how the authors here justify their protagonists' actions, perhaps legitimizing their criticism. These feminist discourses also focus less on the criminal act itself and more on the domestic and familial circumstances leading up to and after the violence.

This writing emphasizes the necessity for reevaluating women's familial and personal narratives in conjunction with political history–the murders would have been publicized, giving the woman a certain, albeit biased, public presence. I analyze works specifically written on the mid-late nineteenth century: Ann Hébert's *Kamouraska* (1970) [14], Toni Morrison's *Beloved* (1987), Margaret Atwood's *Alias Grace* (1996), and Jane Harris's *The Observations* (2006)., My analysis pays particular attention to the Gothic elements as well as British colonialism and immigration in relation to the crimes. Britain figures prominently in the woman's historical novel pertaining to violence and crime.

In *Kamouraska*, Elisabeth and her domestic servant Aurélie Caron, both French and living in Québec, face the law of the British Queen Victoria and are sentenced to prison for murder. Grace Marks in Atwood's novel and Bessy in Harris's *Observations* are Irish immigrants in British dominions, Canada and Scotland respectively, and each enters into domestic service. [15] Only Sethe in *Beloved* does not face British colonialism because the United States is already independent at this time. Nevertheless, Sethe is a slave born into domestic servitude prior to abolition. Thus, she is part of Britain's/America's slave-trade legacy and compared to an immigrant, who has few rights, she has none.

All of the protagonists in this chapter are historical or, in the case of Morrison's *Beloved* and Harris' *The Observations*, inspired by historical figures and events. Bessy is loosely based on Hannah Cullwick, an eccentric English domestic servant who kept a diary in the Victorian era called *The Diaries of Hannah Cullwick, Victorian Maidservant* (Harris, "Interview" n. pag.). Morrison's *Beloved* is imaginatively inspired by the historical figure Margaret Garner, a pre-Civil War slave who murdered her own daughter before being caught by US Marshalls; she later died from typhoid while working as a slave on a planta-

---

[14] I am using the English translation by Norman Shapiro of the original French text *Kamouraska*.

[15] A related sub-genre includes novels on women during the potato famine in mid-late nineteenth century Ireland and their subsequent mass migration and displacement, for example, Jonatha Ceely's *Mina* (2005) and *Bread and Dreams* (2006) and Pat Kelly's *Galway Bay* (2009), which describes a family's emigration to America.

tion. Unlike the historical Garner, Morrison eventually makes Sethe a free-woman and gives her a life and future outside of and beyond slavery. The novel is a means for recuperating those slaves whose voices/lives have been silenced and have gone undocumented (even by the female gothic tradition) and is aptly dedicated to "Sixty Million and more."

The woman's historical novel reveals that criminality in the nineteenth century did not only pertain to working-class women (for instance, the imagined diary of Mary Surratt convicted of conspiring to assassinate President Lincoln, in Pamela R. Russell's *The Woman Who Loved John Wilkes Booth* (1978)), but they were more vulnerable and likely to be punished because of their low social standing. Roxanne Rimstead argues, "Traditionally, domestic servants in literature have been fixed as icons and stock characters (for instance, drudges, loafers, fools, messengers, mammies, and accomplices), or under-represented as silenced subjects, background fixtures mute as furniture" (44). In these novels, the servant protagonist speaks in her own voice (with the exception of Aurélie in *Kamouraska*, who is not the central character) and, as she encounters these prejudices, we see her internally reject them. Essential to understanding the protagonist's psychological state is the narrative technique of flashbacks between each protagonists' present and past, suggesting a continuity not only between time-frames within the novels but also to the contemporary time in which each author is writing. Thus, power dynamics between race and class and between a competing past and present are at play in each text.

Rimstead, referencing the work of several theorists, posits:

> Of the few existing literary studies on domestics in Western literature, most note that when paternalism was displaced by capitalism and the role of the servant shifted from loyalty to a contractual arrangement, the dramatization of intrusion increased, as manifested in crime writing that featured servants as threats within the household (Harris, Robbins, Trodd). The sexualization of master/servant relations and the icon of the domestic as temptress, the heightened need for privacy in the bourgeois home in the nineteenth century, the social hysteria around contamination by servants and the poor in general as morally and intellectually inferior, the rhetoric of racial purity in national policies to recruit domestics abroad, and the construction of good and bad femininity which helped separate the ladies from the maids-social attitudes like these buttressed the popular icon of the domestic as working-class intruder. (46)

Reflecting recent transnational feminist concerns on the relation between gendered domestic labor and gendered mobility, economic and social boundaries are crossed and blurred in these novels. The woman's historical novel "re-mind[s] the public that a majority of migrant workers are females who provide 'the cheapest, flexible, and most docile labor…for dirty, demanding, and dangerous jobs which locals shun'" (Tenaganita, qtd. in Ong 174). Though class separates the mistress and maid and they often fear, loathe, and avoid one another, they also imagine one another as maternal or sisterly figures and as being transformed by the other.

In Harris' *The Observations*, Bessy's mistress, Arabella, dresses herself in her servant's clothing and Grace in Atwood's *Alias Grace* dons the apparel of a lady when she steals Nancy's, her mistress', clothing. Wallace identifies the cross-dressing woman as important a "figure as the tragic queen" (*Woman's* 21) in the woman's historical novel and argues that she be read as the "woman novelist herself, 'cross-writing' as a man in order to enter into the 'masculine' sphere of history" (21), but this kind of cross-dressing is unique to Gothic writing. By dressing as a woman from a different class, new feminine identities are constructed. This further allows freedoms respective to the different gender expectations determined by social stratum. The issues of gender, race, and class in these novels are brought to the forefront through the analysis of such topics as the servant as criminal, red velvet, matricide and othermothering, the servant as prostitute, and the mistress as murderer.

The Servant as Criminal

Atwood's *Alias Grace*, Harris' *The Observations*, and Hébert's *Kamouraska* focus on "maids as slaves" (Ong 158) and, in these cases, the servant as criminal; Morrison's *Beloved* centers on the slave-servant-criminal. Aihwa Ong's description aptly applies to the theme of gendered divisions of labor, migrancy, and poor working conditions that the protagonists experience within the novels. In *Alias Grace*, Atwood reimagines the life of Grace Marks, who at the age of sixteen was accused and found guilty of murdering, with the help of James McDermott, her former employer Thomas Kinnear in the year 1843 in Richmond Hill, Upper Canada. The novel is a montage of literary and historical documents:

> [It] is pieced together like a patchwork, incorporating ballads, etchings, fictionalized dialogues, archival documents from the Kingston penitentiary, fictionalized letters, inner monologues, transcribed confessions, newspaper clippings, excerpts from Susanna Moodie's nineteenth-century descriptions of Grace, epigraphs from romantic literature, and even chapters titled after quilt patterns. (Rimstead 52)

Beginning in the years 1851 and 1859, an incarcerated Grace is sitting in the Governor's wife's parlor. Grace works as an unpaid servant for the Governor's wife during the day. Unlike her partner in crime, her so called "paramour" (Atwood 89), James McDermott, who hung for Kinnear's and his housekeeper Nancy Montgomery's murder, Grace's death sentence was commuted at the last minute.

Shuttling between the past and present, Grace recounts her tale to a psychiatrist, Dr. Simon Jordan. The reader pieces together Grace's past leading up to and after the murders at the same time as he does. We learn from Grace's meetings with Dr. Jordan that she was born in Northern Ireland, which is likened to a crime in and of itself. Grace's Confession confirms that "*both of the accused were from Ireland by their own admission*. That made it sound like a crime, and I don't know that being from Ireland is a crime; although I have often seen it treated as such" (103). Grace confesses that her mother only married her father, a Protestant Englishman and stone-mason by trade, because she was pregnant. When Grace's older sister Martha leaves home for good, Grace only nine years old says, "all the work Martha used to do around the house was now on me" (106). With Grace's father searching for work and drinking his wages in the taverns, the Marks' are close to starving, save for the charity of her mother's sister, Pauline.

When Pauline becomes pregnant herself and can no longer support Grace's very large family, the decision to immigrate to Canada is made for them. Grace reflects, "Many were doing it, and there was free land to be had in the Canadas, and what my father needed was to wipe the slate clean. Stone-masons were in great demand over there because of all the building and works that were going forward" (110). On the voyage, Grace's mother falls ill and dies; the family, when they arrive in Toronto, is given lodgings by Mrs. Burt, a widow who pities them. Under the pretense of looking for work, Grace's father falls behind on rent and drinks their small savings; he tells Grace, who is nearly thirteen, that she is "almost a grown woman now and [she] was eating him out of house and home, it was time [she] went out into the world to earn [her] own bread" (127). Grace, having mastered sewing from her mother, begins her first job working as a lowly servant for Mrs. Alderman Parkinson.

While working for Mrs. Parkinson, Grace meets her soon beloved fellow servant, Mary Whitney. Working in the laundry, Mary reminds Grace, "remember that we [are] not slaves, and being a servant [is] not a thing we were born to, nor would we be forced to continue at it forever, it was just a job of work" (157). Like the narrator in Amirrezvani's novel *The Blood of Flowers*, Mary instructs Grace on how, by saving their wages for a dowry, they can hope to marry into good households. Though Mary cautions Grace that men are liars and not to trust them, she becomes a victim to her own warnings and finds herself pregnant with her employer's son. Discrimination against an unwed mother is clear and flies in the face of Victorian ideals of women's moral purity and virtue. If Mary has the child, she will be forced out onto the streets and her reputation, which these novels suggest is the most important thing a young unmarried woman has, will be ruined.

Unable to face her dismal future prospects, Mary has an abortion and soon after dies. Grace, too reminded of Mary's death, takes up a new position with Mr. Dixon and, thereafter, a series of employers for whom, despite the increasing amount of immigrants, there was a persistent belief that were never enough to make up the shortage. As an immigrant, Grace is suitable to work as a servant in a wealthy "Canadian's" home, but her immigrant status also explains why it is used as leverage against her when she commits murder. The immigrant is considered suspicious and rightfully lower on the social strata. Dependable servants the novels intimate, are seemingly scarce and, thus because Grace is trained and has a reference, she is paid more. It is while working for Mr. Watson that she meets Nancy Montgomery, who tells her that she is Mr. Thomas Kinnear's housekeeper and he is in need of another servant (201). Despite having to leave the city for the country, Grace, desiring female companionship, takes the position.

Though Nancy feigns friendship and sisterhood in the beginning, Grace begins to realize that Nancy "did not like being crossed, and most of all she did not like being put in the wrong by Mr. Kinnear" (Atwood 223) with whom, according to Grace, she has a rather inappropriate and intimate relationship. While working for Mr. Kinnear Grace also meets McDermott, formerly from Ireland and an ex- English and Canadian soldier. McDermott, surly and insolent, is given notice to leave by the end of the month by Nancy. McDermott tells Grace that "he did not care to stay any longer with such a parcel of whores" (255). Grace does not understand his meaning, so McDermott explains that "it was only common knowledge that Nancy had a baby when she was working over at Wrights', by a young layabout who ran off and left her, only the baby died. But Mr. Kinnear hired her and took her in anyway, which no respectable man would have done; and it was clear from the first what he'd had in mind" (255). Learning about Nancy's illicit sexual past, Grace loses respect for her (though she should remember her love for Mary Whitney, Atwood also provides valid reasons for why a reader might think Grace herself is really Mary Whitney) and begins to argue and speak back to her, which coincides with McDermott's increasing frustration and anger towards Nancy–to the extent that he voices his intention to kill her and Mr. Kinnear.

McDermott's words cause Grace to reflect on her own situation. She says, "no prospects before me except the drudgery I'd been doing; and although I could always find a different situation, still it would be the same sort of work, from dawn to dusk, with always a mistress to be ordering me about" (260). Trapped within patriarchal gendered divisions of labor, Grace tells Dr. Jordan about how she discovered Nancy was pregnant with Mr. Kinnear's child. She also describes the murders: hitting Nancy on the head with an axe, strangling her with a neckerchief that had once belonged to Mary, and McDermott shooting Mr. Kinnear and tossing him into the cellar with Nancy's dead body. This part of the narrative neither absolves nor inculcates Grace in the murders, but suggests that she suffers from amnesia (a recurring problem from the time when Mary Whitney dies). After the murders, Grace explains how she and McDermott planned their escape to the United States and she took Nancy's dresses across borders is present in all the novels discussed in this chapter).

Arriving in Lewiston, the pair, quickly caught by the authorities, are arrested. In Grace's defense, her lawyer Mr. MacKenzie coerces Grace into saying,

> I was little more than a child, a poor motherless child and to all intents and purposes an orphan, cast out upon the world with nobody to teach me any better; and I'd had to work hard for my bread, from an early age, and was industry itself; and I was very ignorant and uneducated, and illiterate, and little better than a halfwit; and very soft and pliable, and easily imposed upon. (361)

Grace's propensity for transgressing the law is explained by her working-class status and implicitly, by her gender. As a young woman, without a mother to instruct and guide her, Grace is ultimately left to fend for herself. Ruth Beinstock Anolik writes that "the absence of the mother from the Gothic text allows for narratable deviance to flourish in the text, a deviance that in turn allows the text to thrive" (98).

Dr. Jordan's attempts to fact-check many of Grace's claims are, likewise, inconclusive. Upon visiting the lawyer who secured Grace's pardon, for she was never tried for the murder of Nancy Montgomery, the lawyer tells Dr. Jordan, "in my opinion, she was guilty as sin" (378). Dr. Jordan also visits the old Kinnear house and the Adelaide Street Methodist Church in order to see Mary Whitney's gravestone. Though the stone validates Grace's story, he knows it proves nothing:

> The Mary Whitney buried beneath it may not have any connection with Grace Marks at all. She could just be a name, a name on a stone, seen here by Grace and used by her in the spinning of her story. She could be an old woman, a wife, a small infant,

anyone at all. Nothing has been proved. But nothing has been
disproved, either. (387-88)

As Grace's innocence or guilt remains unresolved, Dr. Jordan asks her to be
hypnotized by a Dr. Jerome DuPont (a former peddler Grace was acquainted
with).

Under hypnosis, Grace purports to be speaking as Mary Whitney; Mary
Whitney, the sexually liberated half to Grace Mark's sexually repressed one,
inhabits Grace's body and reveals: "I told James to do it. I urged him to. I was
there all along!" (402). That Mary Whitney has been periodically taking over
Grace's body, unbeknownst to her, exonerates Grace's involvement in the
murders. It is after this experience that Dr. Jordan hastily leaves, knowing he
will have to make a report of what he has witnessed, though he confirms "the
truth eludes him. Or rather it's Grace herself who eludes him" (407). In a letter,
one of Grace's supporters writes that "as a result of this session [hypnosis], and
the astonishing revelations it produced, Dr. Jordan gave it as his opinion that
Grace Marks' loss of memory was genuine, not feigned–that on the fatal days
she was suffering from the effects of an hysterical seizure brought on by fright,
which resulted in a form of *auto-hypnotic somnambulism*" (432). The novel
ends with Grace's pardon and departure on August 7th, 1872 to a home provided in New York.

Atwood maintains that "the true character of the historical Grace Marks remains an enigma" (465), but she invents for Grace a marriage to her former
neighbor at the Kinnear's, Jamie Walsh, who testified against her in court.
Though Walsh now believes in Grace's innocence and begs her forgiveness, his
interest in Grace, Atwood suggests, is suspect and is possibly/probably no different than any other member of the public (including Atwood herself and the
reader) whose curiosity motivates an unusual interest in a woman who transgressed Victorian Canadian ideologies of sex and gender.

Red Velvet

The presence of the Gothic found in the contemporary women's historical novels discussed in this chapter also resonate with a re-evaluation of the historical
Mary Queen of Scots which begins with Lees' *The Recess* (1783) and continues with current works like Philippa Gregory's *The Other Queen* (2008). The
maternal genealogy these texts create supports Rayne Allinson's research that
argues Mary's body symbolizes three aspects: "the immortal body of the sovereign, the immaculate body of the female martyr, and the polluted body of the
criminal" (100). At her execution, Mary's clothing played an essential role in
her refusal to renounce herself as the rightful ruler of England. Wearing a

sumptuous black gown, she heightened her status and the injustice she faced. Allinson associates the "petticoat of crimson velvet" (107) that Mary wore underneath her gown with a subversive invocation of martyrdom: "Although it is possible Mary wore red to strengthen her resolve and reinforce her monarchical status, its omission from the Earl's report suggests that it was interpreted as yet another act of resistance against the criminal identity imposed on her by the block and axe" (Allinson 108). Red velvet is a symbol for social status, sexuality, and blood in Mary's life and continues to be used in the contemporary woman's Gothic novel, such as Emma Donoghue's *Slammerkin* in which aservant murders her mistress in 1763 London. Mary Saunders desires, like many women in these novels, velvet and lace and fine clothing. Her obsession with a red ribbon leads her to a life of prostitution and criminal behavior. Just as Grace in Atwood's novel "–"is a violent deviant who fails to uphold her role as moral purveyor" (Siddall 88), so too are Aurélie Caron in Hébert's novel *Kamouraska* and Sethe in *Beloved* described.

Caron, who agrees, like Grace, to murder her employer, is an interesting and prominent figure in Hébert's novel. She is seen through the eyes of her mistress, the narrator of the tale, Elisabeth d'Aulnières. Like the other texts, Hébert's narrative technique of recollections shuttles the reader between Elisabeth's present, which is with her dying second husband, Jerome Rolland, and her past when she married the violent, abusive, and unfaithful Antoine Tassy, the squire of Kamouraska, and plotted to have him murdered. As *Alias Grace*, Hébert's novel also takes place in pre-Confederation Canada, but in French-speaking Québec during the late 1830s. Elisabeth, in the early pages of the novel, describes the warrant for her arrest and the indictment followed by:

> Two months locked up, and then home. Reasons of health. Family reasons. Good-bye, prison. And good-bye to you, dear warden. You poor bewildered man. Well you have my maid to console you. Justice can hold her as long as it likes. Two years behind bars. Poor Aurélie Caron. But time wipes the slate. And now you're free, as free as your mistress. A new life, a new start .... (3)

Caron, clearly a servant, has served longer in prison than her mistress. Hébert writes, "Her dying husband Jerome, who, incidentally, wants their current maid Florida by his side rather than his wife, confronts Elizabeth about Caron. Delirious, he asks about the girl 'who used to smoke a pipe? … Aurélie Caron … Wasn't that her name? … Yes, I remember now …'" (21). Rolland's question catches Elisabeth by surprise as she has tried to bury her past and possibly her guilt surrounding the murder; Hébert, however, suggests leaving the past behind is impossible.

Elisabeth recounts her past living in Sorel with her three aunts, her mother, and her servants, including Caron, even after her first marriage. Caron's observations within the house, however, inculcate Elisabeth in her husband's murder: "'Madame would always go and lock herself in one of the bedrooms with Dr. Nelson' …. It's written down on paper, with an official stamp. Aurélie Caron's sworn deposition. That lying child" (40). The ambiguity and play between fact and fiction entails asking whose words count as truth. The novels suggest that it is those spoken by an established local-national (though, of course, former immigrant), white, wealthy gentleman and, in this chapter, also the "native" white, wealthy woman are those whose words are not questioned. In *Kamouraska* as well as *Alias Grace*, the blurring of facts legitimizes why the historical novel, an inherent mixing of the real with imagination, is a most suitable genre for these feminist texts. In contrast to Caron's damning testimony is Elisabeth's aunt Mademoiselle Angélique Lanouette's statement, which exonerates Elisabeth based on her good breeding, piousness, and class, not to mention her devotion as a wife.

Hébert writes: "And as for Aurélie Caron, everyone knows what a reputations she has. Elisabeth's worst mistake, the only thing she can be blamed for, was keeping that girl on. That shameless, unprincipled liar … That drunken beast … That … That slut…" (41). Aurélie, like the other servants discussed in this chapter, is portrayed in the stereotypes of her class, time, and place: fond of drinking, sexually loose, and prone to immoral-illegal activities (Lacelle 49) in contrast to the good wife and respectable mother stereotype. Claudette Lacelle claims that in Canada during the nineteenth century servants did not commit any more crimes than other groups (49) and the most common crime committed in Québec was military desertion (151); therefore, women servants, the majority of which were mobile and between the ages of sixteen and twenty-five, constituted a very small percentage of criminals (56), particularly murderesses. Nonetheless, they had a reputation for being immoral and vulgar. Also worth noting, in terms of the ethnic-immigrant stigmatism Grace encounters (and Bessy in *The Observations*), is that, in Québec City (1871-75), Irish servants, followed by French Canadians committed the most crimes (Lacelle 123).

The second aunt, Adélaïde, confirms her sister's testimony: "Aurélie Caron … Nothing but a liar … A slut, a drunkard …" (43). The third aunt lays her hand on the Bible and whispers, "'Madame was never alone in her room with Dr. Nelson. Her mother, Madame d'Aulnières, was always with her.' All at once Aurélie's laugh chills me to the bone" (104) because Aurélie Caron says, "I swear, Madame spent a lot of time alone with the doctor. With the doors closed. As soon as her mother went out" (105). A class barrier discredits much of Caron's testimony though the reader knows she is telling the truth. Racism is also at play. Rimstead believes that Caron is "a mixed-blood" (47); is she Métis? Is this another reason why Elisabeth separates herself from the working class: "I won't be brought to trial before the likes of them! Servants, innkeepers, boatmen, peasants! Good for nothing witnesses, every one! None of them can stand up against me. And as for Aurélie Caron …" (53). Even before Elisabeth's marriage to Tassy, Caron troubles her.

Both fifteen years old, Elisabeth says, Caron "taunts me, this child, and makes me green with envy" (55). Elisabeth envies Caron for her physical and sexual freedom and asks her several times about boys because she is married to the respectable Antoine Tassy, squire or *seigneur* (which in the French text plays on the word "Lord") of Kamouraska (66). Subject to her husband's violence, womanizing, drunkenness, and extended disappearances, Elisabeth takes her two children and moves back to Sorel with her mother and aunts. Elizabeth reflects, "The first thing I do, back in Sorel. Hire Aurélie Caron. Despite my mother's and my aunts' entreaties. To play Milady and her maid. Until …" (100). Fascinated by Caron, Elisabeth remarks, "they say you have yourself a merry time, Aurélie! Down by the river, out on the islands. Is it true? Tell me, what do you do? Tell me everything!" (ibid.). Elisabeth's dissatisfaction with her marriage influences her feelings when she meets Dr. Nelson, her husband's former school friend. Elisabeth falls in love with the doctor, and, thus, their affair begins. Caron serves as an essential part of the affair as she carries messages between the lovers and even drives Elisabeth to the doctor's home.

The situation leads Elisabeth to send Caron to go fetch the doctor: "Please, Aurélie, you have to. I'm pregnant. …" (144). Elizabeth, first, needs to make peace with Antoine so "the blameless wife can announce that she's pregnant again by her husband" (145). It is during this time that Elisabeth tells Dr. Nelson that they must kill her husband. When Dr. Nelson learns the child is his, he decides to do her bidding. Hébert writes, "The poison is Elisabeth's idea. A pregnant woman's obsession. Send Aurélie to Kamouraska with poison, so she can …" (166). In order to convince Aurélie to undertake the mission, Elisabeth bribes her with money and material possessions: "Now I'm giving Aurélie some cakes. And ribbons too. Red ones and green ones. In an instant her sullen face lights up. Like a child, in tears one moment and laughing the next" (176). Dr. Nelson and Elisabeth dress Aurélie in beautiful clothing; she "claps her hands. Begins to stir. To flutter. Struts about the room. Comes back to the mirror. Declares, in a shrill little drawl: 'I'm absolutely gorgeous! Just like a high-class lady!'" (181). Dr. Nelson tells Aurélie she will go to Kamouraska, seduce Antoine, and poison him. He describes her reward should she succeed: you'll "never have to work again for the rest of your life, Aurélie. You'll live like a lady. Red velvet and all" (182). He tells her, "I'll give you a place of your own,

with beautiful things" (ibid.). Thus, the dream of one day getting married that
Mary Whitney envisions, tempts Aurélie. Elisabeth sweetens the deal by calling Aurélie her friend and her sister. Moved by flattery and the promise of a
change in status, Aurélie consents to their wishes.

Lee Skallerup argues that "she has totally embraced the values of the upper
class, and when she is presented with a possible way in, she takes it. But the
class that she longs to be a part of ultimately betrays her" (150). Antoine manages to survive Aurélie's poisoning and, when she returns, Dr. Nelson declares
he must take the act into his own hands (Hébert 191). He murders Tassy on
January 31, 1839. On the morning of February 7th, the day after Dr. Nelson
returns to Elisabeth, he is to be arrested by the authorities, but he escapes via
the American border. Elisabeth, with her aunt's help, goes searching for her
lover, but is arrested. She declares:

> You're not my friend anymore, Aurélie. I told you to lie when
> they put you in the box. Anything, so long as you didn't betray
> us. Now look what you've done. Here you are in prison, just
> like your poor mistress. I'm so afraid this awful place is going
> to taint me, Aurélie. … Your Honor, this girl is a liar, a shame-
> less slut. (249)

Though Dr. Nelson makes it to Burlington, Vermont, it is suggested by Elisabeth that he is captured and taken back to Canada, where he and Elisabeth
seemingly accuse one another of the crimes. Two months after being imprisoned, Elisabeth is released and quickly marries Jerome Rolland. Dr. Nelson is
extradited back to the United States and disappears. Aurélie's fate after she is
released from prison remains unknown.

Red velvet also plays an important part in Morrison's *Beloved*. The work
opens in 1873, Cincinnati, with Sethe and her daughter Denver being haunted
by a baby's ghost. Extrapolating upon Mitchell's work, means interpreting the
ghost who "remaining spectral to the historical record, is given flesh in the
world the text" by Morrison (128). The mother and daughter live at 124, the
former home of Sethe's mother-in-law Baby Suggs, who dies shortly after
Denver's two brothers leave home. Sethe explains that the ghost is Beloved,
her baby who died. While discussing the ghost and thinking back to her lost
child, Sethe encounters Paul D sitting on her porch; he is the last of the Sweet
Home men and Sethe and Baby Suggs were slaves with him eighteen years ago
in Kentucky.

Sethe, now a cook at a restaurant who sews on the side , explains to Paul D
how, pregnant with Denver who is named after a white girl who helps her give
birth), she made her dangerous escape from Sweet Home. Amy M. Green argues that Amy, the run-away white girl who finds and helps Sethe, a run-away

slave, "harbors an obsession, a near physical craving for red velvet, a powerful symbol of blood spilled in both acts of cruelty and childbirth, both of which relate directly to Sethe" (120). In Hébert's novel, Elisabeth tells her servant, "You'll live like a lady. Red velvet and all" (182); thus, red velvet can be considered a symbol for a woman's escape from the margins, her desire for upward class mobility, her dangerous sexuality, and for blood spilled.

Irigaray uses the term "sang rouge" to signify not just class or sexuality but red blood as a link to the maternal:

> The red blood refers to the possibility of a maternal genealogy, which would take its place alongside, and in fertile conjunction with the paternal genealogy, which is the only genealogy recognized by patriarchy. Red blood may also refer to the unacknowledged debt to the mother, on which patriarchy depends. (Whitford, "Section I" 18)

With Amy's help, Sethe and Denver make it to Baby Suggs' house. Baby Suggs, the reader learns, is a free-woman because her son Halle, who also worked at Sweet Home, bought her freedom. When Suggs leaves the farm, Sethe replaces her and it is during this time that she begins a relationship with Halle, marries him, and bears his children.

Experiencing the trauma of being a female slave, Sethe describes how prior to running away "those boys came in there and took my milk. That's what they came in there for. He held me down and took it" (16). Later Paul D tells Sethe that it is this sight that breaks Halle and the reason she couldn't find him on the day they planned to escape together. Following her traumatic experience in the barn, Sethe tells her white owner Mrs. Garner, who is physically and symbolically unable to speak up on Sethe's behalf; instead she ineffectively cries and the boys and a man known only as Schoolteacher beat Sethe severely leaving scars that look like a tree. Paul D asks, when she ran, did Schoolteacher ever find her, to which she replies yes, but that under no circumstances was she going back. Sethe explains, "I don't care who found who. Any life but not that one. I went to jail instead. Denver was just a baby so she went right along with me" (42). Though the reader reflects on the contradiction of sending a slave to jail when the slave has no legal rights in and of him or herself and, thus, is outside of the system, Sethe seems to give little thought to her prison sentence. It is also possible, as Lorna L. McLean and Marilyn Barber surmise in their work on nineteenth Irish immigrant domestic servants in Canada, that incarceration, though it impeded one's liberty, could be preferable to a harsh patriarchal, racist, and poor economic situation awaiting one's existence outside.

Matricide and Othermothering

In *Beloved*, Sethe neglects to tell Paul D that, when the men came for her, she was in the shed with her children: "Inside, two boys bled in the sawdust and dirt at the feet of a nigger woman holding a blood-soaked child to her chest with one hand and an infant by the heels in the other" (149). With the two boys breathing and Denver still alive, Sethe breastfeeds her; "she took her mother's milk along with the blood of her [dead] sister. And that's the way they were when the sheriff returned, having commandeered a neighbour's cart" to take her to prison (152). Baby Suggs brings Sethe food in prison and tells her that The Colored Ladies of Delaware, Ohio, "had drawn up a petition to keep [her] from being hanged" (183). Approximately three months later (because Denver is ready for solid food), Seth is released. Upon release, Sethe is ex-communicated and sentenced to a life of exile from the black community, both for her perceived pride and for her denial of any wrongdoing. Sethe, however, buys a modest gravestone with only the child's name, which overlaps with the arrival of the ghost in the house.

The ghost, temporarily extricated from the house while Paul D lives with Sethe, coincides with a strange woman appearing. The imagery of giving birth is prevalent in her arrival—not only does Beloved emerge from the water as if she has just been born, but, when Sethe sees her for the first time, she proceeds to release water as if her water is breaking. Paul D asks the woman what her name is and she calmly replies, "Beloved" (52). Clear to the reader, but unknown to Paul D, is the link between this girl and Sethe's deceased child by the same name. The return of Beloved, the daughter, also symbolically signifies Morrison as a daughter returning to the legacy of slavery from "a black female point of view" (Rody 23). A bridge "between the authorial present and the ancestral past" (24), the novel emphasizes a daughter haunted by her connection to her enslaved maternal ancestors.

Taking comfort and joy in Beloved's initial arrival, "Sethe learned the profound satisfaction Beloved got from storytelling. It amazed Sethe (as much as it pleased Beloved) because every mention of her past life hurt. Everything in it was painful or lost. She and Baby Suggs had agreed without saying so that it was unspeakable" (58). It is while Beloved and Paul D are living with Sethe and Denver that the past reveals itself. Denver, who has little memory of her early childhood, is asked by a local boy about her mother: "Didn't your mother get locked away for murder? Wasn't you in there with her when she went?" (104). Paul D is also shown a newspaper photo and article by their neighbor Stamp Paid who witnessed the murder. Though refusing to believe the photo depicts Sethe, Paul D confronts her and can't understand how, even out of love,

she committed murder. Sethe, "your love is too thick" (164), says Paul D and
he moves out of her house and into town.

It does not take Sethe long to realize, "BELOVED, she my daughter. She
mine. See. She come back to me of her own free will and I don't have to explain a thing" (200). Beloved symbolizes the loss of children born into slavery
as a collective. As Shirley A. Hill points out, "enslaved black women ... give
birth to 'property'" and were "especially victimized by motherhood" (109).
Jeannette King declares "wider, however, than the gulf which racial ideology
established between black female sexuality and the idealized asexual white
woman is that established between black and white experiences of motherhood,
perceived by nineteenth-century scientists to be the defining purpose of the
female body" (164). Whereas the white woman usually could keep her child,
the black woman rarely could. Denied a meaningful and loving relationship
with her mother and as a mother, Sethe says, "I'll tend to her as no mother ever
tended a child, a daughter. Nobody will ever get my milk no more except my
own children" (200). For Sethe, the painfulness of slavery is traced back to her
own mother who worked in the rice field and wasn't able or allowed to breast
feed her. Her body was considered her master's property. Sethe was fed by a
nursemaid and only given leftovers, after the white children were full. Seeing
her own mother maybe once or twice in her life, the last image of her Sethe
remembers is her hanging.

Sethe claims a role for herself that has been denied slaves: mother. Yi-Lin
Yu argues that, despite persistent racism and sexism, "black motherlines are
also restored and maintained through other forms of maternity operated mostly
in female-affiliated network and connection" (136). This is clear from Sethe's
own experiences with her mother. Patricia Hill Collins, constructing an Afrocentric perspective on motherhood, argues that, unlike white motherhood,
which is conceived as a private experience, black motherhood is "a public and
'collective responsibility' performed within 'cooperative, age-stratified, wom-
an-centred, 'mothering' networks'" (Collins, qtd. in Yu 137). Collins identifies
four themes that express an "Afrocentric ideology of motherhood view" (ibid.):
"1) Bloodmothers, othermothers, and women-centered networks; 2) Providing
as part of mothering; 3) Community othermothers and social activism; 4)
Motherhood as a symbol of power" (ibid.). Thus, Morrison's work is a counter-
novel to violated and disrupted matrilineages and provides, through the woman's historical novel, a revolutionary notion of othermothering.

The balance, however, between mothering, working, and having time for
one's self is a problem that still plagues twenty-first century society. Morrison
writes that Sethe's life/history is meant to relate "to contemporary issues about
freedom, responsibility, and women's place" (xvi). Motherhood, while a gift

and joy, can also consume. This is evident in Sethe's increasingly problematic relationship with Beloved. Giving her entire self to Beloved, Sethe loses her job at the restaurant. When Denver realizes that her mother is overwhelmed because of her guilt, she takes matters into her own hands and asks for help. Morrison writes, "Denver thought she understood the connection between her mother and Beloved: Sethe was trying to make up for the handsaw; Beloved was making her pay for it. But there would never be an end to that, and seeing her mother diminished shamed and infuriated her" (251). When Denver explains to one of the neighbors that Beloved has returned in the flesh and is pregnant with Paul D's child, the community rallies itself for a rescue.

After eighteen years of solitude, judgment, and avoidance by the neighbors, thirty women in solidarity (a relationship that is not possible in slavery–though the bond of experiencing slavery becomes a familial bond) make their way to 124 to save Sethe and chase Beloved away. Paul D also returns, asking for forgiveness, much in the same way Jaime Walsh pleads with Grace Marks in Atwood's *Alias Grace*, so that he and Sethe can have not only a past, a past confronted, exorcised, and spoken, but a post-slavery future together.

The Servant as Prostitute

Harris's *The Observations* is told from the point of view of Bessy, who, like Grace in Atwood's *Alias Grace*, is a young Irish domestic servant. Working in Victorian Scotland for a Mrs. and Mr. Reid, similar to Grace, Bessy's metanarrative patches "together versions of reality and events" (Wisker 75). With competing claims for truth and lies, it becomes clear the narrator is unreliable. Bessy, glossing over the truth to Arabella Reid, explains that she's been living in Glasgow (Harris 3), working as housekeeper for a Mr. Levy of Hyndland, but is now seeking employment because her employer has died. Short a servant, Arabella hires Bessy. Bessy impresses her mistress because she is literate, and informs Arabella that her late mother taught her to read and write.

The reader, however, knows this is a lie: "my mother was alive and most likely blind drunk down by the Gallowgate as usual and even she was sober she barely have wrote her own name on a magistrate's summons" (Harris vii). While working, Arabella asks Bessy to keep a diary of not only her daily events but also her feelings. When Bessy's matter-of-fact entries are not elaborate enough for her mistress, she begins to invent. For example, she writes of her mother and compares her to a smiling angel. Bessy later discovers, however, that her mistress is secretly writing a book called *Observations on the Habits and Nature of the Domestic Class in My Time*. As Ann Heilmann and Mark Llewellyn note "in the period in which Harris's novel is set, observation was considered essential to the scientific project [and…] 'facts obtained by positive observation and investigation'" (*Neo-Victorianism* 117). The gothic's genre's interest and fascination with science is highlighted by Mrs Reid experimenting on Bessy as she has done with her former employees – all for the sake of science and the pursuit of scientific discovery. Though of course given gender restrictions at the time, her scientific lab is restricted to her domestic world and her subjects not surprisingly are limited to her servants.

Heilmann and Llewellyn continue to suggest that "the concept of observation and the scientific gaze is here appropriated by women across the class-divide: by the frustrated upper-middle-class wife in quest of a meaningful occupation (before her marriage Arabella aspired to a philanthropic teaching career) and by the domestic servant, otherwise the subject of scrutiny and investigation" (*Neo-Victorianism* 119). Bessy becomes a capable observer when she reads the entry written about herself: *"The Most Particular Case of a Low Prostitute"*. Arabella reveals in her notes that she has received a letter from the late Mr. Levy's brother who confirms that Bessy, whose true name is Daisy, was not really a housekeeper, but, in the manner of Nancy in Atwood's *Alias Grace*, was kept there under "IMMORAL CIRCUMSTANCES" (121).

Arabella also learns (and, hence, so too does Bessy and the reader) that she "was reputedly sold into his brother's [Mr. Levy's] care by an elder sister, who in return collected a weekly payment" (Harris 124). As Bessy begins to think about her past, she reveals that her so-called sister is really her mother. Bessy discloses her early life with her mother Bridget, a prostitute, in Dublin. Meeting a man named Joe Dimpsey, Bridget falls in love and, after he tells her he is sailing back to Scratchland, Scotland, she tells her eight or nine year-old daughter she's going with him, but that she can't afford to take her: "You'll be all right here on your own for a few years until you grow up, will you not?" (149, 150). Pleading with her mother not to leave her behind, Bessy convinces Bridget to agree that she will do whatever is asked of her. Pretending to be Bessy's older sister, Bridget pimps out her daughter for the entire week in order to raise Bessy's boat fare.

Arriving in Glasgow together, Bridget takes a room off Stockwell Street and quickly puts Bessy to work, including making her perform incestuous acts with her. As Daisy notes, many of the prostitutes in Glasgow are also "from across the water anyway so there was a bond there in common" (239). The narrative then switches back to the present and Bessy is piecing together the unusual circumstances in regards to the previous maids being dismissed by Arabella. The maid who stands out is Nora. The reader learns that she died mysteriously on the railway tracks one night after being hit by a train. While Bessy plays tricks on her mistress, pretending that Nora's ghost is haunting the house and slowly driving Arabella mad, a real "ghost" also appears to Bessy in the form of her mother (300).

Bessy awakens to see someone in her room: "even without looking I knew that the person was my mother" (301). The appearance of Bessy's mother coincides with several notices in the local paper asking for help in the whereabouts of a certain Daisy O'Toole: "*STRAYED from her home on Wednesday the 2nd September last, DAISY O'TOOLE, also known as ROSEBUD or POD*" (359). At this point in the narrative, Arabella is convinced that two people, Mrs Gillfillan and her hunchman McDonald, who run a Register Office for servants and are interested in "what makes a maid loyal and obedient" (375), have come to experiment upon Nora (376).

The woman, who has been lurking around Castle Haivers and who Arabella imagines as the woman wanting to hurt Nora, is in fact Bessy's mother. Bridget explains that a local man, Reverend Pollock, answered her newspaper ad and told her about a young girl working at Castle Haivers who fit her description. For Arabella, in her confusion, he is the supposed henchman. It becomes clear that Bridget has come to claim Daisy/Bessy in order to make her work for her again: "she wanted *me* back" (422). Arabella imagines the events happening to Bessy as happening to her dead servant Nora, suggesting that she confuses Bessy with Nora and that one servant is the same as the next; every servant is replaceable and interchangeable. In reality, however, it is truly Bessy's life that is at stake, as she foresees a terrible future back in Gallowgate. Bessy reveals:

> Now I realized that no matter where I went, she would track me down … She'd never let me be. It was only a matter of time before she got me fired. And then where would I go, with no character and no money? She'd only come after me again and even if I found another job, she'd spoil it for me by telling them what I was. Of course, my missus didn't care about all that. Dear lovely missus! She didn't mind what I'd been. (424)

Unable to escape her past and her path, Bessy resigns and agrees to go back to Glasgow with her mother. Before she is able to leave, however, her mistress Arabella, the aspiring-thwarted scientist who has been locked inside her room due to her illness and madness, turns the tables. Disguised in Bessy's servants' clothing, Arabella makes her way into the center of town set on killing both Mrs Gillfillan (Bridget, Bessy's mother) and McDonald (the Reverend). In true Gothic style, Bessy's mother is found dead on the rail tracks, in the same place where Nora, Arabella's former servant, died.

The Mistress Murderer

With the death of Bridget, Bessy in *The Observations* is free from a life of shame and prostitution. Though Arabella could not save Nora (who was pregnant at the time of her death and dismissed from the house because of it by Mr. Reid, therefore, very much a Mary Whitney figure from Atwood's *Alias Grace*), she saves Bessy by pushing her mother in front of a train. She also injures Mr. Pollock, who was the father of Nora's unborn child. Thus, the feminist perspective Rimstead writes of in *Alias Grace* is applicable because *The Observations* "focuses on the sexual exploitation of female domestics by privileged men as the dark side of class power" (52). It is, also, only by engaging in sexual relations with powerful men, as Nancy or Bessy does with Mr. Levy and as perhaps Nora does with Mr. Pollock, that social mobility is possible. Arabella is moreover proclaimed mad by her husband and doctor and sent to an asylum, which is similar to Grace, who spends time in an asylum after the murders, though Arabella is absolved of any criminal charges because she is, like Elisabeth d'Aulnières, an upper-class woman. Arabella's asylum is a private facility, unlike the terrible conditions and sexual exploitation Grace describes. Feeling devoted to her mistress for saving her life, Bessy takes up a job working as a kitchen maid in the asylum until she is promoted to attendant. It is here that Arabella functions as a mother for Bessy and the two are able to share a relationship outside of patriarchal restraints and society.

Similarly, Elisabeth in *Kamouraska* is depicted as imprisoned, both physically and psychically, in her everyday life prior to her actual imprisonment. Elisabeth, however, never meaningfully relates to the social restrictions that women across different classes and cultural backgrounds are subjected to, such as not being able to own property or participate politically. Her personal, internal, and fragmented voice expresses a narrow social definition of femininity associated with middle-to-upper-class respectability and reputation. Identifying with notions of love, marriage, and children exemplified by Queen Victoria, Elisabeth has 11 children: two from her first husband, one by her lover, and eight by her second husband. Anolik argues that "fantasy has its limits in posing resistance to the actual dispossession of women" (108) and that, although "warning female readers of the dangers of patriarchal systems, the Gothic avoids endorsing any truly revolutionary resistance to these systems" (109). This is clear when, finding herself unable to cope with the realities of her dismal and violent life with Antoine, Elisabeth turns to her lover Dr. Nelson. She invents him as a fairy-tale inspired rescuer, much like Simon Jordon imagines himself to be in *Alias Grace* by freeing Grace Marks from prison.

Hébert, heightening Elisabeth's imprisonment through tensions between French and English as languages and as peoples in Canada throughout the novel, describes Elisabeth facing charges for murdering her husband. She is read her indictment in a foreign-tongue, the same tongue of her American lover. The charge is one of the few instances of English in the original French text: "The indictment ... Court of King's Bench. Session of September 1840. The Queen against Elisabeth d'Aulnières-Tassy" (Hébert 2). Elisabeth has rebelled against the Queen. Hébert suggests that Elisabeth cannot embody the traditional and antiquated French ways associated with her husband, Tassy, or embrace a foreign, rigid Victorian gender identity; nor can she escape the limits of the Gothic narrative–all of these imprison women.

Murray Sachs adds that "Kamouraska" is also the name of the Québec town in which Hébert saw "the word 'amour' imprisoned within the walls of the harsh sounds of the two *k's*." (115). Thus, desperate to escape her husband's violence and to experience what she considers ideal love with Dr. Nelson, Elisabeth organizes Antoine's death and never expresses guilt, sadness, or regret. The only emotions of regret and loss she shows occur when she reflects on Dr. Nelson escaping across the border: the border symbolizes finality as it separates physically and emotionally; her hopes for a future together are dashed. Unsurprisingly, Karen S. McPherson describes Elisabeth as "a haunted narrator" (107), who commits to romanticized ideals of love and ideals of honor . *Kamouraska* is, thus, not a celebration of the domestic and Victorian ideals but is an argument against gender restrictions, unrealistic notions of romance, and expectations within the family, especially those which deny woman a public-political role/voice by confining her to the domestic realm.

Conclusion

A revamping of the eighteenth and nineteenth century woman's Gothic novel, whereby the heroines either married, died, or went mad, these works continue to express the past as dark, supernatural, fairytale-like, sexed, mysterious, criminal, and whereby women seek escape from a pre-assigned role in order to construct her own version of women's history. Devoted to the mid-late nineteenth century, each work narrates a historical figure publically accused of criminal activity or murder. In Morrison's *Beloved*, the murder occurs as an act of love devoted to familial and personal escape by a mother; in *The Observations*, Arabella, suffering from madness, murders her servant's mother in the belief that she is protecting-mothering Bessy from a future of prostitution and poverty; and in *Alias Grace*, we can see a desire for escape from a life of drudgery as a servant. Hébert in *Kamouraska*, however, brings to light a mother committed to and imprisoned by the ideals of femininity defined by a patriarchal society. In addition, each work reexamines the relationship between mistress and maid, which I explicated through the femino-centric topics of the servant as criminal, red velvet, matricide and othermothering, the servant as prostitute and the mistress as murderer: importantly, "this refiguring of the female gothic represents its continued ability to engage with contemporary anxieties about womanhood, and to function as a device to rewrite and understand both historical and contemporary versions of the female subject" (Cooper 167). Expressing recent transnational fears and concerns about rebellious and violent women, the novels reveal the dynamics and convergence of class, sexuality, and race through a distinct gendered lens that powerfully protests against inequalities between the sexes. At the same time the works resist the relegation of women to the domestic and being violently excluded from history not just in the nineteenth century but in today's twenty-first century.

CHAPTER SEVEN

Feminist Mothering: The Woman's War Novel

> History does not happen of its own accord. It is up to us to
> build it
> — Luce Irigaray, *I Want Love, Not War*

There is a common belief that only men can write authentic war novels (Higonnet, "Cassandra's Question" 144). Margaret Higonnet believes "the a priori identification of war with masculinity symbolically exiles women from war fiction" (160); thus, "no other genre is so highly gendered. The exploits of men in the formation and defense of a people or nation, though they may provoke the 'tears of women,' do not justify their tales" (144). Historical novelists and feminists (Cockburn, Gibbons, Fenton Stitt, Higonnet, Liston Liepold, Logsdon-Conradsen) recently have been re-evaluating and contesting the genre from a plurality of transnational voices. Actively addressing the persistence of patriarchal violence and militarism in the lives of women, the genre's masculine, Eurocentric parameters and notions of an authentic narrative are being challenged by contemporary women's writing.

Most women's historical war novels concentrate on the time frame between the American Civil War (1881-65) and, the period that appeals most to women writers, WWII (1939-1945). War novels also typically fall within at least one of the following six categories:

1) women's contributions as nurses in war, for instance Hilary Green's novel *Never Say Goodbye* (2006), in which Diana, who serves in the FANY program, is also an agent for the Special Operations Executive.

2) women's resistance during WWII against Nazi Germany, both within Germany and Occupied Europe. Examples include the women in Thaisa Frank's *Heidegger's Glasses* (2010), the protagonist Elsie in Sarah McCoy's *The Baker's Daughter* (2012), and the sisters in Lucretia Grindle's *The Villa Triste* (2010), who, in Nazi-occupied Florence, Italy, undermine the occupation.

3) civilian life on the North American and European home front during WWII. For instance, in Marge Piercy's *Gone to Soldiers* (1987), American women's sacrifices are narrated. As Angela Huth emphasizes in her British novel *Landgirls*:

If half a million men were withdrawn from the munitions industries to fight, and the industries had to expand by one and a
half million, who would work in the factories to equip the newly swollen forces? Answer: women. A million and a half of
them would have to leave their children, their kitchens, their
darning, jobs such as running a local post office, and go into
the factories. (148)

4) women as persecuted victims of WWII, seen, for example, in novels on
the Japanese occupation: Belinda Alexandra's *White Gardenia* (2002) narrates
a woman arriving in a village on the China-Russia border after fleeing the Russian Revolution. Facing imminent occupation by the Japanese in WWII, she
has to return to Russia and leave her child Anya behind in China. Rani Man-
icka's *The Rice Mother* (2004) describes a Ceylonese woman who, after marrying, moves to Malaya before World War II and Kate Furnivall's *The White
Pearl* (2012) also discusses the occupation of Malaya.

5) the breakup and separation of families either through death, adoption,
remarriage, relocation, or evacuation. Rosie Alison's *The Very Thought of You*
(2009), Catherine Hall's *Days of Grace* (2010), and Ruth Hamilton's *That Liverpool Girl* (2011) all cover the topic of familial separation by evacuation and
Alyson Richman's *The Lost Wife* (2011) chronicles two Jewish lovers in Pra-
gue prior to the war and their miraculous reunion years later in New York.

6) the immediate post WWII years in which family members attempt to reunite or reconcile, for instance Anne Valery's *Tenko Reunion* (1985) which is
about the internment of western women, after Singapore falls to Japan.
Xinran's *Sky Burial: An Epic Love Story of Tibet* (2004), Susan Abulhawa's
Mornings in Jenin (2010) , and Rosalind Laker's *The House by the Fjord*
(2011), which describes the visit of an English war widow to her father-in-law
in Norway in 1946 also fall into this category.

The recent popularity of women's writing on war suggests the genre is being reconceptualized to suit women's needs. Differing from earlier writing such
as Margaret Mitchell's sumptuous historical romance *Gone With the Wind*
(1936), which is set in the South during the American Civil War, post 1970
novels, as the categories above suggest, recuperate the lives of women actively
engaged in and experiencing the devastation and hardships of war but also the
possibility for post-war forgiveness and reconciliation. The novels analyzed
here Joy Kogawa's *Obasan* (1981), Angela Huth's *Land Girls* (1994), Simone
Zelitch's *Louisa* (2001) , Sara Young's *My Enemy's Cradle* (2008), Margaret
Dickinson's *Suffragette Girl* (2009)and Robin Oliveira's *My Name is Mary
Sutter* (2011),adhere to what Higonnet calls subversive war writing. Women's
writing displaces "stock conceptions" by contesting "the boundaries drawn

between battlefront and homefront, war and peace, public and private, white and black, nation and people, men and women. By mining such boundaries, these texts explode the narrow conceptions of war on which their own exclusion from the literature of war has rested" ("Cassandra's Question" 151-52). Half of these novels portray women as heroic participants on the battlefield and homefront (*My Name is Mary Sutter*, *Suffragette Girl*, *Landgirls*), while the other half portray women as anti-war trauma victims and survivors of the Second World War (*Obasan*, *My Enemy's Cradle*, *Louisa*).

The woman's historical novel alerts us to how war can radically transform, challenge, reinforce, or put into crises traditional gender expectations. Stereotypical images of women as "maternal, emotional, and peace-loving" are complicated by the "monstrous" woman capable of violence (Sjoberg and Gentry 1). Laura Sjoberg and Caron E. Gentry suggest that the woman who commits violence is "incompatible with traditional explanations of all women as the 'peaceful people' whom 'war protects' and who 'should be protected from war'" (3); a "woman is expected to be against war and violence, but to cooperate with wars fought to protect her innocence and virginity" (4). While identifying how gendered tropes, particularly motherhood and the maternal, are used dichotomously either to valorize soldiering and legitimize conflict and combat (even for causes such as abolishing slavery, fascism, or Nazism) or to invoke an anti-war, in which after the death of her son, Joe, a mother walks from Liverpool to London to protest the government allowing underage boys to serve as soldiers in WWI) is worthwhile, the focus in this chapter is on how war contributes to what Andrea O'Reilly refers to as feminist mothering ("That is What Feminism Is" 191).

Feminist mothering challenges feminists claims from the 1960s and the early 1970s (Beauvoir, Friedan, Morgan) that argued motherhood is "a bitter trap' for women" (Shulamith Firestone, qtd. in Nathanson 244) and/or "the very source of women's oppression" (ibid.). By contrast, feminist mothering today re-validates motherhood as a viable feminist choice, evident in women's historical novels. In these maternal texts, mothering is central to one's identity but is "understood as lived resistance to the normative –stereotypical –expectations of both motherhood and womanhood" (O'Reilly, "Introduction" 5). Seeking to "redefine motherwork as a socially engaged enterprise that seeks to effect cultural change through new feminist modes" (7), in the first group of texts on heroic women, two of the novels (Oliveira's, Dickinson's) portray the feminist aunt as ostensibly resisting but then choosing the role of mother. Meanwhile, Huth's novel challenges the image of the idealized farmwife Mrs. Lawrence who, acting as a stand-in mother, is loved but rejected as a viable figure by the protagonists in their future lives as mothers. In the second group of maternal texts on persecuted war victims, the biological mother, as in the former group, is either absent or dead. There is an added exploration of betrayal, which is central to understanding this kind of feminist mothering. Kogawa's work is a search by a daughter for the mother who disappeared; Young's novel is about a woman who raises her Jewish child with an ex-German soldier and Zelitch's text portrays a Jewish mother-in-law stepping in as mother to her German daughter-in-law. A better grasp of the complexity of feminist mothering in women's historical war novels, is evident in the following femino-centric topics: ethic of care theory, maternal mortality and the aunt, maternal reconciliation, mothers as foreign enemies, and the homefront.

Ethic of Care Theory: Nurses on the Frontlines

During the Victorian era, women were expected to be in "the domain of the home and serve as the ornamental wife" (O'Reilly, "Maternal Activism" 7). This belief resulted in the "invention of full-time motherhood" (7). Restricted to middle-class white women, "this gendered schism converged to construct mothering as *essentially* and naturally the identity and purpose of women, and the family as fundamentally a private unit separate and distinct from the larger, political and social world" (ibid.). Defying preconceptions, for instance women's physical and emotional weakness when compared with men, for their times and places (the American Civil War and World War I respectively), the feminist heroines of Oliveira's and Dickinson's novels pursue entering and transforming the strictly male profession of medicine.

Both Mary and Florrie challenge traditional gender roles for women and reveal an emerging feminist consciousness, which Judith Stadtman Tucker calls "a feminist ethic of care." Stadtman Tucker writes that "as with maternalism, a feminist ethic of care designates caring for others as an essential social function. But rather than valorizing maternal sensitivity and altruism as an innate vital resource, a feminist ethic of care aims to liberate caregiving from its peripheral status and reposition it as a primary human activity" (212). This conception of care is supported by Oliveira in *My Name in Mary Sutter*, when she writes of the historical women who:

> Braved disease, despair, devastation, and death to nurse in the
> Civil War hospitals ... nearly twenty women became physicians
> after their experiences nursing in the Civil War; it is to honor
> them and their collective experience that Mary Sutter lives.
> (xiii)

In the novel, the protagonist, Mary, is a famous mid-wife—"*she is good, even better than her mother*" (1), and muses that "everything of consequence that had ever happened in her life had been because of babies" (173), though she never gives birth herself.

Midwifery runs through Mary's maternal family: "her mother had been a midwife, and her mother before her, in a line that extended back to medieval France. Her great-great-great-great-grandmother had once delivered a dauphin" (21). Though she is adept in midwifery, Mary, an avid reader and learner of medical texts, desires to attend medical school and become a doctor . A shift towards the medicalization of childbirth in the novel coincides with an increasing historical trend away from women's importance in the birthing process. The shift to the authority of male physicians possibly explains Mary's determination to become a surgeon. Judith Mintz suggests that in Canada, for instance, "by the mid twentieth century, physician attended hospital births were normalized and midwifery care had become all but obsolete" (39). Thus, Oliveira's work, reappraising mid-wives, historically and contemporaneously, suggests that "midwifery is a vital part of the motherhood movement. Midwifery, ... puts mothers at the centre of the family and birthing process" (Mintz 37-38); this is evident when Mary assists Dr. James Blevens, who in the midst of a difficult birth, requires her expertise.

An authority in birthing matters, Mary requests to be apprenticed as Dr. Blevens' medical student, but he refuses under the ruse of joining President Lincoln's war against the South: "I'm going to enlist. They'll need surgeons" (8). Dr. Blevens isn't the only man, however, to enlist. Mary's younger brother Christian and the husband of her twin sister, Jenny, Thomas Fall, with whom Mary secretly loves, also join. The war, as other women's historical novels suggest, precipitates the work of women. Mary's own involvement takes shape when she reads a news article from Miss Dorothea Dix, Female Superintendent of Army Nurses. Miss Dix calls on "ladies to serve in [the hospitals] in the tradition of Florence Nightingale in her recent successful work caring for British soldiers in the Crimea" (83). Renouncing the stigmatism and conflation of "camp follower as prostitute" (Sjoberg and Gentry 44), Miss Dix uses a maternal feminist argument espousing women's superior ability to care and nurture. Florence Nightingale, being the quintessential example, convinces the President to allow women to serve as nurses in the war.

Despite her mother's trepidations, Mary arrives in Washington City ready for service. Rejected by Miss Dix on the basis of her young age and her lack of formal references, Mary is, nevertheless, determined to work in the hospitals. She eventually secures herself a meager position working for Dr. Stipp in the Union Hotel Hospital. As for teaching her to become a surgeon, he, like all the other doctors, outright refuses. Oliveira, depicting the dire conditions Mary is working within, includes a Report from the Sanitary Commission (1861). It states: "there are no provisions for bathing, the water-closets and sinks are in-sufficient and defective, and there is no dead-house. The wards are many of them over-crowded, and destitute of arrangements for artificial ventilation" (128). Mary's wish for being more useful comes when Dr. Stipp, desperate for aid, must perform his first amputation.

Working from *The Practice of Surgery*, Dr. Stipp, with Mary by his reluc-tant side, performs the first of what will later become thousands of amputa-tions. Stipp tells her, "Go home, Mary Sutter. You don't need to be here. You don't need to witness any of this" (154). Mary, determined to contribute to the war effort, proves she is as capable and emotionally strong as a man. Mary muses:

> No one, not even Mr. Lincoln, could ask anything more of them. Albany would think well of her, too. The woman who had gone to war. And she would go on delivering babies. She would apply to medical schools and wait for their letters of re-jection. Her life would be certain. Safe. And with time, the noise of the saw might diminish, and she would no longer hear boys crying for water, for their mothers, for release. (155)

Resolved to continue working to show how a feminist ethic of care "can ex-pand the language of care as a public good beyond the maternalist paradigm" (Stadtman Tucker 201), Mary recognizes, "she had left the world of women, and now all she had was tomorrow, and men, and their unreason" (Oliveira 156). The casualties of the war affect Mary most deeply when she learns that her brother Christian has died. Though her mother, Amelia, begs her daughter to return home, especially because Jenny is due to give birth–"*I am her mother, not her midwife, and I trust only you*" (183), Mary refuses.

Oliveira highlights the predicament women with careers face: as Mary's family situation worsens, her professional situation improves. Seeing first hand Mary's commitment to the war and saving men's lives, Dr. Stipp overlooks traditional gendered divisions of labor and trains her as a surgeon. Yet, when a patient dear to Mary's heart dies, she decides she must return home to assist with Jenny's birth. By the time she arrives, however, Mary sees on the bed "a man who had planted one knee between Jenny's splayed legs. He was gripping silver handles that disappeared into Jenny. *Forceps*. Jenny's mouth was gaping, her eyes staring unseeing at the ceiling" (242). Dismissing the surgeon, Mary decides to "open her pelvis. Unhinge it at the notch" (243). Oliveira suggests that Mary, like many contemporary women, believes that "misogyny is, and always has been, systemic in obstetrics" (Christensen 90). Envisioning a femi-nine-centric and more nuanced approach between midwifery and biomedical technology, she rejects the aggressive and tool dominated techniques of her male peers and, though she desires to be a surgeon, she works to find alternatives that are more beneficial to the mother and child.

The outcome is that the baby, a girl, lives, but Jenny, whose last word is "*Mother*" (Oliveira 285), dies. The emphasis on the maternal is clear and "Mother" can be read as referring to Jenny's newly earned social designation, her biological mother Amelia, and even a paradigm shift to a new definition for that word in women's lives. Unfortunately for Mary, Amelia cannot forgive her for not coming sooner and reprimands her behavior. Grief-stricken, Mary returns to Washington and, with the army in short supply of men, decides to go to the field and work alongside Dr. Stipp as one of the few female nurses and the sole female surgeon at the front.

In *Suffragette Girl*, Florrie Maltby also works on the front lines, but not before spending several years prior to WWI as a Suffragette in London. Paraphrasing Lukács, Diana Wallace believes that World War I, in particular, made it concretely possible "for [*women*] to comprehend their own existence as something historically conditioned, for them to see history as something which deeply affects their daily lives and immediately concerns them" (*Woman's* 25). This sense of history, reflected in novels like Sandra Birdsell's *The Russländer* (2001), in which the Mennonite protagonist Katya narrates her family's immigration to Canada from tumultuous 1910 Russia, is also seen when Florrie ponders her sense of history from a gendered perspective. She wonders, "Begin? Where should she begin? The war? No, no before that. When had it all started? And then she remembered. It had all started the day she'd refused to marry Gervase" (15). Florrie's refusal to marry her best friend Gervase in Lincolnshire, England, 1912 not only defies her father's orders but also traditional expectations of women to become wives and mothers.

In reaction to her more pressing desire to go to London with Gervase' sister Isobel to join the Suffragette Movement (Dickinson 19), her father forebodingly tells her, "Go then. I wash my hands of you. I just hope your brother never disappoints me in this way" (45). Florrie challenges patriarchy both privately and publically when she joins the Suffragettes. Despite peaceful demonstrations, however, England's political system remains unaltered; no woman, not even property-owning women, are permitted to vote, resulting in the implementation of violence and more extreme measures. Rebelling against Florrie's father, her grandmother Augusta claims, "We can't change the past, Edgar dear. But we can change the future. And that's just what your lovely daughter is trying to do. She's trying to make the world a better – fairer – place for women. You should be proud of her, not condemning her and trying to marry her off to the nearest available eligible bachelor" (73). Florrie's involvement in the Movement becomes public knowledge when, "caught slashing a painting in the

National Gallery" (87), she is arrested and sentenced to prison for twenty-eight days.

In prison, Florrie's militant tactics continue and she goes on a hunger strike. Similar to Kate Walbert's *A Short History of Women* (2009), which describes a woman who starves herself to death for women's suffrage, after two weeks Florrie is force-fed by a tube inserted into her nostril (95). For the next two years, Florrie's and Isobel's activities within the Movement resume until, in 1914, both are arrested for "trying to hand in a petition to the King" (127). Upon release from prison, they are told about the Archduke Ferdinand and his wife being assassinated: "war looks inevitable now" (133). Dickinson writes, "Mrs Pankhurst feels that, if war does break out, we should suspend our activities for the duration of the war. England's need is greater than our own. We should devote ourselves to serving our country in a time of crisis. Florrie and Isobel never question the patriarchal nature of the war, nor if their feminist belief in equality is at odds with an involvement in war. As Wallace points out, during this time "the sense of sisterhood between women developed by the suffrage campaigners … is lost at this point, as women constructed themselves instead as 'sisters' to their soldier 'brothers'" (*Sisters and Rivals* 23). With the men in Isobel's and Florrie's families volunteering for the war, the women turn their feminist endeavors away from the vote towards working in the hospitals.

Isobel declares: "Gervase dear, you can't possibly go, because I'm going to offer my services as a nurse. Lady Lee says they'll be badly needed" (150). Determined to earn her qualifications, under the guidance of Sister Blackstock, Florrie is admitted as one of a handful of nurses to go to France. Gervase warns, "you'll be in as much danger as the men in the trenches" (191). Much like Mary in Oliveira's novel, Florrie is shocked by the devastating effects of the war upon the soldiers. Working under Dr. Ernst Hartmann, Florrie goes to the Front to set up a field hospital and takes on the dangerous job of driving an ambulance for the wounded between stations. As Higonnet notes, "when a woman enters a field hospital, she enters an in-between zone, both of the war and not of it. Wartime nursing is an ambiguous domain, quasi-domestic and maternal but in the public service. It is a role that calls on women to care for men as well as to cure them. Should a nurse restore a man's ability to fight and wound others, or should she as a nurse-writer try to cure society of the disease of war?" ("Cassandra's Question" 156). Thus, Oliveira and Dickinson highlight a paradoxical situation for women in war: women's activities, both on the battle front and the homefront, can lead to feminist opportunities and social change such as new professions, rights, and the "birth" of citizenship (Moura and Santos 588), but only at the expense of men and women risking and losing their lives.

Maternal Mortality and the Aunt as Mother

In *My Name is Mary Sutter* and *Suffragette Girl*, the two protagonists, Mary and Florrie, enact feminist mothering by becoming mothers via adoption. When Mary's brother Christian, who has been fighting in the American Civil War, dies and her sister Jenny dies from complications during child birth, Amelia, Mary's mother, is left with only one daughter and granddaughter. Amelia initially blames Mary for Jenny's death because she didn't return to perform as Jenny's midwife when summoned and Mary returns to the front broken-hearted. Jenny's death also causes Thomas, the father, to desert the army, but he is found by patrolling cavalry: "the judge ordered him returned to his regiment. By two o'clock that afternoon, Thomas Fall was back at Fort Marcy standing on a barrel in the middle of the fort near the bomb-proof for everyone to see" (266). As the war intensifies, Amelia, with Jenny's daughter Elizabeth in her care, re-examines her position, using maternal language, in regards to Mary:

> A hundred times over, she'd relived Elizabeth's birth. A choice changed here, a detail there. It was impossible not to despise herself. What mother chastises one twin for the death of another? Insatiable, a mother's need to save her children. Any means possible, including, it would seem, betrayal. Elizabeth would be dead now, but for Mary. (317)

While Amelia considers writing to Mary for forgiveness, Mary is mustering courage for performing another amputation. She "cut off thirty-five legs a day," but recognizes that the man on her table now is Thomas: "He opened his eyes, fearing death, and instead saw Mary Sutter, aproned and bloodied staring at him as if he were dead" (342). For Mary, Thomas "was Christian and Jenny both, and Amelia too" (344) and saving his life is a chance for familial redemption. When Thomas develops a fever, Mary decides to leave the front and take him home. She explains that "[she's] already broken [her] mother's heart" (356) and is not prepared to do so again.

That Mary saves Thomas' life strengthens the maternal bond between the women in her family: "In their embrace, mother and daughter could feel all the members of their family gone now but for Elizabeth; they sank into one another, linked with regret and grace, as are all the reconciled" (Oliveira 358). Like so many women's historical novels, Oliveira focuses on a family torn apart by war and in the process of healing and rebuilding.

The end of the novels skips ahead five years to 1867. Dr. Stipp is in New York standing outside of a house with an oval plaque which, "announced, *Doctor M. Sutter, Physician and Surgeon*" (359). Welcoming him into her home and business, Mary introduces him to her six year old niece for whom she acts as mother. The novel concludes with Mary, after the war, having attended Elizabeth Blackwell's School of Medicine, achieving her professional and feminist goals. It is only after this professional fulfillment that she is able to truly become a mother to Elizabeth and express a romantic interest for Dr. Stipp that began when they had worked together during the war.

Similarly, Dickinson's novel *Suffragette Girl* concentrates on several of the themes addressed in *My Name is Mary Sutter*. There is a war-time romance between Florrie, a nurse, and Ernst, the doctor she works with at the Front and, similar to Mary who loses her brother Christian, Florrie loses her brother James during the First World War. James does not die fighting but by firing squad for attempting to desert. Unlike Thomas in *My Name is Mary Sutter*, who is shamed and sentenced back to his unit, James faces the ultimate penalty under the law. Thus, the character of James in *Suffragette Girl* is, ultimately, a combination of Christian and Thomas from Oliveira's work. Before he dies, James confides in Florrie on why he left his post. Centralizing the crossover between the domestic and war zone, Dickinson writes, "It's not like they're saying. I didn't desert my post. Someone was supposed to do my duty for me. I arranged it, but he let me down" (306). James explains that he left to find Colette, his pregnant girlfriend: her "family has disowned her. Thrown her out" (307). James claims "I *had* to see her. I had to try to take care of her" (307) and he makes Florrie promise to find Colette and take care of the baby. Reluctantly, following James' death, Florrie makes her way to Colette's village.

Florrie finds Colette in the midst of giving birth in an abandoned farmyard. Just as Jenny dies in childbirth in Oliveira's novel, Colette dies in Dickinson's work, but the child named Jacques survives. Both novels express concerns for confronting maternal mortality. These narratives show the danger women are put in when not given adequate treatment or healthcare and that this lack of care stems from cultural-political beliefs that women's lives are not as valuable as men's (Comerford 136). Resolute, Florrie brings Jacques up under the ruse that he is her own son and faces the social stigmatism of being sent home from the front disgraced, letting everyone believe the father is a deceased soldier. Her own father declares her a fallen woman and refuses to acknowledge Jacques as his legitimate heir.

Sarah Trimble suggests that an unmarried pregnant woman in this context is conceptualized "as a lawbreaker" (180). Quoting Nicole Pietsch, Trimble writes: "She is seen as mutinous, a rebel who knows the boundaries of female sexual propriety and maternity and actively violates them" (180). Florrie not only sacrifices her social standing but also refuses to feel the expected remorse, regret, or shame that social norms dictate. Dickinson states: "She'd promised

James she would care for Colette and their child. But Colette was gone and only their son remained. But now he would be hers. Hers completely. It would be as if she really had given birth to him" (345). Though Florrie vows to be a mother to Jacques, in reality this places restrictions upon her opportunities, such as returning to the front, which she resents. When the war ends and women over the age of thirty gain the right to vote in 1918, Florrie's restlessness is clear; "being a –a *mother* isn't enough" (383) and she transgresses the norms of institutional motherhood by leaving Jacques in her family's care while travelling to London for weeks at a time.

Jacques' health, however, symbolizes Florrie's failure as a mother according to patriarchal culture; she has rejected normative mothering and her punishment is that Jacques is ill. Gervase declares, "He needs his *mother*. Florrie, if he were fit and well and busy – robust would be the word – with a young boy's activities, it would be different. ... but he's not. He's sickly. He needs to be seen by a doctor and he needs you with him" (406). Rather than blame unrealistic or stifling patriarchal definitions of the "good mother," Florrie, instead, consents: "Gervase was right. She had neglected James' son" (407). Thus, the novel picks up from its opening in 1932 with Florrie and Jacques on route to Davos, Switzerland where Dr. Ernst Hartmann runs a sanatorium for patients with tuberculosis.

During his treatment, Florrie finally tells Jacques the truth about how his parents died. For Jacques, Florrie's sacrifices outweigh any anger he feels upon being deceived all these years. After Jacques receives a clean bill of health, Florrie, restored to a position of respectable mother, gains the courage to tell her parents and grandmother, also, the truth about Jacques not being her biological son. The novel concludes with Florrie, like Mary, finding happiness as a mother and aunt to her deceased sibling's child and with a man who respects her feminist principles. In a reverse of the opening, when Florrie rejects Gervase's marriage proposal, Florrie asks Gervase for his hand in marriage.

Both Oliveira and Dickinson suggest that marriages whose purpose "is not reproduction or the acquisition of property but the realization of flesh, spirit and History, in peace, felicity and fecundity" (Irigaray, *I Love to You* 146) celebrate a new possibility between the sexes. Luce Irigaray argues that "a real democracy must take as its basis, today, a just relationship between man and woman" (*Democracy Begin* 118). This feminist thinking can lead to a renewed civility between the sexes: "through a more emotional and physical relationship, it could escape the exploitation of the other, male or female, avoid reducing them to being an object at one's disposal or a means of production, whether of manpower or of children" (107). Oliveira and Dickinson describe Florrie and Mary as unconventional aunts/mothers, thereby constructing a "shared maternal genealogy of siblings" (Wallace, *Sisters and Rivals* 67). This kind of feminist mothering, predicated on romance, mutual love, respect, and civility, embodies a transnational feminist project committed to a democratic sense of love.

Searching for Maternal Reconciliation

While working for the war cause is unquestioned by the protagonists of Oliveira's and Dickinson's novels, by contrast, Kogawa's *Obasan*, Zelitch's *Louisa*, and Young's *My Enemy's Cradle* all concentrate on women who are considered the enemy and are struggling to survive during World War II. Supporting a revaluation of war novels from a gendered perspective, Paula J. Draper believes that "women's capacity to bear children and become mothers [makes] their memories and experience of survival gendered in particular ways" (405). Survivor narratives are also "concerned with historical trauma and the articulation of the long-term psychological – individual and collective – effects of a historical displacement on the processes of identity formation" (Sywenky 166). In Kogawa's *Obasan*, when Japan joins Germany in its war effort, Naomi, though a third generation Canadian of Japanese descent, experiences the effects of racist nationalism.

The novel opens in 1972 in Alberta, Canada with Naomi as an adult and a war survivor, reflecting on her life. She pieces together the lives of her family both within Canada during the time of the war and the lives of her maternal family in Japan. Meredith Shoenut writes: "Naomi's purpose becomes to explore this political language, to question and deconstruct official versions of Canadian history, and to analyze Canada's past as though it were fiction" (481). Essential to rethinking this past is Naomi's connection to her mother. Elleke Boehmer categorizes searches like Naomi's as "the matriarchal yearnings of dispossessed women seeking their own place in nations and in history" (3). Naomi's mother leaves for Japan during the war, but mysteriously never returns. When her uncle dies in 1972, Naomi sorts through her family's belongings while simultaneously sorting through her memories.

The past, still very much in Naomi's present, lends support to Draper's theory about the challenges in interpreting the memories of survivors of traumatic events. She writes: "Understanding history then becomes not only learning 'what really happened' but also gaining a sense of how past events continue to influence and shape the lives of individuals and groups who were in the midst of those events" (Draper 399). Aunt Emily, an active member in calling for redress by the Canadian government, has supplied Naomi with important documents. These documents acknowledge the rights of Canadians with Japanese descent and publicize the Canadian government's heinous actions during and after the war. Kogawa writes:

> Our short harsh history. Beside each date were the ugly facts of the treatment given to Japanese Canadians. 'Seizure and government sale of fishing boats. Suspension of fishing licences. Relocation camps. Liquidation of property. Letter to General MacArthur. Bill 15. Deportation. Revocation of nationality.' Whereever the words 'Japanese race' appeared, Aunt Emily had crossed them out and written 'Canadian citizen.' (34)

Kogawa, like Zelitch and Young, challenges the meaning of nationality and who constitutes a Canadian citizen as well as the geography of the Second World War—it is not being fought solely on European soil but Canadian lands as well.

Naomi and her family must try to survive this war at home. Because Canada is at war with Germany and Japan, Canadian citizens and residents with Japanese origins are persecuted and expelled from British Columbia in 1941. Kogawa asks: "Why in a time of war with Germany and Japan would our government seize the property and homes of Canadian-born Canadians but not the homes of German-born Germans?" she asked angrily. 'Racism,' she answered herself. 'The Nazis are everywhere'" (40). Naomi's family in Vancouver loses its property and they are forced into work camps. Eventually, the family is separated and Naomi is shipped to Canada's interior, first Slocan B.C. and then Granton, Alberta with her brother, uncle, and aunt or *obasan*, from whom the novel's title is attributed. The novel, thus, tackles two coinciding narratives: Naomi and her family enduring threats of being sent to Japan, forced labor, racism, poverty, and loss within Canada and reclaiming the life of her mother and grandmother who returned to Japan at the beginning of the war in order to look after her great-grandmother.

It is this latter story that is most relevant for understanding the role of the maternal in the woman's historical war novel. Sorting through her family's letters, Naomi sees a rare photograph of herself clinging shyly to her mother's leg on a street in Vancouver. Emphasizing the maternal bond, Naomi reflects, "where she is rooted, I am rooted" (69). Shoenut argues that "[t]he presence of her mother represents the cultural values of a 'mother country': unfaltering strength, protection, rootedness, everything that is pure and right with the world, and, more specifically, nature" (485). The novel is, thus, a means for Naomi to write back to hegemonic history through learning her mother's story; it is a way for reconnecting with the mother she has lost and for finding her own identity/autonomy as a survivor.

Eva Karpinkski, drawing on Shoshana Felman's reading of Albert Camus' novel *The Plague*, believes that *Obasan* is a "'narrative as testimony': a mode of writing capable of mediating the relationship between narrative and history, and which makes it possible 'not merely to record, but to rethink and, in the act of its rethinking, in effect transform history by bearing literary witness' to trauma" (47). Supporting this viewpoint, Shoenut writes:

> Vocalized trauma does not distort the facts ... 'Narrative memory' ... 'is not passively endured; rather, it is an act on the part of the narrator, a speech act that defuses traumatic memory, giving shape and a temporal order to the events re-called, establishing more control over their recalling, and help-ing the survivor to remake a self' (489).

Naomi's trauma, largely due to the loss of her mother, entails that she even imagines herself as her mother: "with my eyes averted, I am my mother pulling the drawer open to look for the black darning knob, or a spool of thread, or scissors" (Kogawa 72). The imagery of the thread is a meaningful way for Kogawa to express the link between the daughter and mother and one that, like the umbilical cord, is cut or broken when the protagonists are separated.

Though Aunt Emily declares that her mother and grandmother must be dead, Naomi discovers they did indeed survive the war. In a sense, her mother has betrayed her by feigning death. Naomi also reads a letter written to her grandmother informing her that her application to return to Canada has been rejected because Japanese nationals are not permitted to emigrate to Canada. The other letter explains that her mother, who is Canadian-born, is permitted to re-enter Canada but the Japanese child she hopes to bring with her will be re-fused. Naomi questions why her mother never wrote to the family or tried to make contact; though the more urgent question as to why her mother chose another child over her Canadian family is left unasked and unanswered in the text. Instead Kogawa shows Naomi reflecting on the year 1954, when Aunt Emily (living in Toronto for twelve years) comes to visit the family, which has recently moved off of the beet-farm where they worked to their own house in Granton. Hearing Aunt Emily whisper words about her mother, she sees her tie the letters in a folder. Naomi, now in 1972, after the death of her uncle, holds them for the first time.

She reads letters written by Grandmother Kato from Japan, including one from Nagasaki in 1949. In the letter, her grandmother describes the horrors of the atomic bombs on the city, how "men, women, in many cases indistinguish-able by sex, hairless, half-clothed, hobbled past. Skin hung from their bodies like tattered rags" (261). Just as Naomi is separated from her mother, so too does her grandmother describe being separated from her daughter during the

bombs. Her search for her daughter, Naomi's mother, continues until one even-
ing she sees a disfigured woman:

> Her nose and one cheek were almost gone. Great wounds and
> pustules covered her entire face and body. She was completely
> bald. She sat in a cloud of flies and maggots wiggled among
> her wounds. As Grandma watched her, the woman gave her a
> vacant gaze, then let out a cry. It was my mother. (263)

Di Brandt writes that "it is adult male violence, again, multiplied a billionfold
in the dropping of the atomic bomb on Nagasaki" (115), which Karpinski argues "is responsible for Naomi's mother's disfigurement and silence" (58).
Reading *Obasan* in relation to other women's war novels such as *Suffragette
Girl*, *Landgirls*, or *My Name is Mary Sutter*, can we really believe only male
violence is responsible for the atrocities committed against the Japanese? Is it
not more accurate to suggest that it is patriarchal violence/nationalism in which
women, as well as men, participate and even benefit from (rights, vote, materi-
alistic gain, territory, etc.) that powers the war between the Allies and Japan
and causes Naomi, like many other daughters, to lose her mother?

Naomi learns her mother, though denied the right to come initially, has effectively chosen not to return to Canada. Naomi comments, "Silent Mother,
you do not speak or write. You do not reach through the night to enter morning,
but remain in the voicelessness. From the extremity of much dying, the only
sound that reaches me now is the sigh of your remembered breath, a wordless
word. How shall I attend that speech, Mother, how shall I trace that wave?"
(Kogawa 265). Both Irigaray and Julie McGonegal suggest that the revolutionary potential of silence as an act of feminist mothering. Irigaray argues that
"this silence is space-time offered to you with no a priori, no established truth
or ritual" (*I Love to You*, 117). To be truly listening to another and to let another speak on their own terms without presuppositions requires silence (ibid.
118). For McGonegal, silence intimates reconciliation and forgiveness; we
"enter the realm of possibility by attending silently to her mother's version
rather than dogmatically imposing her own interpretation. … practising atten-
tive silence is how Naomi makes possible the process of rebirth and recovery
from (maternal) loss" (McGonegal 121). At the same time, Naomi's mother
symbolizes the missing voices within Canada's war history.

Karpinski aptly notes that readers cannot ignore "the presence of racism as a
trauma pervading the whole text, including Naomi's pre- and post-war experiences" (55). The novel competes for a voice in Canada's history, a history
which has been silenced on both the national and personal level (after all Naomi's mother prefers silence as a means of protecting her children) and is expressed in the novel through Kogawa's play with women's voices: Aunt Emi-

ly's scathing speech, Obasan's few words, Naomi's mother's silence, and Naomi's narrative. McGonegal argues that "this text alternately displaces and fulfills the promise of reconciliation: that is, it actualizes the possibility of maternal reconciliation but defers the possibility of national reconciliation ... reconciliation is contingent on genuine openness to the position of the other, on what Kogawa might refer to as 'mutual recognition' or 'mutual vulnerability'" (120). Naomi's narrative, bearing witness to Canada's history, "enables us to see that the nation-building project is erected on the bodies of racialized and gendered 'others'" (Karpinski 47). The certainty of Naomi's mother's death is that her name is included on an undated and geographically indeterminate plaque for the dead, whereby a Canadian maple tree, ironically not a Japanese maple, grows.

Hearing her mother's story, Naomi reimagines the life of her "martyr mother" (Kogawa 265), a Christ-like figure, with whom she feels connected and present, despite the distances of time and space: "Young Mother at Nagasaki, am I not also there?" (266). Knowing her mother is dead, Naomi's closure signals the end of her narrative. Kogawa, however, includes an excerpt in support of the fundamental rights of Japanese Canadians from "the Memorandum sent by the Co-operative Committee on Japanese Canadians to the House and the Senate of Canada, April 1946" (272). Kogawa's novel, thus, raises difficult questions about the nature of nationalism and, while the family *is* Canadian, this sense of Canadian nationalism is not without its own problems.

The novel's "repeated appeal to the myth of Canadian civility, its use of linear narrative, and its strong historicizing gesture" means that problematically it is "fatefully entrenched within the nation-state" (Zacharias 14). A strengthening of the notion of national identity is a means for separating one's self and peoples from another, much like Canadians who justified their actions against Japanese Canadians. As Edward Said warns, "nationalism is an assertion of belonging in and to a place, a people, a heritage. It affirms the home created by a community of language, culture and customs; and, by so doing, it fends off exile ... All nationalisms in their early stages develop from a condition of estrangement" (*Reflections on Exile* 176). Rather than read Kogawa's novel as a straightforward narrative of sympathy and justified anger at the treatment of Japanese Canadians during WWII, I argue that it is a transnational feminist critique of uncritical and patriarchal nationalism. The work highlights the dilemma Naomi's maternal family faces when they return to the mother-country to care for a relative. The unfortunate reality is that Japan is Canada's enemy and both Canadian Japanese and the Japanese will face trauma and hardship as long as national and racial identity continues to be the fundamental basis of war.

Mothers on Enemy Soil

In Young's novel *My Enemy's Cradle*, which focuses on Sarah, a Holocaust survivor, national identity and the loss of a mother converge. Cyrla, the protagonist, is a Polish Jew sent, in 1941, to live with relatives in Holland in order to avoid Nazis persecution. Her father tells her, "go to your mother's world. Learn to fit inside her life, and you will find how she fits in yours" (Young 7). With the Germans increasingly mandating restrictions on the lives of Jews in occupied Holland (1), the work, like Kogawa's novel, focuses on a maternal separation. Not only is Cyrla's Dutch mother dead, but Cyrla too will face the possibility of being separated from her own child.

All of this arises when Cyrla's cousin Anneke becomes pregnant by a German soldier named Karl. The family unravels in a parallel fashion to the political order. The reader learns Karl has another fiancée in Hamburg and is "being sent back to Germany" (22-23). With increasing German checkpoints, Cyrla, a half-Jew (though her identity is masked by her blonde hair), is, nonetheless, at risk: "the world was cracking in two, and I was falling into the void" (26). Cyrla's uncle, learning that his daughter is pregnant, sends the family into panic, until he declares, "I have found a solution ... A maternity home" (42). Ordered by her father into a historical Lebensborn facility, Anneke is told the Germans will take her in until the child is born and, after the birth, the baby will be adopted by a German family. Cyrla's Jewish activist friend and lover, Isaak clarifies,

> Those are dark cradles. '*Have one baby for the Führer*' is the slogan. All German women, whether they're married or not, are expected to have children. Every place they take over, they will want to fill with their own. And they'll always want troops. ... Babies aren't babies to the Nazis, Cyrla. They're resources. And now they're taking them from occupied countries'. (50)

Taking control over women's bodies through the maternal is, thus, a means for furthering Germany's territorial gains.

When Anneke, however, performs an abortion at home using a knitting needle, she disrupts and challenges Nazi power by refusing to give birth to a German child. Anneke's death also gives Cyrla the chance to survive by taking her identity. The aunt, as in *My Name is Mary Sutter*, *Suffragette Girl*, and *Obasan*, plays an important maternal role and, supporting the decision, risks her own life. She claims, "I've lost one child. I will not lose another" (68). Though Cyrla miraculously becomes pregnant by the time the German soldiers come to collect her for the Lebensborn home, it is unclear if the father is Isaak or a

German *Oberschütze* who rapes her. Cockburn argues that rape by the German forces during WWII was extensively practiced "on both Western and Eastern fronts" (192) and she attempts to "bring to the issue of sexual violence in war a language" (189) that expresses how "war rape is characteristically collective, and being a soldier very much involves identification and 'belonging.' Rape in war, like war itself, is nothing if not social" (ibid.). The practice of rape further connects with increased bodily control over women during times of war.

A twist in the novel is that Cyrla is not entering a home in Nijmegen, Holland, but one in Steinhöring, outside of Munich. Trapped in the country of her enemy, Cyrla describes a particularly terrible visit by Heinrich Himmler. Himmler tells the women, using patriarchal nationalistic rhetoric, "You carry within you our nation's greatest wealth Germany's future strength … Every war involves a tremendous letting of blood. It is the highest duty of German women and girls of good blood to become mothers, inside or outside the boundaries of marriage" (159-60). He likens the soon-to-be mothers to brave soldiers who also risk their lives and blood. This suggests sacrifices for the war effort by both sexes on both the battlefield and homefront are necessary.

After Himmler's visit, Cyrla's time passes rather uneventfully until the home makes contact with Karl, the father named in Anneke's paperwork. For Cyrla, Karl symbolizes everything she hates about the Germans; he is a soldier, like the one who raped her, and she holds him responsible for abandoning and causing her pregnant cousin's death. Karl, however, seems genuinely ignorant of Anneke's fate until Cyrla tells him about how her uncle arranged for Anneke to come here: "You killed her, Karl. You murdered her. You broke her heart and left her alone, so she tried to carve your baby from her body and she bled to death. That's how you murdered her" (227). For several weeks Karl seeks Cyrla's forgiveness and friendship until he finally tells her, "Listen to me. I didn't walk out on Anneke. I swear to you I didn't know she was going to have a baby.… I told her I was leaving for Germany and that I wanted to end things because I wasn't in love with her" (267). Though Cyrla still holds Karl responsible for Anneke's death, she lets him help in planning her own escape. Karl even offers to marry Cyrla or adopt the child straight after the birth so that Cyrla can use Anneke's papers to get back to Holland.

Cyrla, however, knowing the pain of being sent away by family members believing they are acting in her best interest, refuses to give birth to her son on German soil. She cannot face betraying her Jewish peoples: "The German girls often married their boyfriends, of course, but I hadn't heard of any girls from other countries doing it. It was one thing to sleep with the enemy. Quite another to marry him and move to the Fatherland" (277). Refusing to marry Karl, even after learning his story prior to being conscripted by the Germans, she does slowly begin to trust and care for him. As German persecution against the Jews intensifies, Cyrla's life as well as that of her unborn Jewish child's become increasingly endangered. Her identity is finally compromised after a small velvet bag containing some of her belongings is stolen. Nine months pregnant, Cyrla phones Karl knowing she must flee and he drives her to the Dutch border. Young writes:

> They were on him. I lay in the muddy ditch and watched as two cars and a jeep skidded to circle him. Soldiers ran from each, shouting, guns and lights drawn. Karl stood calmly at the center of the chaos. He held his arms out straight, giving his wrists up to them. For the briefest second as they bound his hands behind him, in the arcing beam of a flashlight, I thought I saw the faint curve of a smile on his lips. Then they dragged him away. (354)

The novel concludes in 1947 with Cyrla and her daughter Anneke standing on the doorstep of Karl's sister's house. Cyrla explains how she managed to make it to England with the aid of papers Isaak prepared for her prior to his death and, from Erika, she learns that Karl is alive, though the Nazis broke his hands and imprisoned him in a work camp for the remainder of the war. Reuniting with Karl in an unnamed place after departing from Hamburg, Cyrla remarks, "We have been apart so long! People can be lost to each other in so many ways … The brush drops from his hand. And in his eyes I see my home" (360). Young's novel, like Kogawa's, ends by invoking the metaphor of space and imagination premised on forgiveness and reconciliation. Cyrla, a half-Jewish woman who faces Nazi persecution during the war, finds her home unexpectedly and controversially within the love of a former German soldier.

Mother and Daughter-in-Law: Identities in Crisis

Like Young's novel *My Enemy's Cradle*, Zelitch's *Louisa* tackles Jewish identity in terms of space and a sense of home; examining the complexity of national, religious, familial and racial identity, Zelitch opens with the narrator, a Jewish Hungarian woman named Nora and her German daughter-in-law, Louisa, leaving Hungary after the war has ended and arriving at a refugee camp in Israel, 1949. Zelitch suggests that prior to 1949 the nation of Israel did not formally exist, evident when Louisa claims, "'But you're an Israelite,' she cried. I stroked her hair and whispered, 'Shh, shh. There's no such place'" (142). That the land is to be recognized as a nation, however, is foremost in the mind of many Jews in this context. During the war, Nora's cousin, Bela argues, "What do you want us to do? Get into our Jewish airplanes and bomb Berlin?

We don't have Jewish airplanes. We don't have an army. We don't have a state. And that's why we're here–not to save Jews but to build a state where we can be Jews" (287). Jewish identity is thus at the core of the novel, not only in the sense that Nora is declared an enemy of Germany but also because Louisa as a German is considered the enemy in Israel.

Faced with outrage from the other refugees, Nora explains that similar to Karl in Young's novel, Louisa has saved her life: "I'd lost my parents and my husband and my son. I had only Louisa. I owe her my life. It was Louisa who had kept me hidden during the German occupation" (4). She confesses, "for this was Louisa's story from the start; she was its heroine. It was Louisa who threw herself into forbidden love, who saved my life, and who saved my cousin's life, I suspect" (357).

In Israel, Rabbi Shmuel Needleman asks Louisa why she has followed her mother-in-law, to which Louisa replies, "Because I love her" (41). Louisa, like Naomi in *Obasan* and Cyrla in *My Enemy's Cradle*, loses her biological mother (she is disowned by her parents), but she effectively adopts her mother-in-law as her new mother. She is likened to the biblical protagonist Ruth: "the daughter of a cursed nation, far from home, clinging to her mother-in-law and taking on her people and her God" (42). Committed to staying in Israel, Louisa desires to become a Jew and to speak Hebrew, a language neither she nor Nora speaks.

In fact, German is the common language between Nora and Louisa and is Nora's preferred language when she writes her cousin Bela, a Zionist, who has been living in a commune in the area since 1925 and to whom Nora intends to locate. The polyphonic narrative fuses several languages (English, Yiddish, German, Hungarian, Arabic) to highlight the impact of the Holocaust upon diverse cultures–and unfolds when Nora cannot find the telegram she has been keeping in her sock, which has Bela's new address; apparently, the old kibbutz he founded is no longer on any lists.

Without Bela's address or contact, Nora has no definitive plan for resettlement, which highlights the refugee's permanent stasis in dislocation. In the process of Nora searching for her cousin, the novel switches between her past reflections and her present situation with Louisa in the camp. The reader learns that Nora grew up in Kisbarnahely but was forced to move to Budapest when her father was murdered in 1919 during the revolutions of the Romanians against Hungarian communists and Jews. The Hungarians "were shot, hanged, or exiled" (76). While living and working in Budapest, Nora meets her husband Janos, who, after marrying, confesses, "I'm a Communist. My friends are Communists" (103). With Janos working secretly in Russia and, essentially, an absentee husband and father, Nora lives in Budapest with her son Gabor, an amateur composer, who, one day in 1943, meets Louisa, a German singer.

Partly for German protection, Gabor reluctantly marries the pregnant Louisa, although she later miscarries, symbolizing that a Germany-Hungary union will never come to fruition. However, a victim of the war, "in March of 1944, Gabor died. He died along with many young men pulled from trams or found in train stations or airports in the days after the Germans invaded Budapest" (314). After Gabor's death, Nora is forced to live in a Yellow Star House and, realizing her imminent danger, hides in Louisa's cellar until the end of the war (56). Following the war's ending, Zelitch describes Nora's brief reunion with Janos, who also survived the war, but then her decision to leave him in order to locate her cousin in Israel. As already noted, Nora cannot initially find Bela and it is only towards the end of the novel that the reader learns Louisa, who has stolen the telegram, is secretly meeting with Bela, now known as Jonah.

The novel, thus, follows closely the biblical tale of Ruth, a Moabite woman and enemy of Israel who transforms herself and becomes a direct ancestor of David, King of Israel, "from whose line will come the Messiah, may it be in our lifetime" (216). Louisa forsakes her German family and nation and, by doing so, is forgiven for her "German" sins. Accepted as a convert to Judaism, she marries Jonah, adopts the new name Leah, and gives birth to a girl. Resonating with novels like Walker's *The Color Purple* and those discussed here, Zelitch suggests identity is fluid: being a mother or being Jewish is not necessarily dependent on one's blood or birth, but on one's state of being, one's choice of self, and the love one has for others. Zelitch shows this transformation through Louisa, a German girl living in Hungary during the war who casts off her former identity in order to join her Jewish mother-in-law in Israel to live as a Jew.

The War at Home

Juxtaposed with the life of a foreign woman on enemy soil, Huth's novel *Land Girls*, like Oliveira's *My Name is Mary Sutter* and Dickinson's *Suffragette Girl*, focuses on and gives credence to the war effort of women, in this case three young patriotic British Land Girls in World War II named Prue, Stella, and Agatha. Literary descendants of Mary Sutter and Florrie Maltby, with a shortage of men to do the farming, women during WWII took up men's positions. Huth's work focuses on the arrival of three lands girls to the Lawrences. The Lawrences, and their son Joe, an asthmatic denied a chance to fight, though uncomfortable with undermining gendered labor on their Dorset farm, out of necessity call upon the Land Army plan.

Huth reads the running of the farm as an essential part of the war effort, equal to the combat, and she blurs the line between civilian and soldier: "Think about what you are doing. Someone's got to organize the massive job of feeding the country. Hallows Farm is making the sort of contribution you shouldn't undervalue" (172). She suggests that, just as not all men fought on the battlefield, not all women (like Mary and Florrie) remained on the homefront. The homefront and battlefield were sites occupied by both sexes.

Huth uses the traditional domestic work of women like Mrs. Lawrence as a mirror for men's battle activities. Higonnet identifies this technique in Mary Borden's *Forbidden Zone* (1929) in which she domesticates war by writing "'just as you send your clothes to the laundry and mend them when they come back, so we send our men to the trenches and mend them when they come back again'" ("Cassandra's Question" 156). Huth, recuperating this technique, "translates the whole machinery of war into the language of the housewife" (156) and upholds the traditional role of women in the domestic sphere as not only equal to women entering into fields previously held by men but also the fighting of men on the battlefield. For instance, Mrs Lawrence is admired and respected by all of the girls. Ag comments:

> This is what it must be like every day for Mrs Lawrence, she thought: sudden silence, the looming of domestic plans, lists of tasks to be accomplished by nightfall. There was no freedom from the discipline of deadlines: food must be on the table by midday, no matter how much ironing. The pile of socks to be darned must be kept under control; the grading of eggs, in the stone-chill of the scullery, was necessary before sending them off twice a week. For the first time, Ag began to reflect on the life of a housewife, doubly hard if you were married to a farmer. (208)

Feminist change, however, problematically is propagated by the war.

None of the girls desire to take up the role of Mrs Lawrence in their imagined future lives. Mrs Lawrence, thus embodies a kind of maternal feminism which no longer resonates with the lives of young British women. Huth writes:

> None of the land girls could remember a time when, if they came upon Mrs. Lawrence by chance, she would not be engaged in some form of work. She never grumbled about her endless duties. In fact, disparate jobs that occupied her, both indoors and out, from early morning till late at night, seemed to give her pleasure. She was an example of a married woman totally preoccupied by the narrow confines of her life, and happy with them. This gave the girls food for thought. Prue, whose

respect for Mrs Lawrence was infinite, was not for one moment deflected by her example: to swap such a life for her own dream of servants and cocktails did not occur to her. Ag has been romantically tempted by the thought of ironing Desmond's future shirts (all that white linen, so Lawrentian). But of late she had begun to think about becoming a barrister: she would be willing to undertake household duties, but they would have to be arranged around a post-war life at the Bar. Stella, too, was inspired by the living energy Mrs Lawrence put into every loaf and pot of home-made jam: something her own mother, a useless cook, had never instilled into her. But, like Ag, she was determined to go out to work when she and Philip married. Life would certainly not consist entirely of looking after his needs. Perhaps, she thought, when the war was over, a new and enlightened breed of women would feel much the same. (290)

Changes in British values, evident in gender expectations, thus, lead to increasing questions as to whether women can adequately fill the roles once held by men.

Comments throughout the novel by the farm-help Ratty express the inevitability of new opportunities for women, including signing up for the Land Army. Expected to help out with all of the chores, the girls from very different backgrounds (Prue, a hair-dresser from Manchester, Stella, a wealthy girl in love with a naval officer, and Ag, a Cambridge graduate) adapt to working long hard hours often endured only by romantic fantasy and desires (both real and imagined i.e., a local RAF dance).

While engaged in their farm work there is the initial sense of protection and shelter from the actual war. Ag notes, "we're lucky here. Hardly aware of it" (Huth 78) and for Stella, "in Dorset, the only evidence of war was the sight of women working in the fields. She caught a glimpse of a row of land girls bent over hoes in a mangold field, and smiled" (187). The proximity of the war, however, intensifies as the novel progresses, again suggesting a rigid demarcation between war and peace, homefront and battlefront, is false.

After a few weeks, an early siren signaling a raid warning is juxtaposed with the equally disappointing notice that Prue reads in the chemist's shop: "*Sorry, no lipsticks or rouges*" (110). By the end of the novel, however, the reality of war hits home: Prue learns that her pilot boyfriend Barry has been killed in action and German bombs begin falling in the English countryside. Huth writes that "a new feeling of unease, which even the hardest physical work could not quite obscure, affected everyone at Hallows Farm" and:

> By harvest-time, the customary peace at Hallows Farm was disturbed more frequently by passing planes: sometimes a Spit-fire, sometimes the dreaded shape of the Luftwaffe monsters. Since the occasion of the incendiary bombs, the old, foolish sense of security in remote country was never quite recaptured. Living in anticipation of the next disaster became part of daily life. (357)

Experiencing the threat of danger and hearing on the radio that the Japanese have bombed Pearl Harbor, Ag begins to doubt whether her work on the farm is, after all, equal to the work of those men and women on the front lines.

> She tried to imagine the distant carnage, the destruction, the horror, the terrible suffering and pointless loss of life. She felt impotent, anger, fear. This was followed by feelings of equally impotent guilt at her own lot, which was comparatively safe … a place where the war scarcely touched them, but there was al-so never a day when she did not wonder if she should not vol-unteer for some less protected field of action. Should she not join the Red Cross, or drive ambulances in the Blitz, rather than milk cows and feed on Mrs Lawrence's secure stews. Should her courage not be tested? And yet, while the men were fighting, girls to work on the land were vital: she had chosen the job, she loved it. (210)

Huth's novel revisits the World War II for the purpose of discussing an over-looked and undervalued event: women excelling in previously male dominant fields such as in the factory and on the farm. She suggests that, though women did not often engage in combat, their work was instrumental to the success of the Allied Forces. Huth values not only Mrs. Lawrence's traditional work, but expresses hope in imagining new opportunities for women as expressed by three British Landgirls. The novel shows how times of war can create and lead to flexible social-political constructions of gender and mothering.

Conclusion

There is such a thing as a woman's war novel. Women's historical novels attest to the complexity of this subject matter and challenge masculinist assumptions about authentic war writing. Ranging typically from the Civil War to WWII, women are depicted on both the homefront and battlefront, essentially blurring a neat division between them. Taking up a variety of roles from nurse, surgeon, factory worker, and farmer for the war cause, we also see women enduring and resisting the hardships of war and struggling to stay alive. Novels like *Obasan*,

Louisa, and *My Enemy's Cradle*, by focusing on the maternal, exemplify not only how families can become dislocated, separated and lost to one another during wartimes but also their ability to endure and survive. *My Name is Mary Sutter*, *Suffragette Girl*, and *Landgirls*, by contrast, show that women's war efforts can lead to unprecedented opportunities, such as entering new professions and gaining citizenship. The femino-centric topics of ethic of care theory, maternal mortality and the aunt, maternal reconciliation, mothers as foreign enemies, and the homefront create a fluid maternal genealogy of war. In all of these feminist works, the nation and national identity is put either implicitly or explicitly into question. A transnational maternal genealogy seeks a beyond the nation and criticizes national boundaries for separating women, particularly during patriarchal wartimes. A transnational feminist reading of these works therefore identifies the necessary role women play in postwar solidarity, forgiveness, and reconciliation.

CHAPTER EIGHT

Love For/Against Art: Rebirthing our Foremothers

> Only that which has no history is definable
> – Friedrich Nietzsche, *On the Genealogy of Morals*

This final chapter surveys transnational novels on women artists. Following in the feminist footsteps of Anna Banti's pioneering novel *Artemisia* (1947), post 1970s novels, in an attempt to create a female artistic tradition that has been forgotten, overlooked, ignored, and rejected, have been avidly recuperating and rebirthing the lives of historical women artists. While some novels take the approach of focusing on the hidden life of a male artist's wife or mistress–such as Tracy Chevalier's *Girl With a Pearl Earring* (1999), Sylvie Matton's *Rembrandt's Whore* (2003), Agnes Selby's *Constanze, Mozart's Beloved* and Juliet Waldron's *Mozart's Wife* (2001), the last two of which both write the life of Konstanze, the wife of composer Wolfgang Amadeus Mozart, the women remain defined by their relation to men of genius. I call women's art novels those that centralize and celebrate the woman artist; For simplicity, the umbrella term "artist" signifies women in a wide range of arts from dance, poetry, and theater to music, opera, art, and so on.

Establishing an artistic-literary-historical genealogy serves to displace and disrupt a patriarchal hold on the art-world that, to this day, poses a challenge for women artists. Transnationally, organized feminist activism against the art world emerged in tandem with a proliferation of women's art in the 1970s (Broude, Garrard, Westen, Reilly, Parker, Pollock). The purpose was:

> Undermining the foundations of art institutions and renowned art publications ... feminism [also] established ties between women, and connected female artists with female art historians and art critics. What had begun as loose, informal networks now consolidated in alternative, more strategic, and more cohesive, forms of collaboration. (Westen 9)

Following essays like Linda Nochlin's "Why Have There Been No Great Women Artists" (1972), activist groups, such as the 'Guerilla Girls' since their inception in 1985, "began putting up illegal posters displaying razor-sharp one-liners and using playful forms of protest to signal skewed gender and race relations in the art world" (Westen 9). In addition, Susan McClary, Catherine

Clément, and Wendy Heller have been pioneering feminist theorists of musicology and opera and Karen Nicole Barbour and Ann Daly have provided insightful feminist criticism on dance.

The woman's historical novel questions the meaning of art from a gendered perspective. In many of these works, the woman artist is faced with choosing between creation in terms of her art or by having a family and children. For example, in Margaret Forster's *Keeping the World Away* (2000), Gwen John disdains a maternal life:

> It was strange, she could not help thinking, that seeing Ida's child made her own work more important, not less so. She did not look at their baby and pine for one of her own, nor did the baby make her work seem irrelevant. On the contrary, he made it seem vital. She herself was not going to create a baby. All her creative talents had to go into her painting, all her feelings and emotions, all her ideas and plans, all her hopes and fears, all the turmoil within her, everything that was precious. (42)

In the midst of her tumultuous love affair with the sculptor Auguste Rodin she writes that "[a]ll around she saw women artists whose work seemed to stop by giving birth–look at Ida, look at Edna, look at Dorelia. None of them producing anything now except sketches" (Forster 61). Thus, deciding between motherhood/marriage and being an artist is at the forefront in these novels.

In addition, each work shows the challenges women artists cross-culturally and cross-historically have faced in having the merit of their work recognized. Strongly suggesting that art can change women's lives, Westen, referencing Lucy Lippard's view in the 1970s, argues that "the influence of feminism did not extend only to art itself, but also to discussions about the role of art in society, as more and more artists were striving to bridge the gap between art and life … feminist art meant art that was engaged in society" (11). Thus, in the woman's historical novel, art is a powerful means for political self-expression and social contestation.

In *The Madwoman in the Attic: The Woman Writer and the   Nineteenth-Century Literary Imagination*, Sandra Gilbert and Susan Gubar read the woman artist in relation to Plato's infamous "Allegory of the Cave" and Sigmund Freud's analysis of it as a "female place, a womb-shaped enclosure, a house of earth, secret and often sacred" (93). Gilbert and Gubar point to "the plight of woman in patriarchal culture, the woman whose cavern-shaped anatomy is her destiny. Not just, like Plato's cave dweller, a prisoner of Nature, this woman is a prisoner of her own nature" (Gilbert and Gubar 94). Yet, the authors also gesture towards another aspect of the "womb-shaped cave" – full of mythic possibilities and rebirths. They write: "The female artist makes her journey into what Adrienne Rich has called 'the cratered night of female memory' to revitalize the darkness, to retrieve what has been lost, to regenerate, reconceive, and give birth. What she gives births to is in a sense her own mother goddess and her own mother land" (99), which the authors compare to a lost Atlantis of women's literary heritage.

Lucia Aiello argues that Gilbert and Gubar "develop an archetypal theory of matrilineal artistic heritage that can be traced back to the 'mother-goddess-myth' of the Cumean Sibyl" (251). The Sibyl not only speaks and dances as the god Apollo's mouthpiece but also she transgresses the gods by scattering leaves that need deciphering. The leaves are a symbolic source for women's creativity because she can "reconstruct the shattered [and scattered] tradition that is her matrilineal heritage" (98). It is not just a matter of reconstructing the lost voices of the Sibyl: "what belongs entirely to her [the female author] is not the mimetic enactment of the role that once was the Sibyl, but the poetic conception of a new form of art, and therefore of a new time where the new Sibyls can speak in their own voices" (Aiello 254). The novels in this chapter recognize the unique and rebellious power of women's artistic voices and, in doing so, create a transnational genealogy. I survey Sawako Ariyoshi's *Kabuki Dancer* (1972), Julia Alvarez's *In the Name of Salomé* (2000), Anchee Min's *Becoming Madame Mao* (2001), Rosario Ferré's *Flight of the Swan* (2002), Slavenka Drakulić's *Frida's Bed* (2008), and Laurel Corona's *The Four Seasons* (2009). The femino-centric topics discussed include dance as transcendence, orphans and opportunity, education, theatre as politics, subversive women artists, and sister rivalry in relation to maestros.

Dance as Spiritual Transcendence

Dance, perhaps the only medium discussed here, has traditionally been perceived, in differing cultures/time-frames, as an art form suitable for women because the "female dancer epitomizes the cultural stereotype of femininity" (Barbour 29). An "object of beauty and desire" (Daly 279), she is idealized for being "upright (straight), lean, compact, youthful, able-bodied, and feminine" (Carol Brown, qtd. in Barbour 29). In the woman's historical novel, by subscribing to an ideology of femininity, a dancer can achieve the status of a celebrity, seen for example in Ariyoshi's and Ferré's novels. Thus, dance becomes a most suitable medium for exploring gender representation. For the women in these novels, dancing, in its corporeality, leads to communing with the divine. In *Kabuki Dancer*, Ariyoshi writes: "Okuni danced and sang in a blackness that obliterated the boundary between earth and sky. Except for a single point where her foot touched the earth, Okuni's entire body reached out to fill the firmament around her" (296). Communing with the divine, however, depends on an eventual rejection of romantic love and motherhood.

Both Okuni in *Kabuki Dancer* and Anna Pavlova, the Russian heroine of Ferré's novel, marry their managers early in their respective careers and neither have children (Okuni miscarries and Pavlova has an abortion because she was "too young to bear children and the abortion made me [her] sterile" (Ferré 106). The protagonists take their failed romantic relationships as inspiration for their art, which raises it to a new level of incomparable merit. This conflict of interest between the purity of art and the interference of love and children, however, is best shown in Ferré's work.

Patricia Vilches writes that Pavlova and Masha Mastova–the narrator, Pavlova's confidante, and a dancer in her troupe–escape from domestic violence while living in early twentieth century Russia but then self-inflict violence on themselves when they become ballerinas. Vilches clarifies:

> *Sin embargo, encontramos que es el ballet mismo el que se convierte en uno de los opresores maximos de la subjectividad femenina en Vuelo del cisne, puesto que si bien libera a la mujer de la ubicuidad tradicionalista, la convierte en sujeto victimizado por las duras tareas y contorsiones que se requieren del cuerpo.*
>
> However, we find that it is ballet itself which becomes one of the ultimate oppressors of female subjectivity in *Flight of the Swan*, since although free from the ubiquity of woman's traditional role, the subject becomes victimized by the hard physicality and bodily contortions required to be a ballerina. (102)

Ferré suggests that Pavlova only experiences spiritual transcendence by subjecting her body to violence. She confirms:

> *Pero, esta es una libertad coartada por la subyugacion del cuerpo femenino a los entuertos fisicos que debe sufrir la bailarina al tratar de aparecer como un ser etereo, si bien ese arte conlleve una violencia congenita de sufrir y soportar.*
>
> But, this is a freedom constrained by the subjugation of the female body to physical pains that the ballerina must suffer all the while appearing ethereal; so well this art conceals an inherent violence of suffering. (Vilches 107)

Pavlova does not sacrifice her dedication to her art until she arrives in Puerto Rico, the setting of the novel in 1917.

Ferré writes, "Madame embarked on her first South American tour with her company, of which I [Masha] was part, on February 10, 1917. Victor Dandré, Madame's husband and manager had persuaded her to take this trip while we were still performing in New York" (8). Unable to make the Atlantic crossing because of WWI, the troupe heads to South America because "several nations there–including Argentina and Brazil–remained neutral and wanted no part in the bloody European war" (9). Dandré is described by Masha as a difficult figure, but one who is essential to Pavlova's success: "None of the dancers cared for Mr. Dandré very much, and we felt sorry for Madame, who, in spite of being a star, couldn't live without him. He took care of her as if she were a child, and lavished attention on her" (14). Pavlova's mother explains to Masha how the young Pavlova met Dandré after performing at a benefit gala. Agreeing to meet the middle-aged "Frenchified Russian" Pavlova declares, "Our economic problems are over, Mother: now we won't have to starve or sell our home because of the strike. I've finally found the protector the Maryinsky Imperial Ballet School always expected me to have" (47). A marriage of convenience, Dandré handles the business side of the performances, including turning Pavlova into a celebrity, which allows Pavlova to focus on her art.

For Pavlova, "[d]ancing was a spiritual experience … [t]he body was the harp of the spirit, the medium through which [the dancer] achieved union with the divine" (16). Striving to achieve perfection and "spiritual transcendence" (32) with her troupe, Masha recounts, "one day she [Madame] asked us to kneel before the holy icon of the Virgin of Vladimir and made us take a vow: 'A career and love are impossible to reconcile. That's why, when you dance, you must never give yourself to anyone" (22). Madame even has hers and Dandré's marriage certificate burned, commenting, "How could I belong to Dandré and at the same time give myself to my art? My duties as a dancer were sacred. As an instrument of God, my body had to be free" (107). Madame, however, breaks her own vow when she meets Diamantino Márquez, a man half her age who "was looked upon by many as El Delfín, the rightful heir to the [Puerto Rican] throne on which the American governor now sits" (76). When Diamantino joins the troupe as an extra violinist, Pavlova is transformed.

Masha reflects, "I had never seen her dance like that, her sweat-slick body curling and uncurling, her body turned into a sign that could only be deciphered by another body's mute language. She forgot all about our sacred mission. Under Diamantino Márquez's appreciative gaze, Glazunov's *Bacchanale* burned sublime" (89). Ferré suggests that lust/love leads Madame to become unprincipled; she becomes animalistic, less disciplined but also more free. Masha quickly realizes that Madame is, for perhaps the first time, choosing romantic love over art. Madame tells her, "the dancing was important, but it wasn't everything. 'One must constantly give birth to oneself, become one's own creation,' Madame said" (104). The affair, like Diamantino's impact on Madame, however, is short-lived (Madame "believed Diamantino had died a hero's death, persecuted by the police for being a revolutionary" (256). After a few months and with Diamantino presumed/being dead, Madame, Dandré and the troupe leave the island for South America. Some years later, Masha, who stays behind in Puerto Rico to marry and raise a family, sees Madame for a final time whilst visiting in New York. Madame asks, "why cry, Masha, darling? You have a baby and I have my art. What a wonderful thing is love! The world is irreversibly transformed by it" (262). Ferré stresses that a woman cannot be an artist and a wife/mother. Art entails suffering and sacrifice, but Pavlova, like John in Foster's novel, does not question this patriarchal structuring or have regrets, instead she celebrates her choice.

Orphans and Artistic Opportunities

The choice between art and love is also exemplified in Corona's *The Four Seasons*. The work narrates the life of two sisters, Maddalena and Chiaretta, in the late seventeenth and early eighteenth century Venice. Beginning in 1695, the young girls arrive at the Ospedale della Pietà: a convent, orphanage, lace making center, and music school. Timothy S. Miller argues that orphanages, like the Pietà, were springing up throughout Italian cities as early as the mid-fifteenth century and "these Western orphanages … focused specifically on saving unwanted babies" (37-38). The Pietà, in particular, is renowned for preparing an orphan for adult life through its music school.

Abandoned by their courtesan mother, the girls are found with a brief letter and an ivory comb. Like Ahdaf Soueif's novel *The Map of Love* that describes a tripartite tapestry, this comb is comprised of three pieces, one for each daughter and the mother (whose piece fits in the middle). Unlike Soueif's book, however, the pieces–the family–remain fragmented. The mother never returns for her children and her portion remains absent and separate.

This novel suggests, like other women's historical novels pertaining to art, that being an orphan or having/living with the absence of a maternal figure is not unusual. The sisters in Corona's work are taken in as orphans by the Pietà and, as a sign of ownership, branded with a "P" on the bottom of their heels (6). Music is their only solace; in the coro, Chiaretta sings and Maddalena plays the violin. Corona writes, "Chiaretta's voice climbed higher, and Maddalena went with her like an echo. Then they were together again, finishing in unison, their music rising and falling like the sound of God breathing" (163). Though Maddalena is content, especially after being chosen to receive lessons from the priest/composer Antonio Vivaldi, the Congregazzione's new violin teacher, Chiaretta relishes opportunities to perform in Venice. She seeks a life outside and beyond the convent's walls either as an opera singer, what at this time was a "vibrant form of public entertainment" (Glixon and Glixon vii), or a rich man's wife.

In the former, a woman is deemed unrespectable in her "vocality and unfettered sexuality" (Heller 25), but she is publically visible in her profession. The wife, by contrast, is respectable, but Venetian wives were relatively invisible and their public role "highly restricted" (ibid. 14). Though the opera heroine's voice, such as the historical protagonist Annina Giró, who struggles to become an opera singer in Sarah Bruce Kelly's *The Red Priest's Annina* (2009), disrupts and threatens dominant ideology, Heller clarifies that in the end "virtue was to be conceded to women based on their silence and chastity" (13). Maddalena notes, "until then it had felt as if her life and Chiaretta's were entwined into one existence, but now she could not deny that Chiaretta's was taking its own path, one that wasn't always going to include her" (77). Similar to Barbara Quick's *Vivaldi's Virgins: A Novel* (2008) which depicts women violinists whose lives change when Vivaldi becomes the new violin instructor at the Pietà, Maddalena's music thrives under the guidance of Vivaldi. She tells him, "I think if I did not have music... She could not even finish the thought" (Corona 94). Vivaldi responds, "we are kindred spirits … we both see that music is poetry" (88); though he has romantic feelings for his student, he never acts upon them. Thus, while Maddalena suppresses her romantic love, she is permitted to continue pursuing music. By contrast, Chiaretta faces choosing between the convent or marriage and the loss of her right to perform.

Engaged to one of the Congregazzione's sons, Chiaretta is told that "husbands must sign an oath that any bride coming from one of the ospedali will never sing or play an instrument outside her home" (Corona 108). Not only will she be prohibited from performing in public, Chiaretta will also have to leave her sister. This separation occurs when Chiaretta marries and moves into her husband's family home. Coming to terms with her husband's frequent absences, Chiaretta finds herself looking out the window one day at the gondolas below. Hearing the melody of a solo she learned at the Pietà, she is overtaken by the urge to sing. When her husband hears her, however, he shouts, "Sing inside for me, for my family. Sing if I say you can. But until then, keep your mouth shut!" (215). The dream of being an opera singer and a wife are incompatible.

Women's Education

In the women's novels discussed, education is linked with women's sexuality and artistic ambition. The Ospedale della Pietà is instrumental in training young musicians in Corona's *The Four Seasons* (2009), Pavlova's monetary donation to Masha sets up a prestigious ballet school in Puerto Rico, and Okuni's passion for training dancers in late sixteenth century Japan is unrivalled. Alvarez's novel *In the Name of Salomé*, however, gives us the clearest insight into the relation between art, women's education, and sexuality. Alvarez writes about the lives of Salomé Ureña (1850-1897), the famous Dominican poet and her daughter Salomé Camila Henríquez Ureña (1894-1970), a Hispanicist educator in the United States and Cuba. Novels on women writers like the Ureñas, are not as forthcoming as one might expect.[16]

Alvarez's novel switches between its two narrators, covering Salomé's life until her death at a young age from consumption when Camila is only three years old (296) and then Camila's transnational life. After her mother's death, Camila's family goes into exile in Cuba and she later moves to the United States. The novel's ending shows an older Camila returning to her maternal root (her mother and the Dominican Republic) and her addressing the reader for the first time in the first person. It is, however, through the mother's, Salomé's, voice that we first sense both the patriarchal control by men over the women in their lives and the need for women's education.

Salomé, a poet celebrated for writing nationalistic poems in a masculine style, is continually asked by her philandering husband Pancho (Francisco Henríquez y Carvajal (1859–1935, the president of the Dominican Republic briefly in 1916) to suppress her personal desire for the greater good of the nation; in response she tells him, "I am a woman as well as a poet" (Alvarez 177), suggesting there is little room for femininity in either the poetic tradition or the nation. Alvarez intimates that political change in the Dominican Republic is not possible without engaging women and the feminine as political equals to men and masculinity. As long as women remain considered inferior and subordinate to men, privately and publically, the Dominican Republic will remain politically fragile and vulnerable.

Pancho, essentially, betrays Salomé in the novel when he goes to Paris to study medicine and has an affair with another woman; it is analogous to betraying his Dominican Republic, his *patria*. Alvarez also describes how Pancho has his brother Federico spy on Salomé and act as a paternal stand-in—this act is echoed later in the novel when Salomé's son, Pedro spies on his sister Camila. Pedro suspects Camila of having an affair with a man, but is, instead, awakened

---

[16] Notable exceptions include *Las libres del Sur: una novela sobre Victoria Ocampo* (2004) by María Rosa Lojo de Beuter, Alica Gaspar de Alba's *Sor Juana's Second Dream* (1999), about the seventeenth century Mexican nun-writer-poet, Sor Juana Inés de la Cruz, Laura Fish's *Strange Music* (2008) and *How Do I Love Thee?* by Nancy Moser (2009), (both depict poet Elizabeth Barrett Browning), and Susan Sellers recreates the sibling relationship between artist Vanessa Bell and author Virginia Woolf in *Vanessa and Virginia* (2009).

to her lesbian relationship with Marion. Uncertain of her sexual identity, Camila, however, represses her desire for Marion. Alvarez, thus, emphasizes how restricting Dominican women's roles in society can be and her works advocate women's empowerment through education and sexuality.

The former *musa de la patria*, Salomé comes to reject her political poems in favour of personal poems and a peaceful revolution brought about through education. Salomé remarks, "I felt up to the hard work of rebuilding *my patria*, girl by girl" (271) and definitively states:

> I had lost heart in the ability of words to transform us into a patria of brothers and sisters. Hadn't I heard that Lilís [the dictator president] himself liked to recite passages of my patriotic poems to his troops before battle? ... The last thing our country needed was more poems. We needed schools. (187)

Salomé's secondary school for educating girls to become teachers, the first in the country, is continued by Camila, who teaches first in the U.S. at Vassar College and then in Cuba, working to build a *patria* through women's education.

Retiring from her position at Vassar College, la Professora decides to return to Cuba, the country of her childhood, spent with her exiled family. Camila declares, "*I think it is time now to go back and be a part of what my mother started*" (35) and "I'm going to join a revolution" (47). Drawing strength from her own mother's resolve to continue educating despite her illness, Camila spends thirteen years in Cuba teaching "at the university at night and in factorías during the day. Weekends, [she] joined [her] young compañeros, writing manuals and preparing materials for the teachers who came in from the rural schools" (347). She recalls, "literature for all. ... My mother's instituto had grown to the size of a whole country!" (349). Like her mother before her, Camila believes not in Fidel Castro's military revolution but that the "real revolution could only be won by the imagination. When one of [her] newly literate students picked up a book and read with hungry pleasure, [she] knew [they] were one step closer to the patria [they] all wanted" (347). The patria Camila envisions necessarily includes the rights and participation of women. One day, to a group of women sorting coffee beans, she impulsively abandons her lessons on the great male thinkers like Karl Marx and, instead, recites from memory an unpublished poem by her mother (Camila's brother Pedro by contrast chooses not to publish any of his mother's personal and intimate poems).

The poem is about her sleeping son Pedro, whom she is watching so intently that she cannot read a word of the book in her lap. When the women realize the poem was written not only by a mother but by their instructor's mother, "the women began to clack with their wooden scoopers on the side of their tables, until the din of the room drowned out the compañera, shouting for order, in the name of Fidel, in the name of the revolution" (348). After her time in Cuba, Camila returns to her mother-country, the Dominican Republic. She reflects, "It's continuing to struggle to create the country we dream of that makes a patria out of the land under our feet. That much I learned from mother" (350), a sentiment that suits the novel's ending. Camila is visiting her family's cemetery and overseeing her own future gravestone but, because her eyesight is poor, she asks a young boy to read the inscription for her. Alvarez writes, "Not a word from him. Finally, it dawns on me. In Cuba, he would know how to read. He would not be picking weeds on a schoolday" (352). The boy is from Los Millones, which Alvarez argues is "named not for the millionaires who do not live there but for the million poor who do" (353).Taking his hand, Camila traces the letters of her name for him, *Salomé Camila Henríquez Ureña*, suggesting that Camila's life is carrying on the work and name of her mother, and she coaches to boy to repeat the words "until he gets it right" (353). Emphasizing the importance of education, particularly women's, Alvarez's work questions and challenges patriarchal and nationalistic discourses on national identity.

"Theatre is Political and Politics is Theatrical"[17]

Alvarez's *In the Name of Salomé* emphasizes that the theme of love versus art found in women's historical novels is political. Metanarrative lends itself particularly well to this genre, which seeks to politically intervene in masculinist discourses. Intra and extra textually, art is used as a political tool. The following novels take place in the late nineteenth and early twentieth century, within which political turmoil runs parallel with familial upheaval and unrest. In Alvarez's novel and Ferré's *Flight of the Swan*, the struggle for national independence in relation to women's lives is at the forefront; Alvarez focuses on the Dominican Republic's separation from Spain and Ferré's work centers on Puerto Rico's change of hands from Spain to the United States. While these novels raise important questions about national identity, national independence/sacrifice, and how women as artists contribute to the national discourse, the impact of a woman on both art and politics is best seen in Min's novel *Becoming Madame Mao*.

Min's narrative begins in 1991, just prior to the former first lady of Communist China's suicide whilst in prison. One of the unique aspects of this work is its innovative style that switches between first person accounts by Madame Mao and a third-person narrator–though there is certainly slippage and ambigu

---

[17] This quotation is from Xiaomeni Chen and his observations in China.

ity between the two as quotation marks are absent. Eric Hayot notes, "The effect is to suggest either that the first-person narration emerges from the imaginative power of the external narrator or that the external narrator might be the projection of Jiang Qing [Madame Mao] as novelistic character" (620). This technique also shows how the "I" of the text perceives and is perceived by others; thus, there is a private self, the first-person, and the public self, which explains the third person. For an infamous figure like Madame Mao separating one's private self from a public self would be near impossible. This style also makes differentiating between historical fact and imagination difficult, but has the effect of reclaiming Madame Mao from both history and literature as simply "a white-boned demon."

Min humanizes Madame Mao by imagining her defense for her controversial political career. The work follows more or less a chronological account of Madame Mao's past, coming full circle back to 1991. What is unique about Min's retelling is her interpretation of Mao's life as a tragic actress. Min imagines Madame Mao's consent to play what she identifies as a distinct feature of Chinese history: a tragic role for exceptional women. Min writes, "That's Chinese history. The fall of a kingdom is always the fault of a concubine. Why should Comrade Jiang Qing be an exception?" (qtd. in Hayot 618). One can read Min's portrayal of Madame Mao either as regrettably confusing/conflating life with a stage–thus, she is always and necessarily playing the role of a doomed heroine–or in existentialist terms, she brilliantly knows life really *is* only a stage but takes up her condemned role ever more passionately. Madame Mao's roles as an actress both in theater and film are truly no less a reality for her than her infamous life as "the most powerful woman in China during the late 1960s and '70s" (Min 7). Art and politics converge and imitate; they are inseparable.

Likewise, Madame Mao repeatedly envisions herself as a literary leading lady. In her early years with Mao in Yenan, she likens herself to Lady Yuji:

> Sitting by her lover the girl is touched by the operatic quality of her life. Events transform in front of her eyes. On the stage of her mind, Mao becomes the modern King-of-Shang and she is his lover, Lady Yuji. She sees herself follow the king. Ever since she was a little girl it has been her dream to play Lady Yuji. (138)

Madame Mao's successes in embodying the role of tragic heroines onstage and offstage stem from several key events in her life which are unique to women.

Madame Mao uses not only her life to inspire art but art to inspire her life. For example, in feminist terms, she translates into a series of operas and ballets, such as *The Women of the Red Detachment* and *The White-Haired Girl* (Min

7), the pain she endured as a child when her mother tried to bind her feet. The irony here, which we also see in Ferré's novel *Flight of the Swan*, is that ballet though an art form is particularly brutal and physically demanding when it comes to women's bodies.

As a child, Madame Mao also witnesses the violent relationship between her mother, a concubine, and her abusive father. Without any resources, her mother eventually runs away with her daughter and leaves her for good to be raised by her grandparents. Living with her grandparents proves fruitful for Madame Mao as she is able to forget her pain through the operas her grandfather and she attend. Identifying with the pain of the heroines in these operas, her grandfather gives her a new formal name: Yunhe, "'Crane in the Clouds'. The image is picked from his favorite opera, *The Golden Pavilion*. The crane is the symbol of hope" (14). In loving opera so much, however, she ruins her chances for life as a respectable woman by running away and joining a theater troupe: "I decide that I shall be an opera actress so I will get to live a heroine's life on stage" (15). Believing she is destined to become a star, Madame Mao aligns herself with an experimental theatre group of underground Communists. Despite Yun-he's success in her first role, in the year 1930, the theater is shut down. Madame Mao's interest in the Communist Party, nevertheless, intensifies when she is introduced to Yu Qiwei, the student leader and secretary of the underground Communist Party on [Shan-dong University] campus.

Enrolling herself in classes and working in the library, Madame Mao officially becomes a member of the Communist Party. She tells Yu Qiwei, in gendered terms, that "the true poverty is having no choice in life. No choice but to get married, for example. No choice but to be a prostitute or concubine, to sell one's body" (28). Following her marriage to Yu Qiwei, Madame Mao begins performing for a small left-wing troupe–"I help create anti-Japanese plays and take them to the street" (30)–and believes herself to be risking her life for China. When her marriage fails, Madame Mao moves to Shanghai, where she combines her love of acting with her political ideals by making political films. She knows "China is under invasion. The public is sick of ancient romance and is ready for inspiring roles from real life" (45). When arrested, however, Madame Mao, controversially, signs a paper denouncing her role as a Communist (though, historically, she denies ever signing the paper). Released in 1934, she gives herself a new name, Lan Ping, which coincides with her big break; she plays Nora in Ibsen's *Doll's House*.

Identifying with the character of a stifled housewife, "on stage she lives out her eternal despair. Nora's lines fall from her lips like words of her own. *I've lived by performing tricks, Torvald, and I can bear it no more*" (55). Following her success in the play, Madame Mao moves onto acting in low-budget anti-

Japanese films. Unsatisfied with minor roles, she moves to Yenan, where she has heard that Mao Tse-tung, a famous Communist, resides. In Yenan, Madame Mao performs in some small operas, the aim of which is to make the Communist hero fall in love with her. Succeeding in her romantic endeavor, she becomes pregnant and marries Mao in 1938. Her new marriage entails a new name, Jiang Ching, given to her by her final husband. Though the party refuses to allow her to actively participate in politics, she concedes that "to be Madame Mao will be her victory" (148), unwittingly becoming somewhat of a Nora figure in relation to Torvald. Essentially, like many of the heroines in this chapter, Madame Mao considers her husband a god.

Suffocating in her domestic life, Madame Mao resurfaces after Mao falls ill in 1947. Trusted to do his bidding, Madame Mao begins working in a stereotypical feminine and unassuming/unthreatening role, as a secretary. Through her ambition, however, she climbs her way up the political ladder. She is careful to emphasize to her detractors that she has given up a life of drama and luxury as an actress for her commitment to a Communist China:

> For a decade, she [Madame Mao] has worked to create a perfect image of herself through the operas and ballets. A heroine with a touch of masculinity. The woman who came from poverty and rises to lead the poor to victory. She believes that the minds of the Chinese have been influenced. It's time to test the water –the audience should be ready to embrace a heroine in real life. (314)

Thus, Madame Mao's power reaches its heights when she is no longer on the stage but behind the stage.

Art, for Madame Mao, is a means to be Mao's Communist propaganda machine. She claims, "to me art is a weapon. A weapon to fight injustice, Japanese, Imperialists and enemies alike" (90). Resolved to maintain her husband's reputation, Madame Mao sets to work on controlling the media: "I see printing machines rolling, voices broadcasting and films projecting. I feel the power of the media. The way it washes and bleaches minds. I can feel the coming success" (214). In Shanghai, the political campaign continues and she trains what she calls a "'cultural troop'. A troop that Mao will need to fight his ideological battles" (215). Min writes that, in 1966, "in Mao's name I [Madame Mao] organize a national festival –the Festival of Revolutionary Operas … I make the operas bear my signature and personally supervise every detail, from the selection of the actors to the way a singer hits the note" (240). Art not only upholds Mao's power but also what she perceives is her own power. She uses the media to solidify her status as the foundation for her husband's success. Min writes of a newspaper article that claims, "Without a guardian angel like Comrade Jiang

Ching, China's future will shatter" (223) and she becomes known as the head of the infamous Cultural Revolution.

The separation, or lack thereof, between fiction and reality is manifest in the Cultural Revolution. Min argues that "in truth, for Madame Mao, there is no line between living and acting. The Cultural Revolution is a breathing stage and Mao is her playwright" (284). That Mao is her playwright suggests that he is still, ultimately, the man in power and Madame Mao is subject to his whims and desires–she is merely an actress on Mao's stage. This becomes clearer after Mao's death in 1976, when Madame Mao seizes the opportunity to claim power for herself but is defeated. A month after her husband's death, Madame Mao, declared an enemy of China, is sentenced to prison and awaits execution. Min writes of how, with her death sentences always commuted at the last minute, Madame Mao works in prison ironically making dolls to be exported to capitalist markets from 1976-1991.

Amy T.Y. Lai points out that paradoxically, though Madame Mao identifies with Ibsen's Nora "who refuses to be a pampered doll and a slave to her husband" by subversively sewing her name "Jiang Ching" inside the doll's clothing, she effectively "turns herself into a doll. By others, and by her own self-fashioning, she has been fashioned into a disposable object" (565). Just prior to her suicide in 1991, and blurring life as art and art as life, Min writes:

> It is time to empty the stage. Remember, you will always come across me in the books about China. Don't be surprised to see my name smeared. There is nothing more they can do to me. And don't forget that I was an actress, a great actress. I acted with passion. For those who are fascinated by me you owe me applause, and for those who are disgusted you may spit. I thank you all for coming. (337)

Thus, Min's novel joins Mao's narrative as an innovative metanarrative.

The Subversive Woman-Artist: Maternal Roots

Women's historical novels suggest that the woman as artist is subversive to society. The emotional impact of art upon an audience also plays an essential role in this subversion. Madame Mao's appropriation of the means of media production bolsters her and her husband's political career in China by appealing to the masses; Anna Pavlova's poetic dances in Ferré's *Flight of the Swan* have life-changing impact. Ferré, via her Russian ex-patriot narrator, Masha, tells the reader:

> Madame, on the other hand, never danced simply for the money. She wanted to give everyone the opportunity to enjoy the

beauty of ballet, even those who had no money … Europe was
being torn apart, but compassion and love were still possible;
that was Madame's message. *The Dying Swan*, the solo piece
that made her famous all over the world, was a prayer for
peace. (21)

Madame performs the piece whilst stranded in Puerto Rico during the war.
Madame is told: "[you are a] poet in your own right" (Ferré 71). In both Ariyoshi's *Kabuki Dancer* and Drakulić's *Frida's Bed*, however, the woman as subversive artist is connected with her sexuality and the maternal.

In the Translator's Note to *Kabuki Dancer*, James R. Brandon comments on
Okuni's innate desire to dance, in a way startlingly similar to Drakulić's interpretation of the maternal as a natural root in relation to Mexican painter Frida
Kahlo. An old woman in the text tells Okuni: "Lewd women, *kabuki* women,
take money for singing and dancing. *Kabuki* women are plants that haven't got
roots in the ground" (Ariyoshi 80). Brandon believes, as a whole, Ariyoshi is
really asking of her text, "Does something grow from singing? After dancing,
is something left? Is a *kabuki* woman a plant without roots in the earth?" (6).
The temporal and fleeting nature of Okuni's art mirrors her life of wandering,
suggesting that she is indeed without roots.

A sexually and economically "loose" woman is a *kabuki* woman; the practice of her art is not a stable or credible profession, but Okuni's effect on her
audiences complicates this reading. Okuni knows that "people need food, a
place to sleep. These needs aren't satisfied watching people dance or hearing
them sing … Yet tired as she was, Okuni felt the desire to dance racing like a
fire through her body to her toes and fingertips" (82), as "she existed in her
dance alone" (295). Okuni transforms the traditional definition of kabuki,
which, in the text, has clear gendered and sexualized connotations as "a word
used in Izumo to mean strange, indecent, improper" (19), into a celebration of
new artistic expression. Okuni says, "If I'm a woman who likes to dance, does
that make me a *kabuki* woman? Can this bright, happy feeling be bad? Don't be
angry, Granny. Perhaps I *am a kabuki* woman" (20). Her appropriation of the
word also occurs when her sister Okaga tells her: "to run away from a promised
husband is what a *kabuki* woman would do" (56). Okuni replies, "If it's *kabuki*
for me to be the wife of Sankuro, the man I love, instead of Kyuzo, someone I
hate, than I'm glad to be called *kabuki*" (ibid.). Okuni, however, also desires to
turn her innovative art into a respectable form; she strives to touch "a man's
heart more than … his body" (15) and continually entrances her Japanese audiences with creating unexpected comic-erotic roles, many of which involve
cross-dressing.

For example, performing for their patron Kanbei and his guests in Kyoto, Okuni is described as holding an unrivalled sway over her audience. After changing from her monk's robe into a beautiful kimono:

> No one spoke. It was a silence of men struck dumb with admiration–for the brilliant kimono suddenly revealed by an ingenious theatrical technique, for the beautiful full face that appeared in an instant from beneath the black lacquered hat, and for Okuni's effortless, leaping dance steps that melded perfectly with her soaring voice. The transformation of Okuni was so splendid, so attractive, and so unexpected, that for some time the guests did not speak. (51)

Okuni's appeal to her audience's emotions and her own self-identification with the word "kabuki" free of an equation with prostitution leads to a gradual transformation of the term.

Ariyoshi notes, "While in the past *kabuki* had meant someone who was eccentric, and in Izumo the word had been used to shame a person who deviated from the norm, it now indicated a trend setter in the foreign fashion" (132) of "sleeveless vests, bloused pantaloons, round hats, velvet belts, Kirishitan crosses and rosaries of the Southern Barbarians" (ibid.). This new trend for men dressing in foreign western fashions inspires Okuni to incorporate the clothing into her performances and to impersonate men, which has a profound effect upon her audience. Okuni's true success, however, besides her innovative techniques, is that she performs for both the rich and poor and with equal enthusiasm.

The popularity of Okuni's theater leads to yet another shift in the definition of kabuki in the text. Singing and dancing prostitutes adopt the name "Courtesans' Kabuki" for economic and social influence: "Troupes of theaters, one after the other, in Sakai Ward, Fukiya Ward, Hirokoji Alley in Nakabashi Ward, and in other parts of Edo" set up a flag "proclaiming itself Best in the World" (274). Ariyoshi writes:

> The white flag in front of the theater simply meant 'Kabuki is performed here.' The universal use of the phrase signified the important fact that Kabuki no longer belonged to Okuni personally. What she had created as a private artistic expression now belonged to the public. In the future, Okuni would be only one of many dancers and performers shaping the direction of Kabuki's artistic growth. (ibid.)

Disheartened, Okuni bitterly laments that "By now, any street performance, dance, or even puppet play was indiscriminately called Kabuki" (300). The novel concludes with Okuni returning to her birth village, the Iron Mountain, to dance a final time. Making her way alone through the mountain pass, she re-members a question once asked of her: "How long are you going to dance?" (343) and her confident response: "Until the day I die" (ibid.). With this knowledge, she closes her eyes, the snow falls around her, and she awaits death while dreaming of her life as a Kabuki actress.

Similar to *Kabuki Dancer*, *Frida's Bed* takes up the theme of art and self-expression by focusing on the life of Mexican painter Frida Kahlo (1907-1954). Maternal imagery is a connecting thread throughout the narrative. Blur-ring the line between reality and dream, Danielle Knafo argues that Kahlo "transformed her canvas into a mirror in which she reflected a world of exquis-ite tensions, stark beauty, stoic strength, insidious will, and layered self-definitions" (Knafo 6). An epigraph to Drakulić's novel written by Kahlo reads, "*Mi pintura lleva el mensaje del dolor*" 'My painting carries the message of pain.' Frida's pain, not only psychical, stems in part from suffering from polio as a child (3) and a street-car accident:

> Her right leg, the lame one, had been broken in eleven places
> and her right foot has been dislocated and crushed. Her lower
> spine was broken in three places, her collarbone was broken
> and so were two ribs. Her left shoulder was dislocated ... A
> long metal rod–the handrail–had ripped into her stomach near
> her left hip and come out through her vagina. (15)

Unable to express herself verbally after the accident, Frida's mother Doña Ma-tilda, hopes painting will ease some of her teenage daughter's boredom and pain.

Given her father's old paints and brushes (Drakulić 20), Frida begins paint-ing not only "sketches, studies and portraits of the people around her, but most-ly of herself. This was no longer a pastime. Painting completely absorbed her. She assiduously studied the history of European art, especially the work of the great Renaissance masters, and she practiced the steadiness of her hand" (25). For Knafo, Frida's relationship with her mother and motherhood is instrumen-tal in her art. Doña Matilda's lack of emotional support for her daughter is a constant source of pain, characterized by Frida as "unavailability, loss, and rejection" (76). This tumultuous relationship, expressed in her self-portraits, shows Frida's shifting conception of motherhood that moves from her own mother to herself as a potential mother and, finally, to the role of symbolic mother. Knafo writes:

> For Frida, the self-portrait represented an apt, almost self-
> evident, means by which she was able to act as a mirror to her-
> self, reflecting her need for self-definition while simultaneous-
> ly attempting to achieve it. Through her art Frida succeeded in

> repeating the mother-infant dyad with its mutual gazing reci-
> procity. Creating her double in her self-portraits, she became
> her own mirror. (78)

Frida's talent manifests itself when the Maestro, historical Mexican painter
Diego Riviera and her future husband, sees a small exhibition of her work:
"You must paint, he told her seriously. He was looking at her paintings as if he
could not get enough of them. It was as if he could not entirely separate the
paintings from the unusual person who had done them" (30). The Maestro continues to support Frida's painting for "he recognized her talent, that *something*
in her paintings that was personal, intimate, painful and completely individual
and distinct" (45). The paintings referenced in the novel by Drakulić highlight
Frida's confessional style, such as *My Dress Hangs*, which Frida paints during
her first time in New York City:

> It looks so forlorn, this Mexican dress hanging there above the
> garbage and the smokestacks, the skyscrapers and the stock ex-
> change, above the church spire with its dollar sign…. Not a liv-
> ing soul inhabits this painting. There is nothing strange about
> that. What is strange is that Frida is not in the picture. To any-
> one who knows her, this absence, this relinquishment of self,
> comes as a surprise. Instead of doing her usual–painting herself
> to confirm her own existence–she is simply no more (Drakulić
> 47-48).

This absence in Frida's work is juxtaposed with an increasing number of self-
portraits, such as *The Henry Ford Hospital* and *Self-Portrait with a Doll*.

These paintings are testimonies to her miscarriages because "for her painting self-portraits was a kind of magical rite, a kind of exorcism" (Drakulić 51).
Her search for herself through her mother is explored on the canvas, but she
also holds the idea that art has a creative, mother-like power. In paintings like
My Birth, "Frida shows how she gave birth to her art–the only arena in which
she was able to express, rework, and master the conflicted relationship she had
with her mother and her own body" (80). Therefore, Drakulić reads her creative
art as a substitute for her inability to physically give birth to children:

> Using painting as her medium for self-expression, Frida paint-
> ed a broken paintbrush, wounds on the leg, a carved-out heart,
> blood gushing from slashed veins, a body pierced with arrows,
> herself dead, herself planted in the earth. She painted fetuses
> and miscarriages, white bloodstained sheets and birth–legs
> spread open, an infant's head peering out. There was nothing
> gentle or sweet about the scream of the woman giving birth,
> about the cry of the child–she herself–being born. (52)

Frida's paintings are inspired by her pain, both physical and emotional. This is evident when Drakulić argues:

> Had there been no accident there would have been no painting. Or life with Maestro. She would have been a country doctor – she had wanted to study medicine. She would have been somebody else. The experience of pain and all of those operations was the connecting thread between her life and her art, tying them together like a surgeon sewing up a wound. They were like an umbilical cord, the paintings nourished by her placenta, sucking in her life. (126)

Painting is an overwhelming primordial force, evident in Frida's final engagement with motherhood. Knafo suggests that this comes near the end of Kahlo's life when, after her mother's death and unable to conceive her own child, she literally and visually embraces Diego, her husband, as a child.

In several works, such as *The Love Embrace of the Universe*, Frida depicts herself as Diego's mother: "*she is the mother who rocks him, takes care of, and protects him*" (Drakulić 89). In other works, she herself is held by a precolonial earth goddess, a maternal *raíz*, (a reference to her wetnurse) (Knafo 86). Resonating with Ariyoshi's novel, the symbolic mother and the maternal (93) are a connecting thread throughout Drakulić's novel and Frida's paintings and culminates in the work *Roots*. Described by Drakulić as linking the maternal and nature to Frida, green lush plants grow out of her body:

> Thin veinlike little roots spurt from their tips, full of blood. It is only a matter of time before all of her blood seeps into the thirsty soil. Her heart has already been bled dry, so has her womb; you can see a part of the landscape through the hole that is in its place. (128)

This physical view of a dying Frida speaks of her desire. Drakulić writes: "how can people understand her suffering unless this painting jolts them into experiencing it for themselves?" (128). The painting's effect upon the artist and the audience is essential to Frida's philosophy of art. Drakulić writes of the viewer's identification with her work: "anybody could identify with her and feel her pain as *his own*. However dramatic they were, her paintings elicited empathy but also immediate identification with one's own suffering.… When the Maestro looked at her paintings he saw his own pain as well" (121). Art's ability to translate both the painter's inner experience and the viewer's own suffering is clear. Though Frida respects the Maestro, the critic who has the greatest influence on her is American painter Georgia O'Keefe:

> In New York in 1938, O'Keefe, took Frida by the hand –her own was warm –and led her to the painting *My Birth*. She

> stood there, looking at the painting. Nobody ever dared to paint
> this before. You've painted something that is never supposed to
> be seen, that nobody ever dares to witness because they are
> shocked by a woman's power to give life … Frida felt that after
> just one look at her painting, this woman, whom she had never
> met before, had shown a level of understanding that she had
> always dreamed of. (81)

O'Keefe's and Frida's experiences of reality as gendered, and as women artists connects them in a way that others, Drakulić suggests, cannot share.

Commanding her energy, Frida believes that "[s]he had to paint because the emotional pain she felt–which seemed to have settled like sediment on top of her old, physical pain–was too strong to contain" (Drakulić 76). She continues to suggest: "my paintings were a guide into the world of show and duplicity. Painting was the only safe place for me, a place of truth, a refuge. The only place where I could really be myself" (98). The novel concludes with Frida, like Okuni in Ariyoshi's text, in constant pain and no longer able to work. Her "body was being eroded by infection and … [her] spirit was being eroded by drugs" (157). She chooses to take her own life by overdosing on her medication. Drakulić writes, "she was no longer the Frida they knew because what was now was not her. Only her paintings were her" (162), suggesting, once again, the powerful nature of art as a subversive means for women to express themselves.

Maestros as False Idols: Sisters as Rivals

Novels like Katherine Govier's *The Printmaker's Daughter* (2011), in which Oei, the daughter of renowned Japanese artist Hokusai, renounces traditional domesticity by committing herself to her art, remains faithful, at the same time to the will of her father by relinquishing any credit for her work–confirm that the choice between art or love and a family is the center of many women's historical novels on art. As a whole, these narratives are about sacrifice and suggest that a pursuit of art comes at a romantic and often reproductive cost: the two appear irreconcilable. In all of the novels discussed in this chapter, the quest for artistic genius is at the forefront of each woman's mind. This quest, however, becomes complicated by the men, considered maestros, in each woman's life. Samantha Haigh clarifies:

> Women are thus unable to relate to each other as subjects, nor
> can they experience desire in their own right. They must exist
> in a mode of masquerade, experiencing desire only as it is situ-
> ated by male desire, and relating to other women only via men.

> Rivalry for the desire of men, is for Irigaray a prime example
> of such a female relationship, and it is a rivalry which begins
> with mother and daughter. (63)

Most of these novels describe an older, wealthy, and prominent figure, a god, a replacement father, a maestro, in relation to a younger, poor, inexperienced and emerging woman artist.

In Ferré's novel, Pavlova's husband Dandré fulfills this role and in Corona's novel *The Four Seasons*, the Maestro is Vivaldi, whom Maddalena secretly loves. Gwen John, in Forster's novel, for example, has a secret and passionate affair with the sculptor Rodin. As Rodin's lover, however, Gwen's drive to create her own art dwindles: "Alarmingly, she had no desire to produce any work at all. She no longer wanted to paint. Why should she? She was happy and fulfilled without striving to convey emotion and feelings to canvas. It was enough to pose for her master–she liked to call him that, *mon maître*–and make love with him afterward" (Forster 56). When Rodin distances himself, Gwen wonders if life would have "meaning without her master at the center of it? But he was not at the center now, perhaps never had been" (66). Without Rodin, however, Gwen completes some of her best work, a theme echoed in Ariyoshi's *Kabuki Dancer* and Drakulić's *Frida's Bed*.

Frida, problematically, also refers to her future husband, Diego Riviera, as the *Maestro* and makes him the center of her world. When the Maestro, "the most famous painter and ladies' man in all of Mexico" (Drakulić 38), visits her studio, he asserts her artistic talent. Drakulić comments that "after art, politics was the second most important thing in his life, but for her ... ideology was less important than the opportunity it gave them to be together" (30). She continues, "In those first years of marriage Frida only dabbled in painting. She was untrue to herself, ignoring her talent, the very thing that had captivated the Maestro. He became more important to her than painting" (40). Even "the papers wrote about her as his charming wife, not as a painter" (41). Coming to terms with the Maestro's womanizing and affairs, including with her own sister, Frida realizes:

> What a waste of time ... I took away from my painting, the on-
> ly thing I cared about, to make him love me, to seduce him, to
> be by his side" ... There was no balance in our relationship. It
> was me who needed him, me who was always hungry, always
> wanting attention, wanting reassurance. In my world, he was
> the source of light and warmth. He was my food, my drug. He
> was my obsession. Why did I let myself become so utterly de-
> pendent on him? (74-75)

In all of the novels discussed here, the artist's romantic life is challenged by their lovers' affairs with other women. In both *Frida's Bed* by Drakulić and *Kabuki Dancer* by Ariyoshi, however, the other woman is a younger sister.

In Ariyoshi's novel, the protagonist Okuni, a pivotal founding member of Japanese Kabuki, meets her lover's secret wife, Oan, in Kyoto 1591. Having recovered from a miscarriage with Sankuro's child, Kabuki stays near Shijo Bridge where she and her troupe meet Oan, Sankuro's legal wife. Okuni slowly realizes, "this is Sankuro's house. This is where he stays when he comes to Kyoto. I've been in a fool" (92); likewise Oan learns that the much younger Okuni is her husband's lover. Okuni "wanted to shout, I've won, Sankuro is mine, he will never leave me" (94). Okuni pragmatically says, "Please understand. Sankuro plays the drum and I dance. Sankuro doesn't want to change this. He and I will never be apart. You must understand this" (95). Following Okuni's proclamation, Oan disappears "like a ghost" (ibid.). In Drakulić's work, Frida also "steals" the Maestro away from his former wife Lupe and marries him (34). Drakulić notes that "her victory would be short-lived" (37) as she soon learns the bitterness Lupe feels when the Maestro sleeps with not only many other women but also her younger sister Kity.

The sister is an ambivalent literary figure; she is simultaneously loved and envied. Frida describes going to inform Maestro that she is pregnant (her third time as she has miscarried twice before) but, when she opens the door to Maestro's studio, she sees them together (Drakulić 66): "She [Kity] was lying in the bed, naked, beautiful –so much more beautiful than Frida. … For the first time Frida saw her sister through the Maestro's eyes, the eyes of a man and an artist" (68). Bárbara Mujica's *Frida* (2001), for example, is written from Kity's point of view, because she often gets overshadowed by Frida. Frida sees Kity's youth, physicality, and fecundity as juxtaposed with her own illnesses, disabilities, and infertility. She knows that Maestro has lovers, but when she discovers Kity is one of them "something inside Frida changed forever" (69). Following the betrayal, Frida cuts Kity, for all intents and purposes, out of her life. Diana Wallace, though focusing on British novels (1914-39), calls these situations, which "set up a test of gender loyalty" and involve two women and a man, an "erotic triangle" (*Sisters and Rivals* 5); "the rival sisters novel is a special version of the triangle novel where the complex play of similarity and difference between women is doubly intensified" (*Sisters and Rivals* 8). This type of rivalry occurs in both Drakulić's and Ariyoshi's work on women artists.

Wallace's insights that "blood sister relationships so often conflict with the ideal of sisterhood" and that there is a "tension between similarity and difference, closeness and separation, friendship and rivalry" (*Sisters and Rivals* 7) are relevant. Drakulić describes Frida's condition as "an empty womb, wounds,

back pain and the feeling of having been completely abandoned" (72). Deject-
ed, Frida moves out of her apartment adjoining the Maestro's and takes up a
series of lovers, including Leon Trotsky (108). In the cathartic painting *Self-
Portrait with Cropped Hair*, Frida sits, holding a pair of scissors: "She has
already chopped off the long silky mane that the Maestro loved so much and
black locks of hair are strewn all over the floor. ... She is dressed like a man
again. She is punishing the Maestro. Your Frida is gone, Frida is telling him in
the picture" (Drakulić 78). A similar situation occurs to Okuni after her sister
Okiku joins her and Sankuro's troupe.

Okuni trains her sister in song and dance and the pair performs to much ac-
claim until Okiku catches the eye of a certain Lord Tokio. Propositioned to
prostitute herself to Lord Tokio, Okuni argues that "being a *kabuki* dancer isn't
a disgrace" but an art, and one which does not entail selling one's body for
money (183). Okiku refuses to listen and the relationship between sisters becomes strained. Sankuro, however, admires Okiku's determination. Okiku tells
Sankuro, "Okuni doesn't have ambition. I'm different. I want to do better than
dance in *this* place ... I'm younger than Okuni. Teach me. I can dance to your
drum better than she does" (189). During a particular performance in which
Sankuro displays his affection for Okiku, Okuni hears the audience clapping:
"She fought to keep calm. It was not just Okiku's success. She thought of the
hot summer when Oan had been driven to madness. Okuni had been younger
than Oan and Sankuro had needed her. She had driven Oan away" (195). She
resolves, "I am not Oan. I won't go mad. I won't be driven away by Okiku"
(ibid.). Like Frida who sees Kity and the Maestro together, Okuni sees Okiku
and Sankuro making love under the stage and is described by Ariyoshi as "ex-
hausted from running, empty, her emotions washed away. She knew now that
all things in this world change ... Her anger toward Sankuro was gone; her
grudge against Okiku had been washed away" (200). As a final act of cleansing, Okuni realizes that because she and Oan and Okiku were women they suffered, and because Sankuro was a man, he did not.

> I want to be a man, she thought, and then shuddered, as if she
> had touched some deeply hidden, unconscious yearning. Not
> hesitating for an instant, she combed back her long, straight
> hair and cut it to shoulder-length with a knife. ... She ignored
> the woman's kimono Omatsu had laid out for her. Instead she
> put on the large man's kimono Kanbei had given Sankuro, but
> which he had never worn. (201)

This symbolic and cathartic gesture signals Okuni's transformation. When
Okuni's troupe moves on to Kitano, Okiku and Sankuro stay behind and the
sisters never see one another again.

While the rift between Okuni and Okiku is permanent and Okiku later dies an ignoble death in Yanagi Ward (the prostitute's district), Frida forgives and reconciles with both the Maestro and Kity. Admitting the betrayal "shattered all [her] illusions" (159), she notes of the Maestro:

> You were my obsession, my fixation. I equated your name with happiness. Of course you couldn't work miracles, because it wasn't in your power. It is my fault, Maestro, that I turned you into a god, gave you the role of the god and then was disappointed when you didn't act like one. What a poor little fool your Frida is, so unbearably demanding, so unbearably unhappy. (154)

As Frida prepares to die, she recounts with tenderness Kity's devotion through her life-long battle with illnesses and operations and blames herself for loving the Maestro too much; though she also recognizes that, without this love, her artistic genius, evident in her paintings, might never have been expressed.

Conclusion

Women's historical novels on artists emphasize continual anxieties about the role of the woman artist in society. Artists are rule breakers, nonconformists, and their work is often politically charged. Choosing to be an artist, these texts imply, comes at the expense of marriage and children. Love and a family block artistic expression, so procreation is manifested through art and artistic production. There is a questioning of the woman as sexual object, as she is molded by the men/maestros in her life (both off-stage-canvas-page and on-stage-canvas-page) and she struggles to become a subject in her own right. Feminist novels recuperate women who, against the odds, were able to commit their lives to art. At the same time there is a discomfort with the lengths each woman goes to in order to achieve her goal, such as having to sacrifice love and family. This implicit criticism and dissatisfaction with patriarchal society is evident when analyzing from a transnational perspective the femino-centric topics of dance as transcendence, orphans, education, theater and politics, subversive women, and false idols. Within patriarchy, women artists in a variety of mediums ranging from dance, opera, film, theater, and literature, have been ignored, belittled, exploited, and forgotten. The woman's historical novel effectively re-evaluates women's work and establishes an alternative maternal genealogy that combats and contests patriarchal control not only over the art-world but also women's lives in general.

POST-SCRIPT

This comparative study on the contemporary woman's historical novel (post 1970) suggests that a transnational feminist perspective is most suitable for studying the medium. The 1970s marks a definitive turn in women's writing: it represents a shift towards globalization, matrilineal traditions become prominent in black women's writing, Hispanic women begin asserting feminocentric histories and voices, feminist responses to psychoanalysis emerge; postcolonial and marginal voices begin revisioning dominant western discourses, postmodernist perspectives highlighting inherent affinities between history and literature propagate; new bodily rights for women become available and allow for new critical narratives on women's sexuality, historical writing comes under attack for excluding and obfuscating the lives of women; and, finally, the historical novel genre became a politicized medium for feminist women writers across the globe. No longer are women novelists writing from specific national origins or are they focusing on a single nation in their works; instead, women writers are exploring lives both past and present that travel beyond and contest national borders. Gender, rather than nationality, is the common thread that ties the works in this genre together. Thus, a sense of gender solidarity or a gender consciousness, which I deem a maternal genealogy, experienced within and outside of the text crosses and defies national boundaries.

Creating a maternal genealogy, comprised of women's voices and figures, (both known and those previously unknown) reveals that the historical novel, in the hands of women writers, can challenge historical erasures, silences, normative sexuality, political exclusion, divisions of labor, and other patriarchal perspectives. The novels surveyed in this work (for example Margaret Atwood's *Alias Grace*, Alice Walker's *The Color Purple*, Laura Esquivel's *Malinche*, and Maryse Condé's *I, Tituba, Black Witch of Salem*) speak from the margins and spaces of silence within history and the genre. As much as the works contest masculinist master narratives, however, they also create and envision new genealogies.

As evidenced in this book, women's historical novels follows four basic criteria: an atypical female is the protagonist, history is visible in the text and allows the heroine or the author to counter patriarchal values, and lastly, a maternal connection exists between the milieu/personal history of the writer and the subject matter/history of the novel. A maternal genealogy emphasizes how in recalling and reclaiming the past, we rewrite the present. In recuperating the past, the contemporary woman's historical novel puts forth a counter text or a counter version of history, and assumes, contrary to the post-modern techniques many feminist novels, for instance Anne Hébert's *Kamouraska*, employ, a historical reality and a gendered reality extends beyond the text and grounds the text.

A maternal genealogy comprised of a transnational corpus is imperative for countering the genre's current masculinist Eurocentric status; it also updates and revises women's writing which has in the past, whether consciously or not, overlooked and marginalized differences such as race, ethnicity, class, etc., between women. Acknowledging differences between women as transnational feminism does creates a firmer sense of feminist solidarity and the movement's potential for studying critical politicized literature, like the woman's historical novel.

The goals of this work were, to reiterate: 1) to acknowledge and analyze a body, transnational in scope, of contemporary feminist women's historical fiction (post 1970); 2) to compare the political potential of the maternal and maternal possibilities in women's historical novels transnationally; 3) to provide a deeper understanding of the relation between transnational feminism and feminist literature. The preceding multi-national, multi-lingual, and multicultural chapters have articulated transnational themes specific to women: 1) Revisionist Writing: Mothers of the Americas; 2) Modernity: Matricide, Gynocracy and Matrophobia; 3) Matrilineal Narratives: Race, Memory, and Survival; 4) Transnational Mater-Familial Sagas: The Matriarch; 5) A New Sexual Politics of Space: Working Mothers; 6) Violent Women: Revamping the Gothic Novel; 7) Feminist Mothering: The Woman's War Novel; and 8) Love For/Against Art: Rebirthing our Foremothers. The transnational feminist ideas contained within these chapters when read together create a politicized femino-centric space which centralizes the maternal.

The title of this project *Writing Back Through Our Mothers: A Transnational Feminist Study on the Woman's Historical Novel* signals my belief that writing back through our mothers is a collective and personal argument for feminist changes; this study has argued that a transnational feminist knowledge project on the contemporary woman's historical novel makes visible the political strategy of writing back. Furthermore, the phrase "writing back through our mothers" expresses continuity with the past, which we have inherited from both historical and literary women.

As noted in the Introduction and supported throughout this book, this project pays homage to women writers from the past, those of our present and future, and the women represented in the novels, both fictional and factual. In the beginning of the Introduction, I referenced Virginia Woolf's powerful words in *A Room of One's One* stressing the need for a genealogy of women writers – "we think back through our mothers if we are women" (76) and "a woman writing thinks back through her mothers" (96) – this need still exists in terms of the genre of historical fiction. An ever-growing body of feminist scholarship, and to which this work contributes, however, seeks to remedy this gap. As Woolf, with her typical gift of foresight, asserts:

> What one must do to bring [woman] to life was to think poeti-
> cally and prosaically at one and the same moment, thus keep-
> ing in touch with fact– that she is Mrs Martin, aged thirty-six,
> dressed in blue, wearing a black hat and brown shoes; but not
> losing sight of fiction either–that she is a vessel in which all
> sorts spirits and forces are coursing and flashing perpetually.
> (44)

Woolf's words about bringing forth a maternal genealogy, dependent on the inherent mixing of fact with fiction, encapsulate the ideas found in this transnational feminist project on women's historical fiction.

In addition to inventing and retrieving a lesser known past, women writers, transnationally, are rewriting familiar figures and changing the very ways in which we understand the past. Women's novels also challenge the two most accepted approaches to historical fiction: masculine master narratives and postmodern narratives. The former erases or downplays women's contributions to history. Like postmodern theories of history, the novels also resist what constitutes history and who makes history, but, defiantly hold onto a shared sense of gender and historical reality. Continuing to acknowledge and analyze this transnational corpus is, therefore, imperative in creating a transnational feminist knowledge project and for expanding and updating the genre. By revealing how the contemporary woman's historical novel creates a maternal space or matria within the genre of historical fiction, an unexamined women's literary tradition and its recent development is recognized. This study contends that previous scholarly criticism has been inadequate in understanding women's historical fiction and specifically how writing back through our mothers is a political act which has the power to contest and disrupt patriarchal history, literature, and society. An initial foray, this feminist project creates a transnational maternal genealogy of contemporary women's historical fiction, but there is still much more work to be done.

WORKS CITED

Primary Sources

Allende, Isabel. *Inés of my Soul*. Trans. Margaret Sayers Peden. New York: Harper, 2006.

Alvarez, Julia. *In the Name of Salomé*. Chapel Hil: Algonquin, 2000.

Amirrezvani, Anita. *The Blood of Flowers*. London: Headline, 2007.

Ariyoshi, Sawako. *Kabuki Dancer*. Trans. James R. Brandon. Tokyo: Kodansha, 1994.

Atwood, Margaret. *Alias Grace*. Toronto: McClelland, 1996.

Banti, Anna. *Artemisia*. Lincoln: U of Nebraska P, 1988.

Bernhard, Virginia. *A Durable Fire*. New York: Avon Books, 1990.

Birch, Carol. *Scapegallows*. London: Virago, 2007.

Cato, Nancy and Vivienne Rae Ellis. *Queen Trucanini*. London: Heinnemann, 1976.

Condé, Maryse. *I, Tituba, Black witch of Salem*. Trans. Richard Philcox. Charlottesville: UP of Virginia, 1992.

Corona, Laurel. *The Four Seasons*. New York: Hyperion, 2008.

Dangarembga, Tsitsi. *Nervous Conditions*. London: Women's, 2001.

D'Eaubonne, Françoise. *Moi, Kristine Reine de Suède*. Paris: Encre, 1979.

Dickinson, Margaret. *Suffragette Girl*. London: Pan. 2009.

Donoghue, Emma. *Slammerkin*. Toronto: HarperPerennial, 2009.

Drakulić, Slavenka. *Frida's Bed*. London: Penguin, 2011.

Duong, Uyen Nicole. *Daughters of the River Huong*. Oakton: Ravens Yard, 2005.

Esquivel, Laura. *Like Water for Chocolate: A Novel in Monthly Installments with Recipes, Romances, and Home Remedies*. Trans. Carol Christensen and Thomas Christensen. New York: Anchor, 1992.

___. *Malinche*. New York: Washington Square, 2006.

Ferré, Rosario. *Flight of the Swan*. New York: Farrar, 2001.

Forster, Margaret. *Keeping the World Away*. London: Vintage, 2007.

Gleason, Judith. *Agotime*. New York: Grossman, 1970.

Gunn Allen, Paula. "Pocahontas to Her English Husband, John Rolfe." *The Longman Anthology of World Literature: Volume F, The Twentieth Century*. Ed. Damrosch, David and David L. Pike. Toronto: Pearson, 2009. 670-71.

Harris, Jane. *The Observations*. London: Faber and Faber, 2006.

Hébert, Anne. *Kamouraska*. Trans. Norman Shapiro. Toronto: House of Anansi, 2000.

Hernando, Christina. *Isabel la Católica: Grandeza, Carácter y Poder*. Madrid: Ediciones Nowtilus S, 2007.

Huth, Angela. *Land Girls*. London: Constable, 2012.

Kogawa, Joy. *Obasan*. London: Penguin. 1983.

Kyung-sook, Shin. *Li Chin*. Trans. Jacques Batilliot and Jeong Eun-Jin. Paris: Edition Philippe Picquier, 2010.

Lebra, Joyce. *The Scent of Sake*. New York: Avon, 2009.

Lehr, Helene. *Star of the North: A Novel Based on the Life of Catherine the Great*. New York: St. Martin's, 1990.

Marlatt, Daphne. *Ana Historic*. Toronto: Anansi, 1988.

Min, Anchee. *Becoming Madame Mao*. Boston: Houghton, 2000.

Morrison, Toni. *Beloved: A Novel*. New York: Vintage, 2004.

Norris, Bett. *Miss McGhee*. Ann Arbor: Bywater, 2007.

Oliveira, Robin. *My Name is Mary Sutter: A novel*. London: Penguin, 2011.

Piat, Colette. *Filles du Roi*. Paris: Éditions du Rocher., 1999.

Rhys, Jean. *Wide Sargasso Sea*. New York: Norton, 1992.

Scott, Manda. *Boudica: Dreaming the Serpent Spear*. Toronto: Knopf, 2006.

Scott, Sir Walter. *Waverley: or, 'Tis Sixty Years Since*. Ed. Claire Lamont. Oxford: Oxford UP, 2008.

Soueif, Ahdaf. *The Map of Love*. London: Bloomsbury, 2000.

Starling, Belinda. *The Journal of Dora Damage*. London: Bloomsbury, 2008.

Sundaresan, Indu. *The Twentieth Wife*. New York: Washington Square, 2003.

Vidal, Elena Maria. *Trianon: A Novel of Royal France*. University Park: Mayapple, 1997.

Virgil, Publius Maro. *The Aeneid*. Trans. David West. London: Penguin, 1991.

Viswanathan, Padma. *The Toss of a Lemon*. Toronto: Random, 2009.

Walker, Alice. *The Color Purple*. Orlando: Harcourt, 2003.

Weir, Alison. *The Lady Elizabeth*. New York: Ballantine, 2008.

Woolf, Virginia. *Orlando: A Biography*. Ware, Hertfordshire: Wordsworth Editions, 1995.

Young, Sara. *My Enemy's Cradle*. Orlando: Harcourt, 2008.

Zelitch, Simone. *Louisa*. New York: Berkley, 2001.

Secondary Sources

Acker, Joan. "Gender, Capitalism and Globalization." *Critical Sociology* 30 (2004): 17-41.

Aiello, Lucia. "Mimesis and Poiesis: Reflections on Gilbert and Gubar's Reading of Emily Dickinson." *Gilbert and Gubar's The Madwoman in the Attic:*

After Thirty Years. Ed. Annette R. Federico. Columbia: U of Missouri P, 2009. 237-56.

Alexander, Jacqui M. and Chandra Talpade Mohanty. ed. *Feminist Genealogies, Colonial Legacies, Democratic Futures.* New York: Routledge, 1997. 23-45.

___. "Cartographies of Knowledge and Power: Transnational Feminism as Radical Practice." *Critical Transnational Feminist Practice.* Ed. Amanda Lock Swarr and Richa Nagar. Albany: State U of New York P, 2010.

Alexander, Jacqui M. *Pedagogies of Crossing Meditations on Feminism, Sexual Politics, Memory, and the Sacred.* Durham: Duke UP, 2005.

Allen, Ann Taylor. *Feminism and Motherhood in Western Europe 1890-1970: The Maternal Dilemma.* New York: Palgrave, 2005.

Allinson, Rayne. "The Queen's Three Bodies: Gender, Criminality, and Sovereignty in the Execution of Mary, Queen of Scots." *Practices of Gender in Late Medieval and Early Modern Europe.* Ed. Megan Cassidy Welch and Peter Sherlock. Turnhout: Brepols, 2008. 99-116.

Amireh, Amal and Lisa Suhair Majaj. Introduction. *Going Global: The Transnational Reception of Third World Women Writers.* Ed. Amal Amireh and Lisa Suhair Majaj. New York: Garland, 2000. 1-26.

Anderlini-D'Onofrio, Serena. "Is Feminism Realism Possible? A Theory of Labial Eros and Mimesis." *Journal of Gender Studies* 8.2 (1999): 159-80.

Anderson, Benedict. *Imagined Communities: Reflections on the Origin and Spread of Nationalism.* London: Verso, 1983.

Anderson, Linda. "The Re-Imagining of History in Contemporary Women's Fiction." *Plotting Change: Contemporary Women's Fiction.* Ed. Linda Anderson. London: Arnold, 1990. 129-41.

Anderson, Perry. "From Progress to Catastrophe." *London Review of Books.* 33.16. 28 July 2011. Web. 20 March 2012.

André, María Claudia. "Breaking Through the Maze: Feminist Configurations of the Heroic Quest in Isabel Allende's *Daughter of Fortune* and *Portrait in Sepia.*" *Isabel Allende Today: An Anthology of Essays* Ed. Rosemary Geisdorfer Feal and Yvette E. Miller. Pittsburgh: Latin American Literary Review, 2002. 74-90.

Androne, Mary Jane. "Tsitsi Dangarembga's *Nervous Conditions*: An African Woman's Revisionist Narrative." *Negotiating the Postcolonial: Emerging Perspectives on Tsitsi Dangarembga.* Ed. Ann Elizabeth Willey and Jeanette Treiber. Trenton: Africa World, 2002. 271-80.

Anolik, Ruth Bienstock. "The Absent Mother: Negotiations of the Maternal Presence in the Gothic Mode." *The Literary Mother: Essays on Representa-*

tions of Maternity and Child Care. Ed. Susan C. Staub. Jefferson: McFarland, 2007. 95-116.

Araújo, Helena. *La Scherezada Criolla: Ensayos Sobre Escritura Femenina Latinoamericana*. Bogotá: Centro Editorial, Universidad Nacional de Colombia, 1989.

Arteaga, Alfred. "Aesthetics of Sex and Race." *Feminism, Nation and Myth: La Malinche*. Ed. Rolando Romero and Amanda Nolacea Harris. Houston: Arte Público, 2005. 60-6.

Babb, Valerie. "Trading Male Literary Traditions for Female Oral Ones." *Women's Issues in Alice Walker's the Color Purple*. Ed. Claudia Johnson. Detroit: Greenhaven, 2011. 74-80.

Barbour, Karen. *Dancing Across the Page*. Chicago: Intellect, 2001.

Bay, Edna G. "Protection, Political Exile, and the Atlantic Slave-Trade: History and Collective Memory in Dahomey." *Rethinking the African Diaspora: The Making of a Black Atlantic World in the Bight of Benin and Brazil*. Ed. Kristin Mann and Edna G. Bay. London: Cass, 2001. 42-60.

Bennett, Caroline. "The Other and the Other-Worldly: The Function of Magic in Isabel Allende's 'La casa de los espíritus.'" *Modern Critical Views: Isabel Allende*. Ed. Harold Bloom. Philadelphia: Chelsea House, 2003. 171-82.

Bennett, Judith M. "Feminism and History." *The Feminist History Reader*. Ed. Sue Morgan. Oxon, UK: Routledge, 2006. 59-73.

___. *History Matters: Patriarchy and the Challenge of Feminism*. Manchester: Manchester UP, 2006.

Bhabha, Homi K. "Cultural Diversity and Cultural Differences." *The Post-Colonial Studies Reader*. Ed. Bill Ashcroft et al. London: Routledge, 2006. 155-57.

Boccardi, Mariadele. *The Contemporary British Historical Novel: Representation, Nation, Empire*. New York: Palgrave, 2009.

Boehmer, Elleke. "Stories of Women and Mothers: Gender and Nationalism in the Early Fiction of Flora Nwapa." *Motherlands: Black Women's Writing from Africa, the Caribbean and South Asia*. Ed. Sushiela Nasta. London: Women's, 1991. 3-23.

Braidotti, Rosi. *Metamorphoses: Towards a Materialist Theory of Becoming*. Oxford: Blackwell, 2002.

___."A Critical Cartography of Feminist Post-Postmodernism." *Australian Feminist Studies* 20.47 (2005): 1-15.

___. *Nomadic Subjects: Embodiment and Sexual Difference in Contemporary Feminist Theory*. Chichester: Columbia UP, 2011.

Brandt, Di. *Wild Mother Dancing: Maternal Narrative in Canadian Literature*. Winnipeg: U of Manitoba P, 1993.

Broude, Norma and Mary D. Garrard. "Feminism and Art in the Twentieth Century." Introduction. *The Power of Feminist Art*. Ed. Norma Broude and Mary D. Garrard. New York: Abrams, 1994. 10-29.

Butler, Judith. *Gender Trouble: Feminism and the Subversion of Identity*. New York: Routledge, 1999.

Butler, Pamela and Jigna Desai. "Manolos, Marriage, and Mantras, Chick-Lit Criticism and Transnational Feminism." *Meridians* 8.2 (2008): 1-31.

Butterfield, Herbert. *The Historical Novel: An Essay*. Cambridge: Cambridge UP, 1924.

Cantero-Rosales, María Ángeles. *El Boom Femenino Hispanoamericano de los Anos Ochenta: Un Proyecto Narrativo de Ser Muje*. Granada: Universidad De Granada Editorial, 2004.

Cassidy-Welch, Megan and Peter Sherlock. "Reflecting and Creating Gender in Late Medieval and Early-Modern Europe." *Practices of Gender in Late Medieval and Early Modern Europe*. Ed. Megan Cassidy-Welch and Peter Sherlock. Turnhout: Brepols, 2008. 317-26.

"Cave." *Merriam-Webster Dictionary*. Merriam Webster Inc., 2014.

Chow, Rey. "Postmodern Automatons." *Feminists Theorize the Political*. Ed. Judith Butler and Joan W. Scott. New York: Routledge, 1992. 101-20.

___. "Where Have all the Natives Gone?" *Writing Diaspora: Tactics of Intervention in Contemporary Cultural Studies*. Bloomington: Indiana UP 1993. 27-54.

___. "In the Name of Comparative Literature." *Comparative Literature in an Age of Multiculturalism*. Ed. Charles Bernheimer. Baltimore: Hopkins UP, 1995. 107-116.

Chrisler, Joan C. and Cynthia Garrett. "Women's Reproductive Rights: An International Perspective." *Feminism and Women's Rights Worldwide*. Ed. Michele A. Paludi. Santa Barbara: ABC-CLIO, 2010. 101-28.

Christensen, Penny. "Birth Trauma Canada: Advocating for the Rights of Childbearing Women." O'Reilly, *21st Century* 89-101.

Christie, María Elisa. "Gendered Space, Gendered Knowledge: A Cultural Geography of Kitchenspace in Central Mexico." *Laura Esquivel's Mexican Fictions*. Ed. Elizabeth Moore Willingham. Eastbourne: Sussex Academic P, 2010. 105-120.

Christopher, Renny. "A Cross-Cultural Context for Vietnamese and Vietnamese American Writing." *Of Vietnam: Identities in Dialogue*. Ed. Jane B. Winston and Leakthina Ollier. New York: Palgrave, 2001. 69-84.

Cockburn, Cynthia. *From Where We Stand: War, Women's Activism and Feminist Analysis*. London: Zed, 2007.

Cohn, Dorrit. *The Distinction of Fiction*. Baltimore: Hopkins UP, 1999.

Comerford, Lynn. "The White Ribbon Alliance for Safe Motherhood: Confronting Maternal Mortality as the Health Scandal of Our Time." O'Reilly, *21st Century* 129-140.

Condé, Maryse. Interview by Ann Armstrong Scarboro. *I Tituba, Black Witch of Salem.* Trans. Richard Philcox. Charlottesville: UP of Virginia, 1992. 198-213.

Cooper, Katherine. "Things Slipping Between Past and Present: Feminism and the Gothic Tradition in Kate Mosse's *Sepulchre.*" *The Female Figure in Contemporary Historical Fiction.* Ed. Katherine Cooper and Emma Short. Basingstoke: Palgrave Macmillan, 2012. 153-68.

___, and Emma Short. "Histories and Heroines: The Female Figure in Contemporary Historical Fiction." *The Female Figure in Contemporary Historical Fiction.* Ed. Katherine Cooper and Emma Short. Basingstoke: Palgrave, 2012. 1-20.

Cosslett, Tess. "Feminism, Matrilinealism, and the 'House of Women' in Contemporary Women's Fiction." *Journal of Gender Studies* 5.1 (1996): 7-17.

Cypress, Sandra Messinger. "'Mother' Malinche and Allegories of Gender, Ethnicity and National Identity in Mexico." *Feminism, Nation and Myth: La Malinche.* Ed. Rolando Romero and Amanda Nolacea Harris. Houston: Arte Público, 2005. 14-27.

Daly, Ann. *Critical Gestures: Writings on Dance and Culture.* Middletown: Wesleyan UP, 2002.

Dalmiya, Vrinda and Linda Alcoff. "Are 'Old Wives' Tales' Justified?" *Feminist Epistemologies.* Ed. Linda Alcoff and Elizabeth Potter. New York: Routledge, 1993. 217-44.

Danytė, Milda. "National Past/Personal Past: Recent Examples of the Historical Novel by Umberto Eco and Atanas Sileika." *Literatūra* 49.5 (2007): 34-41.

Dobrian, Susan Lucas. "Romancing the Cook: Parodic Consumption of Popular Romance Myths in *Como Agua Para Chocolate.*" *Latin American Literary Review* 24.48 (1996): 56-66.

Draper, Paula J. "Surviving Their Survival: Women, Memory, and the Holocaust." *Sisters or Strangers? Immigrant, Ethnic, and Racialized Women in Canadian History.* Ed. Marlene Epp et al. Toronto: U of Toronto P, 2004. 399-414.

Dufour, Pascal, Dominique Masson, and Dominique Caouette. Introduction. *Solidarities Beyond Borders: Transnationalizing Women's Movements.* Ed. Pascal Dufour et al., Vancouver: UBC P, 2010. 1-34.

DuPlessis, Rachel Blau. *Writing Beyond the Ending: Narrative Strategies of Twentieth-Century Women Writers.* Bloomington: Indiana UP, 1985.

Elbert, Monika M. "Toni Morrison's *Beloved*: Maternal Possibilities, Sisterly Bonding." *Women in Literature: Reading Through the Lens of Gender*. Ed. Jerilyn Fisher and Ellen S. Silber. Westport: Greenwood P, 2003. 38-40.

Ellis, Vivienne Rae. *Trucanini: Queen or Traitor?* Melbourne: Brown, 1981.

Engels, Friedrich. (1884). *The Origin of the Family, Private Property and the State*. London: Penguin, 2010.

Faderman, Lillian. *Surpassing the Love of Man: Romantic Friendship and Love Between Women From the Renaissance to the Present*. New York: Morrow, 1981.

Fleishman, Avrom. *The English Historical Novel: Walter Scott to Virginia Woolf*. Baltimore: Hopkins P, 1971.

Fletcher, Lisa. *Historical Romance Fiction: Heterosexuality and Performativity*. Burlington: Ashgate, 2008.

Frame, John M. "Christianity and Culture." *Lectures given at the Pensacola Theological Institute*, July 23-27, 2001. 1-47. Web. 20 August 2012.

Garey, Anita Ilta. *Weaving Work & Motherhood*. Philadelphia: Temple UP, 1999.

Garza, Efraín "*Como Agua Para Chocolate*: La Escritura Femenina y Los Olores a Través de la Narrative" *Arenas Blancas* 6 (2006): 8-15.

Gilbert, Sandra M. and Susan Gubar. *The Madwoman in the Attic: The Woman Writer and the Nineteenth-Century Literary Imagination*. New Haven: Yale UP, 2000.

Gillespie, Carmen. *Critical Companion to Alice Walker: A Literary Reference to Her Life and Work*. New York: Facts On File, 2011.

Gillespie, Jeanne L. "*Malinche*: Fleshing out the Foundational Fictions of the Conquest of Mexico." *Laura Esquivel's Mexican Fictions*. Ed. Elizabeth Moore Willingham. Eastbourne: Sussex Academic P, 2010. 173-96.

Glissant, Edouard, J. *Caribbean Discourse: Selected Essays*. Trans. J. Michael Dash. Charlottesville: UP of Virginia, 1999.

Glixon, Beth L. and Glixon, Jonathan E. *Inventing the Business of Opera, The Impresario and His World in Seventeenth-Century Venice*. New York: Oxford UP. 2006.

Goodwin, Sarah Webster. "Cross Fire and Collaboration among Comparative Literature, Feminism, and the New Historicism." *Borderwork: Feminist Engagements with Comparative Literature*. Ed. Margaret R. Higonnet. New York: Cornell UP, 1994 247-66.

Gordon, Linda. "Response to Scott." *Signs* 15.4 (1990): 852-3.

Green, Amy M. "Crying, Dancing, Laughing: The Breaking and Reunification of Community in *Beloved*." *Critical Insights: Toni Morrison*. Ed. Solomon O. Iyasere and Marla W. Iyasere. Pasadena: Salem P, 2009. 117-26.

Green, Mary. "The Maternal Order Read Through Luce Irigaray in the Work of Diamela Eltit. *Luce Irigaray: Teaching*. Ed. Luce Irigaray and Mary Green. London: Continuum, 2008. 93-102.

Grewal, Inderpal and Caren Kaplan. "Transnational Feminist Practices and Questions of Postmodernity: Introduction" *Scattered Hegemonies: Postmodernity and Transnational Feminist Practices*. Ed. Inderpal Grewal and Caren Kaplan Minneapolis: U of Minnesota P, 1994. 1-35.

Groot, Jerome de. *The Historical Novel*. New York: Routledge, 2010.

Gyssels, Kathleen. "On the Untranslatability of Tituba Indian, An Intercultural Subject." Trans. Victoria Bridges Moussaron. *Emerging Perspectives on Maryse Condé: A Writer of Her Own*. Ed. Sarah Barbour and Gerise Herndon. Trenton: Africa World, 2006. 63-86.

Haggis, Jane. "White Women and Colonialism: Towards a Non-Recuperative History." *Gender and Imperialism* Ed. Clare Midley. Manchester: Manchester UP, 1998. 45-78.

Haigh, Samantha. "Between Irigaray and Cardinal: Reinventing Maternal Genealogies." *Modern Language Review* 89.1 (1994): 61-70.

Handley, George B. "'It's an Unbelievable Story': Testimony and Truth in the Work of Rosario Ferréand Rigoberta Menchú." *Violence, Silence and Anger: Women's Writing as Transgression*. Ed. Deirdre Lashgari. Charlottesville: UP of Virginia, 1995. 62-79.

Harris, Jane. Interview by Judith Kinghorn. *Judith Kinghorn: Writer*. February 27 2012. Web. 10 August 2012.

Hart, Patricia. "Magic Feminism in Isabel Allende's *The Stories of Eva Luna*". *Multicultural Literatures Through Feminist/Poststructuralist Lenses*. Ed. Barbara Frey Waxman. Knoxville: U of Tennessee P, 1993. 103-36.

Hassan, Waïl S. "Agency and Translational Literature: Ahdaf Soueif's *The Map of Love*." *PMLA* 121.3 (2006): 753-68.

Hayot, Eric. "Immigrating Fictions: Unfailing Mediation in *Dictée* and *Becoming Madame Mao*." *Immigrant Fictions: Contemporary Literature in an Age of Globalization* Ed. Rebecca L. Walkowitz. Spec. issue of *Contemporary Literature* 47.4 (2006): 601-35.

Heiland, Donna. *Gothic and Gender*. Oxford: Wiley-Blackwell, 2004.

Heilmann, Ann. "Elective (Historical) Affinities: Contemporary Women Writing the Victorian *Contemporary Women's Writing* 3:1 (2009): 103-11.

Heilmann, Ann and Mark Llewellyn. Introduction. *Metafiction and Metahistory in Contemporary Women's Writing*. Ed. by Ann Heilmann and Mark Llewellyn. Basingstoke: Palgrave Macmillan, 2007. 1-12.

___. *Neo-Victorianism: The Victorians in the Twenty-First Century, 1999-2009*. Basingstoke: Palgrave Macmillan, 2010.

Heitlinger, Alena. "Émigré Feminism: An Introduction." *Émigré Feminism: Transnational Perspectives*. Ed. Alena Heitlinger. Toronto: U of Toronto P., 1999. 3-16.

Heller, Wendy. *Emblems of Eloquence: Opera and Women's Lives in Seventeenth-Century Venice*. 2003.

Heng, Geraldine. "'A Great Way to Fly': Nationalism, the State, and the Varieties of Third-World Feminist." *Feminist Genealogies, Colonial Legacies, Democratic Futures*. Ed. Jacqui M. Alexander and Chandra Talpade Mohanty, 2003. 30-44.

Hiền, Nguyễn Thị "'Seats for Spirits to Sit Upon': Becoming a Spirit Medium in Contemporary Vietnam." *Journal of Southeast Asian Studies* 38.3 (2007): 541-58.

Higonnet, Margaret R. "Cassandra's Question: Do Women Write War Novels?" *Borderwork: Feminist Engagements with Comparative Literature*. Ed. Margaret R. Higonnet. New York: Cornell UP, 1994. 144-61.

___. "New Cartographies, an Introduction." *Reconfigured Spheres Feminist Explorations of Literary Space*. Ed. Margaret R. Higonnet and Joan Templeton. Amherst: U of Massachusetts P, 1994. 1-19.

___. "Comparative Literature on the Feminist Edge." *Comparative Literature in the Age of Multiculturalism*. Ed. Charles Bernheimer. Baltimore: Hopkins UP, 1995. 155-64.

Hill, Shirley A. "African American Mothers: Victimized, Vilified, and Valorized." O'Reilly, *Feminist Mothering* 107-122.

Hirsch, Marianne. *The Mother/Daughter Plot: Narrative, Psychoanalysis, Feminism*. Bloomington: Indiana UP, 1989.

Hochberg, Gil Zehava. "Mother, Memory, History: Maternal Genealogies in Gayl Jones's *Corregidora* and Simone Schwarz-Bart's *Pluie et vent sur Télumée Miracle*." *Research in African Literatures* 34. 2 (2003): 1–12.

hooks, bell. "Writing the Subject: Reading *The Color Purple*." *Alice Walker*. Ed. Harold Bloom. New York: Chelsea House, 1989. 215-28.

Hughes, Helen. *The Historical Romance*. London: Routledge, 1993.

Hutcheon, Linda. *Poetics of Postmodernism: History, Theory and Fiction*. London: Routledge, 1988.

Irigaray, Luce. *The Irigaray Reader*. Ed. Margaret Whitford. Oxford: Blackwell, 1991.

___. *I Love to You: Sketch of a Possible Felicity in History*. New York: Routledge, 1996.

___. "Women on the Market." Trans. Catherine Porter and Carolyn Burke. *The Logic of the Gift*. Ed. Alan D. Schrift. New York: Routledge, 1997. 174-90.

___. *Democracy Begins Between Two*. New York: Routledge, 2001.

___. *Key Writings*. New York: Continuum, 2004.

___. *An Ethics of Sexual Difference*. Trans. Carol Burke and Gillian C. Gill. London: Continuum, 2005.

Jackson, Shelley. "Of Dolls and Monsters." *Points. Interviews, 1974-1994*. Ed. Elisabeth Weber. Stanford: Stanford UP, 1995. 385-86.

Jain, Jasbir. "Feminist Writing and the Question of Readership." *Comparative Critical Studies* 6.2 (2009): 221-32.

Jalazai, Zubeda. "Historical Fiction and Maryse Condé's *I, Tituba, Black Witch of Salem*." *African American Review* 43.2-3 (2009): 413-25.

James Alexander, Simone A. *Mother Imagery in the Novels of Afro-Caribbean Women*. Columbia: U of Missouri P, 2001.

Jameson, Elizabeth. "Connecting the Women's Wests." *One Step Over the Line: Toward a History of Women in the North American Wests*. Ed. Elizabeth Jameson and Sheila McManus. Edmonton: U of Alberta P, 2008. 5-28.

___. "Ties Across the Border." *Finding a Way to the Heart: Feminist Writings on Aboriginal and Women's History in Canada*. Ed. Robin Jarvis Brownlie and Valerie J. Korinek. Winnipeg: U of Manitoba P, 2012. 65-80.

James, Heather. "John Milton." *The Norton Anthology of Western Literature*. Ed. Sarah Lawall. 8th ed. Vol.1, New York: Norton, 2006. 2550-54.

Jay, Paul. *Global Matters: The Transnational Turn in Literary Studies*. Ithaca: Cornell UP, 2010.

Jennings, Hope. "Dystopian Matriarchies: Deconstructing the Womb in Angela Carter's *Heroes and Villains* and *The Passion of New Eve*." *MFS* 21 (2008): 63-84.

Jones, Gareth Stedman. Introduction. *The Communist Manifesto*. Trans. Samuel Moore. Ed. Gareth Stedman Jones. London: Penguin, 2000. 3-187.

Jordan, Constance. *Renaissance Feminism: Literary Texts and Political Models*. Ithaca: Cornell UP, 1990.

Kaplan, Caren. "The Politics of Location as Transnational Feminist Practice." *Scattered Hegemonies: Postmodernity and Transnational Feminist Practices*. Ed. Inderpal Grewal and Caren Kaplan Minneapolis: U of Minnesota P, 1994. 137-52.

Karimi, Zahra. "The Effects of International Trade on Gender Inequality in Iran: The Case of Women Carpet Weavers." *Veiled Employment: Islamism and the Political Economy of Women's Employment in Iran*. Ed. Roksana Bahramitash and Hadi S. Esfahani. Syracuse: Syracuse UP, 2011. 166-90.

Karpinski, Eva. "The Book as (Anti)National Heroine: Trauma and Witnessing in Joy Kogawa's *Obasan*." *Studies in Canadian Literature/Études en littérature canadienne* 31.2 (2006): 46-65.

Keen, Suzanne. *Romances of the Archive in Contemporary British Fiction*. Toronto: U of Toronto P, 2001.

___. "The Historical Turn in British Fiction." *A Concise Companion to Contemporary British Fiction*. Ed. James F. English. Oxford: Blackwell, 2006. 167-87.

King, Jeannette. *The Victorian Woman Question in Contemporary Feminist Fiction*. Basingstoke: Palgrave Macmillan, 2005.

Knafo, Danielle. *In Her Own Image, Women's Self-Representation in Twentieth-Century Art*. Cranbury: Associate UP, 2009.

Knezevic, Djurdja. "Affective Nationalism." *Transitions, Environments, Translations: Feminisms in International Politics*. Ed. Joan Wallach Scott, Cora Kaplan and Debra Keates. London: Routledge, 2004. 65-71.

Koontz, Claudia. "The Review of Gender and the Politics of History." *Women's Review of Books* 6.4 (1989): 19.

Kristeva, Julia. *Women's Time*. Trans. Alice Jardine and Harry Blake. *Signs* 7.1 (1981): 13-35.

Lacelle, Claudette. *Urban Domestic Servants in 19th-Century Canada*. Ottawa: Minister of Supply and Services Canada, 1987.

Lagos, María Inés. "Female Voices From the Borderlands: Isabel Allende's *Paula* and *Retrato en Sepia*." *Isabel Allende Today: An Anthology of Essays*. Ed. Rosemary Geisdorfer Feal and Yvette E. Miller. Pittsburgh: Latin American Literary Review, 2002. 112-28.

Lai, Amy T.Y. "Images of Theatre and Theatricality in Anchee Min's Works." *Tsing Hua Journal of Chinese Studies* 36.2 (2006): 543-82.

Lashgari, Deirdre. "To Speak the Unspeakable: Implications of Gender, 'Race,' and Culture." *Violence, Silence and Anger: Women's Writing as Transgression*. Ed. Deirdre Lashgari. Charlottesville: UP of Virginia, 1995. 1-21.

Lauret, Maria. *Alice Walker*. New York: Palgrave, 2011.

Lee, Janet and Susan M. Shaw, eds. *Women Worldwide: Transnational Feminist Perspectives on Women*. Corvallis: Oregon State UP, 2011.

Lennox, Sarah. "Some Proposals for Feminist Literary Criticism," *Women in German Yearbook*. Lincoln: U of Nebraska P, 1991, 91-97.

Light, Alison. "'Young Bess': Historical Novels and Growing up." *Feminist Review* 33 (1989): 57-71.

Lionnet, Françoise. "Cultivating Mere Gardens? Comparative Francophonies, Postcolonial Studies and Transnational Feminisms." *Comparative Literature in an Age of Globalism*. Ed. Haun Saussy. Baltimore: Hopkins UP, 2006. 100-13.

Lokke, Kari. "Charlotte Smith's *Desmond*: The Historical Novel as Social Protest." *Women's Writing* 16:1 (2009): 60 -77.

Long, Ryan F. "Esquivel's Malinalli: Refusing the Last Word on *La Malinche*." *Laura Esquivel's Mexican Fictions*. Ed. Elizabeth Moore Willingham. Eastbourne: Sussex Academic P, 2010. 197-207.

Lorde, Audre. "The Master's Tools Will Never Dismantle the Master's House." *Sister Outsider: Essays and Speeches*. Darlinghurst: Crossing, 1984.

Lukács, Georg. *The Historical Novel*. Trans. Hannah and Stanley Mitchell. Harmondsworth: Penguin, 1962.

Macklin, Audrey. "Particularized Citizenship: Encultured Women and the Public Sphere." *Migrations and Mobilities: Citizenship, Borders, and Gender*. Ed. Selya Benhabib and Judith Resnik. New York: New York UP, 2009. 276-303.

Manzoni, Alessandro. *On the Historical Novel*. Trans. Sandra Bermann. Lincoln: U of Nebraska P, 1984.

Martínez-Ortiz, María Teresa. "National Myths of Archetypal Imagery in Laura Esquivel's *Like Water for Chocolate*." *A Recipe for Discourse: Perspectives on Like Water for Chocolate*. Ed. Eric Skipper. Amsterdam: Rodopi, 2010. 167-84.

Marx, Karl. (1867) *Capital*. Trans. Ben Fowkes. London: Penguin, 1990.

Marx, Karl and Friedrich Engels. (1848) *The Communist Manifesto*. Trans. Samuel Moore. London: Penguin, 2000.

Maxwell, Richard. "The Historical Novel." *The Cambridge Companion to Fiction in the Romantic Period*. Ed. Richard Maxwell and Katie Trumpener. Cambridge: Cambridge UP, 2008. 65-88.

___. *The Historical Novel in Europe, 1650-1950*. Cambridge: Cambridge UP, 2009.

McGonegal, Julie. *Imagining Justice: The Politics of Postcolonial Forgiveness and Reconciliation*. Montreal: McGill-Queen's UP, 2009.

McLean, Lorna L. and Marilyn Barber. "In Search of Comfort and Independence: Irish Immigrant Domestic Servants Encounter the Courts, Jails, and Asylums in Nineteenth-Century Ontario." *Sisters or Strangers? Immigrant, Ethnic, and Racialized Women in Canadian History*. Ed. Marlene Epp et al. Toronto: U of Toronto P, 2004. 133-60.

McManus, Barbara. *Classics and Feminism: Gendering the Classics*. New York: Simon, 1997.

McPherson, Karen S. *Incriminations: Guilty Women/Telling Stories*. Princeton: Princeton UP, 1994.

Menton, Seymour. *Latin America's New Historical Novel*. Austin: U of Texas P, 1993.

Merali, Noorfarah. "Arranged and Forced Marriage." *Feminism and Women's Rights Worldwide*. Ed. Michele A. Paludi. Santa Barbara: ABC-CLIO, 2010. 81-100.

Miller, Timothy S. "The Early History of Orphanages: From Constantinople to Venice." *Home Away From Home: The Forgotten History of Orphanages*. Ed. Richard B. McKenzie. New York: Encounter, 2009. 23-42.

Mintz, Judith. "Empowering Women to Become Mothers: Midwifery in Ontario, 1990-2010." O'Reilly, *21st Century* 37-49.

Mitchell, Kate. *History and Cultural Memory in Neo-Victorian Fiction*. Basingstoke: Palgrave Macmillan, 2010.

Modleski, Tania. *Feminism Without Women: Culture and Criti* feminist' Age. New York: Routledge, 1991.

Mohanty, Chandra Talpade. *Feminism Without Borders: Decol Practicing Solidarity*. Durham: Duke UP, 2004.

Morgan, Sue. "Writing Feminist History: The Theoretical Deba Practices." *The Feminist History Reader*. Ed. Sue N Routledge, 2006. 1-48.

Moss, Jane. "Postmodernizing the Salem Witchcraze: Maryse (ba, Black Witch of Salem." *Colby Quarterly* 35.1 (1999): 5-1'

Moura, Tatiana and Rita Santos. "No Body, No Crime? The M and the Struggle for Justice and Non-Violence." O'Reilly 574-92.

Muller, Nadine. "Sexual f(r)ictions: Pornography in Neo-Victo Fiction." *The Female Figure in Contemporary Historical Fic* erine Cooper and Emma Short. Basingstoke: Palgrave Macmillan, 2012. 115-33.

Murray, Stephen Butler. "The Absence of God and the Presence of Ancestors in Laura Esquivel's *Like Water for Chocolate*." *Laura Esquivel's Mexican Fictions*. Ed. Elizabeth Moore Willingham. Eastbourne: Sussex Academic P, 2010. 90-104.

Nathanson, Janice. "Maternal Activism? How Feminist Is It?" O'Reilly, *Feminist Mothering* 243-56.

Newman, Julie. "The Untold Story and the Retold Story: Intertextuality in Post-Colonial Women's Fiction." *Motherlands: Black Women's Writing from Africa, the Caribbean and South Asia*. Ed. Sushiela Nasta.London: Women's, 1991. 24-42.

Oakley-Brown, Liz. and Louise J. Wilkinson. Introduction. *The Rituals and Rhetoric of Queenship: Medieval to Early Modern*. Ed. Liz Oakley-Brown and Louise J. Wilkinson. Dublin: Four Courts, 2009. 11-19.

Ong, Aihwa. "A Bio-Cartography: Maids, Neoslavery, and NGOs." *Migrations and Mobilities: Citizenship, Borders, and Gender*. Ed. Selya Benhabib and Judith Resnik. New York: New York UP, 2009. 157-184.

O'Reilly, Andrea, ed. *Feminist Mothering*. Albany: State U of New York P, 2008.

___. Introduction. O'Reilly, *Feminist Mothering* 1-24.

___. "'That is What Feminism Is –The Acting and Living and Not just the Told': Modeling and Mentoring Feminism." O'Reilly, *Feminist Mothering* 191-204.

Maternal Activism as Matricentric Feminism." O'Reilly, *21st Century* 56.

. *The 21st Century Motherhood Movement Mothers Speak Out on Why Need to Change the World and How to Do It*. Toronto: Demeter, 2011.

." *The Concise Oxford Dictionary of English Etymology*. Oxford UP, . Web. 15 February 2012.

avio. *The Labyrinth of Solitude*. New York: Grove, 1985.

lette. "Les Filles du Roi sont des filles formidables." *Histoire Nationale -1760: Nouvelle-France*. 1 June 1999. Web. 5 May 2011.

dele. "Historiography that Breaks Your Heart: Van Kirk and the Writ- f Feminist History." *Finding a Way to the Heart: Feminist Writings on ginal and Women's History in Canada*. Ed. Robin Jarvis Brownlie and ie J. Korinek. Winnipeg: U of Manitoba P, 2012. 81-97.

Antonio. "El Realismo Mágico Hispanoamericano Ante la Critica." ui 17.1 (1988): 9-23.

Poumeks, Elizabeth and Andrea O'Reilly. "Maternal Literatures in Text and Tradition: Daughter-Centric, Matrilineal, and Matrifocal Perspectives." *Textual Mothers/ Maternal Texts: Motherhood in Contemporary Women's Literature*. Waterloo: Laurier, 2010. 1-30.

Pratt, Mary Louise. *Imperial Eyes: Travel Writing and Transculturation*. New York: Routledge, 2007.

Purvis, June. "'Women Worthies' to Poststructuralism? Debate and Controversy in Women's History." *Women's History, Britain 1850-1945: An Introduction*. Ed. June Purvis. London: UCL, 1995. 1-22.

Purvis, June and Amanda Weatherill. "Playing the Gender History Game: A Reply to Penelope J. Corfield." *The Feminist History Reader*. Ed. Sue Morgan. New York: Routledge, 2006. 124-27.

Radway, Janice. *Reading the Romance: Women, Patriarchy, and Popular Literature*. Chapel Hill: U of North Carolina P, 1991.

Rama, Angel. *Writing Across Cultures: Narrative Transculturation in Latin America*. Ed and Trans. David L Frye. Durham: Duke UP, 2012.

Rich, Adrienne. *On Lies, Secrets, and Silence: Selected Prose 1966–1978*. New York: Norton, 1979.

___."Compulsive Heterosexuality and Lesbian Existence." *Signs* 5.4 (1980): 631-66.

___. *Of Woman Born: Motherhood as Experience and Institution*. New York: Norton, 1986.

Richards, Constance S. *On the Winds and Waves of Imagination*: *Transnational Feminism and Literature*. New York: Garland, 2000.

Rimstead, Roxanne. "Working-class Intruders: Female Domestics in *Kamouraska* and *Alias Grace*." *Canadian Literature* 175 (2002): 44-66.

Rody, Caroline. *The Daughter's Return: African-American and Caribbean Women's Fictions of History*. Oxford: Oxford UP, 2001.

Rogers, Deborah D. *The Matrophobic Gothic and Its Legacy: Sacrificing Mothers in the Novel and in Popular Culture*. New York: Lang, 2007.

Rye, Gill. "Maternal Genealogies: The Figure of the Mother in/and Literature." *Journal of Romance Studies* 6.3 (2006): 116-26.

Sachs, Murray. "Love on the Rocks: Anne Hébert's *Kamouraska*." *Traditionalism, Nationalism, and Feminism: Women Writers of Québec*. Ed. Paula Gilbert Lewis. Connecticut: Greenwood, 1985. 109-23.

Said, Edward. *Orientalism*. New York: Random, 1979.

---. *Reflections on Exile and Other Essays*. Cambridge: Harvard UP, 2000.

Salazar Parreñas, Rhacel. *Servants of Globalization, Women Migration and Domestic Work*. Stanford: Stanford UP. 2001.

Sandoval, Anna Marie. *Toward a Latina Feminism of the Americas: Repression and Resistance in Chicana and Mexican Literature*. Austin: U of Texas P, 2008.

Scarboro, Ann Armstrong. Afterword. *I, Tituba, Black Witch of Salem* by Maryse Condé. Charlottesville: UP of Virginia, 1992. 198-213.

Schor, Naomi. "The Essentialism Which Is Not One: Coming to Grips with Irigaray." *The Essential Difference*. Ed. Naomi Schor and Elizabeth Weed. Indiana: Indiana UP, 1994. 40-62.

Scott, Joan W. "Experience." *Feminists Theorize the Political*. Ed. Judith Butler and Joan W. Scott. New York: Routledge, 1992. 22-40.

___."Feminism's History." *The Feminist History Reader*. Ed. Sue Morgan. New York: Routledge, 2006. 387-98.

Shaw, Carolyn Martin. "'You Had a Daughter, but I am Becoming a Woman': Sexuality, Feminism, and Postcoloniality in Tsitsi Dangarembga's *Nervous Conditions* and *She No Longer Weeps*." *Research in African Literatures* 38.4 (2007): 7-27.

Shoenut, Meredith. "'I am Canadian': Truth of Citizenship in Joy Kogawa's *Obasan*." *American Review of Canadian Studies* 36.3 (2006): 478-97.

Siddall, Gillian. "'That is What I told Dr. Jordan …' Public Constructions and Private Disruptions in Margaret Atwood's *Alias Grace*." *Essays on Canadian Writing* 81 (2004): 84-102.

Sjoberg, Laura and Caron E. Gentry. *Mothers, Monsters, Whores: Women's Violence in Global Politics*. London: Zed, 2007.

Skallerup, Lee. *Anne Hébert: Essays on her Works*. Toronto: Guernica, 2010.

Skipper, Eric. "The Mexican Revolution as an Active Participant in Esquivel's *Like Water for Chocolate*." *A Recipe for Discourse: Perspectives on Like Water for Chocolate*. Ed. Eric Skipper. Amsterdam: Rodopi, 2010. 185-96.

Smith, Anthony D. *Nationalism and Modernism: A Critical Survey of Recent Theories of Nations and Nationalism*. London: Routledge, 1998.

___. *The Cultural Foundations of Nations: Hierarchy, Covenant and Republic*. Malden: Blackwell, 2008.

Spivak, Gayatri Chakravorty. *Outside in the Teaching Machine*. New York: Routledge, 1993.

___. "Subaltern Studies: Deconstructing Historiography." *The Spivak Reader*. Ed. Donna Landry and Gerald MacLean. New York: Routledge, 1996. 203-36.

___. *Critique of Postcolonial Reason: Toward a History of the Vanishing Present*. Cambridge: Harvard UP, 1999.

___. *Nationalism and the Imagination*. London, Seagull, 2010.

Staub, Susan C. "'My Throbbing Heart Shall Rock You Day and Night': Shakespeare's Venus, Elizabeth, and Early Modern Constructions of Motherhood." *The Literary Mother: Essays on Representations of Maternity and Child Care*. Ed. Susan C. Staub. Jefferson: McFarland, 2007. 15-32.

Stevens, Anne H. *British Historical Fiction Before Scott*. Basingstoke: Palgrave, 2010.

Sywenky, Irene. "Displacement, Trauma, and the Use of Fairy Tale Motifs in Joy Kogawa's Poetry and Prose." *Joy Kogawa: Essays on Her Work*. Ed. Sheena Wilson. Toronto: Guernica, 2011. 159-204.

Thomas, Jennifer R. "Talking the Cross-Talk of Histories in Maryse Condé's *I Tituba, Black Witch of Salem*." *Emerging Perspectives on Maryse Condé: A Writer of Her Own*. Ed. Sarah Barbour and Gerise Herndon. Trenton: Africa World, 2006. 87-104.

Thompson, Katrina Daly. "The Mother Tongue and Bilingual Hysteria: Translation Metaphors in Tsitsi Dangarembga's *Nervous Conditions*." *Journal of Commonwealth Literature* 43.2 (2008): 49-63.

Thornham, Sue. *Women, Feminism and Media*. Edinburgh: U of Edinburgh P, 2007.

Trimble, Sarah. "(Un)usual Suspects: Mothers, Masculinities, Monstrosities." O'Reilly, *Feminist Mothering* 177-90.

Torres, Antonio Torres. "*Malinche*, de Laura Esquivel: los mitos revisitados." *Huellas del mito prehispánico en la literature latinoamericana*. Ed. Magdalena Chocano et al. Madrid: Iberoamericana, 2011. 371-84.

Tucker, Judith Stadtman. "Rocking the Boat: Feminism and the Ideological Grounding of the Twenty-First Century Mothers' Movement." O'Reilly, *Feminist Mothering* 205-19.

Turner, Joseph W. "The Kinds of Historical Fiction." *Genre* 12.3 (1979): 333–55.

Ueda, Makoto. Introduction. *The Mother of Dreams and Other Short Stories*. Ed. Makoto Ueda. Tokyo: Kodansha International, 1986. 7-20.

Vara, Maria. "The Revenge of the Stereotype: Rewriting the History of the Gothic Heroine in Alice Thompson's *Justine. Metafiction and Metahistory in Contemporary Women's Writing*. Ed. Ann Heilmann and Mark Llewellyn. Basingstoke: Palgrave, 2007. 172-81.

Vickery, Amanda. "Golden Age to Separate Spheres? A Review of the Categories and Chronology of English Women's History." *Historical Journal* 36 (1993): 383-414.

Vilches, Patricia. "La Violencia Pública/Íntima Hacia la Subjetividad del Cuerpo Femenino En Julia Álvarez y Rosario Ferré." *Taller de Letras* 32 (2003): 99-112.

Von Dirke, Sabine. "Feminist Criticism and the Historical Novel: Elisabeth Plessen's *Kohlhass*." *Seminar* 34.4 (1998): 410-27.

Walker, Alice. *In Search of Our Mothers' Gardens*. San Diego: Harcourt, 1983.

Wallace, Diana. *Sisters and Rivals in British Women's Fiction, 1914-39*. New York: St Martin's, 2000.

___. *The Woman's Historical Novel: British Women Writers, 1900-2000*. Houndmills: Palgrave, 2005.

___. "Letters." *London Review of Books*. 33.16. 25 August 2011. Web. 20 March 2012.

___. "Difficulties, Discontinuities, and Differences: Reading Women's Historical Fiction." *The Female Figure in Contemporary Historical Fiction*. Ed. Katherine Cooper and Emma Short. Basingstoke: Palgrave, 2012. 206-21.

Wang, Veronica C. "In Search of Self: The Dislocated Female Émigré Wanderer in Chaung Hau's *Crossings*." *Multicultural Literatures Through Fem-

inist/Poststructuralist Lenses. Ed. Barbara Frey Waxman. Knoxville: U of Tennessee P, 1993. 23-36.

Weldt-Basson, Helene Carol. *Subversive Silences: Nonverbal Expression and Implicit Narrative Strategies in the Works of Latin American Women Writers*. Madison: Fairleigh DickinsonUP, 2009.

Wesseling, Elisabeth. *Writing History as a Prophet: Postmodernist Innovations of the Historical Novel*. Utrecht: Benjamins, 1991.

Westen, Mirjam. "Rebelle." Introduction. *Rebelle: Art & Feminism 1969-2009*. Ed. Mirjam Westen. Arnhem: Mmka, 2010. 5-23.

White, Hayden. "The Historical Text as Literary Artifact." *Clio* 3.3 (1974): 277-303.

Whitford, Margaret. ed. *The Irigaray Reader*. Oxford: Blackwell, 1991. 1-15.

___. "Section I." Introduction. Whitford, *Irigaray Reader* 23-9.

___. "Section II." Introduction. Whitford, *Irigaray Reader* 71-8.

___. "Section III." Introduction. Whitford, *Irigaray Reader* 157-64.

Widdowson, Peter. "'Writing Back': Contemporary Re-visionary Fiction." *Textual Practice* 20.3 (2006): 491–507.

Wilkinson, Louise J. "The Imperial Marriage of Isabella of England, Henry III' Sister." *The Rituals and Rhetoric of Queenship: Medieval to Early Modern*. Ed. Liz Oakley-Brown et al. Dublin: Four Courts, 2009. 20-36.

Wisker, Gina. *Margaret Atwood's Alias Grace*. New York: Continuum, 2002.

Wittig, Monique. *The Straight Mind and Other Essays*. Boston: Beacon, 1992.

Wolff, Janet. "The Artist and the Flâneur: Rodin, Rilke and Gwen John in Paris. *The Flâneur*. Ed. Keith Tester. London: Routledge, 1994. 111-37.

Woolf, Virginia. *A Room of One's Own*. London: Penguin, 2000.

Wright, Derek. *New Directions in African Fiction*. New York: Twayne, 1997.

Wynne, Catherine. "Navigating the Mezzaterra: Home, Harem and the Hybrid Family in Ahdaf Soueif's *The Map of Love*." *Critical Survey* 18.2 (2006): 56-66.

Zacharias, Robert. "Citizens of the Exception: Obasan Meets Salt Fish Girl." *Narratives of Citizenship: Indigenous and Diasporic Peoples Unsettle the Nation-State*. Ed. Aloys Fleischmann et al. Edmonton: U of Alberta P, 2011. 3-24.

Zapata, Mónica. "La déconstruction de l'Histoire et les 'histoires de bonne femme' les récits d'auteures hispano-américaines au tournant du xxie siècle." *Lectures du genre* N° 2: *Femmes/Histoire/histories* (1999): 69-77.

Zwicker, Heather. "The Nervous Conditions of Nation and Gender: Tsitsi Dangarembga's Challenge to Fanon." *Negotiating the Postcolonial: Emerging Perspectives on Tsitsi Dangarembga*. Ed. Ann E. Willey and Jeanette Treiber. Trenton: Africa World, 2002. 3-24.

INDEX